NEGLEY FARSON

Behind

God's Back

To

MY WIFE

My sole companion on the drive
from coast-to-coast across Africa;
she was better than any man

Author's Note

AT the beginning of this book I state the major conclusion I reached at the end of it: I believe that it is under the Englishman that the native will have the best chance of progress in Africa. The definition of this progress you will see in the book. The British *moral* attitude towards their African holdings and protectorates is above any except minor criticisms. Their economic conception seems—just absent. And, in their Colonial Service, the British will find the same faults they are now trying to eliminate, under the pressure of war, from their home Civil Service. If they do this with their African service, a new and vigorous life will spring up in Africa.

What value this book may have (aside from its entertainment) lies in the fact that it is the last eyewitness survey that could have been written on the territories I traversed. I began in South-West Africa, the first German colony, then went down through South Africa, then made a coast-to-coast drive across Africa through Tanganyika, Kenya, Uganda, Ruanda-Urundi, the Belgian Congo, French Equatorial Africa, the French Cameroons. And I sailed on an Italian tramp steamer from the Gold Coast just two months, to the day, before this war began.

This book will seem to lack "form," and be full of paradoxes and contradictions. But so is Africa. I have made no attempt to pull it into shape to please the purely literary critic. I won't blame them if they get after me. On the other hand, this is, without distortion and bruising of facts, Africa as I saw it. The raw material and the people "behind God's back"—waiting for the brave new world.

Contents

ix

X CONTENTS

AT five o'clock one green dawn, when the stars were paling and the pea-fowl were screaming from the thickets across the tracks, another man and I waited to be picked up from a railway station in upper South-West Africa. He had a sullen face. It was not he who told me he had just come from serving twelve months in prison for stealing Government funds. Seeing that I was a stranger, he talked in a grand way about his farm.

"When I get a new boy," he said, "the first thing I do is walk over to him and twist his ear."

With a terrible thumb and forefinger he showed me how he walked across to a new black laborer, took hold of the man's ear, and screwed it around.

"But doesn't that humiliate them?" I asked.

"Sometimes I make them cry."

"Don't they ever try to hit back?"

"Sometimes a Herrero will. They've too damn much cheek; two words for every one of yours."

"What do you do then?"

"All you've got to do is guard your head. They fight with sticks. They'd kill you, when they get mad—so you go for them."

He had grown up, he said, in the Karoo, fighting with black boys. And he knew stick fighting.

"After a minute or so I always get the stick away from them —and then I let them have it! I make them understand I'm *baas*. Then we get along fine."

Then he added: "But I always tell them why—why twisted their ear. You see, I always find some good e: for it."

"Sort of make them see reason?" I suggested.

"That's it. You've got it!" he said. "Exactly!"

INTO MODERN AFRICA

1. New Land in "Closed" Africa

WITH three Angola Boers we were looking for new farmland on which to settle thirty Boer families in the uninhabited territory above Utjo in South-West Africa. North of us there was nothing for hundreds of miles, except a few native tribes along the Portuguese border. Part of that country had never been explored. There was plenty of land, but it was deceptive.

The farms were to be twelve thousand acres each.

A couple of days before, we had passed the last farm, owned by a Boer named Pretorius, who claimed that during the last year he had lost sixteen hundred of his two thousand astrakhan sheep, from worms. Pretorius declared that either the rams which the Government sent him were wormy, or the soil was poisonous, and therefore should be condemned. He was sure of the latter; the Government should put him on new land.

He said this without passion, almost dreamily, as if he had taken a strong sedative and was already half-asleep. He got up then and left the shack, with the bitter remark to van D. that the Government was spoon-feeding the other settlers. This was meant for the Angola Boers, who looked at one another unhappily. To let down the tension, van D., who represented the Land Board, stroked his black, curling side-whiskers (which he had grown for the recent "Voortrekker" celebrations), and said to Pretorius's wife:

"But aren't you glad now" (now that the Pretoriuses had been ruined) "that you *didn't* have any advances from the Government, money that you would have to pay back?"

"What's that? What's that?" said the woman, staring him

straight in the eye. "Don't you let Pretorius hear you say that —we always pay our debts."

Then she added: "Since *you* came on the Board, all we've had is a big mouth."

The Angola Boers squirmed. It was exciting to hear a mere woman talk to a man like that, a Government official, a man whom they considered a "softie" because he lived in a settlement where there were twenty-five white men. But they did not want van D. put into a peevish humor.

The woman's brown, beady eyes were now fixed on the seams of a child's trousers she was opening with a safety razor blade. Her forehead was creased with worry. She looked fifty, but was probably around thirty-five—blowzy, swollen, with long breasts that sagged under a purple cotton print. To make matters worse, her lank, black hair had been bobbed. The farm was just four walls of mud and plaster, with a galvanized iron roof, slanted to shed the rains. The luxury of big clusters of ostrich feathers, being used as brooms, only added to the note of despair.

"My man's lost heart," said the woman. "But I won't let him give up. He is going to work now; build a dam for Mr. Cohen. I stay here. If *he* goes from this farm, *I* go—but not with him."

This was too much for the Angola Boers, who got up and went out. Out there Pretorius had spread some things that he hoped would catch our eye. Some things we might buy. There were three lion skins, a leopard, seventeen springbok, two purplish gemsbok (the original of the unicorn); a four-foot lizard, and some twenty small rock rabbits. We bought none.

I suppose we were all thinking the same thing, that when a man had fallen upon such hard times as this, it would be insulting charity to give him the price of a mere skin.

"Coffee," said the woman, reappearing at the door.

"Oh, no, we don't want any," said van D.

"You come in," she demanded. "If you don't drink a cup of coffee with me now, you'll never have coffee in my house again."

The windmill and the wretched house of Pretorius lay among some prickly pear in a valley that was flat as a floor. It was a baked, outcast scene. The straw-colored grass was enlivened here and there by a solitary thorn tree, and everywhere on the horizon rose the monstrous shapes of dead and deserted white anthills. It would be difficult for a thinking man to keep his reason in a landscape such as that, even if he did not know it was ruining him. And Pretorius, whom I had at first taken to be old, and taciturn, I now saw was young, and beaten.

His thick hair had become tow-white. His beard was white, streaked with orange. High cheek-boned, still proud, and sucking stoically on an unlighted pipe, he watched us while we drank the humiliating coffee. There was no tobacco in the pipe —until one of the Boers, quick to see what was up, casually handed him his pouch.

Several miles across the valley, another range of gray, thorn-dotted mountains lay along the sky. At its foot ran an encouraging belt of green thorn. That indicated at least a seasonal dampness of some sort. But when we got to it, after the low shack of Pretorius had elongated and vanished in the mirage, we struck a clay pan that broke like piecrust under the wheels of our lorries. A powder shot up, as it does from a puff-ball when you kick it playfully in some pleasant meadow. The Boers looked alarmed.

"I condemn this," said van D. "There is land enough for four farms here, but we condemn them, here and now."

They were marked off on the imaginative map we trusted to: Land unsuitable. The Boers declared that during the rainy season they could never get their butter, milk, hides out through the mire this land would become. And a cow caught in that, and struggling to get itself clear, would die. They always did. They complimented van D. on his wisdom, and to make him forget some of the things that Mrs. Pretorius had just done to him.

"But what a woman!" whispered the youngest Boer to me. "With a woman like that, no man could fail—*he wouldn't dare!*"

The land changed with startling rapidity, owing to its chemicals (or lack of them), but it was chiefly in variations of arid, whitish, limestone country, dotted with immense white anthills among the spare grass, with only an occasional patch of the reddish soil that meant fertile land.

Among the thorns, flocks of guinea fowl scampered like monstrous insects into the protecting thickets. It would be impossible to flush them without a dog. Black and white knorhaan rose from the grass with their scolding "kak-kak-kak," flew desperately to outpace the lorries, then fell back into the plain with legs dangling and wings outspread, in perfect helicopter descent. What appeared to be small, thatched roofs in the lonely trees were the huts of "society birds," with dozens of them living within one nest. Wild pig, with stiff tails erect, trotted off at the heads of their prolific families. An obscene ostrich hen went off at its zig-zag, jolting gait, fetching the remark from my English companion, "Finest pair of bare legs south of Leicester Square!" Little stembok darted off, deer no bigger than hares. And, in the trembling distance, a great herd of springbok began to leap, flashing like jewels in the burning sun. All of this under the immensity of a cloudless sky.

This valley, I was glad to hear, would be safe from man for a long, long time to come, because of its pie-crust entrance. The Boers' eyes lingered hungrily on the fat white rumps of the fleeing springbok.

These Boers had a romantic history. They were the last remnant of a great tradition—the last section of that Great Trek which, fleeing in 1835 from British rule, left the Cape.

At the time of our trip, all South Africa had just been undergoing a hysteria of emotions during a national celebration based upon a reproduction of the Great Trek. All the way from Cape Town to Pretoria, where a monument to the "Voortrekkers" had just been unveiled in the center of thousands of shouting horsemen, women wept as the great oxcarts lumbered once again through the streets. There was not a Boer woman in South Africa worth the name who had not made for herself a "Mother Hubbard." Men, in preparation, had grown long, curly beards (such as van D. refused to dispense with, now that he was actually himself leading in the last stage of the original trek!). And they wore the old flapping, black veld hats. The excitement had been so great that, fearing the old antagonism might be roused once again between Boer and Britisher, General Smuts and other personalities in South African life had appealed over the radio for calm.

The original trek of ten thousand "Voortrekkers" had crossed the Orange River to form the Orange Free State and the Transvaal. From there, as civilization seemed crowding in on them, another more space-hungry group inspanned again, and, with their long whips cracking, drove their ox-teams and their families north-west. They came into that arid, riverless land which is now known as South-West Africa. Here some remained. And, with the Biblical encouragement of "going into their flocks," these Boers cohabited so enthusiastically with their Hottentot women servants that they bred that race of salmon-colored people who are now known as the Bastaards, and have something like a self-governing community of their own around Rehoboth.

The progenitors of our lot of Boers pushed on again. They were heard of in 1883, when they established an independent republic at Grootfontein on the edge of the Kalahari desert. But then, possibly because they felt suffocated if they saw the smoke of another man's fire on the horizon, a group from this community inspanned and trekked up into Portuguese West Africa.

They had been there ever since. Old "Mooie," the Elder of our party, had been on that trek. For something like forty years they rode transport for the Portuguese, even carrying supplies between remote native villages in the deep interior, shooting elephants for their fat and ivory, making walking sticks out of rhino tails, until, in 1928, the administration of South-West Africa decided to repatriate them.

There was violent opposition to this, principally from the German settlers in the Mandate, who declared that the 301 Boer families were being brought down from Angola to swamp the German vote. It was a German renegade, a former millionaire speculator, who owed the administration a large sum of money (and also owed money to Germany), who, desperate and broke, cast the deciding vote in the Legislative Assembly to bring the Boers down—and after that lived in fear of his life from all the other Germans.

Even the apparently romantic protest of General Smuts was ignored. He said: "Let the Angola Boers stay up in Portuguese Africa. This is the first retreat in their history-long trek, the first time the Boer trek has not been to the North. They should remain in Portuguese Africa, and make their names there."

"It was not a pretty story," said a man in the administration, when I found I was lucky enough to be included on this expedition. "They were brought back here for political reasons, and then some of them (our lot) were given the worst farming land in all South-West Africa—which is saying something."

He then said that, to tempt the Angola Boers down, an old Boer had been sent up, who told them that "milk was flowing, cattle were only two or three pounds (actually they had to pay six pounds), and they would receive such Government assistance to get settled on their fine farms that they could regard them as a gift." Only forty of the Boer families in Angola elected to remain.

The rest found themselves unlucky pawns in the game. The

South-West African farmers were undergoing a slump at that moment. Also, their ability to repay loans that they themselves had received from the Government had been based upon too high estimates of their farms. Most of them were on the verge of being ruined and having to sell out. Instead, they sold their cattle to the Angola Boers (at £6 a head), and saved themselves. This, as it happened, did not cost the Angola Boers much in real money; the Cape had advanced £700,000 for their repatriation. But many of them had brought their own cattle down from Angola. And the land which had been given to this branch of the Boers to settle on was so bad that seventy-five per cent of their breeding cattle had died during the nine years they were there.

Our expedition was the resolve of the present administration to make amends for this and to give the last members of the Great Trek a new and happy life.

But even old "Mooie" admitted to me, as he sat on a crate of tinned food around the campfire, that he would never, never have left Portuguese Africa had it not been for the Portuguese. "It was a lovely land!" he said, passionately. "Just river . . . after river . . . after river. . . ." The pauses were to allow for dramatic waves of his hand to indicate the many streams of fresh water running through the high uplands. Water, game, solitude—all that the voortrekking Boer demands; the very memory of this country made his voice shake. For these Boers love land that has never before been tainted by a white man. They don't count the blacks as human. And there is not a river in all South-West Africa that holds water the year round; only the dried beds of watercourses which flush with the seasonal rains, and hold water for only a few weeks, days, even hours, every year.

Angola was a great land. "Mooie" loved it. He had had ten children born there during his forty years. But the Portuguese Government would never allow the Boers to own any land—no more than the actual plots on which their houses stood, or which they plowed. And the Angola Boer hates a plow; he must have fine, open land where his cattle may roam. Even so, said old "Mooie," he would have stayed in Angola had the Portuguese not tried to close their schools and churches, and make their children Portuguese.

"And that," said old "Mooie," "we could not stand!"

We found one ideal valley. But it was only large enough to make one farm, and so rimmed in by a hem of high hills that hardly a breath of air seemed to get down to it. " 'Mooie,' " shouted the old Elder, "that's fine!" But the second eldest Boer shook his head. "Do you think enough wind can get in over those hills to turn a windmill? I don't."

We went on.

Suddenly, in a red defile that promised good farming land beyond, I saw that the head lorry had stopped. The Boers were out, holding their .303 Mausers. And van D., looking a bit helpless, was clutching a .22.

"I dislike meeting them face to face," he was saying, wiping the sweat off his bald head. "You see, you can't do anything *to* an elephant—but he can do anything he wants to you!"

That seemed very sensible, from a man armed with nothing but a .22. But the Boers could hardly contain themselves. It was obvious that their hearts were aching to come up with this elephant while van D. was still chaperoning them, because he, being a Government official, and nervous, would be only too glad to testify they had shot the great animal in self-defense. They were suffering from their incurable lust to kill everything within sight. But van D. wasn't having any.

"No," he said, putting back the flat black hat he had worn for the "Voortrekker" ceremonies, "we go back."

And so, I thought, just a few steaming balls of fresh elephant dung (about the size of large grapefruit) have turned us back from a promised land.

There were, of course, no roads in this part of the world. We had been following the game trails. Now we turned our lorries painfully among the rocks of the pass, and broke out into the open again by simply crushing the trunks of the weakest thickets under our front axles. I have never seen cars take such punishment. We went down along the near side of the glinting, sun-smitten gray mountains, with occasional baboons barking at us from the scant shelter of their trees. Then we reached a pass which, I hope, will one day become known on the map as "Farson's Nek." For one of the delights of this trip had been naming mountains, valleys, passes, after ourselves. And whether eventual cartographers will perpetuate our titles is a matter that still holds my interest. Van D., I feel sure, will get at least a sizable mountain range named after him. Part of his stoicism on this, to him, painful trip came from his bitter resolve to achieve such immortality.

Then I saw that the lorry ahead had stopped again. The Boers were out again. This time, although they were still holding their rifles, their arms were pointing to something far off and below them. And their hands were trembling.

"Well, there it is," muttered the Englishman. "My God, just look at it!"

Stretching off in the sun was a valley so broad that its far range of mountains was just a low, blue silhouette on the horizon. And a broad belt of green, across its surface, showed that at least some time in the year this valley held a river.

Down below us was a *vlei*, a sunken depression, still holding the dampness from seasonal rains. And its grass was so green I wanted to go down and eat it!

✦

I was too new and impatient to take the invariable midday siesta that the Boers, their nerves frayed from excitement, now seemed to think was doubly necessary. They were already lying down, dozing, under the shade of an omborombongo tree, the tree which is supposed to hold the souls of the Herrero and Ovamba tribes. But when I took out my shotgun old "Mooie" said that he would stroll along with me.

When we had got out of sight of the others, he announced that he had already been in this valley. He had made a secret survey, all by his old self. But the Angola Boers did not want van D. or the Land Board to know that. They did not want to appear too anxious. What they wanted to happen was to have van D. "find" this place himself; then he would be all for them when it came to dealing with the Government. It would be *his* idea.

"Why," said old "Mooie," "I saw twenty-eight giraffe in this valley! When I was lying under a tree, seventeen of them walked so close I could have spit on them!"

"But why do you always want to kill the giraffes?" I protested. "They're such beautiful, even useless creatures."

"Giraffe?" "Mooie" looked amazed. "Why, for whips! Didn't you know that giraffe make the best whips?"

"And elephant fat is so sweet," he continued, walking on, "that, when you render it, you can eat it with a spoon and not get sick!"

He left, and I went on along the red, pitted trail, marked with the tracks of all the game in that part of Africa. "Mooie," who had a photographic mind formed from a lifetime of registering maps of new country in his memory, had said that this trail would meet one coming down from the pass where we had turned back. It did. I came on a damp spot where an elephant, very likely *the* elephant, had tarried only a short time before. I did not want to meet an elephant face to face; not with a shotgun. I can think of no sound more terrifying than the squeal of an elephant when he flaps forward his ears, preparatory to a charge.

A gemsbok, big as a horse, and I faced each other for a few silent moments. He was standing under a thorn tree. He shook his head once or twice, as if to clear his eyes, as if to make sure he really was seeing such a thing as I. Then, when I moved, he flung up his lovely, horned head, and with a plunge like a horse galloped off in his own dust storm.

I went back to camp with three Namaqua partridges and eight doves.

We camped that night on a grassy slope and slept under the open stars. And what a lot of them there were! The sun had been brutal during the day, so hot that I felt always half-afraid my cartridges would go off when I slipped them into the blistering shotgun. As the sun slid down now, it shot the fire of its orange flame against the clouds. The clouds threw it back against the earth. The result was bewildering. It was as if the world around us had suddenly turned to gold. The green leaves, nevertheless, had become a peculiarly resonant green. The vivid Italian blue of the sky had taken on a green tinge, across which now slowly floated islands of pale flamingo clouds. Towards the direct set of the sun the trunks of the forest above us were an ebony fretwork against flaming orange. In these few minutes a hyena brayed and laughed ironically. Then it was night.

I heard young van D. (who always addressed his father in the third person), say: "When pappy is ready for dinner, dinner is ready for pappy."

The Angola Boers, with their veteran camp technique, already had their blanket rolls out, and were lying there, gossiping, almost before the lorries stopped. They just shook the worn bed things out from ordinary burlap sacks. The two elders were unmistakable "Voortrekkers," with long, pointed, gray beards and goatees, and sunken blue eyes in sunken cheeks, that years of sun and rain had tanned like leather. All three wore veld shoes which they had made themselves from kudu skins. Thick leather, reddish, but pliable as a stiff glove. Their luggage they had also made themselves; of slabs of rhino hide, painted gray as a battleship, with trumpery tin locks they had riveted on. In a strange way all this primitive equipment spoke of contentment and security; the ability of the men, in almost any circumstances, to fend for themselves. They were very close to mother earth.

Their rifles seemed attached to them. When they moved away from a lorry, they automatically picked up the rifles. During a rest at midday, when lunch was being prepared, they sat on sacks and drew beads on distant objects—just to enjoy the feel of their firearms. They seemed unwilling to part with them, even to go to sleep, and, from a lifetime of caution required on veld and in jungle, the rifles were always laid within reach of their blankets before they lay down. Old "Mooie" always went to sleep wearing his broad veld hat, and with his pipe in his mouth. This beloved pipe had a perforated metal cap, which, I am sure, had often saved him from setting himself on fire when asleep.

We were now well over a hundred miles from the nearest store. I had looked forward to this meal. It would be the first one, recently, that we had not had from tins. As I plucked and cleaned the birds, the youngest Boer squatted beside me and translated some of the talk that was going on.

Van D. was indulging in an emotional orgy, in Afrikaans, the Dutch African tongue, playing Boer with the Boers. It was about their new life. Van D. had found a hitch at the start. The sketchy map we carried indicated that there was enough land for only twenty-seven farms in this valley; at least, that was all the Land Board had allowed for. But the Angola Boers quickly disposed of that. There were, they said, three Boer family heads among them, who were the "weaker brethren." Either because of illness, or lack of character, they could not be expected to work a 12,000-acre farm. They could couple up with three stronger Boers.

They would, of course, all draw lots for the farms.

Then, van D. had forgotten about the school. This should be on a big central farm, with 2,500 acres for itself. As nearly as it could be made, it should be self-supporting. A school teacher could be sent up from Windhoek, the capital; the children on outlying farms could live in the house which the Boers would build for the master and school; and each Boer family head would give to the school farm as many cattle and sheep as he could afford.

The communal school fees, they estimated, would work out at around two shillings and sixpence a month each. If a Boer didn't have that much, the wind would be tempered to him. They had their own predikant for the church. All children must go to school until they were sixteen, or had passed grade six.

In fact, van D. found himself being swept along on the easy flow of talk in which the Angola Boers discussed the establishment of this new life. The Boers were careful to pin him down to a promise that the Government would pay for the cost of well drilling (which, in South-West Africa, costs £1 a foot, usually goes down 250 feet, and more often than not requires several such borings before water is struck); and, in return, the Boer elders agreed they would allow none of their flock to attempt to put up a house until water had been found.

This is a written law now in South-West, wherever any Government aid is involved; and I had passed too many abandoned homesteads, on my way up from the desert coast, not to know what stout hearts had been broken by disregarding this precaution.

During the months they were drilling for water they would live in their oxcarts, as the Boers had been sleeping for over a

century. From the excited way in which the youngest Boer told
me this, I could see the romantic picture that this idea brought
to him.

A neat bit of political skulduggery was uncovered here.
Van D. had brought along a friend of his, a professional well-
driller, a coarse, hairy man, with fat forearms, a fat belly, fingers thicker than bananas, and the most boorish manners in
camps I have ever met. His presence spoiled the day. It seemed
to me that even he ought to see that the Angola Boers detested
him. Yet, unless something could be done to prevent it, he was
going to get that well drilling contract. He was in on the
ground floor, without competition. "You can get started drilling
here next week?" asked van D.

"Wait a minute," I heard the Englishman saying. He had
been a farmer in South-West for over fifteen years, one of the
mere handful of authentic Englishmen in that Mandate, which
is larger than all France. Wounded in the battles of the Somme,
he had ended the war as a major and liaison officer at G.H.Q.
in Paris. The oafish well-driller just hated his guts, and the
Englishman knew it.

The Englishman talked Afrikaans, but I heard him address
van D. coolly, in English: "You can't do that, you know. This
is Government work. Competitive bids will have to be opened
for the well-drilling."

"Look here," began the well man.

"Yes?" The Englishman waited to hear what it was that he
had to say.

"Do you think so?" said van D.

"Absolutely. He—" The Englishman nodded curtly at the
well-driller. "There is no reason why he shouldn't have the
contract, if his bid is right."

When my fire was nothing but rose-red embers I arranged
three stones and put on the pot. I had cut the birds into sec-

tions, and generously (as it wasn't mine) filled up the pot with tinned butter. The birds couldn't help but be good. I had been neither fish, flesh nor fowl on this expedition and I thought it was about time that I displayed *my* hand at something. The Boers had been almost too kind when I returned, taking doves and partridges out of every pocket of my shorts.

They had brought biltong (jerked meat) with them, and coffee, but they were now having a farewell banquet, which van D., with pontifical hospitality, produced from the back end of his car. It was as if they had been turned loose in Fortnum & Mason's.

Perhaps, I thought, as I occasionally stared into the pot at my contribution (which I was cooking for the Englishman and myself) the old far-thrusting spirit of the Boers would peter out if they were put down on a land which gave them a good living? Or perhaps, just when they found that things were going well, too well, the wanderlust might seize them again? They talked, however, as if they had reached the end of the long trek now.

"How's it going?" asked the Englishman.

"Pretty good. They ought to be ready now; I've been cooking them for over an hour."

He lifted the lid. "Marvelous! What a heavenly smell. Put in plenty of pepper and salt?"

"Stab a hunk."

"Blunt fork," he said. "Hold the pot while I have another jab."

I held the pot.

"I say," he said, "don't you think we might offer the Angola Boers some of this?"

I didn't have the courage to call "Mooie," so I beckoned to the youngest. He squatted down, reached in his hand, and pulled out a steaming breast of partridge. He nodded his thanks, and bit. His jaws stayed there. He looked at me inquiringly over his youthful beard and chunk of partridge. Those soft brown eyes—

"Don't try," laughed the Englishman; "we just called you over; we think we've found a new way to make India rubber."

The Englishman and I had made our beds at some distance from the others. We lay there, staring up at the spaces between the stars. The Englishman said he had counted about two million more than he had ever seen before. There was still enough light from the fire of the Herrero boys (who are always afraid of what might come with the dark) for us to enjoy the smoke of our cigarettes. I was full of tinned Vienna sausage. The two Herreros—and they can prize the caps off pop-bottles with their teeth—were still ripping and gnawing at the doves and partridges. For the first time in years I felt completely at peace with the world, and said so.

The Englishman chuckled, and repeated the last words of van D. to me. These were spoken as I stood up from the campfire: "Don't you think, Mr. Farson, that you have been very lucky to have been out with such interesting people as us?"

"Do you find me interesting?" laughed the Englishman.

"Yes," I retorted; "a man of your caliber; you have plenty of money to live where you want. It puzzles me why a man of your stamp should have elected to bury himself on a farm way out here in the heart of South-West Africa."

"I thought that myself for the first seven years. I lived in a hut, you know, made of mud and wattles. For seven years, while I was boring for water. . . ."

"And then?"

"Well, by that time, I'd got my back up. When you've been *fighting* your farm; putting up fences, then putting them up again, after the kudu, and the wildebeest, and the giraffe have been knocking them down; when you've bored for water until you're damn near broke—and *then* hit it. Well, about that time

you begin to feel towards your farm as you do towards a woman
—*you've got her!* Understand?"

"And now, you do not need the world any longer?"

"No. I can go back to it . . . if I want to . . . every two or
three years."

"And this—this life in South-West Africa?"

"Oh, damn you!" he said. "Self-expression, if you want it!"

I had been living with him on his lovely place, below the
glinting granite kopjes. He would not allow anything to be shot
on his 30,000 acres. A big herd of kudu frequently invaded the
flower garden which his wife had built around his cement swimming pools. That preciously treasured water (usually scummy
as a cattle dip) where we had a quick dive, then a few glasses
of sherry and cubes of iced grapefruit before lunch. His kraals
were full of cattle, having their legs roped before being milked
by the Herrero boys. He was "settled."

"But these Angola Boers?" I said. "It seems a pity for people
like them to settle down. It's the end of something epic!"

"You needn't worry," he said. "If I know anything about
these chaps, they'll never stay put. As soon as they've killed
every living thing in this valley, they'll get restless. They'll
pack up and move on. These Boers will go on, and on, and on—
just as long as there is any new land left in Africa."

2. Germans in South-West Africa

SOUTH-WEST AFRICA is not a "sahib's" country. It is a land of strictly professional cattle farmers (a third German and the rest South African), with the most unpretentious set of Government officials you will find in any territory.

It was Germany's first imperial colony, the land which launched Bismarck out on the scramble for the partition of Africa. It is larger than all France, and lies almost wholly without the tropics. In 1914 there were fourteen thousand Europeans there, of whom twelve thousand were German. That was double the number of all the Germans in all the rest of Africa, just one-half the German colonists in all the world. After the World War, six thousand of these Germans elected, and were permitted, to remain there.

They stayed on their own farms. In 1920 the Union of South Africa received the Mandate. At the outbreak of war in 1939 there were, roughly, 9,600 authentic Germans in South-West Africa.

In other words, there were more out-and-out Germans in South-West Africa than there were white men, officials included, in all the remaining African Mandates.

This fact had a bearing on the future of Africa. For these Germans were good settlers—so long as they remained settlers. But they would not. Even before Hitler, their Germanism was making it difficult to work the limited amount of self-government that the Union of South Africa granted to South-West Africa under the Mandate. After Hitler the situation became so unbearable that the growth of the colony came almost to a standstill. Banks in Capetown were refusing to lend money to so uncertain a territory. The life, the peacefulness for which many of the Germans themselves had come to Africa, was shattered. And—this is a very important point—the very quality of colonial life was being lowered.

Germanism, not mere Hitlerism, was beginning to appear as a menace to the authentic life of Africa. For the natives, of course, all the individual tribal developments which the South Africans (not notably overgiven to pampering black people) were fostering in the South-West Mandate, seemed up for sacrifice, if the German rule came back.

"Our kraals," one headman told me, "our chiefs, our headmen, our fields—all these will go. We will become just so many black 'boys' again."

The natives, to be honest about things, do not recognize much difference between a German and an Englishman. They are all just "the whites." But in the highly developed native territory of Ovamboland, for instance, the chiefs and headmen were aware of an interest in their welfare; they knew a good thing when they saw it—and they could not fail to recognize the independence of their tribal life, which the South Africans were deliberately trying to consolidate.

This is not merely my personal tribute to the good and wise things I saw the South Africans doing for the natives in Ovamboland. It was the Italian delegate to the League of Nations, a nobleman (who visited Ovamboland before Mussolini's Abyssinian depredation) who stated that, in that territory, the South Africans had established an indirect rule which could be both a model, and a laboratory, for any Mandate in Africa.

But South-West Africa is different in several essential details from any other mandate, protectorate, or colony in Africa. I have already implied this when I said it is not a "sahib's" country. It is unlike an English colony; you will find there no class of retired army or navy officers; there are no "society" settlers, who might write letters to *The Times*, or who might have "connections" in London who could get a question asked in Parliament; there are no careers there, in baked South-West, for the bright young men of the British Colonial Office—for this is a South African Mandate.

Settlers in South-West Africa are, almost entirely, dependent for their livelihood upon the earnings of their farms. This is as it should be; the farmland of the country is being developed because of it. There are a few English settlers, but they are so few that you could count them upon the fingers of your two hands. And even these good men are referred to derisively by the South Africans as "check-book" farmers, because they have some private means. They are, however, a good leaven in any colony, because of their humanity. As personalities in South-West Africa, their presence is, in some cases, strong enough to prevent German settlers in the neighborhood from exercising too ruthless a policy toward native labor.

But South-West Africa's chief characteristic—aside from the fact that there is not a river in it that holds water all year—is that it is a classless colony. There is a complete, and refreshing, absence of the class obsessions which still clog the lives of all British colonies overseas—usually from people who have no class.

And there is no such institution as the club.

The modern German settler had no class consciousness. Or, if he had, he took damned good care not to show it. *His* quirks were all focused upon being merely politically objectionable. Inflamed with reports of a continual succession of Nazi successes in Europe, the average German in South Africa was an impossible person to talk to. The South African farmers, on the other hand, of whom there were 21,000, took no interest in politics. In fact, many of them were of the indefatigable "trek-Boer" type, living on red, desert land that would have broken an English or German farmer's heart. And they were making a living from it.

In the desert country of the South, it was estimated that it took at least 25,000 acres to give one family a decent living;

from ten to twelve thousand acres are required in the central thorn-scrub territory; and in the extreme North, the only place where any plowing can be done (and that with seven spans of oxen), there is some land sufficiently fertile to make five thousand acres a practical farm.

The average farm in South-West Africa covers thirty-two square miles.

For this reason, people are spread far apart, and very little of their life is lived in towns. You are constantly struck, in South-West, by the emptiness of the settlements' sandy streets. There are only three towns with a population of more than a thousand Europeans. The few other settlements have white populations that range anywhere from fifty to the average hundred or so, up to an occasional center with a population of five hundred.

Traveling in the thorn-scrub valleys on the plateau known as the "Police Zone," which is where the Europeans are settled, driving along the red, empty roads at fifty and sixty miles an hour, only once in a while seeing the windmill, dams, and low white buildings of a farmstead—always with the broken blue silhouette of mountains lying somewhere along the skyline— traveling under the vivid, blue skies of this vast, open land, where the kudu will spring at one bound across the red road to vanish into a thicket, you frequently have to force yourself to realize that you are not back in some remote foothills of the Canadian Rockies.

Even the natives, in South-West Africa, do not make their presence felt—not in the farming country. For South-West Africa has only 258,000 natives against 31,600 white men, and only 110,000 of these are allowed to live in the "Police Zone." The rest are confined in reserves, or are up in the free air of Ovamboland. And South-West Africans, therefore, are proud to refer to their home as merely "a European country—with native appendages."

Contrast this with Tanganyika, where there are over 5,000,-
000 natives to 8,500 whites, and you see another, and very
vital, reason why South-West Africa is different from any other
colony.

The proportion of white to black is higher in South-West
Africa than it is anywhere else on the continent. It is the most
"white man's country" in Africa.

The "Police Zone" is a high wedge of plateau, anywhere
from three to five thousand feet high, with some mountains
that reach eight thousand feet, sandwiched between two burning, uninhabited and uninhabitable deserts.

The Namib, nearly a thousand miles long, on the coast. Inland, the equally terrible Kalahari.

The coast line of South-West Africa is long, low, monotonous,
unbroken by bays or promontories, beaten all the year round
by a heavy surf. An ice-cold current from the Antartic races up
it, bringing seals and penguins, making its foreshore a desert,
just as the Humboldt Current has made a desert of the west
coast of South America. The two regions are strangely similar.

Although there are three little settlements on its water edge,
no white man can live in the Namib desert. Diamond prospectors who ventured inland to establish water caches have been
found two years later, buried with their oxen, their carts, their
boys, like a bas-relief, solidified in action under a shifting sand
dune. The prevailing wind from this waste is a hot blast towards
the sea. On most days this carries a low-level sandstorm that
nearly blinds you. When the wind is more moderate, the hot
air from the sand condenses over the icy Benguela Current.
This dreadful coast is then blanketed in a cold sea fog.

The Bushmen lived there. And then came the Hottentots.
Tiny, hollow-backed, hollow-cheeked, yellow people. And Nature, so that they might exist, had deliberately made them different from other men, particularly the Bushmen. For they

have a protruding rump—*steatopyga* (an excessive accumulation of fat on the buttocks)—on which, like the camel, they can live.

The Hottentots, the Herreros, and the Ovambas of South-West Africa say that on their arrival the Bushmen were found to be in occupation, and that the latter must have been there since the beginning of man. The Bushmen likewise believe that they have been there since the very beginning of things. The white men advancing from the Cape exterminated the Bushmen and Hottentots, like wild game. They organized hunts for them.

And then the Germans came.

In 1882 an enterprising Bremen merchant, A. E. Lüderitz, obtained a concession on this coast from the Hottentot chief, Joseph Fredericks of Bethany. He was assisted by German missionaries who had been there since 1840. Whether he got the concession "for one hundred rifles and £200, or two hundred rifles and £100" makes no difference, says a pamphlet prepared by the British Foreign Office for use at the Peace Conference in 1920; "this territory was lost to Britain through lack of decision and want of foresight."

For what happened was this: Bismarck had been declaring that he did not want colonies. He claimed they were expensive illusions. In 1871, at Versailles, he said: "I want no colonies. They are only good for providing offices. For us, colonial enterprise would be just like the silks and sables in the Polish noble families, who, for the rest, have no shirts." In 1872, Bismarck said to the British Ambassador in Berlin: "Colonies would be a source of weakness, because they could only be defended by powerful fleets, and Germany's geographical position does not necessitate her developing into a first-class maritime power."

As late as 1881 he was reported to have said (to a Deputy in the Diet): "So long as I am Imperial Chancellor we shall carry on no colonial policy. We have a navy that cannot sail;

and we must have no vulnerable points in other parts of the world which would serve as booty for France as soon as we went to war with her."

But Bismarck was being pushed from behind. Associations for assisting German emigrants had been forming thickly in Germany for over two hundred years. William Penn visited Germany in 1667, and six years later a small body of German settlers crossed the Atlantic and settled near Philadelphia. Large settlements were established in Brazil; the colonists adhered closely to the old German customs. In Brazil, in 1906, there were 345,000 inhabitants of German descent or parentage. There was even an organization, founded in 1842, the "German Association for the Protection of German Emigrants to Texas."

But to trade or settle—not to annex—had been the cautious, unimaginative German official policy. Both British and German Governments seemed, around the 1880's, to have failed to distinguish the vital difference between official policy and private action—in Germany.

German explorers were performing prodigious feats in exploring North and Central Africa. They were backed by powerful trade bodies, notably the Hamburg merchants, and these last were openly demanding of the Government, "For how long must Germany do nothing but dot Africa with the bones of her explorers?"

In 1878, Stanley returned from his second expedition to Africa, and offered his services to King Leopold II, who, in that year, formed his *Association Internationale du Congo,* which this unscrupulous king soon twisted into a purely Belgian enterprise. As late as 1881, German official opinion was so hostile to a colonial policy that Bismarck failed to get the German Diet to vote a grant guaranteeing 4½% interest on £400,000 German property in Samoa, which had been mortgaged in London. Private German sources had to redeem this almost lost German enterprise. And the action of the Diet was taken as sufficient warning that German Parliamentary opinion was not as yet ready for colonial experiments costing public money.

In 1882, a powerful German Colonial Organization was formed by such influential personages as the traveler, Baron von Maltzan, and Prince zu Hohenlohe-Langenburg. Its express aim was to divert German emigration overseas from the United States, Canada, and the South American republics, to small factory settlements *under the German flag*. First secure small trading stations, then secure Government "protection" for them—which is precisely what came about, in 1884, at Lüderitz.

Adolph Lüderitz (whose end is obscure, but who, one of his early friends in South-West Africa told me, was drowned in the Orange River while prospecting for diamonds), had opened a factory at Lagos, on the Guinea Coast, about 1881. "Trade was so good, and *public* opinion in Germany was so favorable to the colonial movement" that Lüderitz decided to set up more factories, and then apply to his Government for "protection."

His concession at Lüderitz (then known as the Angra Pequena region) was for a twenty-mile coastal strip, running northwards from the insignificant, rocky harbor. In 1882 he applied to Bismarck for "protection." In February, 1883, Bismarck sent a note to England, asking if she exercised any jurisdiction over the Angra Pequena region, as, "if not, Germany intends to offer her subjects in that region the protection which they need."

England sent a vague reply, three weeks later, saying the Cape Colony had certain establishments along the coast; England "did not know" the exact location of Lüderitz's factory, and "it is impossible to say whether the British Government could afford this protection, if required."

England had a peculiarly obtuse Ambassador at Berlin in those years, Lord Odo Russell, afterwards Lord Ampthill. He continually assured his Government that Bismarck would never embark on any colonial enterprise. He was insisting upon this on the very day when a German naval officer, at Lüderitz Bay, was informing the British commander of a gunboat hurriedly rushed up from the Cape, "You are now in German waters."

But even then the position was still fluid!

In December, 1883—nearly a year after Lüderitz had enlisted Bismarck's attention—the Germans sent another note to Great Britain, notifying them officially that Germany assumed she was justified in according protection to Lüderitz. The British did not even take the trouble to reply to this note. Bismarck, by this last official query, had complied with all the polite requirements of diplomatic etiquette; in 1884 the German flag was hoisted at Lüderitz, and Bismarck officially annexed it to the German Empire.

The British Foreign Office pamphlet of 1920 is correct, as this chronology shows so incontestably, when it says:

"England could have had this colony not only without the objection but with the active good will of Germany. That it ever passed into German hands was due to the continued inaction of the home Government and the Cape Colony."

Südwest Afrika launched Germany in the scramble for colonies. Once Bismarck had been shoved into the partition of Africa, he carried through with a rush. Within less than five years Germany had annexed Togoland, the Cameroons, and all that delectable territory around Kilimanjaro known today as Tanganyika.

Kilimanjaro itself, as a matter of fact, should belong to Kenya. Queen Victoria gave Kilimanjaro to her nephew, Kaiser Wilhelm II, as a birthday present.

Such was the attitude of those days toward Africa.

3. Ticket for Walvis Bay

THE first time I heard of Walvis Bay I was on the bridge of a Norwegian whaling steamer between the Shetlands and Faroe Islands. We were towing back to the land a dead fin-whale we had just shot off the Gulf Stream. And as the lookout barrel on our mast swung in its arc across the stars, the gunner became reminiscent:

"Ever been to Walvis Bay?"

I asked him where it was.

"Why, that's where the whales go to make love!"

"Nonsense!"

"Absolutely! I've seen them at it! Though what the hell fun *they* get out of it, I don't know!"

When I bought my ticket in the Haymarket for South-West Africa, I found that it was for Walvis Bay. There was no other port. I had chosen a German ship deliberately, as I was anxious to study what type of German it was that still went out to their former colonies. I need not have been so particular; there was no other boat. No British line of any class whatever had thought it worth while to have one of its ships call at this colony.

Even some South Africans on the boat thought it amusing that I should be getting off at Walvis Bay. There was nothing there, they insisted, except a lonely wharf, and one crane. They made me promise not to look until they could lean over the rail beside me—and watch my face.

(They were wrong; there were five cranes.)

But they need not have worried. There was a fog that morn-

29

ing. And so my first sight of Africa, after seventeen days out from Southampton, was what it should have been. It was two bargeloads of tattered natives, being towed out by a tug to take off ourselves and our baggage.

And the sight was frightening.

"There they are!" suddenly shouted a young Rhodesian mining engineer beside me. "Black diamonds! The most overtaxed man in Africa!"

Certainly I had never before seen, except in prison, a body of men whose lot in life seemed obviously so uncongenial to them. Part of their plight was the fault of the climate; for all these sullen natives had been brought from the dazzling sun-country inland—Zulus, Damaras, Herreros, Ovambas, Portuguese boys—even the few yellow Hottentots among them ordinarily lived far back among the burning coastal sands. This fog would be the death of them. And, to stave it off, they were wearing every conceivable rag and castoff of European clothing. Macabre, in this dejected harlequinade, were the raucous stripes of Old School blazers, scarlet berets, Buster Browns, and tam-o'-shanters.

"Where they should get those tams from," said the Rhodesian engineer, "is by me! But last voyage, a passenger from this ship suddenly knocked down a native he saw on the wharf. 'By God!' he said, 'he's wearing a Royal Scot!' But you won't see any Old Etonians about; these blazers are mostly from the universities down in the Union."

The Portuguese "boys" had their teeth filed sharp as needle points—a relic of cannibalism.

It may sound farfetched to say that such a spectacle of broken natives could be frightening. But if you talk with many thinking people down in the Union (particularly those of English extraction) you will find that occasionally one will admit that the attitude of the white man towards the native *is* based upon fear. You may do anything you like to him, but he is still there—by the millions.

His capacity for suffering, his vitality, his faith that one day things must come all right for him, are indestructible. They shame you. What *are* you going to do with him? In Africa, the black man, by his very presence, has made the white man do mean things. Demean himself. And the white man hates him for it.

It was a sidelong look which passed between us as these doleful natives silently climbed up the gangway to enter our ship.

"It is absurd," growled the young engineer, disturbed by the sight, "to think that the native has taken everything that has happened to him, and then forgot. You will find that look of resentment, however skillfully it may be veiled, throughout Africa."

There was a horrible girl in the ship (I still think she was a Bastaard), who came from Johannesburg. She said she had no use for Durban—"because they let the blacks ride in trams there!"

After she had left us one night, an Englishman, who lived in Durban, called for a double whisky.

"There you are," he said despondently; "you can just imagine what the Zulus feel—finest men in Africa!" Then he told me of a scene he had come on in a Durban back street. It was an old Zulu, addressing his fellows.

"Don't despair, brothers, don't despair," the old Zulu was saying; "we know the white man has us down." He made the gesture of kneeling upon another man, whom he was holding down in the gutter. "But don't despair—when *he* stands up, *we* stand up!"

The old Zulu arose and stood to his full, proud height. "To show," said the Englishman, "that when we are holding him down in the gutter—we are down there with him! When we become decent, then he will have a chance."

"*'You had the Bible—and we had the land; now we have the Bible—and you have the land!'*"

That was another Zulu saying, said the Englishman, which took some answering. "One of these days, if we keep on the way we are, we'll be having the Zulus sending missionaries to England—to teach *us* Christianity!"

He said that in South Africa the English had betrayed their trust to the natives, when, politically, they subscribed to the Boer slave tradition.

Very few white men go to the tropics to live—not in Africa. It is either to make a career or enough money to retire upon. And there are three broad types of white man's life.

There is the Gold Coast, or Nigeria, where practically all the cultivation is in the hands of natives, and the white men are merely Government officials or employees of the big trading companies, mines, or plantations, nearly all of whose capital is held by a few financiers in London. That, in the right sense of the word, is not colonization; it is exploitation.

The same holds more or less true for Togoland, the Cameroons, and French Equatorial Africa. These countries are the tropics (sometimes at their very worst), and white men are lucky if they get away from there without their health being ruined. No white man ever believes he will have the bad luck to have to retire there. That would be a calamity.

And leave, usually for six months, at home, is granted after every eighteen months or two years.

Then there is the Belgian Congo—just one vast, Big Business concern. The entire Congo is being exploited and developed to-day by four huge business companies. They build the roads, establish the aerodromes, run the railways and river steamers, the plantations, the mines, the hotels, the general stores—and, indirectly, they also run the natives of the Congo. For in the huge financial holding company, which embraces all these other companies and their subsidiaries, the Belgian Government itself is a half-share owner.

In the Belgian Congo an *administrateur* has to be out on

safari in his district for twenty-one days out of every month. Out on business. To see that the natives, in that region, are producing the stipulated amount of cotton, oil nuts, or whatever it is that that particular locality has been allocated to produce.

White keepers of small shops, traders, settlers, hotelkeepers —and particularly diamond or gold prospectors—are not encouraged in the Congo. In fact, they find, for one reason after another, it is almost impossible to exist.

And the natives? Well, church, state, and big business, in the Belgian Congo, are all united in one grand co-operative effort to "lay hold of the native," to put him on the inexorable belt of progress, in spite of himself.

But don't let this statement, at this early part of the book, prejudice you against the Belgian colonial administration. Let it be said that the native laborers in the Belgian Congo live in better villages, and receive more and better medical attention, than natives do anywhere else in Africa. And the realistic Belgians make no sentimental bones about why they are doing all this; they state frankly that it is to conserve, and keep happy and healthy, a dangerously limited black labor supply.

Then there are the alleged "white man's" countries, such as Kenya, Tanganyika, and South-West Africa. Opinions still differ as to the suitability of the African "white highlands" for a white civilization. For example, with white children in Kenya, all born above 6,000 feet, many from 7,000 to 8,000 feet, none of them is old enough yet to provide any accurate knowledge of what will be the effect of the high altitudes and the actinic rays of the sun—directly on the equator—upon them. It struck me that all the people I met in Kenya were a little daft. Nevertheless, if I had to live in Africa, that is where I should go— to majestic Kenya.

In these "white man's" countries the settlers have come to live. Their farms are their homes. They bring children into the world with the hope that they will carry on with the farm. The

English (and German) settlers, in the white highlands, love their farms.

Perhaps nowhere else in the world will you hear an Englishman (of all people!) speak with unashamed passion in his voice, as the English settlers always do there when they talk of their farms in Kenya. They speak with real tenderness about it.

In Tanganyika, British settlement has, up to date, been carried on in spite of the British administration. That is the English settler's chronic complaint: That Dar es Salaam interprets too literally the mandate that the land of Tanganyika must be held in trust for the native. Nothing could be more honest, in that respect, than the Whitehall handling of the Tanganyika Mandate. But it has cramped British settlement.

In Kenya there are about two thousand farms, where the owners are improving the land with children as well as livestock. There are four thousand such farms in South-West Africa, and it is, therefore, the largest colonial white settlement in Africa.

The landing of the Germans from our ship had the quality of that of an Evangeline. They had been home to the fatherland; tears and waving handkerchiefs from the tug's bridge now welcomed their return. I watched them, although it was none of my business, with a curious mixed feeling of admiration and resentment. They were such solid folk! Yet I knew that some twenty young men among them were just returning after their "finishing" education in Germany; and this included, aside from the usual six months in the labor corps, two full years in the German army. They were returning to the Mandate of South-West Africa as trained Nazis.

And while their Nazidom made conversation unpalatable on the boat, I also knew that the arrogant man, who looked like the Crown Prince, was a regular German cavalry officer; that he had been with his regiment when the Germans took over Austria; that he had ridden with it into Sudetenland; and that he was now, on six months' leave, returning to his farm in South-West Africa, up around Grootfontein.

And the South Africans, I had also discovered, did not say a word against any of all this. This easy—and, considering the times, dangerous—state of affairs came from the hereditary feeling of friendship for the German, felt by one section of the population. And so, even before I set foot ashore, I was to witness the outstanding characteristic of the Mandate—the tolerance of the South Africans, both past and present, of the German inhabitants.

This was a real homecoming. The Germans' well-kept cars were waiting for them on shore. And while I was still trying, vainly, to clear a rifle and shotgun through the customs, I saw them, in whirls of red dust, streaking off across the desert to their homes, their shops, and their well-run ranches on the high tableland.

It would be two or three days before some of them reached their front doors, and put down the Christmas trees they had brought all the way out from the fatherland.

I was prepared for the vacuity of life at Walvis Bay, but not for such a complete vacuum.

The wharf, with a semi-circle of fifteen miles back into the desert, has always been a British enclave in this former German colony. But shockingly little has been done with it. It is still just a railhead for the train that twice a week crawls across the orange desert to where the blue mountains of the "Police Zone" mark the range for Europeans in South-West Africa.

On some raised land across the sea were the warehouses and customs shed, the vast cement block of "The South-West Africa Storage and Stock Farmers Ltd.," as the welcoming slogan of that slaughterhouse reads from the sea. Then there were the three shining, aluminum tanks of the Shell Oil Company. Finally, the stack and disused sheds of the abandoned whaling station, from which, every October, seven Norwegian factory ships, each accompanied by eight little whale chasers, go down to the Antarctic "ice."

Inland from this was a dreary depression of salt-crusted sea mud, so impregnated with chemicals that when, a few years ago, the bodies of some German soldiers interred here were exhumed for reburial at Windhoek, the corpses were found to be perfectly preserved.

Facing this was Walvis Bay's main street, with all its one-storied buildings facing one way. They were, with the exception of Barclay's Bank, all German shops, or places managed by Germans. There was one hotel, run by a German. And, in it, my window looked out into the sandy compound of Herr Ernst Baumgart, the grocer and ship chandler.

The compound was neatly stacked with empty beer barrels and packing crates. Mr. Baumgart, like the Germans all over Africa on the eve of this war, seemed to be standing on his dignity. He was very self-conscious, very irritating about it. Somehow, in that evil climate, he always managed to look clean and fresh. Most of the South Africans at Walvis were content with shorts and an open shirt—that is, unless they had to put on their official uniforms to receive a ship. But Mr. Baumgart always wore a stiff white collar. And he always wore a white linen dust coat over his gray business suit.

One-quarter mile behind this main street, at the minimum sanitary distance observed all over South Africa, was the native "location."

This sandy settlement was composed almost entirely of huts made from rusty, flattened-out, gasoline tins. There were two rows of white, plastered barracks set up for the black railway workers. But Europeans informed me at Walvis the native prefers the former abode made of the tins. It is more airy. Some seventeen hundred assorted natives were living out, here, their deformed lives. Each has to carry a pass card. And curfew, although it may not ring, is 10 P.M. for him.

If he is caught outside the "location" after that hour without a signed permit from his master he is locked up.

In this, the South African goes several pegs lower than the American South. But his problem is different. In the United States, the Negroes number only about one-tenth of the population. In South Africa, there are nearly seven million natives to two million whites. And the South African feels, correspondingly, more strongly on the subject.

It was while at Walvis that I first became aware of that thing which I shall call "South Africanism." It exists, all right—in fact, it is very, very strong. Its fragrance is something like the combination of "the odor of sanctity" and a dead buffalo, depending largely upon how you yourself feel upon certain subjects. *Tolerance* is certainly one of its outstanding characteristics.

When I made a speech before the University Club at Cape Town, I nearly blew the "English" out of their seats with that remark. "For heaven's sake, man," whispered one of them to me afterwards (he was an Irishman, by the way), "don't talk about *them* like that!"

"Who's *them?*"

"Why, they—the Dutch South Africans."

"Well, aren't you a South African?"

"Yes, but—"

"They tolerate you, don't they?"

He laughed, and slapped me on the back. "Yes, I suppose you're right there; it must get on their nerves to hear all this talk of 'we' and 'they'—but they do the same thing with us. Yes, I suppose you *could* say there was a certain amount of tolerance in this team-up. But not on the back veld!"

I have already spoken of the tolerance shown by the South Africans towards the Mandate's German inhabitants. It is not so widely known that the German farms in South-West Africa were not confiscated after the World War, as they were in Tanganyika, Togoland, and the Cameroons. On the contrary—when

the German forces in South-West surrendered to the South
Africans in 1915, General Botha, that great Boer commander,
told all the legitimate German farmers that they could immediately return to their lands. The South Africans, as they withdrew from the country, found the Germans already at work
again.

The Germans in South-West were not repatriated when the
South Africans received the Mandate in 1920, which could easily have been done under the Treaty of Versailles. On the contrary, many who had left the country, or who had been deported, were allowed to come back.

And when the dual nationality showed itself unworkable under the limited self-government that the Union gave the Mandate, the South Africans even offered the Germans South African citizenship. All Germans of six months' residence could accept this unless they declared otherwise. Out of the 3,489 adult
Germans eligible, only 227 declined naturalization.

In 1926, when the first elections were held, the Germans actually succeeded in getting seven out of the twelve elected votes,
and thus held a majority in the Legislative Assembly.

There is no need to go into details. Disputes were constant
along racial lines. With the advent of Hitler they became intolerable. In January, 1939, at Windhoek, the *Deutsche Südwest Bund,* strongest political body in the territory, voted two
resolutions: One was that any German accepting British citizenship was a traitor to the fatherland; the other was that all Germans in South-West owed allegiance to the Third Reich, and
that the full moral and legal right of Germany's claim to her
former colonies should be recognized. .

Such resolutions as those could be expected under a Mandate.
There was nothing illegal or unethical about them, except for
one thing: The South-West African Germans who voted these
resolutions, unanimously, *had all previously accepted South
African citizenship.*

Most of them had two passports: A South African one, and a Third Reich passport, supplied, pressed upon them by the German Consul General at Windhoek.

That was the answer of the Germans, the reward they returned for the tolerance of the South Africans. Since 1923, when General Smuts reached an agreement with the German delegates in London whereby the German Government agreed to have its nationals throw in their lot with the South Africans in the Mandate, and accept South African citizenship, the Union of South Africa had even been paying some of the old imperial pensions to former officials in Südwest Afrika.

When South Africa came off gold, the Union increased these pensions, in pounds, so that the pensionnaires, in Germany, should receive the same number of marks.

As to the Negro question, it is recognized by all South Africans that this is their most dangerous political problem. But even there the South Africans are not so intolerant as we Americans are in some of the Southern States; they don't lynch Negroes in South Africa. And while, in the States, we now seem to be solving the problem, regionally, by the passage of time, the position of the Negro has been definitely shelved as a national political question. Thus, we Americans are doing nothing about it.

The South Africans are doing something—even if, in the eyes of most of the rest of the world, they seem to be doing the wrong thing.

The point is—and this is a very important thing to remember about South Africa—the South Africans regard it as part of their problem of security to safeguard the "South African brand" of white civilization *at least up to the equator*. They would like a political understanding with the Rhodesians, to bring this state of affairs about. The sight of natives bearing arms, even of native clerks and technical workers in some of the territories adjoining the Union, has an alarming effect upon the average white South African.

It was a South African senator who proposed a scheme whereby the Union should become the head of a Pan-African League, with the object of extending white civilization to all Africa 10 degrees south of the equator—by which he meant that South African native policy should be applied up to there. And a disarmed black zone should be proclaimed between 10 degrees south and 10 degrees north of the equator.

The labor policy of South Africa today is to make native labor cheaper, not dearer. Hut and poll taxes have already been established to make the Negroes leave their reservations and seek work. The confiscation of native lands under the 1913 act had forced large blocs of natives into the labor market. And increasing apprenticeship restrictions are debarring, ever more stringently, all natives in South Africa from even the unskilled trades which a "poor white" might be induced to take on.

Behind all the camouflage of various measures, the fact remains that the future for the black man in South Africa grows blacker every day.

If the Negro men at Walvis were scarecrows, their women were birds of paradise. The Herrero women, whom I came on at the very start, were the most beautiful native women I found in Africa. Their skins were an attractive light brown, not black. Instead of wearing tatters, as did their men, they walked the sands like Victorian fashion plates. They wore scarlet and magenta turbans; their high-waisted dresses were pleated around slender torsos, and billowed and waved like plumes as they walked. Their necks were tall columns, ringed with rows of colored beads or shells. They had tapering, aristocratic chins. It took twelve yards to make one of their costumes, of the favored, flowered tobralco cloth—that cost two months' wages of any "boy" on an up-country farm. And when you watched these vivid women, with their long, slender fingers, saucily handling bales of wool beside a sea which was the color of a fizzing lemon squash, you expressed your thanks to God that He had not left you color-blind.

They were an enjoyable sight, these Herrero girls, who laughed among themselves whenever a tolerable-looking white man passed by. The merry sluts!

"For they're all tarts," sighed a South African, covetously. "They're there for any man who's got the money in the 'location.' The Zulus never marry here; they never have to, they can always pair up with one of these Herrero girls. But just consider what it must have been like in German times."

In hot South-West Africa the beauty of these Herrero women seems an everlasting taunt to the lonely white men. Yet, although I heard a lot of talk about it, I never came across any case where I knew they were "living in sin," as it is so enviously put.

"In German times," went on the South African, "they say they used to make the Herrero women wait on the mess, naked. I suppose that must have been the N.C.O.s? But they say it is absolutely true that up in Fort Mamutoni the officers used to make a pretty Herrero girl strip and then lie on the table, and they would play cards on her stomach."

The Herreros, who, possibly, were one of the finest tribes of Africa, were decimated by the Germans as a race. But infinitely worse than the usual German "atrocity" story are the numerous accounts of the ways the German settlers and traders tried to swindle the Herreros out of their magnificent herds of cattle. In 1904, when the Herreros rebelled, the Germans killed sixty thousand of them. The tribes began with a population of ninety thousand; in 1907, when the rebellion ended, there were less than thirty thousand Herreros. They had been "crushed."

Yet it is a queer thing—I find, in drawing down the answers I got to my persistent question, "Would the natives like to have the Germans back?" nearly all the affirmative answers were coupled with the Herreros' name.

"It is understandable," said a South African. "When the Germans annihilated them as a race, as a tribal organization, the remnants fled into the Kalahari desert. Many of them lost their children on the way. The Germans took these orphans— some, perhaps, from pity or remorse, but most simply because they did not have to pay them. They began as servants around the house. Eventually, they were put into uniform, as soldiers or police. The Herreros were always the ruling caste; they had their own slaves, the Damaras. So they fitted into the German overlordship nicely. And there's many a Herrero walking about South-West Africa today, or sleeping his life out in a Reserve, who looks back sadly to the days when *he* had a colored cockade in his felt hat! The Herreros never did like manual labor; they'd much rather have a gun, or a stick, and be allowed to boss other people about—there's the romantic appeal of the German for them. We South Africans will never put a native into a soldier's uniform!"

The resentment of the Herreros is still so strong against the whites that Herrero men will often pretend that they do not understand English or German when you try to talk to them. They appear to be stupid, on purpose. "We just don't want to have anything to do with a European," a Herrero boy told me. "If you can't talk to us, you can't 'get across' to us, can you? And so you can't impose your ideas upon us. The language can be a barrier of self-defense."

That, he said, went for the old people. He was one of the "new" Herreros—those who had been born since 1915, when the British came in. He wanted to take the best of everything that the white man had to give. He was a philosopher, this boy, with an eager mind. When he came, after a furtive glance backward at the closed door, into my room in Windhoek one baking afternoon, I think, perhaps, the only reason why I received him was that he was holding a little fox terrier, lovingly, in his arms.

A few minutes later I was ashamed of myself. For he said: "I've found you. I heard you were here. And I wanted to talk."

And what he said was like opening the book of the Herreros' heart.

The story goes, in South-West Africa, that the Herrero women refused to have babies, after the German massacre. They are supposed to have said, "We are not going to bear any more children into slavery." It is claimed that the Herrero women have such a knowledge of abortion that many of its secrets are still a mystery to their own men.

Whatever the truth of the story, the fact is that it seems extremely difficult for a Herrero woman to have a baby, and they seldom have more than one. More than that, their fecundity seemed to stop during their rebellion against the Germans. And they have never been fertile since. Officers who fought with Botha told me that when they went into the country in 1915, they were astonished by an amazing gap in the Herrero population.

"You hardly ever came on a child younger than eleven. There just weren't any. It was as if, since 1904, the Herrero women had stopped breeding. And now they say they can't have children any more!"

"But it is a lie," said this boy, "to say that we Herreros don't want babies. We talk about it all the time. It has broken up our whole life. And the women don't care what they do. A young girl of fifteen will marry an old man of sixty, then she will go about with a young man. But nothing happens. Married or unmarried, all the young girls go about. The men are also promiscuous. They have several sweethearts—but no children!"

He wrung his hands.

"In a hundred years there won't be any Herreros if they are not helped *now!*"

"But what can anyone do?" I asked.

"I don't know. If a Herrero girl *is* lucky and has a baby, it is nearly always conceived at the very first time she has contact with a man. Now, here is another thing: If I sleep with a Berg-Damara girl, I can give *her* a baby. If my wife should sleep with a Berg-Damara man, he can give *her* a baby. How can you explain that?"

"There doesn't seem to be an answer."

"Yes, there is," he said. "That is one reason why I wanted to come and talk to you. You might tell the people here. Because some of us Herreros, we think we have found the answer. The Herreros have become devitalized by their lazy life in the Reserves.

"We get no exercise, no work; the old people won't let us work. They say, 'The Reserve is the place to rest.' Before the Germans came, we at least had to draw water. Now we have windmills. We don't hunt any more; we are not allowed. The women build our huts. We won't even plant seed!"

He said that the Berg-Damaras, whom the Herreros formerly considered a contemptible tribe, their slaves, were now leaving the Herreros behind in civilized life.

"We Herreros," he said, scornfully, "are *too lazy to work to eat!* We just think we can get along on less. But you take a Berg-Damara; he thinks he's just got to fill his belly three times a day. He gets frightened if he can't. So he works. In Windhoek, here, they are sportsmen, these Berg-Damaras. They play football. They have children. We Herreros, we're jealous; if a Berg-Damara woman has several children, we say of her contemptuously, 'She breeds like a Kaffir—that Berg-Damara woman!'"

"What is the thing the Herreros want most?"

"Cattle. The old people would be very happy if they were allowed to have three hundred cattle—*and the holy fire!* But then, there is no hope for them."

"But what do you *need?*" I asked.

His aristocratic, lean, level-browed face contorted with pain. He shook his head. "We cannot have it," he said, at last. "We would like to have our country back, sir. But a book education, sir, is no good for a native in our position. It only makes him want things he can never get. I have a practical idea."

Together, all that hot afternoon, we worked upon it. In its finished shape, it emerged something like this:

The Herreros should have an institution something like Tuskegee Institute, in the United States. It was he (who knew more than I did about Tuskegee) who told me this.

"There we should be taught *manual* trades—carpentry, and practical agriculture. Then we should not just be turned loose. We, the young graduates, should be *made* to go back to the Reserves. *We should be made to stay there for five years.* Then —you watch the result! When the rains came, we just wouldn't sit around doing nothing; we would plant. We'd build houses. We'd just have to, we couldn't just sit still, with all our energy —*and knowledge!*

"Then, they should keep the young girls away from the men until they are of a marriageable age."

Then he told me that he, himself, was a half-caste. "My name is Otto Schimming. I was born on a German farm near Gobabis; my father owned the farm. I can still drink the milk from the sacred cattle in the tribal calabash—but I could not if my mother had been a German and my father a Herrero man. The idea is that I've had *everything* in my mother's stomach. I am a Herrero."

He said with scorn: "You can't pass between the sacred fire and the Elder's hut! But I pass right through it. I think it's rubbish. Waste of time. I believe in a Christian God; my mother's father, a Herrero, was an elder of the Rhenish Church.

"We understand that the Negroes of the United States are very clever?" he half asked. "They become lawyers and doctors, and they go to Yale?"

"They do," I said; "but be careful when you make comparisons; all Negroes in the United States don't have chances like that. You must know more about things. Then, perhaps, you won't be so discontented with your life here. I am having dinner tonight with Mr. X. I will talk with him about all this, your idea for the school."

He stood up. "Thank you, sir."

"Well, don't thank *me,*" I said, gruffly. "It's none of my business; you thank yourself. You are doing some good. You ought to be a leader among the Herreros."

He put his back against the door.

"Tell me, sir; is it true that the Germans are coming back?"

"Are you frightened?"

He nodded. "Yes, I am. Then everything would go; we would have no hope."

"You believe that?"

He nodded again.

"The Germans are not coming back," I said. "I think the South Africans would go to war before they would permit that. Where did you hear that?"

"The Germans here; they tell us that."

"Don't listen," I said.

That night, X said: "Yes, I know him. Good lad. And what we are trying to do is very much what you were talking about, all except that idea of *making* the graduates remain on the Reserves. That boy himself was a school teacher; he had three years at Lovedale. But his eyes are weak. I don't know whether you noticed it or not; but he is nearly blind. He's just a clerk in a store, now."

"Well, that little fox terrier certainly loves him," I said. I felt sad for Otto Schimming.

But there will not be many more Otto Schimmings, or native half-castes any more—not in South-West Africa.

"It's a queer thing," ran the conversation one night at Walvis, "this new miscegenation law. Up here, in South-West, it's now illegal to cohabit with a native girl—yet you can *marry* them!

One of the first results of this new law was that a lot of the fellows married their Damara and Herrero girls—when they found they could not go on sleeping with them any other way. You know, on some of these farms way up-country a man gets lonely as hell, whereas, down in the Union, you can roger any native girl who's willing, but it's a legal offense to marry the girl!"

"Still," said one, "I wouldn't mind taking a crack at one of these Herrero girls. They tell me they can't have babies; something wrong with them."

"You try it!" came the chorus. "You'll be doing two years, like that German's doing now. He must feel a fool!"

I have heard an argument go on for forty minutes as to just what was an authentic "Bastaard." By the inclusion of an extra "a," or just leaving off the "d"—they sometimes call them Bastars—both the early South Africans and the Germans attempt politely to camouflage the fact that there is now, in South-West Africa, practically a new race of people, salmon-colored people with kinky hair, called Bastaards. Rehoboth, their main town, with its red, sandy streets and fine houses, is the capital of Bastaardland.

They are, by origin, the result of a free-for-all mating between early Boer and native Hottentot—a mixture which, incidentally, has produced some of the most brilliant personages in South African life. So, the term Bastaard carries no offense in South-West Africa.

"On the contrary," I was informed during this argument, "an authentic Bastaard considers himself an aristocrat—one of the oldest families in South-West Africa. And everyone knows they have the finest land in this God-forsaken, flea-bitten territory."

But modern "breeds" do not come within this category. Down at the far end of Walvis Bay's main street, just on the edge of the green lagoon, was a sullen colony that illustrated the argument. They were "Cape Whites." They were resentful of the term, Bastaard; they claimed to be white. And they stared at you, angrily, as you passed—passed on your way to that green lagoon, so mossy green, whose edges were rimmed with islands of pink flamingos, where, all day long, the pelicans spread their wings, and played at "gliders"—always, with never a flap, soaring, swooping, rising again in the hot upward currents of air from the blazing sand dunes.

No man could live there. The dunes were pitted with jackal tracks. At night the flamingos moved out into the water, and slept on one leg, to avoid being eaten.

Eight miles below, untroubled yet by any archaeologist, lay some kitchen middens of the early Bushman. It took me half a day to get there, going down along the sandy shore. And there I found a bone knife, a perfect ivory needle, and hundreds of tiny perforated disks, the beads the Bushmen made from ostrich eggs, uncovered by yesterday's winds.

There is a strange beauty and irony in the Herrero calendar. They do not use the European time table, but, like the Chinese, know the periods of the year by their seasonal effects, and years by events. For instance:

January: OTJITARAZU, Rainy Month.
March: ETENGARINDI, First Deaths to be Attributed to Rains.
May: KOZONJANGA, Month of the Lilies.
August: KOMBUNDU, Misty Month (Time of the Bulbs).

The year 1881 is known as "The 'year' of the battle of a frontage of two hours"—obviously, in a native war.

1886: OJORUNDUMBA, The Year in Which the Dogs and the Cattle Went Raving Mad (Drought).
1887: OJOUROMBU, The Year of the Caterpillars.
1902: OJVURANDE JOVINEJA, The Year of the Traders and of Fraud.

The year 1902 was the one leading up to the Herrero rebellion of 1904, when the Herreros were driven mad by the unscrupulous methods of the German traders and military, who were trying to take their cattle away from them, and began that three-year war which reduced them from 90,000—possibly the finest tribe in West Africa—to 30,000 broken men and women. The cattle-raising tribes of Africa are always the aristocrats. But by 1903 the Germans had got half the Herreros' cattle away from them. And after the rebellion ended, in 1907, the Germans forbade the Herreros to graze cattle any more. As an example of German methods (which seem to me far more brutal than mere physical atrocities and massacre, from which no white race can be absolved in Africa), I quote from a certain Captain Schwabe's book, *Mit Schwert und Pflug*, to show the German traders' methods which gave the Herrero name to the year 1902:

As an example of the ignorance of the veld-living Herrero as to the value of money, I may quote the following: A trader camps near a Herrero village. To him are driven the oxen which the Herrero wishes to sell. "How much do you want for the oxen?" says the trader. "Fifty pounds sterling," says the Herrero. "Good," says the trader; "here you have a coat valued at £20, trousers worth £10, and coffee and tobacco worth £50." The Herrero is satisfied; he knows that according to the custom of the traders he cannot expect more for his cattle. He may probably exchange the coat for a blanket, and get some sugar in lieu of tobacco, and he will also (as is customary) by begging get a little extra; if, however, he does not succeed, the transaction is closed. It will be admitted that this sort of trading is quite exceptional and original; it requires to be learned, and the newcomer will have to pay for his experience before he is *able to emulate the dodges and tricks of the old traders*. (Italics mine)

The Herrero account of all this indicates the desperation which drove them, at last, to rebel against the heavily armed Germans; it is shown in the following sworn affidavit of Under Chief Daniel Kariko, which deals with the reasons for the Herreros' attack on the Germans in 1904:

Our people were being robbed and deceived right and left by the German traders. Their cattle were taken by force, they were flogged and ill treated, and got no redress. In fact, the German police assisted the traders instead of protecting us. Traders would come along and offer goods. When we said that we had no cattle to spare, as the rinderpest had killed so many, they said they would give us credit. The trader would simply off-load and leave the goods, saying we could pay for them when we liked, but in a few weeks he would come back and demand his money, or cattle in lieu thereof. He would then go and pick out our very best cows. Very often one man's cattle were taken to pay another man's debts. If we objected, and tried to resist, the police would be sent for, and what with floggings and threats of shooting, it was useless for our poor people to resist. If the traders had been fair and reasonable like the old English traders [the Germans made most of the old English traders leave when they annexed South-West Africa] of the early days, we would never have complained, but this was not trading at all; it was only theft and robbery. They fixed their own prices for the goods, but they would never let us place our own evaluation on the cattle. They said a cow was worth 20 marks only. For a bag of meal they took eight cows, which to us were the equivalent of 16 oxen, as the Herreros would always give two oxen for a cow, as she is a breeder, and we loved to increase our herds. For a pair of boots a cow was taken. Most traders took only cows, *as they were farmers also and wanted to increase their herds.* Often, when credit had been given, they came back and claimed what they called interest on the debt. Once I got a bag of meal on credit, and later the trader came back and took eight cows for what he called interest; thus, it cost me 10 cows altogether. Just before the rebellion in 1903, things got worse than ever. All traders came around and began to collect debts. . . .

What the official Germans in charge of *Südwest Afrika* thought of these methods is made unmistakably clear by Professor Karl Dove of Jena (sometime director of land settlement for the colony) in his book, *Deutsche Zuid West Afrika.* He declares:

Leniency towards the natives is cruelty to the whites. . . . As to the ideas of their sense of justice, these are based on false premises.

It is incorrect to view justice, in regard to the natives, as if they were in the same *kultur-position* as ourselves. They have no conception of what ownership of the ground means.

A nice position for the (white) director of land settlement to take! Professor Dove's *kultur-position* was taken some thirty-three years before Hitler. It is German. There is nothing new, or Nazi, about it. Marshal Goering's father was the first Governor of German South-West Africa.

4. Dead Copper Mine

THERE was not one blade of grass at Walvis. Not a vestige of green. The wife of the chief of customs told me that the silicon in the sand had cut everything off a maidenhair fern that she had tried to nurture in her bungalow. And conversation at Walvis was, not unreasonably, almost confined to what a filthy female Mother Nature is.

The bed of the sea, for example, played some ghoulish tricks. One morning, during the last war, an island suddenly appeared in Walvis lagoon. It remained long enough for an adventurous trader to row out, stand up, and have his photograph taken. A day or so later, it had gone.

But about once a week the sea bed rumbles and emits a belch of poisonous gas. It did this the week I was there. I discovered this the next morning, when, walking along the lonely beach, I noticed that the highwater line was marked for miles and miles with a silver, irregular line of dead fish. They were so tainted with the poisonous gas that not even the ravenous guano birds would touch them.

Then, though the sands of this thousand-mile desert are so blazing that a white man could not bear to walk upon them in his bare feet, the Benguela Current which races up its coast is so icy that you feel your arms and legs congeal. It is highly dangerous to swim there, numbed, in the long, diagonal waves that sweep northwards, pushing mountains of quivering sud across the slimy sand.

And the coast line is always changing. Before the last war the Germans had built a steel pier at Swakopmund, twenty miles above, to take the trade away from Walvis Bay. The pier was meant to unload oceangoing liners. It was a thousand feet long. People were charged sixpence to fish from it.

When I swam at Swakopmund, riding like a gull as the current carried me up toward the equator, the ocean end of that pier, when I passed it, was at least sixty yards back on dry land. The people at Swakopmund now use that pier for their sunset promenade. It is the only use left it by the incorrigible sea.

Between Walvis and Swakopmund there are some shifting sand dunes which are still a mystery. No scientist has yet been able to explain how they got there, nor why they are not blown away. For they are always in motion, forming and re-forming, within this area of exactly twenty miles. When the wind is particularly dry, sucking the last vestige of moisture from them, they explode.

"*Vrooooom!*" they go, with loud booms. And you know that another sand precipice has toppled over.

These dunes, by day, are orange. At sunset they take on the most beautiful shadows of violet and gentian blue. Only the jackal lives among them.

On my first evening, when a port official had led me to the edge of the desert, and asked me to look at it, I asked him what lay above, below, and out beyond us.

"Nothing!" he said, with a note of hysteria in his voice. "It's just miles, and miles, and miles—and *miles!*—of Sweet Fanny Adams!"

The port pilot told me that when it was blowing he had to wear goggles to bring a ship in. "The difference between a fog and a sandstorm," he said, "is that with the former you can usually make out *something* in the murk, some blur that will give you some idea where you are. But with a sandstorm it's sometimes a complete blackout. I've brought a ship right in under the cranes on the wharf before I knew where I was."

During the last war he had run cargoes over all the seven seas. One of these was 14,000 tons of high explosives. They discovered that they were being chased by a submarine.

"But we didn't worry. We knew that if it did hit us, we'd all meet on the horns of the moon."

He appeared at my door one morning and said: "I have no ship to bring in. What about the desert? There's an old German copper mine up in the bed of the Khan River."

The inland desert is swept bare by the wind, like a threadbare carpet, and its undulations are filled with the blues of false mirage lakes. They appeared or disappeared if you raised or lowered your head only a few inches or so. Against them, standing on a ridge, I saw my first two springbok. They were lovely; and when I mentioned this to the port pilot, he began to mutter. It was "The Hound of Heaven." Next he gave me some Edith Sitwell. Then, still staring ahead as he drove the car, he said:

> O Love, are spirits ever old?
> Your dust shall mingle with the earth
> Like mine, and men shall count its worth
> As land to plough, in which to sow
> Their yearly seed.
>   How can they know
> That earth they bruise with heavy tread
> Was once an altar, at which bled
> This heart of mine?

"Yes?" he said.

"Who wrote that?" I asked.

"I did. Why?"

"Mmmm," I said. "I knew you swing compasses for the Norwegian whalers here, that you are considered to be the best compass adjuster on the West African coast, and I have seen you balance a billiard cue on the end of your toe—but I didn't know that you went in for that sort of thing. 'Do you think, at your age, it is right?' "

"You are too young, too young," he said sadly. "You want movies and shops, you do. You've got to know more before you can appreciate a place like Walvis Bay."

It then came out that he had contributed several times to the London *Mercury* while Jack Squire was editor. And that one of his diversions at sea had been reviewing books for one or two of the London literary weeklies. "But I got fired because I wrote that *If Winter Comes* was all bollicks!" He had been at sea since the age of sixteen, and had some very pungent stories of the Chinese coast.

The dead copper mine in the dry bed of the Khan River was something that you might have expected to find in the Valley of the Moon. Its sun baked buildings lay at the foot of bare, crumbling mountains whose black ridges of ironstone glinted with a heat you could almost *see*.

The mill buildings had been looted. Only the cement bases of the big crushers remained. Even the window sills had been prized out. The roofs had been ripped off for their timber and tiles. A massive chain of solid copper still adorned the empty shell of the house where once the heavy foot of the German manager had trod. (Its green massiveness, somehow, indicated that he was a ponderous soul.) And nothing remained worth taking away, except that in the sun-smitten walls of what had been the office we came on some old records of the *Deutsche Kolonial-Gesellschaft für Südwest Afrika.*

It would be hard to describe just the exact start that these papers gave us—this sensation of having abruptly stepped back into Time. The papers were brittle as cigar ash, and full of scorpions; but they held a story.

It was the tale of a German carpenter, William Loeffel; his full contract, signed at Duisburg, Germany, 22nd Jan., 1913. He had been engaged, at 350 marks a month, to go out to

South-West Africa to the *Khan-Kupfergrube*. He was to get
250 m. a month while the steamship *Windhuk*, sailing from
Antwerp, took him to South-West. He signed on for two years.

Next letter in the file was the copy of a letter from Herr
William Loeffel. It was written to the *Deutsche Kolonial-Gesellschaft* head office in Germany. It explained how on Christmas night, just when he was about ready to sail, he had his
pockets picked in Cologne.

> I was a bit drunk [he wrote to the head office]. I came home
> and must have left the doors open. In the morning my landlady said,
> "Your pants are in the hall." And there was nothing in them! I had
> there three 100 m. notes; spent 15 marks for drink. Please do not
> write this to Africa and give me a bad reputation.

But they did. It was a typewritten copy of his letter which
I read in that pitiless sun, a copy that had been sent out to
Africa. And he came. Later I read the manager's report, for
the mine's records, of an accident to William Loeffel. It re-
corded how *Zimmermann* Loeffel was accustomed to bring timber down to the manager's house, and then ride back on the
little railway truck downhill. With Loeffel, this day, there had
been a native inside the bucket of the truck. The brakes did
not work; Loeffel and the native hit the bumper at the foot
of the mine buildings. Loeffel got a cut on the head; the native
complained his feet were injured, and he could not work.

Later I read the mine doctor's report on the two cases.
Loeffel's wound, he said, was not of any consequence, and the
native was now "ready for tropical duty." All very thorough,
echt deutsch, and quite macabre to read in that dead valley,
after all these years had passed. Water now fills the shafts of
the abandoned copper mine; the machinery is dismantled; the
pit props still hold open a yawning slit of dangerous mountain.
Some green thorn and mimosa trees stand sentinel.

I would have stayed at Walvis longer, had it not been for
another discovery. My bedroom was nothing to cling to, for its

only window opened out into a sand compound. And this compound held nothing but pyramids of those empty beer bottles. The barefoot Klip-Kaffir who served my morning tea I saw, I think, only once. For he never knocked, never said a word; he must have given me just a slight nudge and run for it, after he had put the tray on the chair beside my wire-spring bed. But the boy who cleaned my shoes I might summon at any time of the day, to get the sand and mud off them. And this watery eyed little Hottentot did not look good to me.

"That boy's sick," I said to my German host.

"Hmph! That one? Oh, he's got syphilis."

"*What?*"

"*Ja.* But it don't hurt nobody. When they get syph I always make 'em go to the doctor. He fixes 'em up so they can't give it to anybody."

"*They!* Do many people around here have syph?"

"About ninety per cent," said the German.

"Well!"

"You needn't worry. I don't ever let 'em touch any food."

I felt like retorting he couldn't have made the food any more poisonous, if he had. I didn't worry. There was a train the next day, and I took it, for Swakopmund.

5. *Führers* in the Mandate

TWENTY miles north of Walvis Bay is the Mandate's summer capital, Swakopmund, as German as any Baltic seaside resort. Its sandy, unpaved main street, the Kaiser Wilhelmstrasse, was intersected by the Moltke Strasse. Its homes were stucco bungalows, red roofed, with gardens and green shrubbery, and bougainvillaea banked against their white sides. Its main hotels were the Kaiserhof, Fürst Bismarck, Hansa, Faber, Europäischer Hof—and then the little Strand, run by Herr Ohlmann. The most imposing structure was a baroque German church. The most pleasant, nestling among its fan palms, overlooking the botanical gardens and the icy Benguela Current, was the long, low, buff, summer home of the Administrator for South-West Africa; always a South African, appointed by the Governor General of the Union. This one was a Pretoria lawyer.

And outside the residence still stood the old German war memorial. (Which, of course, must have been put up by the Germans since the last war.) It was a life-size bronze of a wounded German soldier, his bayonet fixed, his head bandaged, standing guard over the body of a dying German sailor. It was very moving.

And, such is the tolerance of the South Africans, I suppose it is still standing there; a statue which, aside from its original purpose, is a monument to South African patience.

Throughout the Mandate, and down in the Union, I was continually struck by this tolerance (it might be called blindness) of the liberty-loving Boer South African to the menace of Nazi aims. They refused to believe that Nazi ideology would, if successful, wreck their own domestic lives—which, when all is said and done, is the final thing we live for. This race, which has added some of the most fascinating pages to history—the Great Trek, the Boer War—these stout-hearted people, who would rather die than be *policed* by anybody, even their own statesmen; these fearless men and women—could not see the menace which would make every one of them a servant of some *Gauleiter*. The reason was (or is), perhaps, that their honest, placid minds were not capable of imagining such a servitude. They were, mentally, too far from Europe.

The night I arrived, the local Nazis boycotted the dance in my hotel, because they had discovered there were some non-Aryans among its five-piece band. They stood at the door and took the names of people going in. This was the main hotel; and it, also, was being punished by the Nazis because its owner had applied for South African citizenship. Still, one of the oldest Germans in the colony, one of the original settlers of Südwest Afrika, was staying there. He told me that when he came they had to be put ashore in a surfboat. Now he had over forty thousand head of cattle. Yet even he cut me dead, and refused to speak to me afterwards, when he heard that one of the men I intended to see up at Windhoek was a Jew.

"You *shouldn't* talk to men like that!"

"And why not?"

"I have nothing to say," he said.

So we left it at that.

There was not much more to be said for Swakopmund, except, as the one South African I found there (aside from the Administrator) put it: "Swakopmund is just 120 per cent Nazi!" My local paper was the *Swakopmunder Zeitung*, which changed its name to the *Deutsche Beobachter* when I was there.

It was the most violent of the three big German newspapers in the Mandate (there was only one English one, *The Windhoek Advertiser*, which, at that time, had a circulation of only

750); it was printed in German script, was full of verbatim excerpts from the Third Reich press, putting, as they did, the usual reverse-English spin on all foreign comment.

And the meals were very German: Bismarck herring, roll-mops, frankfurters, potato salad, and bouillon *mit Ei* served by a German fräulein with bare and sunburned legs and plaited hair. (The beer was heavenly!)

You were thankful, frequently, for this German efficiency, in a raw place like South-West Africa. Wherever you went there were good German hotels; good and well stocked German stores, excellent photographers; and, sinisterly propagandistic, spectacularly well filled book stores. There were German druggists, dentists, and doctors. Whenever you wanted anything done for your car, you could, if you were able to reach a town, be sure there was an efficient German garage, its owner very often the *Führer* of the district.

And (showing dangerous apathy on the part of the South Africans) there was hardly a mechanic of any sort in South-West who was not a German. (Of course, excepting the South African railway workers.)

If you did happen to find a shop with an English name, you usually found, on entering, that it possessed a German manager. The three big international oil companies in the Mandate, none of them German, all had German managers. This was done partly, you learned, to attract German custom, but also because there was always, apparently, an efficient German ready for the job.

Even the ammunition dealer at Windhoek, the capital, was a German. His shelves were stocked with German rifles, German shotguns, German cartridges. These last, he insisted, when I tried to buy English, were much better than the English kind; so he sold me six hundred.

I found a bitter sweetness, a month later, when I came down from Ovamboland, in telling him, before some of his German customers, that when the ducks and geese were coming over thickest, his blasted German cartridges would not go off.

"You'd need a hammer to detonate those caps!" I said.

"But you should have a *German* shotgun!" he replied.

You appreciate this German efficiency, and then it gets on your nerves. You resent the way Berlin is always poking its finger into peaceful African life. To be "Heil Hitlered!" and given the Nazi salute in the African bush was almost too much to bear. Particularly when you knew that many of these Germans did not feel that way in their hearts.

For, despite the fact that even a secret plebiscite would show that about ninety per cent of these Germans would vote for the return of the colony to Germany—they are such invincible patriots—and despite the fact that nearly all Germans there were proud of the way Hitler had brought Germany up again, a great many wanted him to stop there—in Europe.

They did not want the Nazi terror imposed upon them in South-West Africa, for it is no exaggeration to say there was hardly a German in all South-West Africa who did not live in mortal terror of his own kind.

"You must understand," said one old German to me, "there is hardly a German in South-West who has not either some part of his business, or some relations, back in Germany. They are our hostages to fortune. And whatever we do out here is vented upon them. That's why we are all such good Nazis!"

His case was typical. He was one of the Germans whom, after the last war, the South Africans had deported from the Mandate. "They considered me a troublesome character," he said with a smile, "and had had me in a concentration camp. But all I did, when the South African soldiers landed at Walvis, was to plant some land mines along the beach. Then I hid in an empty piano packing crate and touched them off with an electric wire as they passed over them."

In 1926 he was allowed to come back. "That was a bad year

in Germany, and as I couldn't take any money out of the country, I took a stock of goods. I set up a store up-country. I did so well that one day I was foolish enough to say: 'Thank God I am back in South-West Africa again!'

"Someone in the store who heard me went out and told the others that I had said, 'Thank God I am not in Germany!'

"I was boycotted. There were only Germans in those parts. In two months, I failed.

"Then I came here. Now, the local *Führer* here is in my same line of business. He started the story that I was either a Freemason or a Jew. I started to fail again. But I was getting desperate, about then, so I went to him and challenged him in public. I said that he was to have the party look up my antecedents in Hamburg; if they could prove that I was a Jew, or had any Jewish ancestors, or that I had ever been a Freemason —and the Nazis can easily find that out—then I would leave South-West Africa.

" 'But if you don't,' I said to the *Führer*, 'then *you've* got to pay a forfeit; you've got to take three months' earnings from your store and give it to the hospital here. Are you on?' "

This German laughed. "Well, you see, I am still here, and I'm not a Freemason or a Jew any longer; the *Führer* backed down. But it's the young ones who make most of the trouble. Those lads who haven't any stake in this country. They've nothing to lose; if they get kicked out of this country for their Nazi activities, they know they'd be treated like bloody little heroes when they get back to Germany. So they simply raise hell with us out here!"

Another German, a determined-looking young wool exporter, told me that he had just received letters from all his former German suppliers that they would not ship their wool through him any more. They were, they said, receiving better prices from someone else. But one of them, a close friend of his, came to him.

"That's all a lie," he said. "It's not a question of prices. But all of us have been told that, in Hamburg, you are known as an anti-Nazi. And now it is said that if we ship our wool through you, no one will be allowed to buy it in Hamburg. So what can we do?"

The young German told him.

"And he was probably quite right," said a South African. "He makes no bones at all that he is an anti-Nazi. In fact, he's told some of the younger Nazis here that if they get funny with him, he will put a bullet in them. He would, too! And they know it, so he is safe.

"Only," he added, "the man's business is gone."

I have a copy of a letter from the German Consul General at Windhoek to a German in South-West Africa, who had had the temerity to apply for South African citizenship. The letter coldly asks why he has dared to do this, points out that the future of the Mandate is still at stake, indicates that it will one day be returned to Germany, and advises the recipient that if he crosses over, and might one day want to come back, the door will very likely be closed.

The letter is signed under: "Heil Hitler!"

To the Germans, the German Consul General was the most terrifying object in South-West Africa. They lived under his inquisition. And he, it was said, was at daggers-drawn with the ostensible *Führer* for the Germans in South-West Africa.

It was to ask questions of these two men that I crossed the desert up into the high plateau and lingered at Windhoek, the capital of South-West Africa.

They were both hard men. The German Consul General was an ex-cavalry officer, erect and arrogant, his manner tempered with an icy politeness. His attitude was that of a commander of dissenters within a hostile fort. In spite of any other feelings you might harbor towards him, you could not help but feel that he was, *qua* man, as good a man as you would find in the Mandate. He accepted the typed questionnaire that I had prepared, with several duplicates. It asked how many Germans there were in South-West Africa with two passports, what was the extent of their land holdings vis-à-vis the South Africans, how many Germans still possessed only Third Reich passports, etc. Coming to that particular question, he curled his lips under a brazen monocle, and asked me to call again "when I have had the time to study this—this *very* interesting paper!"

When I did, again, pass through the iron-barred, zoo-like doors that protected the German Consul General at Windhoek against any night effort to investigate his premises, this Prussian ex-cavalry captain, who had fought in Südwest Afrika, gave me an ironic handshake, an even more understanding smile, and, holding out his cigarette case, said: "The man you should ask these questions of is Dr. Hirsekorn—a most competent man. I have told him about you."

He smiled again, bowed, clicked his heels.

Dr. Hirsekorn was the *Führer*.

Dr. Hans Bruno Karl Hirsekorn (as I read on his passport) was an attorney who, before the last war, had come out to enter the colonial service in Südwest Afrika. He was heavy-set, blue-eyed, with a natural inclination to be a good fellow; his left cheek was heavily scarred in duels for his student corps, which, he told me with self-deprecating modesty, had been the same as Baron von Neurath's.

"I am afraid," he said at once, "that we cannot answer some of your questions. The Consul General is the only one who possesses some of this information."

I smiled. "I see," I said; "I was afraid you would say something like that. I made several copies, and gave one to the Secretary for South-West Africa. Perhaps he has the information?"

Dr. Hirsekorn gave me what can be described as nothing less than a broad grin. "Please sit down," he said.

He reached into his desk, and handed me his own passport.

It was a South African one. It had been granted to him, under the Union Act of 1910, on August 13, 1928, at Pretoria. This meant that he was a full South African citizen, that within the Union he had all the privileges *and obligations* of any South African, and that wherever South Africa had ministers or consulates abroad, he was entitled to all their services—everywhere, except in Germany.

"I do not even have a German passport!" he said, as if that ought to satisfy all my inquisitiveness.

"Yet you are the president of the *Deutsche Südwest Bund*, and you headed the meeting which passed those resolutions saying that all Germans in South-West Africa owed allegiance to the Third Reich and that any German who applied for South African papers was a traitor to the fatherland?"

"Yes," said Dr. Hirsekorn.

"Paradoxical, isn't it?"

"Yes; it might look like it. But there are grave issues at stake. In days like these, when, at any time, a German in this country might be asked to state definitely to which country he belonged, we want to make our position clear at the very start."

"That you are Germans?"

"Yes; I'm a born German, and, under the circumstances, I can only be a German."

"And this passport; what does it all mean, then?"

The conversation that followed could not have better illustrated what we are fond of calling "German obtuseness" in foreign relations—and calling it quite correctly that! For Dr. Hirsekorn was an honest, likable man. He was quite bewildered that I did not accept his premise, and that his obvious sincerity did not convince me of his impeccable position. Once a German, always a German; that was his contention, and, to him, it explained everything else, justified any treachery to anyone who was *not* a German.

"I admire your patriotism," I said, "but I'll be damned if I can make any sense out of this argument. You've just been saying that one of your major complaints is that a German can now only secure South African citizenship after a residence of five years in the colony. Whereas, a South African may vote in the Mandate after he has been here two years. I can understand that grievance; there's some reason to it.

"But, on the other hand, you have just passed that resolution saying that a German is a traitor who asks for South African papers, and that all Germans here, no matter if they have got South African passports, are still subjects of the Third Reich!"

"The South Africans were beginning to discriminate against us," said Dr. Hirsekorn; "they have been refusing permits to German immigrants."

"But you don't expect the South Africans to sit idly by and watch you create a Sudetenland in South-West Africa? And you also passed a resolution that South-West belongs, and should be returned to Germany," I concluded.

"I am a German," said Dr. Hirsekorn.

I told him that I could see that. I pushed his South African passport back to him, and he dropped it into his desk. Then I suggested that our argument had been useless, beside the point; for it was not questions of ethics which would decide the future of the South-West African Mandate; it would not be settled here. It would be a trial by force, in Europe.

He looked grave.

"Well, I can tell you one thing," he said; "we won't *putsch* here. I know that's what they're all telling you."

I said: "The South Africans are not embarrassed by any of the considerations that may hold England's hand·back, for the moment, in European affairs. The South Africans are very direct, and this seems a simple problem. I don't see how you could get away with it, if you did *putsch;* the South African soldiers would be in here the next day."

"I like talking to you," said Dr. Hirsekorn. "I wish you had more time here; we could have a *Bierabend. Good-*day!"

✦

I talked with the *Führer* of a little town up-country. He was the proprietor of its garage—a young, competent, alarmingly energetic man.

"There will be no war," he said. "Mr. Chamberlain will save us from it."

"Why Chamberlain?"

"Well, he saved us at Munich.

"And the *Führer*," he added quickly; "the *Führer*, he doesn't want a war. The *Führer* wants peace with all mankind."

"Well, you're going about it in a queer way," I said.

"How's that?"

"Well, what about the August persecution of the Jews? That had a terrific effect in the United States; I think it has finally tipped the scales against you."

"Ho!" He gave a genuine guffaw of amusement.

Then he pointed up into the sky. There were one or two little morning clouds still hanging against that incredible blue. They were evaporating, in that heat, even as we regarded them.

"It will all pass, your indignation about the Jews," he said; "just pass, like those clouds."

"And the hell of it is," said an Englishman I was staying with, "it will. I sometimes wonder if those bloody Germans are really as dumb as we think they are!"

6. Food Trouble

THERE are only five miles of paved roads in all South-West Africa. And Windhoek has all of them.

This hilly capital is God's gift to the colored postcard industry. Its sky is just that incredible blue. Its buff government buildings rest on impossibly green hills. They have red roofs. And nearly everywhere you look in Windhoek there are beds of scarlet geraniums and purple bougainvillaea, while even the graveyard, which is one of the showplaces of the town, is laid out with vistas of cypress and classic urns. The zoo, in the park, in whose deep shade you may drink a glass of hock at midday, is a sunless sanctuary of gum and casuarina trees.

The favorite drink here, after dinner, is hock, which the Germans, with robust jocularity, have labeled "Naked Arse." It has five little gnomes, with bare behinds, on the bottle.

A newcomer usually breathes a little hard in the baking summer, at this height of over 5,500 feet. But the winters are cold. The two castles built on two hills overlooking Windhoek have baronial fireplaces of hewn stone. Both the castles, amply turreted, were built by the same man, a German baron, one of the old "aristos" whose epoch ended with the last war. One was for himself, the other he built for his wife. He called upon her every morning, but before doing so he always sent his "boy" across with a card, to see if it was convenient to receive him.

In the old days many of the Germans who came out to Africa seemed to be seeking there the fairyland of their legends. They lived lives of grandiose unreality. Down in the territory still stands another castle that is as turreted as any fortress along the Rhine. This was owned by a count, and his boast was that no house party, no matter how large, could ever drink up his stock of wine for any one year. When this seemed in danger of happening, he would shout, "To horse!" And all his guests, in a shouting cavalcade, would gallop to the nearest settlement. Here the proprietor of the local bottle store, well stocked against such a contingency, would fill his donkey-mobile with crates of champagne and hock, and the house party would race home again.

It was a vast life.

This German had an American wife. They were in the States at the outbreak of war in 1914. He somehow got to Germany, and was killed, in the line, before Christmas that year.

"Sundowners" are what they call cocktail parties in South-West Africa. They are comfortable affairs. Not noisy. And at one of these, easing down after the heat and the political tension of my day's work, I met N'Goni, a Bushman. N'Goni had the reputation of being the best cocktail server in the Mandate.

And N'Goni illustrates a point.

The point is that Africa is the land of idle women. The reason for this is that there are so many "boys" about. A boy may be anywhere from six to seventy; he may be a Kroo, an Angola boy, with his teeth filed; he may be a haughty Herrero, or a Zulu.

With so many white bachelor establishments, a "boy" is expected to run the house.

Some women, in Africa, become so dependent upon their "boys" that they never even bother to enter their own kitchens. When I reached Dar es Salaam, the story was still going the rounds of a woman who thought she had the best cook in Tanganyika. This came out one night, when she complimented her hostess of that evening on the excellent dinner. This woman mentioned the name of the famous cook. "But *I've* got him!"

cried the other. When they went into the kitchen they found that neither of them had him.

He had appeared, in person, at both houses to get the job. He had, presumably, stayed at each a few days, at odd hours, to show the flag, as it were. Then he had hired a cheap substitute to carry on with the work. In case of danger from discovery, the substitute always managed to find an excuse for his absence (and his own presence), and summon his superior.

Then there was the case of a newcomer who, at first, found herself very popular in the colony. After a time she became aware that people were always finding excuses for not accepting her dinner invitations. She went to her best friend.

"My dear," said the other, "do you ever go into your kitchen?"

"No; why *should* I?"

"Because, my dear, your cook is a leper."

N'Goni was discovered under a bush where his mother had abandoned him. This was in the park lands on the edge of the Kalahari desert. When N'Goni was washed, he nearly died from exposure. And so would you, if you had not much more protective clothing than the increasing cake of dirt that a Bushman acquires during his little life.

When I saw N'Goni his mistress had made a little Grecian tunic for him, and shorts, trimmed with red tape. His master was the Secretary for South-West Africa. N'Goni was twelve years old and four feet high; he would never get any bigger. He was the color of peanut butter, with his hair in little balls all over his melon-shaped head. His eyes . . .

"My eyes are little, master," said N'Goni, twinkling; "but they see *every*thing!"

So they did. He was a sprite in the house. By sheer mimicry alone, he aped the retiring Kroo "boy" and learned to wait at table. Listening to the sounds, he rapidly acquired a good working knowledge of English and German. The Courtney Clarkes discovered this when they heard him retailing, in the kitchen, things they had just said at the dinner table. His mistress declared it made her feel ashamed, to witness little N'Goni's linguistic abilities.

He was always at your elbow, irrepressible, anticipating your own wishes before you became aware of them.

When I spent Christmas with the Courtney Clarkes, up at Grootfontein, the first toast of that friendly dinner was, "To absent friends."

In the traditional silence which followed this ceremony, N'Goni noticed that I merely raised the sherry glass to my lips, but did not drink.

I felt a touch, and turned to find some little yellow fingers, delicate as flower petals, tugging at my sleeve. N'Goni's face was close to mine. He pointed at the glass:

"Wantem whisky, master?"

"Ssssh!" I shook my head.

N'Goni shook *his* head; he could not understand. And I could not explain, not to a Bushman, that I was on the water wagon.

The Courtney Clarkes were prominent and very much liked people in South-West Africa. He is an Oxford man, an Englishman, who had been thirty-six years in the South African service, without ever a day's sick leave—one of those sturdy souls which no climate can break.

When Courtney Clarke drives to Government House, many of the old-timers in the street raise their hats. He returns the salute.

One day, when he was driving, with little N'Goni in the dickey seat, he noticed that people always smiled, or looked embarrassed, when he raised his hat. Then he turned quickly, hat in hand, and caught N'Goni in the act.

When master raised his hat, N'Goni raised his. When master bowed, N'Goni bowed.

"The only answer to that," said Courtney Clarke, "was not to take him out; I couldn't stop him mimicking me!"

It is at Windhoek that you become aware of the unobtrusiveness with which the South Africans are administering this Mandate. For the Dutch South African hates being "ruled," or even ruling anybody. From here you see them running all the railways, the posts and telegraphs, all the municipal and civil administration, and native affairs. Up-country from here you begin to meet the resident magistrates whose scope of duties embraces more subjects than even their counterparts in India. These are all South Africans. They are, as I said, the most unpretentious set of officials you will find in any territory. The minimum of ceremony, and no pomp, accompanies their position. They exercise their control with almost an invisible minimum of police. And in all the seven weeks I was traveling in South-West Africa I did not see a single soldier in uniform.

Social life, as such, at Windhoek was nil, except for an occasional, quiet dinner party. And there was not much pleasure to be gained from eating. I think the worst food in the world is served in South-West Africa and down in the Union. It may be my fault (undoubtedly I'm too Nordic), but food just loses all taste, for me, below the equator.

The food at my hotel at Windhoek was tolerable. But every now and then we would have a meal placed before us that seemed nothing less than a studied affront. It both looked, and tasted, as if it had been merely thrown at the stove.

"Can't this cook cook?" I demanded of the waiter.

"She can cook," said the old German, mysteriously, "but sometimes she doesn't want to!"

This remark had a hidden significance. These vile meals usually occurred when there were just a few South African business men in the hotel, and myself. They did not occur on those nights when the tables were full of talkative Germans. And this woman, the wife of the proprietor, was, I had heard, one of the hottest Nazis in Windhoek. It made me wonder if there could not be some connection between the two—was she trying to poison us!

Down in Walvis, when I came in, one night, covered with dust and sweat from the desert, I asked the German frau could I have some bacon and eggs and a cup of coffee.

"What do you think we are?" she suddenly stormed at me. "Do you think we have nothing else to do but wait on you—"

"Americans?" I suggested.

I rather had her there. She thought I was a member of the race which had given her such a frustration complex. Then her husband got up. "All right, all right," he said quickly, "I'll get them for you." And when he put down the meal he said, sotto voce, "You know what women are!"

She was standing there, glaring at us. In the sputtering gasoline light I saw that her blonde hair had a half-inch of black spreading from either side of the parting. He had learned what women were, all right, from her!

And she focused my interest on something very vital, a thing that will have a lot to do with ultimate German resistance in this war; that is, that the woman is often a more bitter Nazi than the German man.

7. Herrero Names for White Men

THE peace of this upland farm was quite unbelievable after the political tension of Windhoek. It was what you expected from Africa. And it was one of the few things I found there that I did expect.

Eric's place was between two glinting granite kopjes, their gray sides a little rusty. A leopard lived on the top of one. But Eric, with easy tolerance, let him live. (Anyway, the kopje's sides were too smooth to climb.) He was a "check-book" farmer, an Englishman. He did not fine his Herrero boys when they lost a calf; it is the chronic complaint of all boys who work for the other farmers that they have been fined two or three months' pay out of their year's wages. In their fairness towards the natives, the English settlers are almost invariably good examples. They are usually well enough off to remain altruistic, so bitterness does not often enter into their relations with their "boys." This accounted for much of the peaceful feeling on Eric's farm.

On the other hand, the loss of a few karakul ewes, whose lamb pelts (to be turned by furriers into astrakhan) might be worth as much as twenty-seven shillings each, would be a matter of first-rate importance to a struggling Boer. He is not always to be blamed if he lets his exasperation get the better of him, especially if he thinks it has been a stupid loss, sometimes a *deliberately* stupid loss. For natives can be like that.

The ideal treatment of the native lies almost in the realms of fancy, contrasted with the immediate, practical problem. And you will often hear, down in the Cape, that the disillusioned Englishman sometimes becomes the most overbearing taskmaster.

"He comes out here with grand ideals. He is going to love the native, be a father to him. Then he finds they are doing him dirt on every side. He gets mad as hell; he thinks they're the damnedest, ungratefulest bastards he's ever met. So he turns cynical and just plays hell with them. But the native has just been a *native* all along."

I've often heard it said that the natives would rather work for a South African than they would for either an Englishman or a German, even though he beats them more and pays them less.

"It's because the natives feel *they can talk with him.* A Boer will chat about the weather, or what's wrong with the cattle, and that sort of gives the native a proprietary interest in the farm. He feels he is part of it; the beggar's *interest* gets aroused—all working together, so to speak. Natives must work in company, even if it's only among themselves. But it's much grander to feel *company* with a white man."

There is something very appealing about that. It shows a loyalty that many intelligent white *baases* appreciate and appeal to.

But many English and South Africans also told me, out there, that the native would rather work for a German than for either of them. A German settler said to me:

"It's because they'd rather have twenty-five on the backside than be fined. In the old days, when we had an unruly 'boy,' we usually sent him along to the police with a note suggesting they give him fifteen or twenty-five strokes where it would do him the most good. He understood that; and a native boy soon gets over pain.

"Now—what happens? You get fined if you touch 'em! Of course, many do, because the 'boy' usually doesn't know enough to complain, and, then, if the *baas* knows his business, the 'boy' won't be able to get a pass to leave the farm and get down to the magistrate while the bruises and blood are still there to show he's not lying. So the *baas* fines him!"

The natives hate that. At Grootfontein, first and last post where the boys recruited from Ovamboland and Portuguese Africa pass through on their way for employment in South-West Africa, they must make a statement before the magistrate (taken down in writing) as to just what treatment they received during that year from their master. By far the most frequent complaint is that the master has fined them one, sometimes two or three, months' pay. When it is realized that a "boy" after a year's work in the South seldom brings back more than £5 for a whole year, it can be seen why they would rather have twenty-five on the backside.

Near Eric's place was a magnificent old South African character, Boodles. Boodles, who was living in the old German military mess, had theoretical possession of several thousand acres, across which wandered an imaginary herd of cattle. Actually Boodles's livelihood came from the amount of firewood that his Herrero "boys" gathered and sold to a nearby settlement. Boodles's wife was a direct descendant of "George Rex" (a natural son of George III, who had been exiled to Africa to prevent him from embarrassing the London scene). Boodles's chief offering, when you drove across his Alice in Wonderland farm to have tea, was to show you the very tree, with the rusted wire noose, from which the German officers hanged the Herrero "boys."

"Hung 'em on any pretext! Fact—there's the very wire!"

The blue flowers of the jacaranda trees were thick as mist around the white walls of the ghostly old German G.H.Q. Boodles has been there ever since he came in, as a policeman, with General Botha in 1915.

"I'm English all through!" shouts Boodles. "And I think we ought to clear all these —— —— Germans out; lock, stock, *and* barrel! But *they* knew how to handle the natives! Made 'em respect 'em; that's what they did! *Look* at that tree!"

Seen in the late afternoon, with the rain clouds hanging over the depressing thorn scrub, with the little cell still standing where the condemned native spent his last night, the picture suddenly became too awful to bear of the poor Herrero or Ovamba, standing there, patiently waiting to be strangled, while the native *askaris* stood at salute.

"A native knew where he was *at*, with the Germans!" said Boodles.

City dwellers often play with the idea of going to live in far-off parts. Luckily, few ever put their dreams to the test. Most white men go to places like Africa for the following candid reasons: To make a career, to make money, to get away from something or somebody else—to get away from themselves. The last is usually a hopeless effort. The silence and loneliness of the bush will only magnify any maggot that is eating your soul. Only a person of supreme receptiveness, or greatness of character, capable of absorbing all the meaning of veld or forest, can ever shed his troubles and begin a fresh and sweet life again. Usually, he just rots from boredom. And his personal devil gets him.

"Even the best of them go bush-barmy!" you will hear frequently in these parts.

Even old Boodles, whose egotism seemed thick enough to isolate him from any situation, fired a revolver through his own roof at times. "There was an owl," said Boodles, "sat on my roof, screechin'. I figured out where he was, *and* took a shot at him. Missed! Fired again. Then he'd come back, sittin' on another side of the roof. Fired. Missed! Never did get him!"

But then there are people like Eric and his two friends. A major from the Somme; a major from the regular Indian Army; a slightly built dilettante, whose spirit had marched its frail body, as a prisoner of the Turks, across Asia, who refused to be exchanged when he found his pals must remain behind, who is described in one book of memoirs as "possibly the

pluckiest member of our outfit," who, when I was driven over
to dine with him, met us in a mercerized suit of robin's-egg
blue.

All of these men had money enough to live in England;
none had enough to live there the way he liked. So they wrote
to each other; from India, from London, from the Riviera.
They forejoined at Windhoek in South-West Africa. They left
there during the night, in their oxcart, because they did not
know how to drive it, and did not want to make a show of
themselves. Fourteen oxen were pulling it. On their way out
of town they took a red lantern from a street obstruction and
hung it on the horn of the leading ox. In this way, when dawn
came over the misty scrub, they were on their three-hundred-
mile trek up into South-West Africa.

Their sense of humor saved them. Because it was years
(actually seven of them!) before any one of the three struck
water. They lived in mud-and-wattle huts they built themselves. They lived out of tins, or on what they could shoot.
They slaved building dams to hold the seasonal rains.

Now, the dark interior of Eric's house has a few restful pieces
of old furniture that he has brought out from England. His
cement floors are covered with leopard mats. Every mail brings
new books and practically all the illustrated weeklies. Around
his house black house domestics gossip in circles in the shade;
the girls about to have babies; suckling the latest; with tiny
pot-bellied "totos" standing up with their thumbs in their
mouths, and nothing but a "shame-string" of colored beads to
hide their sex.

Once he has "struck it," a white man practically ceases to
do any manual labor in Africa; usually he doesn't do much
before he "hits it." All that Eric has to do now is see that his
Herrero shepherds don't let the cattle get away. They roam
25,000 fenced acres. Their cream is driven in a one-ton lorry
to the nearest butter factory; then there is the season for

"slaughter cattle." The skimmed milk is simply poured out into cement troughs, and I watched the big, black pigs wallowing in this.

Eric met me at the railway junction. The country saps the blood out of Englishmen's lips. This made him look particularly close clipped, blue-eyed, his taut skin attractively hardened by wind and weather. Beside his wife in the car sat a cylindrical Sealyham.

"Now, don't say she's fat!" she said as we drove off. "She saved my life once."

Bingo, or whatever its name was, had been lying on its mistress's bed, on her first married day in the house, while she was trying to take a nap. But Bingo was nervous, and got spanked for being so fussy. His wife mentioned it to Eric when he came in. Both watched Bingo, staring accusatively, at something down under, under the cot. Eric got an electric torch and peered under. Then he stood up, very quiet.

"Get up quickly, and rush out the door; there's a cobra under your bed."

"That's the bed you're going to have," she laughed.

When my boys had taken in my things I closed the two doors, and *I* looked under the bed. I didn't trust to Bingo. In the Belgian Congo, later, I sat down on a scorpion.

Eric, always dressed in tropic white, was one of those immaculate Englishmen, who, you knew, if he fell into a sewer, would come up in a dinner jacket. His wife had been married to him a year before she knew what his native name was. They always have one for you—usually too candid.

Eric wouldn't tell her.

So she went to one of the three friends. "What *is* Eric's Herrero name?"

" 'The Man with the Dirty Habits!' "

"Oh, my God!"

Seven years after this, when she retailed this story about Eric at my first dinner with them, Eric became so enraged that he flushed. Afterwards he said to me:

"I don't know what it is that they think is dirty about me, but they certainly do! That's *always* the way they mention me among themselves."

Six weeks later, when I came down from Ovamboland, on my way out of South-West Africa, I told Eric he need not worry. I had one worse than his.

There had been a big tribal dance of the Ovambas; an "effendula," an initiation dance, after which the young Ovamba girls need no longer remain virgins. After this exciting orgy, wherein a hundred or so of the most lovely busts were glistening with red ocher, the tribe decided to "name" me.

I stood there (with the fourteen drums hammering), as proud as ever I had been. I waited. For probably the first time, certainly the last, I was going to hear about a thousand guileless people unite in paying me a compliment. There *are* only eight white men allowed in all the seventeen thousand square miles of "closed" Ovamboland. It was an unusual experience.

Then the chief's last, and favorite, wife shouted a name. The Ovambas went into a frenzy; they sang, they danced; the drummers, "riding" the eight-foot drums, poured with sweat. And the native commissioner was holding his sides.

"What is it?" I asked, apprehensively. "What *is* my Ovamba name?"

" 'The Man with the Big, Strong, White Stomach!' "

"I won't have it!" I shouted.

"But it's a *com*pliment!"

"Not to me . . . not to me, it isn't!"

Eventually they gave me another one, after an old dead chief. But it was a tame affair. It aroused no enthusiasm. And I kept the big, strong, white stomach.

I still have it.

*

8. Bushmen of Kalahari

AFTER being thoroughly exhausted by the amenities of our civilization, it was a relief to meet people who were managing to get along without any of them—the Bushmen. The last 3,000 of them left in the world live in the Kalahari desert and along its rim, in South-West Africa. In two long jumps by motor car from Eric's farm I passed beyond civilization, and got to them.

As late as 1910, the farmers around Grootfontein, in South-West Africa, were petitioning the magistrate to let them class the Bushmen as *Vogelfrei*, vermin—as "game" to be shot all the year round. The magistrate said, "No, they are human."

This remark is still quoted in these parts, with, it seems, a certain element of surprise that the man was advanced enough to make such a statement. For it was not the prevailing opinion. And so, they were not legally classed as a target.

But if a man shot a Bushman he was not tried for murder. The result was that Bushmen got shot.

The result of this was that the Bushman was forced into a secretive life vis-à-vis the white man. He vanished at your approach. No contact was made with them, particularly with their minds. The farmers shot them because in times of drought (when the game had left the country for water holes further north) the Bushmen slaughtered a cow or so to keep alive.

In this the farmers only followed the earlier example in South Africa, of civilization spreading up from the Cape. The advancing Boers shot the Bushmen as if they were baboons. They organized hunts for them—very nearly sporting events. They paralleled the early Scotch sheep ranchers in Patagonia and southern Chile. I have talked with men down there who said: "If you didn't shoot the Indians they shot you; so what did you *expect* us to do?" The result was that there were professional "Indian hunters." They were paid $10 for each pair of Indian's ears—pelt bounty. I have talked with ranchers in southern Chile who, while they denied ever having paid this bounty themselves, admitted they had ranched with men who had.

Such pioneer deeds are usually a secret of those who perpetrated them. But the deliberate extermination of the Bushmen is a matter of record. If you take the trouble to read a few unexpurgated, unromaticized histories of the white man's northward expansion from the Cape, you will see that I have pulled a very small bow indeed, as far as the deliberate destruction of the Bushmen and Hottentots is concerned.

Today it is being realized that these almost extinct Bushmen (South-West Africa is the only part of the world where they still remain) are one of the most interesting species of the human race. It is now being asserted in some scientific quarters that they were the original inhabitants of Dordogne, in southern France. It is realized that their rock paintings, previously accepted without much consideration, indicate an astonishingly high intellectual capacity in other arts. South-West Africanders say the Bushmen have a knowledge of poisons and medicinal herbs far superior to that of any other natives. As I have told in a preceding chapter, in kitchen middens of the Bushmen on the deserted coast of South-West Africa I found a bone knife and an ivory needle seven inches long, whose workmanship made it a delight to handle them. Amid lions' teeth, mounds of rock mussels (none being found within miles of those mud flats today) I uncovered hundreds of minute beads made from ostrich shell, all perfectly round, as delicately made as the jewelry found in the tomb of Tutankhamen.

The Bushmen had obviously killed the lions and eaten them; even today a Bushman will eat a putrefied lion carcass. No one knows when the mounds were formed. "But no Bushman," declared a native of those parts, "would ever walk a couple of miles with a rock mussel, before he sat down to eat it!" As the mounds have not yet been visited by any scientific expedition, the supposition is that the sea was thus far inland then; and the kitchen middens must have been made by the Bushmen's southward trek, which is estimated to have occurred well over five hundred years ago.

Many of these Bushmen in the Kalahari have never seen a white man.

In the eastern territory of Ovamboland, near the Okavango River, we made contact with some Kung Bushmen. They hunt with the bow and poisoned arrow. Stories I had heard that they could hit a tobacco tin at 200 yards I found unconfirmed. The twenty men and young boys shot for fifteen minutes at a red bag of tobacco we hung on a bush only twenty-five yards from them. True, there was a young boy among them, shooting with a wooden-tipped bird-arrow, who grazed the bag several times. They made excited, clucking noises as they lamented their inability to win the tobacco. These clucks, or clicks, came from the Bushman's inability to pronounce consonants. The slender boy (the biggest man did not come up to my shoulder) was the one I wanted to win the tobacco. So, when his turn came around again, I hung my felt hat on the bush, and told him to shoot at that.

His first arrow ripped right through it.

When I stood there, making a mock-rueful face as I pushed my finger through the hole, the entire Bushman tribe responded with a burst of laughter. They had never seen anything quite so funny—they had ruined my hat!

When I laughed, these timid aborigines at once seemed to lose their fear of us.

Similarly, when we managed to make contact with some of the more elusive Bushmen in the park lands rimming the Kala-

hari Desert, all their nervous fear of us vanished when they
started playing a game around their fire that night.

The game, which no white man could play, simply because
he doesn't know the secret of the Bushman stomach control,
produced a physiological phenomenon that was quite startling.

They sat, squatting, in two rows facing each other. They
slapped their legs in chorus, clapped their hands criss-cross
against their breasts, then suddenly held up a hand with one,
two, or three, fingers raised upright. It was a game of guess-
work, of "matching." When a man's opposite number lost, he
had to take a hop forward. When he came near enough to cross
the center line, he was regarded as "captured."

Their yellow, bulge-headed faces were grinning with delight
in the rose firelight. They were laughing and shouting taunts
at each other. Yet all the time a strange mass sound was coming
from them. Where it came from I could not find out. I thought,
at first, it must be a high wind, sweeping through the tips of the
low camel-thorn above us. Then I looked around to see if someone was not working a pair of gigantic bellows. Then I saw that
this peculiar "huffing" sound was coming from their stomachs!

They were doing a thing which no white man can do, not
even the best ventriloquist. For at the same time that they were
jabbering away at each other, even talking (with those grotesque clicks), they were actually using their stomachs as bellows, forcing air in and out their throats between the words; to
be exact, with the words.

It is difficult to make clear this dual vocal function. But you
can imagine how uncanny it would seem if a roomful of Europeans, around bridge tables, were playing an accompaniment to
their talk with their stomachs, in addition to an ordinary conversation.

The tiny women, with breasts either like razor-strops or
peaches, were sitting in a long, solemn line, watching this performance. They showed "an intelligent attention." They wore
little else than beads. And as they sat, with one elbow placed

upon an upright knee, and with chin in hand, their posture was amusingly like a party of school girls watching a matinée!

That night three Englishmen and I watched four Bushman doctors (witch doctors, if you like) dance an initiate into a state of complete hypnosis.

He went completely "out." One of these Englishmen, a man from Dorset, who has lived on this easternmost farm in South-West Africa for fifteen years, had seen several of these Bushmen before, and was, therefore, not so frightening to them. When the initiate fell in his trance, this Englishman stepped into the circle of firelight and tried to open his eyes.

"Prop him up," he asked me, "while I try it again."

But the side of the face towards me made no grimace to keep the other eye shut. The body was icy cold. The little arms were nerveless as pipestems in my hands. It was as if we had gone into a medical college and were trying to examine the eyes of a corpse.

Only the boy's rounded little stomach had any life in it. That, when I placed my hand against it, was fluttering like a bird's wing.

The dance, under a cloudy moon, had the definite element of magic about it. The men alone danced, in a circle around a high fire of thorn branches, a little segment of six Bushmen almost touching each other. The women provided the rhythm by claps of their hands and a high, thrilling chant that went, like a series of steps, "Ha-hoo-ha-hoo-ha-hoo." The flames gilded the branches of the tambuti trees. Sworls of red sparks flew up towards the few stars.

The dance seemed to consist of taking the shortest step possible. The segment of glistening bodies scarcely moved. The four witch doctors stamped, staggered, limped as one. Their eyes were closed. It was bewildering—how little contact we could reach with the meaning of it all! They were exorcising the evil spirit from a sick child's body. An actual case of illness.

For the "initiate" is always broken in on a real case. And the manner of the head doctor was as professional (and probably no more guilty of mumbo jumbo) than that of a specialist from Harley Street.

"He knows what he's doing!" said the Dorset man. "These chaps aren't all fake. Looks like a Chinese philosopher, doesn't he? When he goes over to that child and rubs it, then rubs the boy that he is initiating, he's transferring that illness from the baby to the boy—a sort of distributing it."

One of the witch doctors began to bark and howl like an animal. He ran around the circle, bending over, with his hands touching the ground before his feet. Another doctor suddenly let out a high scream, seized a brand from the fire, and ran among the women with it. He was seized; the burning brand was taken away, and they led him, staggering, off into the darkness, waving the burning brand up and down close before his eyes. He fell, senseless, in the grass.

I let the initiate fall backwards and moved out of the bright firelight. The leading witch doctor came over, professionally felt his stomach, possibly searching for nerve reactions. Nodded. The boy was "out."

Then they danced a kudu hunt, one of them holding his fingers up on both sides of his head, to represent horns.

Two hours later that night, when the Bushmen must have thought all we white men were asleep, I stared from my blankets and saw some of the members of the tribe still working on the initiate to bring him around. They were forcing him to walk, practically carrying him. And every now and then one went back to the fire and brought back a brand, which he moved slowly up and down before the boy's dazed eyes.

These park lands of the Kalahari are a gentle country. The general scene is a sweep of low grasslands as open, and as salubrious as Richmond Park. But instead of horse chestnuts there are clumps of acacia thorns, tall tambuties, and prehistoric bao-babs with trunks at least twenty feet thick. They gave the mon-strous touch to the scene. Fan palms, silvered in the moonlight, were like frozen sprays of water.

We had been shooting duck up there. These lay in the vleis, those watery depressions whose vivid green made oases on this sandy carpet. Giraffe and wildebeest lived in the thickets. The water was warm in the vleis as we waded into them. Ducks got up—huge Muscovies, white breasted, whose iridescent black backs were almost as big as Canada geese; darting flights of teal, black duck, whistlers and spoon-bills. It was nearly always pos-sible to get one or two as they rose off the water. Then, so unaware were they of the menace of man (a man with a shot-gun), they nearly always circled and came over again, if you stood perfectly still.

I got six out of a flight of eight this way. And while I was standing motionless, waiting for them to come over again, I saw a fat zebra standing on the opposite side of the vlei, among the thorns, coolly watching me.

He did not stir, although I fired at two flights again. It was only when I waded out into the vlei to pick up the ducks that he flung up his head. And I watched his fat little rump as he trotted off casually among the thorns.

These vleis held a fascinating bird life. Toucans, black and white, with banana-colored beaks, swooped from thorn to thorn around them. Giant maribou cranes stood, fishing for frogs, so intent that they let me come almost on top of them. Then they merely spread their seven-foot wings and flapped up to a dead tree overhanging the pool. There they stared down at me. On one tree a white eagle sat on a dead branch below a maribou, and both peered down curiously as I stood directly beneath and took their photo. There were flocks of clattering, red-shanked African plover; wisps of snipe; fish ducks, diving in the vleis; kingfishers, no bigger than sparrows, sparkling blue in the blaz-

ing sun. The sandy marge of every vlei was pockmarked with
the prints of wildebeest, eland, gemsbok, and giraffe. These the
Bushmen shot with their poisoned arrows.

No Bushman shoots an arrow to kill anything by impact, except a bird. Poison is their most deadly weapon. Only a few
among the Bushmen themselves actually know the secret of
these poisons. No white man does—not yet. Like some snake
poisons, they cannot be analyzed. As late as 1926 a magistrate
out here was killed by a poisoned arrow. His name was van
Rynefeld; he was accompanying a trio of camel police who had
just run down a handful of Bushmen they were after, for cattle
stealing. The little Bushmen lost their heads. One fired into
van Rynefeld an arrow that was no longer than a pencil. But
its tip was a poisoned thorn.

"Boys, I'm done for!" said van Rynefeld, when he plucked
out the thorn. "Leave me alone."

They worked on him; but he was dead within an hour.
Within less than two hours, I was told, his body began to
putrefy.

With most poisoned arrows the shaft falls out after the arrow
has entered its object. Only the little triangular head of steel
and some distance along the shaft is poison coated. And this
looks, mockingly enough, like that rough, reddish-brown covering of candied almonds.

Nearly all African hunters agree that the Bushman is the
most superb tracker in the world. When he stalks, and shoots
one of these poisoned arrows into a wildebeest, the prey may be
one of a herd that numbers hundreds, thousands. Such herds
are plentiful. You see these gnus standing like black islands under the African sky. And amidst a maze of tracks the Bushman
locates the wounded animal, usually beginning when he has
picked up the fallen shaft. Then the beast is followed until he
drops.

The Bushmen told me (via various interpreters) that the poison almost always kills the wildebeest within two hours. They cut out the part of the flesh around where the poisoned arrowhead remains (this area is usually a five- or six-inch circle of vivid green), and then they can eat the rest of the beast without any harm to themselves.

At Fort Namutoni, a Bushman who works for the solitary policeman there said that, although he did not know the secret poisons of even his own tribe, he knew that *some* herb went into them which the springbok must eat. When I asked him why, he said: "Because the poison does not easily kill the springbok. Sometimes he will run for a whole day. The big wildebeest dies from that poison before two hours."

The Kalahari Bushmen laughed when I asked them to show me how to make fire. It was too easy. A man simply took a strip of dried wood from his pouch, sat down holding it between his feet, and spun the base of a wand in one of its cup-like depressions by rubbing it between his palms. In a few seconds a little ring of brown, powdered wood encircled the spinning wand. In another second it smoked. He blew on it—and there was fire!

Anyone could do it, he intimated, wondering at my stupid curiosity. And now I know I can.

These Bushmen have presented a nice problem to well meaning South African anthropologists. If you leave them out in the open, to take their chance of survival against the white man, they are doomed. And their end will not be long delayed. Yet if you put them into reserves they die. They die almost at once in prison.

One of the latest possibilities, suggested to me by a wealthy English big-game hunter over in Natal, was that they should be allowed to live in the immense game sanctuary of Kruger Park.

"They can't do much harm there," said this man, who is a trustee at the park. "Of course, they'll shoot a certain amount of game with their poisoned arrows. But that is what they have always been doing. They and the game lived together. And, until we came along, both survived. That is where they belong, and that is the way we should let them live now."

Without thinking about it, he had given the precise position of the Bushman in the world today; he is the last wild thing in human form.

The Bushwomen wore a tatter of ragged skins to protect them from the cold at nights. The men wore nothing but a leather G-string. It was no wider than a belt, for which it was used. In the back of this was carried a primitive ax, a piece of steel stuck in the head of a wooden club. And each man carried a three-foot hollow reed.

This was a drinking tube; in the desert, the Bushmen know where they can find moisture beneath the sands. Several years ago, to get rifles and equipment, some Bushmen, offering themselves as guides, led a body of white diamond prospectors out into the Kalahari Desert. The white men were soon dying from thirst in the burning sands, which was what the Bushmen had planned. The whites, puzzled by the fit condition of the Bushmen, kept a secret watch at night. They caught the Bushmen, a short distance beyond their camp, drinking from the pipes they had shoved down through the sands. The white prospectors returned to civilization, with the drinking reeds—but without the Bushmen.

Writing this now, I find it hard to believe that along the rim of the Kalahari are these little half-wild people hunting with poisoned arrows, playing their ancient games and dancing in the moonlight, sleeping like hares in "forms" they make in the prairie grass.

It was a strange experience to move from them, drive up through the red dolomites and mopani forests, and come out into that vast emptiness of sand-flat and water known as Etosha Pan. Here, on these treeless plains, roam some of the greatest herds of elephants, buck, and giraffe left in Africa. And north of here, dotted across the border into Portuguese West Africa, are the kraals of the Ovambas—perhaps, on the South African side, the highest cultural development of the indigenous native life in Africa.

The South Africans are trying to keep Ovamba life intact. Wandering writers are not encouraged. Cape Town journalists find it almost impossible to get permits to enter Ovamboland. But I got a permit; the police at Tsumeb sealed my rifle and shotgun, so that I might not use them until I had passed north of the great game sanctuary of Etosha Pan. The seals were not to be broken until I reached the thatched bungalow of Major H. C. Hahn, the Native Commissioner of Ovamboland, who had invited me to live with him.

9. Murder in Ovamboland

HAHN and I went up to the Kuenene River on the border of Portuguese Africa. It was to be the first flowing water I had seen for over a month. I had expected to experience some of the incredulous joy that Moses—at any rate, his followers—must have experienced when he smote the rock. But the gorge of the Kuenene was baking red heat.

The actual falls of the Kuenene held us spellbound for some time. What happens is that a broad river, flowing sluggishly through the African jungle, suddenly tumbles off a table of red rock. It tears in long veils of coffee cream, thundering slightly, with a perpetual mist rising from their feet.

We watched this from the edge of a mopani forest on the tableland of South-West Africa. Far below us lay the roof of the jungle forest—as level, green, unbroken and illimitable as the Atlantic Ocean—into which the Kuenene River, rapidly quickening below the falls, rushes through the red, unexplored mountains of the Kaokoveld.

Less than a few miles to our left began a ragged country whose natives—a few of them, at least—had never seen any white man. And in there are plants, and some men, that no white man has ever seen.

The Kaokoveld is a "closed" country, like Ovamboland, where no white man is allowed to live, except one or two police officers.

The previous year, in pursuit of some diamond prospectors who were thought to be working near the mouth of the Kuenene River, Hahn had struck in some sixty miles below where we were sitting and staring down into Portuguese West Africa, and had been twenty-five days on foot trekking to the coast.

On that trip he brought back three plants which he had never seen before. For, like many men who live in far-off places, Hahn had acquired a strong, scientific interest in his surroundings. The day we started on this particular trip he chanced to receive a letter from the British Museum, saying that two of the plants which he had forwarded were entirely new plants; their existence had never been suspected before. The third might be a subspecies of euphorbia. Behind us now, as we sat, dreading to go down into the valley of that choking heat, rose some grotesque plants that are only found along this river.

If you can imagine a giant stalk of asparagus, twenty feet high, with a ridiculous, quite unnecessary little fuzz of branches growing at its top, you have it. The Boers call it "the maiden's thigh." They have an aptitude for giving functional names to things; the bird which screams around your camp from 4 A.M. until 7 A.M. every morning, just as regularly as an alarm clock, they call "the daybreaker."

He certainly does it.

The river was lined with rushes, which prevented our swimming. And its red-rocked valley was waving with heat. The clear water came in whirlpools from below the falls, racing at a steady seven or eight miles an hour; it was cool, as was shown by a hippo, snorting ecstatically in his bath. The rushy islands looked sanctuary, if we could have swum out to them. But the river was full of crocs. The grooved traces of their tails were in the red sand. It looked entirely deserted, its swirling surface polished metal-bright by the blazing sun.

Our reason for coming up was that Hahn, as Native Commissioner for Ovamboland, was investigating a murder.

It was a strange case, the date of which would, or would not, make it a punishable crime. And the murderer had believed that he was doing a good deed. He still believed it. For how else could you kill an evil spirit, protested old Chief Muala, unless you killed the person possessing it, as well as all that person's children? Didn't the clever English know that?

He admitted to Hahn, as I sat beside them at the *indaba* under the baobab tree, that he had given the order to kill the woman. His own trusted witch doctor had "smelt her out." So there had been no mistake about that; no innocent person had been done away with. It had all been according to the best practice. So, why all this fuss? Why bring all this up, after twenty-six years? All this had happened way, way back, in the German times.

The Germans had never been able to extend their rule in South-West Africa over the independent natives in Ovamboland. What Muala did then was nobody else's business. Even the British had not succeeded in getting up here until 1915. But after that, as Hahn pointed out now with great solemnity to Chief Muala, if anyone vanished in Ovamboland, the Government must know the reason why—*and how!*

Muala, who professed to be a Christian on the surface—and wore a cap, tattered brown cardigan, and old corduroy trousers to prove it—was a pagan at heart. And a frightened one. He knew the people with whom we had been holding palavers on the way up. One of them, a headman—Festus Hango—Muala knew, was not in love with him. And on top of our camp equipment in the motor lorry sat one of the murdered woman's children his assassins had failed to kill. Now a grown-up woman, suckling a baby; eight months and some days gone with another baby, which, she said, she might have any minute.

She was terrified of Muala, even now. But her story, plus evidence from Festus Hango, plus data given by another chief, fixed the murder in the year 1920. "Master knows the year," said Festus Hango, when he squatted in the sand before us outside his kraal. "It was when the master brought two other masters here to kill elephants."

Hahn knew that date. And then the age of the child that

Muala had failed to kill, this now pregnant woman, clinched the matter. In fact, as we were driving through the mopani forest a native flung himself on his knees when he saw Hahn in the car, and declared (hoping for mercy) that he was one of the two men who had taken the woman off into the bush and knobkerried her to death.

Our quest was a little spiced by the discovery, a few days before, of three pairs of shorts, with no natives in them. These shorts had belonged to returning laborers from the mines, farms or diamond fields of the South. And the only explanation seemed to be that someone had murdered their owners for the money and valuables they had brought back with them. But Muala, who had been very good lately, was not even suspected of this.

Still, Hahn was also determined to find out the whereabouts of the men who *had* been inside those trousers.

It was not a pleasant ordeal for old Muala, any way you looked at it. His apprehensive surliness increased measurably as he tried to see, and dodge, the innumerable pitfalls that Hahn set for him in what appeared to be the most friendly conversation. And, watching the hair-trigger adjustments of Hahn's mind—that beautiful timing which kept him always just this side of the borderline between friendship and familiarity—I saw a perfect exposition of the supervising white man and the savageness that lurks in the heart of the African native to this day.

Muala hotly denied that he had a witch doctor now. But we all knew he had. And Hahn had said to me the previous night, as we camped outside another staked kraal: "Take *us* away, and the witch doctors would be back *openly* in there inside two years!"

Civilization is still a veneer.

Yet Hahn does not have one policeman or soldier to back him up in ruling the 117,000 natives in Ovamboland.

✦

This harrying persistence on the part of Hahn was being made almost an unbearable torture for Muala by another, and living reason, the Princess Shilahula.

While he had been stating his defense, slobbering, "All this— all this happen in German time," Muala's one good eye had from time to time been fixed venomously on a beehive-shaped hut near his stockaded kraal of storage grain.

In that sprawled sardonically a woman who was the cause of all this. She was an Angola princess. She and Muala had never been "churched," or even married in the Ovamba fashion. But there were good reasons to believe that they had been sweethearts, once. In fact, it was the inexplicable illness of her child, which Muala had given her, which caused old Chief Muala to have her servant girl murdered.

Shilahula, this wrinkled beauty, had not yet turned state's evidence against Muala. But she had admitted that she and Muala had discussed the extermination of her servant girl. She declared, on the other hand, that she had had nothing to do with the actual assassination. She had merely broached the sub-ject—and Muala had gone ahead on his own bat.

The fact that her servant girl *did* have the evil eye, however, she insisted had been proved. The proof was that the instant the servant girl had been killed, the child became well. And contemptuous scorn of the Cape detective, who had been three weeks at Muala's kraal, trying to question Shilahula, held more uncomfortable menace than even Muala's poisonous glare. And "poison," as you will see, was just what was in his eye.

The story of Shilahula and Muala is quite African.

A few years before the World War of 1914, Shilahula fled south from Portuguese West Africa before a famine. Being of royal blood, she took quite a large retinue with her. African royalty, like its European counterpart, befriends its refugee members. Therefore, when Shilahula crossed the Kuenene River and entered Muala's territory, she was received as roy-alty. Muala gave her a kraal and a large section of land; he also deputed a considerable number of Ovambas to cultivate her land for her. She set up house.

This neighborly friendship had one result: she had a baby by Muala.

When I went to talk to Shilahula I found a woman of some sixty years, but slender as a girl. She was wearing a *lapi*, a little apron made from the soft skin of an ox belly. From head to toe she was painted red with ocher. Her breasts were withered, and the skin over her flat stomach was wrinkled as crepe. But her shoulders were fine, she had slender arms and legs and long, tapering fingers. The expression on her dignified face was one of bored disgust.

She gave me the impression, an uncomfortable one, that she was ashamed to be in such a position as to have to answer questions from so rude and vulgar a person as myself.

There was nothing "mammy" about old Shilahula.

She had been a beauty in her day. Facing me silently outside that hut of thatched poles, she had all the histrionic dignity of Sarah Bernhardt. She was rimmed around her slender waist and long column of neck, with rows and rows and rows of colored beads made from ostrich eggs. And her high, curly pompadour, which was now a natural white, had been stained with ocher the color of a flamingo's wing.

She looked as if she had been lipsticked all over.

Old Muala was past eighty. As one of the three remaining Ovamba chiefs, his photograph appears in the text-book, *The Native Tribes of South-West Africa*. He was an important figure. And the Ovambas have been interfered with so little by the South African rule that he, too, resented having to answer these embarrassing and dangerous questions. But Hahn knew how to handle him. One of Muala's eyes was sick, protruding like that of a rabbit which has just been struck on the head. Hahn inquired solicitously what was wrong. Muala replied surlily that he did not know, neither did the Finnish missionary doctor, to whom the pain had driven him.

"It just burns," said the interpreter, to Hahn. "Muala says it burns as though he had a red wasp under his eyelid."

They had tried every remedy, including the widely esteemed one of spitting in Muala's eye, but nothing had worked.

As the interpreter continued to translate Hahn's steady succession of leading questions about the murder, old Muala answered with "Aah! aaah! ahh!"—that curious exclamation, of either assent or understanding, that nearly all Africans give when they talk. Then, suddenly, he seized the interpreter's fingers and began to illustrate his *own* points with them. Holding one finger firmly, Muala began to state his case; *that* was a point—he pinned the luckless interpreter's finger to the sand. He laid hold of another. He wiggled it. His mouth slobbered as he went off into an eager, heated protest:

"He says," said the poor black interpreter, looking up; "Muala says, 'Yes'; yes, he tell the men to kill the woman. He don't remember if she was knobkerried or whether they take her and choke her. He don't remember that far back. Chief Muala say all this happen in German time."

Hahn heartily wished that he could find extenuating circumstances. For this eighteen-year-old crime was being investigated simply because a note from the administration of Portuguese Angola had asked what had happened to the black woman who left with Princess Shilahula—oh, thirty years ago! A relative of hers in Angola had just received the news that she had been murdered.

"You tell Muala he had better speak what is on his heart," said Hahn, firmly, to the interpreter. "You tell Muala that the Government will not just let people disappear in this country. It must know what has happened to them. You cannot take a human life."

"Aaaah!" said Muala.

"You tell Muala that the Government's word must be obeyed. When a man or woman disappears in Ovamboland, the Government must know what has happened. The Government will at once take up the spoor—*and it never lets go!*"

"Aaaah!" said Muala, unhappy.

The white detective sergeant, from Cape Town, had been camped under this baobab tree for weeks, trying to make Shila-hula talk, or break Muala's nerve. He complained bitterly of the flies. He tried to convince Hahn that no amount of persuasion would make Muala confess. But Hahn replied:

"Keep the pressure on. I'm sorry for old Muala, but he must learn he can't get away with this. The thing's so old, anyway, he'll probably only be fined fifty cows."

Hahn knew how to handle this chief he had known since 1915. "Well," he said to the interpreter, standing up, "tell old Muala to keep well. Tell him the people down at Ondonga say he is holding the rain back. He keeps all the rain up here."

The interpreter translated this verbatim. Old Muala suddenly seized two of the interpreter's fingers again. The interpreter said:

"Muala say, 'How can I keep the rain back?' Muala say, 'People down at Ondonga always saying I keep rain back!' Muala say, ask master, 'How can I keep back the rain?' "

"Your witch doctor," said Hahn, with the faintest smile.

It was a direct spear thrust in repartee—it went straight to the ritual murder involving the evil spirit. It showed old Muala that Hahn, although he was a white man, could think like an Ovamba, when he wanted to track back in talk.

Muala started. Then he shifted uncomfortably. Then he let his serviceable eye wander slowly to the silent beehive hut containing his former mistress. He slowly bowed his head. . . .

Even the nights were stifling in the bed of the Kuenene. The red bed of the setting sun steamed like slaked embers in a fire.

We enviously watched the hippo taking his sunset bath. "Psst—ahhh!" he grunted ecstatically, floating downstream to stand on convenient sand bars, twitching his cat-like little ears. They were pink as the setting sun shone through them. His was the only voice to break the vast silence. The black cormorants, on a sunken tree in mid-river, sat in heraldic posture, wings out-spread, over the swirling waters. The game had gone inland to eat the grass fresh from a recent rain. Only a herd of beautiful, foolish impala stared at us from the river thickets. It would have been easy to kill them. But we never fired a shot along the Kuenene.

We saw no reason to break its peace.

But our sympathy for old Muala sank somewhat on our way back. The last night, under flashes of lightning and patches of cloud-swept moon, Hahn held another palaver with Festus Hango, outside that headman's kraal.

"All the witnesses around here against Muala have suddenly started to lie," Hahn told him. "Why?"

"Yes, master, everybody round here know that Muala kill that woman in 1920. But nobody going to speak now."

As Festus Hango could talk English, I got the whole of this.

"Muala been threatening?" said Hahn.

"Yes, master. Muala say he poison anyone speak. Any one person come say Muala kill that woman 1920, that person be poisoned."

"Ha!" said Hahn. He stood up. "Well, keep well, Festus. People say one thing, now they say another. I told Muala he had better tell the white *baas* (the Cape detective) what is on his heart. The Government is on the spoor—and it won't let go."

"Yes, master."

The fat headman stood up. Behind him his escort of under headmen stood up under the cloudy sky. They had been sitting, as custom prescribes, well beyond earshot when their chief talked with Hahn. Now they chorused a native farewell to Hahn, saluting him by his native name, "The Whip."

Hahn, who is without doubt the most nimble, daring motor driver I have sat beside, jammed the one-ton American truck through the gripping mopani forest, around reedy vleis, from which black and white ibis, geese, storks, and golden cranes rose with their cries of protest and vanished in the night. Ahead shone the brilliant, pink disks of leaping "spring hares" eyes—the rabbit that is like a kangaroo. Lightning flashed, quivered, and remained like white skeleton trees in the sky. Hahn grunted:

"Poor old Muala! I'm afraid he's a bit desperate. Guess he thinks he's 'in for a penny, in for a pound'—that poison business. Now, we *must* go on."

Poison is a thing which must be always guarded against in native life. And now, after Muala had been foolish enough to circulate that threat, the Government must pursue this case to the very end. No native must ever be allowed to think he could throw the Government off the spoor.

10. Ovambas and "The Whip"

A BOOK could be written about the beauty of native life in Ovamboland. Admittedly, it is only a temporary paradise, as I will show. But in this "closed" country of seventeen thousand square miles, where only eight white officials and a few Finnish missionaries are allowed, the South African Government is encouraging some 117,000 natives to live in their traditional way under an indirect rule that is one of the most altruistic in all Africa.

The Ovambas were enjoying a golden age—for they had no money economy—and their pastoral development was along the philosophical improvement of the indigenous native life.

Ovamboland controverts completely the charge that the South African is cynical towards the black man. The Ovambas were the happiest natives I found anywhere in Africa. The Native Commissioner had not one soldier or policeman, white or black, to enforce his regulations or punish people. His attitude was (except for such major crimes as murder) to let the Ovambas regulate and punish themselves. The 117,000 Ovambas were in seven tribes; three under hereditary chiefs, four under tribal councils which the Commissioner had instigated; and his indirect rule was cautiously administered in a manner which may be best described as "the voice behind the chair."

The personal example of his leadership, of course, played the major part in all this. Hahn went to Ovamboland in 1915 as a young scout, riding for General Botha. He remained as assistant to the first Commissioner that the Cape appointed over these

natives—the first time that any white man had been set to rule
over them. For the Germans, although they had held theoretical possession of this territory since around 1890, had never
been able to extend their rule more than by a "Beau Geste" fort,
called Namutoni, nearly eighty miles south of the bigger
Ovamba kraals. For close to twenty years Hahn had been in
supreme command.

The South Africans have been lucky to have such a man; so
have been the Ovambas. But, if at times it is difficult to distinguish his own personality from the administration's aims, the
fact remains that in the simon-pure effort to give the Ovambas
the best life possible, Cape Town has always backed him up.

This from a Government whose problem of white versus
black is more serious, immediately present, even menacing, than
in the American Southern States.

The land of Ovamboland is in itself not too salubrious. It
is always menaced by drought, and there have been years of
famine, followed by years of whitening skulls across the sandy
plains. But as Hahn encountered a famine almost to begin with
(a famine which "made" him), his foremost effort since then
has been to persuade the Ovambas to store grain. So that today,
as you visit the high stockades of Ovamba chiefs and headmen,
you see a section of their kraal, or a special kraal outside, full
of acorn-shaped baskets, perched on stilts and full of grain,
stored against the year when the rains might fail to come.

Nehemiah had thirteen wives. He had fifteen hundred cattle.
His kraal, a labyrinth of sharp-pointed stakes, was over a hundred yards in diameter. It was a small settlement, built in the
form of a maze to complicate attacks. The stakes were made of
small tree trunks, about twelve feet high, thick as a man's leg,
and presented a bewildering network of spiked tips. There were
walls within walls, and dummy "U" passages that led to no-

where. There were separate beehive huts and compounds for each of his wives. There were establishments for his under-headmen and their wives. There were guest houses. Before the British came, Nehemiah, as the paramount headman, would probably have slept in a different hut every night, so that attackers, searching in this confusion, would not know where to go to kill the leading man. But, as smiling Nehemiah himself was quick to tell me, "Master, the British brought peace," he is freed from those fears at night.

So, smiling at his own happiness, Nehemiah politely led me to a little thatched, mud-walled beehive, where, he told me, he was now sleeping with his favorite wife.

She came in from the fields, bearing a load of fagots upon her head and carrying two strings of red-green-yellow caterpillars that she had collected and would cook for her husband's supper that night.

Caterpillars were very sweet, said Nehemiah. And as she passed by, giving me an astonishingly sophisticated smile, Nehemiah touched her lovingly on her slender, naked waist. Her breasts were like Juno's.

"Yes," said Nehemiah; "yes, master; I am a very lucky man!"

I spent, I think, about three weeks in Ovamboland, a lot of the time with Nehemiah, shooting duck and spur-wing geese, with a couple of futile lion hunts on the treeless flats around Etosha Pan. The last days were really enchanted. For, sleeping at night under the open stars, I woke at dawn, lying with just my blankets spread out on the soil, so close to earth that I could watch the golden sun shining through the vlei grass. And the springbok, which had wandered near us during the night, when our fire had lost its glow, were leaping from sheer ecstasy at the break of another day. In the hot noonday sun the great herds of wildebeest stood out under the open African sky. I find it hard to recall other days when I have been so conscious of the sheer joy of being just alive.

Had it been permitted, and had I not other commitments to obey, I would be there now.

You have to get a Government permit to enter Ovamboland. This is done to preserve the Ovamba life intact. No white trader may venture in there; there is only one store in the seventeen thousand square miles. This is semi-Governmental, run for the recruiting company that gets "boys" to come down from Ovamboland and Portuguese West Africa to work in the mines, farms, and diamond fields in South-West Africa. It is at a little cluster of thatched bungalows known as Ondonga, eighty miles north of Fort Namutoni. And the white, turreted walls of Namutoni are a hundred miles north of the nearest town in South-West Africa. This fort is "held" by one South African police sergeant and his wife, with some Bushman scouts.

North of the fort all is Ovamboland, until, 120 miles above, you reach the Kuenene River on the Angola border. South, in a wilderness of thick thorn and tambuti forests, there are just three farms in one hundred miles.

It took me from 9 one morning until 2 A.M. the next day to do the 180 miles from Tsumeb to Ondonga. This was in a German semi-Diesel motor-lorry, driven by Herr Teitz. In 1936, when there had been a flood in Ovamboland, it took him twenty-four days—twenty-four days in the open bush.

Aside from its remoteness, the principal reason why Ovamboland is such a native paradise at the moment is that its cattle have lung fever. No cattle or dairy products may be allowed out of it. Therefore it has no money economy. The natives do not know this complicated curse; the affliction of their herds has saved them from it. The only money that goes into Ovamboland is that brought back by the "boys" returning from work in South-West Africa. The only tax they pay is five shillings a year, which may be paid in grain, and is spent back upon them.

The "boys" hardly ever earn more than £5 for a year's work in the South. That is what they have when they reach Tsumeb, the last town in South-West Africa. But at Tsumeb there are twenty-six general stores, all owned by Germans, except one, the shop of a South African Jew. These shops get most of the "boys' " money. A new pink celluloid comb (always carried in their kinky hair); an inevitable hurricane lamp; a tin trunk, painted gaudy colors, full of colored cotton cloth for a prospective wife; sometimes a European's solar topee; the boys spend their money, pack these treasures on their heads, and begin the long homeward trek. Some of the Portuguese "boys" walk eight hundred miles before they get back to their kraals in Angola!

There were twenty-four "boys," packed like upright sardines in the back of our motor lorry, who had paid ten shillings each to be transported this 180 miles. Most of them lived in kraals near Nehemiah's, and the thought of being so near home made them this profligate. The "boys" who were setting out to walk 400 or 800 miles were not tempted.

They were an unruly load. They shifted with lurches of the truck, like a ship's cargo in a hurricane, and when we reached the soggy bits they went off under the pretext of finding stones, and hid in the bushes. The two German men carried sticks on their drivers' seats, and I think they frequently wanted to use them. In the forest the black "cotton" soil was soft as butter; the trucks ground themselves in till the rear ends were aground. And we spent two hours in one place, mired in a fresh green swamp. No ordinary passenger car could have got through.

Fort Namutoni was the last German outpost against the Ovamba tribes. They could never extend their rule beyond it. Its castellated, loopholed walls have a tower at each corner. It is whitewashed, blazing in the cloudless sun. It guards the last "drift," the ford leading into Ovamboland.

From its loopholed walls in 1904 five Germans fought off an attacking force of Ovambas all day. A bronze plaque in the fort marks their feat. Firing with rifles, they killed hundreds of natives who were trying to rush the walls from the reeds surrounding the watercourse. They killed so many that the Ovambas withdrew until dark. At dusk the Germans mounted their horses, tied a sick comrade to his saddle, and dashed out of the fort. They reached the mopani forest and, with this sick man, succeeded in riding hundreds of miles down into South-West Africa.

The Ovambas that evening sacked the fort.

It is a haunted spot. Caught there by the rains on my way out of Ovamboland, I stayed two days. I took six dead bats off the floor where I set up my camp bed. At night I felt the bats flying above my face. There is no one living there now but the police sergeant and his wife, with a few Kung Bushmen camped outside it.

It was not difficult to recall the days when the German officers were here. One of them had made a cement-lined swimming pool by surrounding a natural spring of warm water. It lay in a circle of oleander bushes. Beyond the fort is a shallow neck between two vast, shining plaques of water of Etusha Pan. From the walls of the fort you can see the great herds of wildebeest roaming the acrid sands. Skulls of those freshly killed by lions, or bones whitened by years of burning suns, dot the plain. And by them, companions even in death, lie the crushed bones and striped skins of zebra. The place has the fascination of utter solitude. Complete loneliness. It made me wonder if it could be true, the tales of the wild orgies the German officers held inside these blazing walls. I should have thought the place would have tamed them. Well, the officers, and those good old days, are gone now, although Fort Namutoni is unchanged enough to make it full of ghosts.

The first fight the South Africans had with the Ovambas was in 1917, the last in 1932.

This 1917 affair was when a powerful chief named Mandumi, whose tribe numbered 52,000, took to raiding over the border into Portuguese Angola. One of Mandumi's tricks was to make his prisoners fry meat over the fire *on their own hands*. The Portuguese objected. The British warned Mandumi; Hahn took his life in his hands when he insisted upon riding horseback up to Mandumi's kraal, to try to reason with him, persuade him to obey the Government's order to go down to Windhoek and give an account of himself.

Hahn told me that—although the South Africans did not know it then—any Ovamba chief who leaves his own territory automatically ceases to be a chief. It is an Ovamba taboo. So, actually, this war and the death of courageous Mandumi were all due to a misunderstanding. Mandumi would not go to Windhoek.

Hahn was both fond of and admired Mandumi, who was a fine figure of a man. Hahn dismounted outside his kraal and simply sat there. After a while, Mandumi sent out word to ask what he wanted. Hahn answered, "Beer." Some native beer was sent out to him in a calabash. This, to begin with, showed the coolness of Hahn, for he might easily have been poisoned. It had the effect he wanted upon Mandumi, who, smiling, came striding out.

Hahn argued with him for hours. Finally Mandumi shook his head and stood up.

"I can't help it. Something inside me makes me do this; I can't help it when something inside me says 'Kill! Kill! Kill!'" Mandumi made a quick gesture, as if stabbing with a knife. "But Mandumi gives you his word he will not fire the first shot. If British come, I won't fire; they fire first. Then I fight."

Hahn said that was suicide. Both men were facing each other. Then, as Hahn told me, Mandumi reached out his bare arm and placed his hand on Hahn's shoulder.

"I can't help it," he said. *"I am young!"*

Hahn told me that he thought these were probably the saddest words he ever heard. He shook Mandumi's hand, and rode away.

When the expedition of South African Mounted Rifles, military constabulary and a few settler irregulars rode into the park-like grasslands of Ovamboland, Hahn was the intelligence officer. The Ovambas ambushed them, dropping on them from the branches of the marula trees. But for a lucky accident, the Ovambas might have annihilated this column of seven hundred men. Hahn, who had seen the Ovamba main strength crawling up on them through the fields of standing maize, galloped back to the commander and told him the natives were within a thousand yards. That officer, chewing his pipe, seemed undecided as to what to do. Apparently, before the battle, he had made up his mind what it was going to be like, and he could not change it. This ambush had bewildered him.

Then a trooper in the rear of the South African forces accidentally fired a shot. This was the lucky accident. For Mandumi had kept his word about not firing first; it was then that the natives, with knives, began to drop out of the marula trees upon the South African troops. And Mandumi, giving his war cry, led his own troops to charge.

In this excitement there was no use waiting for orders from the hesitating commander. Soldiers had never seen natives dropping from trees. People were being knifed everywhere. The father of Hahn's future wife, a padre, was hurled from his horse, and was probably saved only because he was dragged along the ground with one foot caught in its stirrup. Both the men he had been talking to were at that instant knifed to death. Then an English colonel with the column got his three Maxim guns into action at once.

The men at the Maxims fired blind into the high grass. Suddenly the charge evaporated. The natives were in full retreat. Searching the tall grass, the soldiers found the reason; a native scout came on Mandumi, just in front of a Maxim gun, with seven holes, all in a straight line, across his bare chest.

It was Mandumi's tribe, which never again had a chief, that

is ruled by Nehemiah today. Nehemiah had been one of the braves who dropped from the marula trees during the fight.

Nehemiah was dressed in a dogskin jacket, with a zip-fastener, open shirt, white man's trousers, tennis sneakers, and a topee. Thin-faced, smiling, with a great sense of humor, he was quite well aware of the unbelievable luck which this trick of fortune had brought to him, for he had been a clerk in a Windhoek solicitor's office. *He* knew how hard it was for a white man to get a beautiful and faithful wife, and here he had thirteen of them. Moreover, two of them were of the royal blood. Finally, surmounting even such gifts of the gods as that, although he was the bull of the kraal, he did not even have any family duties!

I have never encountered a man so peculiarly relieved of so many responsibilities, or who had the wit to be so well aware of it. For intelligent Nehemiah was all for keeping up the old Ovamba customs.

In Ovamboland succession is matrilinear. One always knows who the mother is, explained Nehemiah, but the father—well, he might be anyone. Therefore royalty goes down in the female line. Each of his thirteen wives had her own establishment within his kraal, her own patch of land to till, her own cattle, and her own storage baskets of grain.

The children were hers. If, for any reason, she wanted to leave Nehemiah, she would merely walk off with everything. All that would be left behind would be a deserted plot and an empty hut. As Nehemiah seemed devoted to all his wives, she would probably also leave an aching heart. For he was really a good and kindly man. And this fact, that any one of his wives could walk out on him, probably made him more faithful than a European husband.

As it was, each of his thirteen wives took her turn to cook his meals, which insured a certain amount of variety (I thought of the caterpillars); and each contributed her share of grain from her field to his storage bins. Actually, he seemed to possess no personal wealth himself; he merely owned, as a symbol, the kraal and the central store of grain that was reserved for the tribe. The chief purpose of his own store of grain was that it should be used for the tribe's social requirements, for the entertainment of visitors, or for feasts. The life of the half hundred people within the kraal was that of a commune, and he was its titular head.

Like most primitive people, the Ovambas had the equivalent of old-age pensions and sick insurance; they felt the obligation to take care of any member of the tribe who could not look after himself. Orphans were adopted according to an ancient formula. And in a household such as Nehemiah's there would always be native nurses for the children. It was an admirably constructed society. And you wondered, sometimes, at the effrontery of the missionaries. They were doing their level best to tear down this ancient life, especially polygamy; but what could they put in its place?

The eleven Finnish missions in Ovamboland all had women doctors. They served a useful purpose, and the atmosphere of these remote, thatched settlements was that of a happy peace. But this was almost entirely due to the repose of the Finnish women's natures; it was not God. What the two English missions brought I am still wondering. But two zealous Cambridge men were laboring to win the Ovambas away from their evil ways.

The missions claim that about a third of the Ovambas have accepted Christianity. Nominally, perhaps, they have. But it is impossible to tell how many concubines a chief or a headman might have aside from the one wife legalized by the Christian Church. You could usually tell a Christian's kraal by its dilapidated condition; with only one wife to work for him, the very base of a native's life soon began to decay.

To prevent his dependence upon women being a barrier to the acceptance of Christianity, the missionaries were trying to get the native to accept the plow. They would, therefore, force him away from hand husbandry and put him on the basis of a competitive money economy, to the raising of cash crops. And when this comes about the peace of Ovamboland will be at an end.

There is a certain ruthlessness with which the mission disrupts native tribal life, which, you feel certain, would not have been approved by Christ himself.

Hahn, of course, unable to oppose the efforts of the missions, was struggling to perfect the Ovamba life as it was. It was his business to see that the people were well fed and contented, and that they regarded the Government of South-West Africa as a well intentioned and helpful friend. Here, too, the question of his own personality played a major part. If Hahn had, in the past, relied upon the threat of the Government to back up his suggestions or commands, then Ovamboland would have had the usual African quota of soldiers or policemen. But as I have said, there was not one.

His native name, "The Whip," he had won unintentionally at the very outset of his command. Ovamboland had been laid low by one of its historic droughts; the cattle were dying, and the Ovambas had become living skeletons. The South African Government sent up food relief. Hahn, who saw a strong native rush off with a woman's bowl of grain, went after him, brought him down with a dive tackle, and hammered him almost unconscious with his bare hands. The next time it happened Hahn was waiting with a *kiboko*, a rhino-tail whip. This time he did not tackle the robber; he just ran behind him, in full view of the starving natives, and flayed his behind till it bled. *"Shangola!"* cried the natives; "The Whip!"

It was the magistrate down at Grootfontein who gave me the best illustration of Hahn's power. "The natives," he said, "will follow any man as long as he is manly and can inspire respect. Doesn't make any difference whether it's a German or an Englishman; they don't know the difference. They follow Hahn because they know he's got both brains and pluck."

Hahn, he said, had forbidden the natives to bring their rifles with them when he was holding an *indaba*, a big tribal meeting. At first they refused to obey him. At one *indaba*, at which there were some two hundred Ovambas, they all brought their rifles. Hahn suddenly broke off the talk he was giving them, and raced across to the trees.

"And he had smashed six rifle butts before they could get the rest away from him. Now they know that Hahn can out-run, out-shoot, out-fight, and out-think any of them. He's the best man, *as* man, in Ovamboland."

Hahn had been an old "Springbok," a Rugger International, playing for South Africa. And in the Johannesburg games he once did the 100-yard dash in 10 seconds flat. He was quite a good specimen of white man.

But he always led, rather than pushed. It was amusing to watch the way he was opening up new country for the Ovambas. These natives, who are very sociable, are the very furthest thing from pioneers; they *hate* going into uninhabited country. And tribal taboos even prevented them from entering the territory of a strange tribe. To get them to open up land eighty miles to the east seemed an insurmountable problem. If ordered, they would do it; but then the South Africans would have to pay them for building the roads.

So Hahn got hold of Nehemiah and two more of the most intelligent headmen, and "sold" them the idea of what a fine grazing land that would be. He induced one headman to take some people out there and build a kraal for a cattle post. Then, always complaining about the fact there were no roads, he made it a point to drive this eighty miles out through the tambuti and mopani forests to visit them. In effect, he always said something like this:

"Of course, if you did build a road back to Nehemiah's kraal, it would be easy for you people to visit each other."

When I went out eastward to visit this kraal, the last habitation before the wastes of the Kalahari desert, I found all the natives frenziedly at work—at work on the new road. They were building *back* to Nehemiah.

They saw the joke now, and laughed when Hahn said openly: "Of course, I'd never have been able to get you fellows to build *out* to here; you would always have found some good excuse."

"Yes, master," laughed the headman; "that's right, master— we would have found a reason!"

"And now look what a nice life you've got," said Hahn. "I'm ashamed of you."

They knew he wasn't; that, actually, he was very fond of them. We sat on the logs that are the traditional Ovamba seats. A native played a "piano," a little box with sets of steel prongs that he thrummed. We drank the ceremonial "beer." And the headmen and Hahn planned the next development of their new life. Their aquiline, high-cheek-boned faces lighted with intelligent thoughts. A council of white pioneers could not have discussed a program with greater thought or dignity.

As we leaned back against the hot logs of the stockade I watched two golden crane fishing for frogs in a green bottom below us. The talk was, in fact, converging upon them, for Hahn had persuaded the headman to plant rice in that wild bottom. Here, eighty miles from even the most primitive Ovamba kraal, Hahn had planted a new life.

In a long, green vlei near that outpost I got twenty-five ducks and geese one morning. They were nearly all high, flighting shots. Nehemiah and the natives squatted in the thorn bushes and watched the sport. It was in no way murder, for every one of these ducks would be gratefully eaten by the Ovambas, and very welcome they would be in that remote district. I was pleased when, in full view, I got one or two doubles on high Muscovies. When I finished I gave Nehemiah eight cartridges.

A week or so later, passing Nehemiah's kraal, I asked him what had he done with the eight cartridges.

"Very fine, master; I get five ducks with each."

"Nehemiah, you incredible liar!"

"No, master, I no lie. But I don't shoot the way master does; I shoot 'em on the water. I crawl up—bang! Bang! One time I kill ten! Master, he go bang! bang! in the air. When duck drop, that is luck!"

A few days later, one sad morning I faced the four-hundred-mile drive down to Windhoek in South-West Africa. But when we had all my stuff on the one-ton lorry, we found that two of its springs were broken. And as we had to go down through some of the worst country in Africa, we could not chance it.

"You fix 'em," said Hahn to "Boy."

Now, "Boy"—he had no other name—was a Portuguese Ovamba. He had never seen a town, much less a workshop—except the one he had patiently put together himself in Hahn's sheds. Yet, within four hours, "Boy" had made and put in two perfectly good, serviceable spring leaves that he had made from some strips of steel with a vise and a hack saw. Going down, our hydraulic brakes jammed. "Boy" and Hahn dismantled them and put them back again—on the open plain.

I watched "Boy" during this performance. His anxiety to learn everything was nothing less than pathetic; also it was admirable. Many white mechanics, when they take a new contraption apart, have difficulty in putting it together again; they have forgotten the sequence of assembly. But not "Boy." "No, master—*this* way."

"Boy" demonstrated ability to *think* better than scholarly books I had read on the subject. He was an African Edison, a Ford. And that puzzled frown of his, when he was trying to figure something out, was one of the most lovable, and yet sad, expressions I have seen on any man's face.

Yet to watch "Boy" cook a goose was just horrible. He always boiled it in a gasoline tin—a tin full of grease, or whatever it was he had been using it for. He just put in the goose and water, and walked off. Some time during the day, when the idea occurred to him, he would take out the goose and throw it on the sand. He did this to a fine spur-wing I had given him. And I was angry.

"If you didn't want to eat it, Boy, why didn't you say so?"

"No, master, I eat him. I eat him tonight."

He would take the goose and toss it up into the motor lorry among the packs, the crates, the beds, blankets, guns, rifles, tattered clothes, and bare feet of the three Ovambas we always had with us.

My last nights in Ovamboland were under a full moon. The palm trees were silvered in the calm light. There was a diamond brilliance to the constellations in the sky. The crops were all in. And all night long the kraals of the Ovambas boomed like swamp frogs. The black and white ibis flew by with startled cries—and I had seen what was frightening them.

The flaming torches stuck in the sands. The log walls of the stockades gleaming. The girls, painted red with ocher from head to foot, dancing, dancing, dancing. And the drummers, riding their eight-foot hollow logs, thudding out the old blood-stirring chants.

"Boy" forgot all about carburetors and gaskets and spanners, on those nights. He was an Ovamba again. And I could well understand the resentment of the missionaries against the dance, because, they say, "It takes the Ovambas back!"

The last battle in 1932 the South Africans had with the Ovambas was when a local little despot, Chief Impumbu, forcibly removed from the veranda of the Finnish Mission a girl whom he was determined to make his wife. He refused to obey any orders from Windhoek, and three aeroplanes were flown up from the Cape to overawe him.

But, from spies, the South Africans learned that when the planes flew over Impumbu's kraal the Ovambas did not even look up!

Later, after telling the Ovambas to evacuate the kraal, the South Africans bombed it to bits. Impumbu fled, and was captured on the borders of Portuguese Africa. Then, remembering the taboo which had led to the rebellion and death of Mandumi, the South Africans made him live outside Ovamboland for five years. When he went back in 1937, therefore, the Ovambas no longer regarded him as a chief; Impumbu was a broken man.

11. Party Politics in South Africa

THE trouble with South African politics (from England's point of view) is that there is not in them an Englishman of any consequence. And there are no young ones in sight. This gives rise to more trouble than the mere fact that some 60 per cent of the South Africans are of "Dutch" extraction (which might be anything, a Hollander, a German, or a French Huguenot), and that only 40 per cent are English. The few Englishmen of any consequence in South Africa, these days, are content to restrict themselves to their business interests in Cape Town, Johannesburg, and Durban.

As a result, the continual bickering within the South African Parliament along racial lines is a fight among the "Dutch" *about* the English, rather than against them. Were some English personalities present, these debates might serve as a safety valve. Without this escape, these discussions only tend to embitter the Nationalist feeling.

The whole tendency of South African politics has been toward a "super-Nationalist" Party, splitting off from a Nationalist party. General Hertzog left Botha, demanding a republic. Dr. D. F. Malan, perhaps the most dangerous figure (to the British), left his pulpit and joined Hertzog. When Hertzog cooled down on the republic idea, Malan left him, to form another super-Nationalist Party, and led the Parliamentary opposition up to the outbreak of this war. When in this present war General Smuts brought South Africa in on the side of the British against Germany, and Hertzog fell, Malan drew Hertzog further away from the commonwealth idea, although, at this time of writing (January, 1940) Malan and Hertzog have not fused on the republic idea. And there is no real reason to believe that Hertzog has abandoned his political belief that to remain within the British Commonwealth of Nations is, in spite of Nationalism, the best life-insurance policy for the Union of South Africa.

Malan, even his worst enemy will tell you, is the man to be watched. He is intelligent, honest, and fanatic; an easily comprehensible comparison would be to say that he is the South African De Valera. By birth, training, profession, and political attitude, he appeals to the majority of South African instincts. To begin with, he is an ex-predikant of the Dutch Reformed Church, and to most Afrikanders on the veld the Bible is still the one and only book. Finally, he is almost insanely determined to take South Africa outside the British Commonwealth, and there is an alarming number of South Africans who are pro-anything, as long as it is anti-British.

Malan has but to capitalize these two strongest appeals to the South African temperament.

He was born 65 years ago, at Reibeck West, the farming town where Smuts was born. He studied for the church at Victoria College, Stellenbosch, and finished his studies at the University of Utrecht, Holland. His first district, at Montague, S.A., in 1906, was in a rich wine-growing province; yet the young Malan preached, if not strict prohibition, then rigid temperance. His probity was so passionate that his wine-growing religious Dutch congregation forgave him even that. When, before the war of 1914-18, General Hertzog began preaching his advanced gospel of Afrikanderism, practically demanding a republic, and quarreled with Botha, Malan took Hertzog's side. After the World War, when an Afrikaans newspaper was established to help Hertzog's Nationalism, Malan resigned his pulpit and became editor of that. When General Hertzog became premier, Malan became minister of interior in his cabinet.

He was the best minister of interior, even his enemies admit, that South Africa ever had.

When, in 1933, for the safety of South Africa, General Smuts and General Hertzog merged their two political parties together (a union which lasted until the outbreak of this last war), Malan split off and organized a purified Nationalist Party of his own. Malan's party demands:

1. A republic for South Africa.
2. Total segregation of the native and colored races, both territorially and industrially.
3. Complete stoppage of Jewish immigration.

And, as a philosophy, Malan's party holds that there is room in South Africa for one language only, Afrikaans.

There is not one of these demands that does not appeal, strongly, to the heart of the majority of South Africans of "Dutch" extraction.

The violent anti-Semitic program throws light on a curious facet of the South African mind. Its opponents try to deride it by declaring that this sentiment is back-veld. They are wrong.

The anti-Semitic bill itself, which the Malanites brought before the South African Parliament of 1939, was introduced by none other than Mr. Eric Louw, the first South African minister plenipotentiary to the United States.

Before that, Mr. Louw was South African High Commissioner in London; afterwards he was minister to France and Portugal, then minister at Rome. After this "twelve years' pioneering abroad," as he called it (during which he engaged in a bitter controversy with Lord Passfield, Dominions Minister, over the status of the South African High Commissioner at London, Louw claiming wider privileges), Louw resigned his ministership and returned to the Union to side with Dr. Malan.

He is known as the best dressed man on the Nationalist benches.

His anti-Semitic bill rivaled Hitler in its blind harshness.

Known as the "aliens amendment and immigration bill," it proposed, among other things, that no person of Jewish parentage (and this is made to include all naturalized British subjects) should be allowed to enter the Union of South Africa for permanent residence. It refuses even a temporary sojourn to anyone whose passport provides that he would lose his nationality within a specified period or prohibits his re-entry into the country where the passport was issued. This seems to include every possible refugee of Jewish origin.

Moreover, it declares that Yiddish is not a European language. This clause was undoubtedly inserted because the knowledge of at least one European language was a strict requirement of the present immigration act. Louw's act was attempting to block every loophole.

The bill even proposed that all aliens in South Africa would have to carry pass cards (the way the Negroes do now), and that firms employing aliens would first have to obtain official permission, then publish the names on signboards and documents, giving any previous names that these aliens might have held. This retrograde bill was so ruthless that it would require all Jews who had entered the Union under the 1937 aliens act to surrender their permits and take the tests again.

That this anti-Semitic bill had no chance whatever of getting passed, Malan admitted to me himself, when I saw him in Cape Town, in February, 1939.

"The Government members will assure us of their support in the lobbies," he said, sarcastically, "and then they will go in and vote against it out of personal loyalty to Smuts and Hertzog and party politics. We know that. Nevertheless, a large number of them will, in their hearts, wish that they could have voted for it. *And that is what we want to show them.*"

I have heard few unpleasant things put in a more sinister fashion!

Cape Town papers were uniting in calling the bill "contemptible." They declared it only emphasized the racialism that is always an unfortunate side of Union politics. But that was merely another thing that Malan wanted to make apparent. Its opponents also said that it was a low appeal, that it was playing up to the sentiments of the 300,000 "poor whites" in the Union, who are below the "bread-line" status. The more Jews you displace, the more jobs you provide for needy Afrikanders. And that was just another thing that Dr. Malan, expredikant of the Dutch Reformed Church, wanted to make known to everybody.

For he is a politician.

In 1932 a Carnegie Commission visited South Africa, and, after a careful study, reported that 22 per cent of the population of the Union was "poor white"; 34 per cent were below the normal sustenance level; 20 per cent had not risen to the taxation class; and only 3 per cent could be classed as well-to-do.

It is said that the Jews have never been so happy anywhere else in the modern world as they were in Johannesburg. It was literally their golden age, and many an aristocratic British name today is being supported by the money earned by the early, adventurous British Jews on the Rand or in the Kimberley diamond mines.

Today, one person in every sixteen in Johannesburg is a Jew. And one-third the Jews in the Union of South Africa (78,000) live along the Witwatersrand, the gold reefs.

Similarly, as they knew their segregation bill would also meet defeat, the Nationalist Party was merely circularizing it as a "petition" to be presented to Parliament. This bill would make all natives and colored people live outside the towns, or in special areas in the towns. And it would legally bar the blacks from certain occupations.

They are already barred, by the equivalent of a law, from practically every one of the skilled trades or professions in

South Africa. And the term "colored" is not a polite name for a Negro, as it is in the United States; it means someone who has a detectable amount of black blood in him. If Sarah Gertrude Millin is correct, then this debars from all the professions and trades over one-third the entire population of the Cape Province.

In South Africa they say, "You are just as white as you can get away with!"

Malan would risk antagonizing even this large bloc of voters. (The "coloreds" have votes in Cape Province.) For he said to me, "Even if those bills can never be passed, I want to show the majority of South Africans where their hearts lie, and this way will do it."

He then made the statement by which his party hopes to ensnare the white labor vote in the Union:

"Unless white labor is protected against black or colored labor, the white race will go down."

This is the equivalent of saying, "South Africa must be a white civilization, therefore the black man must not be allowed up." And when I pointed this out, Malan made the staggering remark that "the *intelligent* section of the native and colored community would welcome segregation."

In order of importance among the aims of the Nationalist Party, I would say that this holding down of black and colored competition was the chief. It is nothing less than legalized repression. To break with England is really not an aim for many Boers; but advocating political jingoism which may always be counted upon to get plenty of votes at election time—votes from people who know they can play with this fire without ever getting burnt; England will always protect them, if only for her own interests, they feel.

But the South African universities, the intelligentsia, and many honest politicians, like Malan, are working day by day to get a republic; they want to break with England as quickly as possible.

General Smuts assured me that this was all very well; a great number of South Africans liked to "play with this idea"; but, he insisted, the minute the menace of Germanism became apparent, these people would rush for cover within the British Commonwealth. He did not extend this to Malan and the other leaders of the Nationalist movement, but he indicated that it went for about 99 per cent of the intellectuals.

If you study these aims against the "racialism" that is always the background for South African politics, this feeling between Afrikaan and British, you will see many things come into focus that, at first glance, seem quite incomprehensible in far-off England.

The chronic racialism in South African politics, both local and national, arises from something more tangible than the fact that it is a frustration, a hang-over from the Boer War; a great many South Africans sincerely believe today that they *could* exist as an independent state. Not so many, perhaps, now that Germany has shown her attitude towards small neutral states. But, as Hertzog has shown by his speeches, quite a representative section of South Africans believe they could, and should, keep out of Europe's (England's) wars, and that they would not lose their freedom by doing so.

To people of this belief, to cut the painter with England would be the first step to guarantee immunity.

But the desire for a republic comes from something deeper in the heart than that. "It's this," said a group of South African journalists to me in Johannesburg; "we people, whom you choose to call 'Dutch,' are the only real South Africans. We have no other homeland outside this country. When our people came out here from Europe, they came to found a new country —*and this it is!*

"Now, with the 'English' South Africans, they always have

one foot in England. They don't place all their allegiance here. 'There is always England'; that's what's in the back of their minds. They are only half-hearted South Africans. They want South Africa for the empire; we want it for South Africa."

"Well," I asked, "what *real* difference to you does that make?"

"Only this: South Africa, the way things are now, is a machine, with strings attached to its levers, and those strings go to England. Every time we think we are running the machine ourselves, someone in England pulls a string."

"We don't *own* our country!" said another one. "It's not wholly ours."

They said they did not want me to leave South Africa without forming the right impressions. They asked whom I had seen at the Cape. I told them: Smuts, Pirow, Malan, etc., giving them quite a list of personages.

"My God!" gasped one, unconsciously; "why, he's seen *all* the wrong people!"

But that is just where the chronically untenable situation in South African politics comes in. Personalities.

The personalities of General Smuts and General Hertzog, the two outstanding national figures of South Africa, were so strong that a large part of their former United Party followed the *personal leadership* of one or the other. Until the outbreak of this present war, it was the combination of these two men which was the strongest influence holding South Africa within the British Commonwealth.

But, in January, 1940, Hertzog made a speech which shocked his followers. Formerly a man with a "single-track" mind, whom South Africans always believed they understood much better than they did the subtle Smuts, he suddenly revealed an attitude towards European politics that came as nothing less than alarming. In a speech which Smuts characterized on the floor as reading like *Mein Kampf*, Hertzog demanded that South Africa withdraw from the war, declare a state of peace with Germany, and remain perfectly neutral. Smuts said that Hertzog had shamed South Africa. And even the Malanites (who detest the name "Malanazis," as they have come to be called in the Union) recoiled from the wreckage that single speech of Hertzog's made of the Opposition tactics.

On January 27, 1940, Hertzog's "peace motion" was defeated by 81 votes to 59 in the Cape Parliament. The English hailed this as a great victory for Smuts; and it was—for Smuts. But the fact should not be overlooked, or its importance minimized, that 59 members of the South African Assembly thought it right, in crucial times like these, to cast their vote *not* to help England. They numbered 42 per cent of the Assembly. And, in a strange way, this reverses the "racial" composition of South Africa, which is 60 per cent "Dutch" and only 40 per cent "English." The London press, perhaps unconscious of the significance of the vote, declared that the *"personality of Smuts* [my italics] had never reached a higher point in South African politics."

Five months after this war began, when Hertzog and Malan were both in violent opposition against Smuts, Hertzog still refused to accept Malan's bitter program for a republic, with immediate separation from England. Hertzog was still sticking to his conviction that it would be wisest for South Africa to remain within the Commonwealth.

When I talked with Malan in February, 1939, it was the common saying in Cape Town that if Smuts were not alive Hertzog would swing over to the Nationalist movement. This would be an invaluable help to Malan.

"But it would be much better the other way," Malan said to me, seriously. "If Hertzog died, the men who follow him would desert Smuts. There would be so many of them that I would probably have a majority against Smuts."

As the events have shown, Smuts was able to carry the Parliament, voting South Africa into the war on England's side, against both Malan and Hertzog.

Malan is a pale, heavy man, nearly always dressed in black, with intense, brown eyes, behind spectacles, so fanatic that they seem to smolder when he is pressing home some point. His mouth is the stern, dogmatic aperture of the prelate who believes implicitly in the righteousness of his cause. It is said that he never laughs, never makes a joke; but he gave an unconscious heave when I said to him: "To the English, your ideas must seem horrible!"

"I believe that we shall have a republic within our time," he said, solemnly. "I am doing all I can to bring it about. I won't ask for it merely because I shall have a Parliamentary majority; I shall put it to a special vote of the people—a straight vote on whether or not they want a republic. No other political question will be allowed to be mixed with it."

He said he did not fear that a small Republic of South Africa would be attacked by any nation. When I countered by pointing out German rapaciousness, he replied:

"Look at Holland! Look at Belgium! Look at Denmark, Norway, Sweden!"

(That reply reads rather differently now. "Do," I feel like telling Malan; "look at Holland, Belgium, Norway, and, in particular, France!")

But it was substantially the same thing that Hertzog said in Parliament, just one year later; he, too, asserted he did not believe that Hitler was a menace to the small states. He said this five months after this war had been on!

But on July 17, 1940, when Dr. Van der Merwe, Nationalist, a strong supporter of Malan, was trying to organize a mass meeting "to consider active constitutional steps to establish a republic," Hertzog gave a statement to the Afrikaans paper, *Die Vaderland*, in which he said:

I regard the purpose of it in the present circumstances as extremely undesirable and foolish. I therefore express my strongest disapproval, and decline to be a party to it in any way. I wish to warn the people against irresponsibility.

In reply to my request for his reasons for having a republic, Malan said that it was the same desire for full nationhood that had motivated the United States and the Irish Free State, and which the British were repressing in India. He declared it was the natural evolution of all component parts of the British Commonwealth. The right of appeal to the Privy Council, he declared, would soon be abolished in Canada. He was even more specific in indicating certain immediate steps that should be taken to prevent South Africa being drawn into any war of England's.

Simonstown, the British naval base at the Cape, he said, should be put on a different basis. The Union of South Africa should not and could not be asked to defend it. "As it is, if we give shelter to British ships, and no others, in time of any war we are *automatically* drawn into it. South Africa cannot have neutrality with Simonstown the way it is."

He elaborated the analysis I had just been getting from Dr. Karl Bremer, the deputy leader of the Nationalist Party. Bremer, far from being a back-veld South African, went to London University, finished his medical studies at Cornell University, and then served as an intern in St. Bartholomew's Hospital, in London.

"If Germany were able to beat the combined British and American fleets," said Bremer, "and South Africa had taken part on the losing side, then it is our country which would be handed over. In the event of a defeat on the part of, say, Britain, France, and America, then, *if we have not taken part in any war*, we retain our independence."

"Germany would never take a white man's country in Africa," said Malan. "She might take a native country, but not a white country, unless we fought against her. The English are the only country which has made war in Africa against a white race."

I said that his position seemed to be that South Africa was banking on the protection she would get because England would never willingly let her Cape route be menaced by Simonstown falling into foreign hands, but that the South African National-ists were not prepared to make any sacrifice. If the combined fleets of England, France, and America were *not* defeated, then South Africa was sitting safe, anyway.

"You mean that we should go in on the side of the 'democ-racies'? That ideology is not enough. The fact that the world seems to be working up to war is not enough. You, the democ-racies, are quite prepared to ally yourselves with the worst form of dictatorship of all, the Communist.

"On the side of patriotism? Patriotism for England? There is none. As I have said before, the only country which has made war against a white civilization in Africa is Great Britain. There are many Afrikanders in the Hertzog-Smuts United Party today who want a republic for South Africa with all their hearts, but they are playing for safety, for self-interest. They think they will secure this by remaining under the protection of England.

"On the other hand, there is just as much to be said for another fear that is growing stronger every day here; and that is, *that if we are drawn into another European war we shall lose all.*"

I would have been much more impressed by Malan's argu-ments were it not for one of them. He declared that the large settlements of salmon-colored people in South-West Africa, the Bastaards, the Cape Whites, and the undefinable number of people in the Union, who are known as "coloreds," are *not* the mixture of Boer and Bantu.

"No," said Malan, piously, "they are the racial mixture of Bantu and Hottentot."

If Malan can believe *that*, I can also readily understand why he can believe that South Africa would never be endangered if she became a republic. Malan can believe anything.

12. General Smuts and Oswald Pirow

BEGINNING in South-West Africa, and becoming more and more aware of it as I lingered at the Cape, in Johannesburg and even in "English" Durban, I became aware of a distinct South Africanism. And General Smuts, when I talked with him, seemed its embodiment.

"I'll tell you the secret of General Smuts," said a South African telegrapher, who had been side by side with him through three years' political campaigns; "Smuts loves South Africa. Smuts loves South Africa more than any other South African *ever* loved it. That's Smuts!"

At the opening of Parliament, I watched Smuts from the press box—that hollow-cheeked, thoughtful face, with its pointed, white beard. He never once raised his eyes from a spot he had selected on the floor before him. It was as if he had cultivated an air of philosophic detachment. Hertzog sat beside him, but *his* eyes, also fixed on the floor, were frowning with some intense thought—the perfect expression, I thought, of the "man with a single-track mind." These two generals had fought the British to win South Africa; there had been a feud between them for twenty years; and they were both national heroes.

"I wonder what he's up to," came the whisper from a local journalist by my side; "I'm sure Smuts is up to something."

No stranger can visit Cape Town without being asked what he thinks about Smuts. The people seem anxious about it. When I asked the Parliamentary reporter what he thought Smuts was "up to" he declared: "I'll bet you he is writing another volume of his philosophy; *Holism,* he calls it." He added: "Smuts isn't the man to sit around and do nothing!"

I had expected him to say that the enigmatic Smuts was incubating some astute political maneuver, for this man's paper was not friendly to the general. His answer merely revealed how much, despite their efforts to deny it, all South Africans are puzzled by the brilliant personality of Smuts. I found him perhaps the most difficult statesman to talk with I have ever encountered, until—until I mentioned the sight of the springboks, leaping in the morning sun, above Etosha Pan.

"Yes!" he exclaimed, and he let his chair come forward. "Isn't that lovely?"

It was difficult to get him back to politics after that, for (and I knew I was doing it) I had mentioned perhaps the one sight which will stir any veld-loving South African to the heart—the leaping springbok.

"We shall keep South-West Africa," said Smuts. "Our position is both legally and morally unimpeachable. We will go to any extremes. Yes, we would even go to war."

His composure as he spoke, the nice adjustment he gave each word, the way he weighed a sentence before he let it go, all bore out the "Slim Jan" legend about him. It is hard to pin him down. On the other hand, you may take these fine inflections of meaning as nuances of the brilliant mind you are confronting. His voice is light, with an almost flute-like quality that enhances this delicacy. He placed no more emphasis upon this dramatic statement that South Africa would go to war before surrendering South-West Africa than he did in expressing his delight about the springbok—not as much, in fact.

The question of the extent, and danger, of German propaganda in South Africa, had been foremost in my mind, after I got this flat statement from him about the refusal to let South-West Africa go. Smuts was annoyed by my persistence.

"I know better than you do!" he at last said, peevishly.

I bowed my head, in all humility, but pressed on with the

point that, even if the propaganda was a political "racket," it could, and might, cause some serious trouble. He placed his slender finger tips together, leaned back in his chair, and said with extreme quiet:

"As times of test approach, we South Africans stick to our friends. It is not sentiment; it is an economic and defense necessity. The Germans know the weakness of their position here; they know"—he paused—"they know that when their *menace* becomes apparent it will fuse instead of divide the parties. It will sweep away, not create, differences. But until it does become clear that it is a menace, why, people will listen to it. I know better than you do, and I tell you that it is not serious."

It was Smuts who made the agreement with the German delegates in London, in 1923, whereby the German Government agreed to have its nationals throw in their lot with the South Africans in the South-West Mandate. I asked him what had actually taken place. (The Hitler government was now claiming that the words used by their delegates at that Conference only meant "for the time being.")

Smuts smiled: "There was a clause in our agreement in London whereby the South Africans agreed that, if a German became a subject of the Union under the Mandate, he would not be asked to take up arms against Germany for thirty years. That shows you the length of time we were contemplating; it would last for at least this generation.

"Also, when I returned to the Union, I called a meeting of the leading Germans from South-West Africa, together with the German Consul General, here in Cape Town. I did not want them to be able to think, or say, that I had been making agreements with the statesmen of Europe behind their backs. I told them what we proposed to do, and they agreed."

It was only then, said Smuts, that the Union of South Africa passed the 1924 naturalization act, whereby all Germans in South-West Africa, who wanted to, could become Union citizens.

"I do not think," smiled Smuts, "that the Germans would like to raise that 30-year exemption clause. It shows too clearly the length of time discussed, and the mood, in which those London discussions were carried on. *When we took over the Mandate of South-West Africa we intended to keep it for all time.*

"I have said so before, and I repeat it: We will go to war before we give it up."

It was quite obvious that in those London discussions the German delegates had met their match in Smuts. As a negotiator, with an innocent front, he is probably unsurpassed. But he is a much greater international figure than he is a South African. At home, his nimble agility of mind upsets his fellow countrymen. They never know quite how to get hold of him, where he is on any point. Mentally, he is always one or two jumps ahead of them. That is why so many South Africans positively dislike him. At one Cape Town luncheon, where there were several distinguished persons, I asked the wife of one of them why she was so anti-Smuts.

"Because I cannot understand him," she said simply.

"And Hertzog?"

"Oh, yes; I understand him; I like him."

The Negroes of South Africa are afraid of Smuts. But he has a difficult task in trying to placate, at the same time, both aspiring black man and Boer farmer! One day he is working to get more land set aside for the native; the next day he is telling an angry meeting of Boer farmers that the natives will never have enough land to enable them to be free—free from the necessity of having to work a certain number of days for the white man. At Oxford University he delivers a series of lectures, setting out to demonstrate to that uninformed audience that the black man must, and can, develop within his own civilization—inside the Reserves. In Africa, the native knows that these Reserves provide no chance whatever for the exercise of any of the skilled professions, nothing much higher than semi-skilled manual labor. The natives of South Africa fear Smuts; they think he is a dangerous man.

I talked with Negroes of all types and stations in life, in South-West Africa, at the Cape, in Johannesburg, and over in Natal. While it is true that the more primitive laboring class among them look forward to the day when they may own a plot of land, and farm for themselves, to be completely free from the white man, the forward-looking African looks upon such an end as little short of life imprisonment. He wants the chance to get on in life, in any fashion that he wants to get on. At Adams College, in Natal, I talked with a Bantu boy who had been two years at Yale.

When I asked him what it was like, being back in Africa, he smiled sadly and shook his head. "I don't know," he said. "I don't know *what's* going to happen!"

He implied that whatever did happen to him it would only be, in a varying degree, some sort of unpalatable life.

It was Oswald Pirow, the Minister for Defense at that time, who first called my attention to the Union's "Greater Africa" policy. Pirow's recent visit to Berlin had caused a stir in Europe; a large section of the British press firmly believed that he had come to offer Hitler a return, or some spectacular compensation for the German African colonies. Nearly everyone in England was convinced that Pirow was pro-German.

But I had been told that he was the most misunderstood man in South African politics. He was not pro-German at all; he was just 100 per cent pro-Pirow. He saw himself as a leading figure at the Cape; and, surely, he could not envisage himself as that, under any German domination. Therefore, don't write Pirow off too lightly, as merely a Nazi admirer.

Pirow, who has enough energy for any two men south of the equator, nearly swept me off my chair by the vehemence of his outburst. South Africa, he said, would be only too glad to get rid of South-West Africa; but it could not—especially not to Germany. Neither could South Africa afford to let the English, in Whitehall, surrender Tanganyika.

Why? Because to do that would wreck South Africa's plans for the future. South Africa saw herself as the guardian of the white race up to the equator. She would have no political connection, perhaps, with the bloc that must be formed of Kenya, Tanganyika, and Uganda, and that other bloc composed of the Rhodesias and Nyasaland. But she would have a common defense policy and set of communications with them.

Tanganyika was a vital section of the "white backbone" in Africa. If the Germans were ever allowed to have that, they would not make it a colony—the Germans never did that. No; they would make it a little slice of Germany. Then the Union of South Africa would be halted in its "Greater Africa" policy—to say nothing of what the Germans could and would do to the rest of Africa after they had organized the 5,000,000 natives of Tanganyika. German propaganda would sweep the continent!

Of course, the South Africans had to back the English up in hanging on to Tanganyika. In case of a future war, South Africa might have to defend Africa up to the equator. They might have to defend Kenya.

And then, there were the Japs. It would not do to forget the Japs; remember Lothrop Stoddard's *The Rising Tide of Color*. Time is short when measured by history; the Japs were busy now in Manchuria and China, but one day they would come out of that. Then the Japs would look west. When they did that, the African highlands would be one of the first places to greet their covetous eyes. What about Tanganyika then?

Well, if Tanganyika were still firmly held by the British, it might very well be the bastion of defense against the Japanese European invasion. One had to look ahead in these things.

"I think great crises breed their own great men, don't you?" asked the impetuous Pirow.

It was plain whom he was thinking of.

I had asked Smuts if it was true that Pirow had gone to Berlin with alternative proposals to satisfy the German colonial ambitions. It was characteristic of Smuts that he said, "Mr. Te Waater has denied that, in London." Smuts himself did not deny it.

I now asked Pirow.

"Don't talk to me about that Berlin trip!" he exploded. "I won't say a word!"

I had heard that Hitler had treated him with the utmost discourtesy. He had kept Pirow hanging about until the very last moment, and then, when he heard that Pirow was preparing to take a train to leave Berlin, he sent for him. But he did not give him an audience alone; he received him in the presence of several other Nazi officials. And then, so I was informed, he gave the South African Minister for Defense a very bad "quarter of an hour."

"Do you know what Hitler is?" Pirow is reported to have told the people at Dar es Salaam, on his return. "Hitler is John the Baptist in jack boots!"

And another member of the Tanganyika League told me that Pirow said to him, "If Tanganyika ever leaves the British Commonwealth, South Africa goes too—and in the same direction!"

There was no doubt in my mind, after that exhilarating interview, about his not being pro-German. He may have changed since he went out of office with General Hertzog, but I doubt it. On the other hand, I think it is equally sure that he is not pro-British, and that nothing could make him so. He is, I am convinced, at least 120 per cent pro-Oswald Pirow. He sees a great future for himself in a greater South Africa. And I think he will have it.

"But don't forget," said Pirow as I was leaving, "peace will be a dream unless the Allies admit, unreservedly, both the legal and moral right of Germany's colonial claims, and agree to give her adequate compensation for the colonies she cannot have owing to the way aeroplanes, railways, and faster ships have changed the world since 1913. There must be a frank solution."

When I asked him what it would be, he said, "I do not know."

Malan had been equally emphatic in asserting that the Union of South Africa should not surrender South-West Africa. "It is as much a part of the Union," he declared, "as the shires are of England. But Germany must be given compensation."

"What?"

"Elsewhere," said Malan.

"Where?"

"I don't know," said Malan.

South Africa is spinning on a hub of gold. Half the national income comes from gold, half the national life is connected with its production. "Take the gold away," say the Dutch, "and we shall stay—but the English will have to go."

That is true; the Dutch could revert to their early life, become Boers, farmers, again. Many would relish it.

South-West Africa, Mozambique, even Tanganyika, could all become air bases, within striking distance, for any foreign power which wished to seize this gold.

In peace time, fifty ships every day pass the Cape. This is England's alternative route to the Far East. In case of a war in which the Mediterranean became involved, it is almost certain that the Suez route would be unusable. Then over two hundred ships a day would be going around the Cape of Good Hope.

This knowledge on the part of many South Africans that England would never dare let the Cape fall into foreign hands is the reason why so many South Africans feel that they are not playing with fire when they demand a Republic of South Africa.

It is a good thing to keep in mind.

13. "Black Zoos"

LIFE in Africa is like life in a ship—and the white men are the passengers.

It can be taken as an axiom that a white man never intends to do any heavy-duty manual work in Africa. His life's job, as he considers it, is to supervise black labor. He is dependent upon the native for all the manual work in the mines, on the farms, and for all the labor in connection with urban civilization. Until he is willing to do this work himself, he will never be able to free himself from the black man. The black man must, therefore, be kept under control. This reservoir of black labor must be preserved. More than that, it must be made to work. Left to himself, the native would do only the barest minimum of work, merely enough to keep himself alive, if that. Therefore a system of taxation, to make a native work, was invented long ago. Whether it is head or hut tax, the result is the same; a large number of natives must be absent from their Reserves a certain number of months every year, in order to earn enough money to pay this taxation. And any *surplus* of labor which the white man feels he may reasonably do without may be segregated in Reserves.

That, in rough outline, is the position of the black man in South Africa today. This does not apply to Tanganyika, where the British administration is holding the country in trust for the natives, and tribes like the Masai would never labor for the white man. Nor has it any connection with the British West African coast, where all cultivation is in native hands, and the white men are merely Government officials or traders. It holds good, however, to a large extent for the Belgian Congo and

French Equatorial Africa; for while there may be no Reserves in these last two territories the natives are being, one by one, caught up in the mesh of taxation, put on a revolving belt of progress, and made to acquire a money urge, in spite of themselves. With Kenya, it is about half true.

Both Kenya and the Rhodesias are in transition, and seem to be heading towards the South African model.

The chief scandal of these Reserves is the overcrowding. In Natal (always strongly under English influence), 43 per cent of the land has been set aside for the natives; 8.75 per cent in the Cape Province; 3.56 per cent in the Transvaal; 0.2 per cent in the Orange Free State.

In the Transvaal 70 per cent of the population is on 3.56 per cent of the land; in the Free State, 67 per cent is on 0.2 per cent.

These are the "black zoos" which the white man has set up for the Africans.

The Transvaal and the Orange Free State are the most "Dutch" of the South African provinces. Here not even a "colored" man may buy a drink, and all natives (unless they live on the premises of their master) must be in their locations by 9 P.M. Johannesburg and Pretoria have "pick-up" vans, police patrols which pick up and arrest natives found after that time in the streets.

But there are 300,000 natives in the mine compounds on the outskirts of Johannesburg!

If you have seen a recruiter at work, you will remember it for the rest of your life. You will never forget the sight of scrambling, stinking black man power.

"I'm sending down a hundred boys today," said the medical officer in Ovamboland. "Want to watch it?"

Now, Ovamboland is the one place within the South African jurisdiction where the black man need not do any work, if he does not want to. The tax there is only five shillings a year;

it may be paid in either cash or grain; it is all put into a tribal trust fund, and spent back on the native.

Yet there were over four hundred "boys" scrambling outside the employment shed for these jobs.

The scene afforded a diluted impression of forgotten slave markets; like a cattle fair; like the selection of vegetables at Covent Garden. Only, this was a river of black flesh that was banking up outside the door of the Northern Labor Company —a black cargo for the waiting motor lorries.

"Africa's richest asset!" said the doctor. "About half of those 'boys' out there are Portuguese Angolas. They've already walked over four hundred miles to get here. They're much heavier and stronger than the local Ovambas, but their chests are weak; they die like flies in the copper mines."

The local Ovamba "boys" did not want to go to the Tsumeb copper mine, 180 miles below; the deaths had been averaging eight natives a day there, only a few months before. At one time it mounted to as high as 10 per cent of the labor corps. The situation was so bad that the Government had stopped recruiting for ten days, until it had been investigated.

It was then discovered that the mine authorities had been giving the "boys" raw, uncooked food. They had to cook it themselves, after their work was done. One "boy," interviewed by the Government medical officer and the native affairs official, had, on coming off shift, not eaten for twenty-two hours. "I have no time to work, and then cook my own food," he said. As the result of the investigation (which had been made just before I got there) the Tsumeb mine had now installed a kitchen.

This Tsumeb mine was about a 100-per cent German concern, with the bulk of its capital held in Berlin. There were 240 Europeans in the mine, of whom only one was not a German. He was a South African, an electrical apprentice, married, and he was being paid £4 a month.

Many of the "boys"—those who did not die—would return

from the Tsumeb mine ruined for life, from sulphur fumes, lead poisoning, and, until this particular date, from the atrocious food.

"It seems a damned shame to send him down there," said the doctor, having just passed a magnificent Angola "boy." "Break him."

The local Ovambas both did and did not want to go to the fields of the Consolidated Diamond Mines, at Lüderitz. They did not like the tales that the other boys had brought back, of the cold fogs along the South-West African coast, and of the alternative blazing suns. But they knew they would thrive there, for the Lüderitz diamond field feeds its "boys" like fighting cocks. What frightened them most was the new X-ray apparatus which the mines had installed to prevent the natives from smuggling the stones out in their bodies. There had been a big strike in the fields when the machine was first used; the natives were afraid the X-rays would sterilize them!

It was on the damp islands off that coast that the Germans had put their Herrero captives during the rebellion of 1904-07, knowing full well that the natives would die of exposure. The sea was full of bodies being washed up on the mainland. Five hundred, at least, died from cold there.

Outside the "boys" were fighting to be passed.

The doctor who was examining them was supposed to be the medical officer for 25,000 square miles and 150,000 natives; and, as he is always examining recruits, it can be seen what attention he can give to the other natives. He was being assisted by two native clerks, and a German known as "the rodent man" because his particular job in the district was to stamp out the bubonic plague. His macabre little office was full of flea-diagrams, stuffed rats, mongoose, and civet cats.

The "boys" came in stripped.

There was a strange, dank, sour smell about them that

became sinister as it began to flood the room. It was not like white man's sweat; this was different. The doctor made them jump towards him in two enormous leaps, like frogs. This was done to expose the hernia (very common, from faulty cutting of the umbilical cord); it comes down when they jump. The "boys" made every effort to conceal the hernias, putting their hands over the places.

Each "boy" was made to demonstrate that he did not have a common venereal disease. It struck me that they were particularly clever in their effort to evade a revelation. There was an astonishing number of malformed, or not fully formed legs, varicose veins, and the beginnings of elephantiasis. The doctor refused to pass any with roughness on the skin. "This fellow might very likely be a starting leper."

Regarding them, as the hundreds passed before me, I realized the truthful saying that Africa is not a healthy country, even for the native, and that the great majority of African natives have something wrong with them. It wasn't the white man who had debased these bodies; it was the vile climate. Most of the Portuguese "boys," when asked why they were so anxious to go "South," said, "Because I am hungry, master."

Considering the death rate (and "boys" must have brought the tale home), it was amazing how anxious they were to go. A healthy "boy" will try to substitute for his weaker brother; be examined, then pass on the card. For no "boy" may leave Ovamboland without a pass card. In the scramble to be examined, two who had just been rejected succeeded in getting into the room for another examination. The doctor told one by his spotted behind. "I won't look at those with spots on them!" And the other was blind in one eye. It was amazing, the deftness and celerity with which the doctor examined them. He held his hand over one eye of this "boy," then held up the fingers of the other hand. He asked how many fingers he had raised. But the "boy" could not tell.

When the doctor had passed one, he marked, with yellow

chalk, the letter A, B or C on his naked chest. Then the "boy" stepped to the left, and two native attendants clapped a cord around his neck, and sealed it with a lead "plomb." The A's and B's were sent to the copper mines or diamond fields; C's were considered only good enough to work on the farms. Thus was this black humanity graded.

An A "boy," going to the mines, begins at 8*d*. a day for a shift of nine hours. Their average earnings are 25 shillings a month. (A white miner gets over £1 2*s*. 6*d*. a day.) A B "boy" gets the same as an A, if working in the mines. But on a farm he starts at 10 shillings a month, for the first four months; then 11 shillings and 12 shillings for the next two blocks of four months. But not many B's go to farms; it is usually the C's. These start at 8 shillings a month; and, as far as I could make out, that is about all that they ever get.

A year later these "boys" would come back (some of them) to Tsumeb with the usual £5 earned by a year's labor, and, as I have said, buy trinkets for their wives and sweethearts before they began their long trek back into Ovamboland and up into Portuguese Africa. While there is no stipulated tribute, each "boy" would have a few shillings, kept strictly in reserve, which he would give to his headman or chief. Very few "boys" fail to do this. No harm comes to them if they do not hand over this token of fealty. But, as the medical officer pointed out, it was comforting to find savages who willingly gave "money that hurt" rather than break with their old tribal loyalties.

Whenever a naked "boy" hopped before us with a ring of ostrich shell beads around his neck, we knew that he was going South to get the money to be married. This necklace showed that he had just become "engaged."

The records of the Northern Labor Company's recruiting office showed that about 90 per cent of the men who have once been South try to go back again. Some re-recruit the minute they get back to Ovamboland. But the doctor said that the average "boy" remained at his kraal for four or five months. The doctor wanted to make this an obligatory eight months, so that the native would be ingrained with his old customs again, and not become detribalized.

Every one of these natives had perfect teeth. I looked down several hundred throats that day; I have never seen such superb molars. They were not even discolored. But all the local Ovamba boys had the middle lower tooth knocked out—so that they could spit properly. And a great number of the Portuguese West Africa boys had their teeth filed. Why? To get a good grip on their meat? Or for beauty? None knew. They said that it was done with a knife, and that it did not hurt to do it. I examined several sets of these filed teeth closely, and I couldn't discover any discoloration, even where the dentine must have gone, nor was there any sign whatever of any decay setting in. Their smiles were appalling.

There came before us, this day, two proud Herrero "boys." They were much taller than the others, some five feet eight or nine inches. They were "Ovatjimbas," descendants of those Herreros who had fled from the Germans, in the rebellion of 1904-07, into the unexplored Kaokoveld.

They had skins like satin, and the medical officer said they had the finest spines he had ever seen.

When the required number of "boys" had been passed, they were reassembled again in a long line, and passed before the doctor, who gave each an injection of anti-cholera and typhoid serum. Then they romped off, congratulating each other like schoolboys who had just passed an examination. They were then addressed by the recruiting officer.

He told each group of A, B, or C "boys" where it was going; what would be a day's work, and what they would get for it. He told them that food, shorts, shirt, blankets, and medical service would be given to them free. And then he turned over the job to the Government clerk-interpreter. His was the most interesting address. He said:

"If you have any complaints to make over your treatment in the South, if you have a row with your *baas*, or something like that, you must make your complaint to the Native Affairs Officer, or the Magistrate, *at once!*"

"You see," one of the white men at the recruiting office explained to me, "the 'boy' really ought to see the Magistrate while the blood is still showing from any cuts or bruises."

"And yet most of them want to go back?" I said, wondering.

"Yes; but damned few of them ever want to go back to the same master. Their optimism about us white men is humiliating. They always think they'll find a better one!"

UP THE EAST COAST

14. The Indian Problem in Africa

IT was six days in the British India boat from Durban to Dar es Salaam. And for five of them the Swami told me how the Union of South Africa was going to decide the fate of the British Commonwealth. This was on the handling of the "Indian question." For one day I did not see the Swami; he had taken some medicine, and lay prostrate in his bunk.

There were twelve white passengers in the ship, and below decks there were several hundred assorted Indians. Both in crew and passengers we were a Noah's ark. The air, even on deck, was as steamy as in a Turkish bath. Between decks it was suffocating. Yet down there the Mohammedan women were keeping *purdah* in stuffy enclosures made from flour sacks; and Hindu males, each wearing the one suit of pajamas that would suffice for the twenty-one days between Durban and Bombay, sat on camp beds, in the encampment which their wives were setting up around each family's pre-empted section of living space. As there were so many tongues and dialects, without one common denominator, the toilets were marked with little painted statues in bas-relief. Aside from their artistic merit, they served to indicate which was for males and which was for the other sex.

We had taken fifty goats aboard for the Mohammedans. But the Hindus, who would not eat fish, flesh or fowl, anything which had been killed, sat around trays of sticky, yellow sweetmeats made from sugar and rancid ghee, and bowls of saffron, curried rice.

In my own bunk, in the muggy nights, the heat was so

sweat-producing that my pajamas stuck to me as if I had fallen overboard. Below decks it was even more intolerable, and the stink was unbelievable. The Hindus and the Mohammedans, most of them, moved about with a lime in their hands. They did not eat it; they merely squeezed it slightly to get its scent, to avoid being sick.

Perhaps a roster of the crew might give some indication of the complications that we carried. There were eighteen white officers and one white steward; then came a "cargo staff" of eight Parsees; two Chinese carpenters; forty-five Hindu deck hands, fishermen from the Gujerat; fifty-one Goanese waiters and saloon men; twenty-five Moslems in the engine room; fifteen Hindu cooks; fourteen Mohammedan cooks; and three Hindu laundrymen.

"Mixed lot," said the first officer. "Idea is that they'll never all get together in case of a mutiny or a riot."

A turbaned Sikh wandered despondently about, staring covetously at the steaming coast of Africa he saw through portholes —staring regretfully, for he was being taken back to India, not having had the two hundred shillings which are required as a deposit for an Indian landing in British East Africa.

None of these communities would have anything to do with each other. For they were going back to India, where the class and creed and caste distinctions would be drawn sharply again. And yet the little Swami, in his arguments, always spoke of them as one—one indivisible, liberty craving, Indian mass.

The Swami had been sentenced to three years in prison in British India, for aiding Gandhi's *satyagraha* (passive resistance) campaign. Yet, he kept on assuring me, Gandhi's "back to the loom" movement was no good for modern India. It was behind the times.

Talking with the Swami, I saw that I was in the presence of a serene and noble mind. His was one of the rewards of foreign travel, definitely. He was a Hindu, a holy man, who had given away all his worldly wealth in order to serve mankind. He was the president of the South African Indian Congress. He had written fourteen books on Indian metaphysics and politics. The South Africans had also thought enough of him, his nuisance value, to imprison him for three months; three months' hard labor, in 1913, with his wife, Jag-rani, and child, Ramdutt, for organizing an Indian strike at Newcastle. And he was deep, unfathomably intelligent, with an easy command of wit and irony. In short, he was one of the most exhilarating boat companions I had met in many voyages.

One green sunset, when we were leaning over the rail, watching two rows of Mohammedans on the aft hatch bowing towards Mecca and chanting their prayers, the peaceful scene was broken by an ungodly thumping of Hindu drums and whining stringed instruments from between the decks. He saw the look of appalled annoyance on my face, and smiled.

"It's funny, how unmusical everybody else's music sounds!"

The Swami was going to India to protest against the new segregation bill, being proposed by the Minister of the Interior for South Africa, the Hon. R. Stuttaford, a Durban department-store owner. The bill, in brief, provided that if seventy-five per cent of the people of any area in South Africa protested, Indians could not own property in that area; they could neither live nor conduct business there; and, if they were there, they could be dispossessed.

It may seem odd, at first glance, that the Swami should be going to India to protest against a South African measure. But the technique was simple, and is invariably followed by the Indians in Africa when they wish to bring England's pressure to bear in Cape Town politics—which is always.

The Swami, by his speeches in India, would create a popular agitation in India. Then the Indian Congress would take it up with the Indian Legislature. Then, as the plan was, the Viceroy would become alarmed, and take it up with the India Office in

London. The India Office would call the attention of the home Government. And, as Indians are supposed to have equal rights as British subjects anywhere in the Commonwealth, the British Secretary of State *should* take it up with the South African Government.

"But," I protested to the Swami, "the British have enough trouble on their hands, without putting their fingers into South African politics. That's the last thing they want to do. The position of South Africa within the Commonwealth is one of absolute independence."

"It is a very grave issue for England," said the unmoved Swami, "whether she will maintain India within the Commonwealth, or whether she prefers *to satisfy public opinion* in South Africa. England can lose her empire in the handling of the Indian problem—and she can lose it in South Africa!"

That was his mission. That was his threat. And I sat beside him on the platform at Lourenço Marques while he inflamed an eager meeting of Indians of Portuguese East Africa on this embittered, and apparently insoluble, problem.

For the "Indian problem" in South Africa, these days (to say nothing of its danger in Tanganyika and Kenya), is probably more immediate and puzzling than the Negro question can ever become in the United States.

The threat of the African Indians, to use India as a club to browbeat England into taking a hand in African politics, is a constant menace to England's pleasant relations with the South African Government. In Kenya, it once brought matters to a point where the white settlers were going to kidnap the Governor! In Tanganyika (an Indian paradise, these days), the only place in the world, perhaps, where the Indians are given a fair and equal chance against white men, the clever, exultant Indians would seem to be a bar across the road of all lower levels of advancing black and white civilization.

The Indians in British East Africa have a powerful friend in

English politics. There are so many of the adherents of the Aga Khan in Tanganyika, Kenya, and Uganda, that this part of Africa might just as well be called "the Aga Khan country." When he visited Nairobi, a few years ago, his admirers weighed that fat lineal descendant of the Prophet (and race-horse owner) in solid gold. They put him on a scale. His followers even bought his bath water, after he had used it. The Aga Khan always has a thick, powerful finger in the British political pie; so there is no knowing how far he may be able to hold open the east coast of British Africa for Indian free development.

But in South Africa itself it is just the sheer fecundity of the Indian which makes him, in South African eyes, so ever-growing a menace—his multiplicity, and his ability to underlive and undersell the white man wherever he comes into competition with him.

The South Africans feel they have many problems, Bantu, British, "colored," and Indian. And of them all, the last is the only one which enlists your sympathies on the South African's side. For this is a black man's country, not a white man's; and if the white has had the arrogance to pre-empt it, there is no reason why he should turn sentimental and let cheap Asiatic labor prevent him from getting full value from it.

That's the way you feel at first. Then you meet some of the higher-class Indians on the east coast, you see what pleasant, reasonable, intelligent, even desirable people they are, and your heart is torn.

It is a wretched problem, a thing which never should have been allowed to happen; the present efforts to solve it are unquestionably cruel and inhumane. It presents the same opportunities for savagery that Hitler seized upon in the case of the Jews. It was his twenty-one years' South African experience that turned Gandhi from an ordinary, aspiring Indian, a barrister of the Inner Temple, anxious to emulate English ways, into a loinclouted ascetic, fighting his continual battle for Indian rights.

✦

Put briefly, the South African "Indian problem" is this: In 1860, the sugar planters in Natal got permission from the Government to import Indian labor. The Indians, they declared, would be more useful and reliable than the black man. To encourage Indians, they gave them land and allowed them to settle on it, after their days of indenture were over. The Indians poured in like locusts; they multiplied like locusts.

Then, in the 'nineties, the white people in Natal who were not planting sugar began to be alarmed. If the Indians continued to increase like this, there would be no room for the white man. Nevertheless, the vested sugar interests were so strong that they managed to perpetuate the system until 1911. In 1911 immigration was prohibited.

Today there are 220,000 Indians in South Africa. Over 184,-000 of them are in Natal. This is only 6,000 less than Natal's entire white population. Over 85 per cent of these Indians were born in South Africa and are South African nationals. What can be done with them?

Young, ambitious white men in South Africa find it hard to get business positions, because of: (a) very little industrial development; (b) cheap Indian competition; which, of course, the white employers use ruthlessly.

Not only has the Union of South Africa itself imposed a ban against any further Indian immigration, the Provinces themselves have also imposed bans. They have placed restrictions upon the ownership of land, restrictions upon trading facilities. These bans vary in intensity. In the Transvaal, by establishing certain "proclaimed areas," the authorities have been trying persistently to exclude Indian trading competition from the mining districts. But there are 25,000 Indians in the Transvaal.

On the other hand, there are only fifty Indians in the Orange Free State, and they are all hotel waiters.

In the Transvaal, the Orange Free State, and Natal the Indian has no vote. He cannot possess, or drink, liquor in either the Free State or the Transvaal; yet in Durban the Indians have their own bars, which no Bantu or "colored" man may enter. In the Cape Province alone do the Indians have any vestige of political or municipal franchise. And, so the Secretary of the South African Indian Congress told me in Durban, of the 30,000 "colored,".who have a vote in the Cape, 18,000 are Indians.

A. I. Kajee, this Mohammedan secretary, told me, as we sat at his door, that, although immigration had been stopped, and 30,000 Indians had accepted repatriation to India, under the various schemes with which the South Africans have tried to solve the Indian problem, the population of Indians in South Africa had increased by 35 per cent since the census of 1921— figures which, if correct, are sufficiently alarming proof of the threat from mere Indian fecundity. The population of Durban itself (230,000), he said, was composed as follows:

> 100,000 Europeans
> 90,000 Indians
> 6,000 "coloreds"
> 34,000 black men

Seventy thousand more Indians live within a radius of seventy miles in a semi-circle around Durban, working on the everlasting sugar plantations, living in fantastically wretched hovels, running, it seems, every shabby shop in the country districts.

Yet Durban is far and away the most "English" city in South Africa, more English than England would dare to be, in these days. And it is these very "English," not the Boer South Africans, who are frantically making these repressive segregation laws to "settle the Indian problem."

The problem of the two million whites in South Africa against the eight million blacks and "coloreds" is a long-range and more ponderous problem; it does not have the immediate intensity of the struggle between the almost equally balanced numbers of Indians and whites in Natal.

"Our hopes must lie with Hertzog and the British press,"

said this Secretary of the South African Indian Congress. "We cannot hope for anything from the Englishman in South African politics. The Englishman, out here, is a man who gets disheartened too quick. He is a defeatist!"

It struck me at the time that it would be a good thing when, either in England or in South Africa, the Englishman criticizes the South African for his attitude toward the color problem, for him to look at the Englishman's attitude, in Natal, toward the Indian problem.

One of the possible outcomes of these two problems, each adding weight to the other, is a combined front, which would include the thousands of disgruntled "colored" people in South Africa.

At the Cape and in Natal I heard quite a lot of talk about a non-European front which might be formed one day in South Africa. Labor intellectuals said that the South African Labor Party (its leaders all "English") had got the color bar bill, practically prohibiting all black men from any skilled occupation in South Africa, for their support of Hertzog in his successful 1923 elections.

If Malan's proposed "colored segregation" petition ever became a bill, extending, as he openly declared, this industrial segregation to all the "colored" inhabitants of the Union, then the "coloreds" would turn, in desperation, away from their historic ambition to be considered as whites—*and organize the Bantu natives*.

And, embittered by segregation bills such as the "English" Minister of Interior, the Hon. R. Stuttaford, was proposing, a large section of the South African Indian Congress was asserting that the Indians should join such a common front of "colored" and black men.

"With Hertzog and Smuts you can talk," said a prominent Durban Indian to me. "With Hertzog particularly, if you win a point from him you are aware of how much you have advanced; you can 'get somewhere' with him. And Smuts, I suppose, for all his evasiveness, is trying to help us. But Stuttaford—*he is a heartless man!* He is hopeless! He has the soul of just exactly what he is—a Durban shop-keeper!"

The little Swami, in our long, moon-lit talks, told me he did not want the non-European front. He did not want the Indians to mix themselves with the "colored" or Bantu men; he wanted their problem to be clear-cut and distinct. He wanted the Indians' battle fought in a larger arena, with England as their champion.

While we crawled slowly across the muddy waters of Delagoa Bay, with the Lascar leadsmen whining their high cries, a deputation of Indians of Portuguese Africa awaited the Swami on the quay. That night I sat beside him on the platform while he spoke to them of his mission in India. They had hung a wreath of marigolds and colored field flowers around his neck, and thrust a bouquet into his hands, as they did to me. And I felt that I looked like a corpse prepared for burial.

"The Union of South Africa is going to decide the fate of the British Commonwealth," he began, in a high, incisive voice. "Gandhi declared the independence of India, after twenty-one years of South African experience. . . . An empire which often says 'an equal right for every native, nation, and creed' . . . But, in South Africa, and in British Africa, the Indians are treated like helots! . . . Mr. Stuttaford's bill will create great agitation in India. . . . It is a breach of the Smuts-Gandhi Cape Town agreement. . . . It is an unbearable insult to the Government of India!

"I am going to India," said the little Swami, "to put this blunt question to the Government: 'Do you intend to help—or leave alone—the Indians in South Africa?' The Government of India must be made to demand an explanation of South Africa. . . ." And so on.

But what seemed to me so arresting about the little Swami's speech was not his dark threats to hit England in the eye if she didn't make the South Africans behave more generously to their little brown brothers; it was this attentive audience he was lecturing to. In Lourenço Marques, not quite a community of lily-white Europeans, I caught myself wondering why the Indians did not sometimes take it into their heads to draw the color line against the white man. For certainly these two or three hundred I regarded in this schoolroom seemed the most respectable and purest-blooded people I had encountered in that Portuguese port.

Back aboard ship I found the captain dutifully doing the honors for some sun-rotted Lourenço Marques Englishmen. There were a "busty" brunette who was the epitome of the common Englishwoman who, in the tropic countries, has risen far above her natural level—plenty of servants, and that sort of thing—and her shriveled little husband, who, in spite of his monocle, was just a second-rater, whatever he was.

She guffawed when she heard I had been to the Indian "do." "Oh, my, those wogs! they're no good to anybody!"

(A wog, in case you don't happen to know it, is a *pukka sahib's* term for any Indian; a Wily Oriental Gentleman.)

"Hummm!" said the man, wisely; "I know sumpin' about 'em!"

Whatever it was (and we asked him) he could not reveal; it was just *something*. But what he did not know was that the Indians were by far the most intelligent and wealthy class in Lourenço Marques, a class by themselves, and that he could not possibly be included on either count.

We coaled at "L.M.," as they call Lourenço Marques, from little wicker baskets, holding a few lumps of coal, on natives' heads. "Low-grade labor, directed by low-grade white men," said one of the ship's officers, "and you have to use plenty of the former to make up for the latter."

The tally clerk told me that our cargo was 9,876 bags of cashew nuts. Each bag was handled by the natives fourteen times—all with the aid of song. The nuts go all the way to

India, because only the Indians around Bombay and the Kathia-war States know how to prepare them. Then they go to the cocktail bars of London and New York.

The wind shook in hot rasps through the wooden screens over the forward ports in the dining saloon. When we left Lourenço Marques we were 7,308 miles from London via Cape Town, 8,414 via the Suez Canal. Just about as far from England's comfortable green fields as it seemed we could get; far enough to make spotted trout in clear chalk streams seem a memory of another planet. The captain, to keep his reason, polished some flakes of turtle shell that the ship's agent had given him; another officer etched Japanese designs, with a sailing needle, through the blue enamel of cigarette tins. A fat woman, dressed in greasy black, and with battered sun helmet, revealed that she was bound for Kenya, to look after a concentration camp of some Abyssinian refugees. Poor refugees! The young Irishman who had been prospecting for diamonds on the Gold Coast appeared at dinner with an Eton tie, produced the photograph of his South African girl, after a few drinks, said he *must* find diamonds or gold, somehow, so that they might get married. This Eton tie had a remarkable effect upon an Englishman (in the colonial service) who at once asked him to share a bottle of wine. A sedate man, with his gray hair in a bang, who always dressed for the evening in a dinner jacket and whom I had accepted as a judge, turned out to be merely an up-country bank manager, with just one story to his credit: "My dear sir, *have* you ever shot a lion with a shotgun?" He then added, with great solemnity, "I *have!*" He said this as if it had been his one purpose in life since birth. I was rude to him; no, I positively had not shot a lion with a shotgun, I said, and why the hell should I!

It was the time of a full moon. Sometimes we were fifty miles off the coast of Africa, yet, even then, an occasional gray mountain inland showed up in the west. Sometimes we ran in close, within a mile, to avoid the five-knot Mombasa Current. In this way we lost a German ship, the *Wangoni,* which had trailed us from L.M. The chief said, "The engines did 310 miles today; the ship did 200."

At L.M., the Eton-Irishman and I had a swim in the 200-yard wire inclosure (to keep off sharks) in water that was as hot and filthy as kitchen slops. Behind Mozambique Island, where the ship dropped anchor in a lagoon whose shallows flashed green and sapphire under the burning sun, we swam at night, walking cautiously on the carpet-like reefs of coral, seeing the big fish, like black shadows under the moon, dart away from our nakedness. That Irishman was quite mad; he said, as a horrid black thing rasped itself against our legs, "I suppose this water *is* too shallow for sharks?"

And below decks the Indians sweated, steamed, and stank. "It costs 'em only £5 to get across from Mombasa to Bombay," said the sweating white steward. "With their passports, they can stay in India three years, and then return. I don't think the British would like to get rid of Gandhi, in India—not if they'd seen this lot! Gandhi's a sort of policeman for them."

At Mozambique, the Swami addressed another meeting of Indians. On that lovely island, I walked along a beach of golden sand. Young girls, their faces painted white, were washing themselves for their circumcision ceremonies; bloated Portuguese officials were being hauled past in rickshaws, or sprawled in a state of coma in cafés. Two spick and span little Jap merchants came off to our ship at Mozambique. The Swami frowned.

"After 1905, when the Japanese defeated the Russians, we Indians looked up to them as the saviors of the East," he said. "But not now; now we look upon them as animals. The way the Japanese have treated the Chinese has turned all India against them. We no longer look to them to lead us in our struggle against the West."

"And Gandhi?"

He shook his head. "No; Gandhi is a fine man; we all love

him. I have written his biography. But he has not the modern view."

Jawaharlal Nehru, he said, the Harrow and Cambridge graduate, was the strongest man in India. He would lead.

"Look here, Swami," I said gently, "I've been listening to you telling other Indians that *if* England doesn't make South Africa back down on her 'segregation' program, *you* will try to take India outside the British Commonwealth. Yes?"

"That is quite right," said the Swami, with a smile.

"But you have always *been* trying to do that!" I said, with an answering smile. "That's why they sentenced you to three years in prison during the 1930 *satyagraha* campaign?"

He nodded his pink turban.

"So there is nothing new in what you are doing?"

He looked up, and that beautiful, ascetic face widened into a boyish laugh. "There is always hope," he chuckled.

"And you will," I carried on, "use Mahatma Gandhi as a stalking-horse, as the Indian 'moderates' have always been doing? Use Gandhi to gain independence from Britain, and *then* drop him?"

He didn't like that.

"And who will protect you, you Indian ascetics, against your own business men, those noble Indian mill owners, who work indentured Indian children fifty-seven hours a week in Bombay?"

He did not like that. He shuddered slightly.

The sunset had gone. Huge masses of dark clouds hung over the mainland, and their valleys were lighted up by flashes of lightning. They filled with dark orange. And then became black.

Rain fell. And the ship, with its British officers on watch, plodded slowly up the coast.

COAST-TO-COAST ACROSS AFRICA

15. "Haven of Peace"

IT is no wonder that the early Arabs called Dar es Salaam the "Haven of Peace." Its blue, palm-fringed lagoon is one of the most perfectly protected and welcome harbors in the tropics. The floating dock, which the Germans scuttled in the entrance during the last war, still bars part of the channel. It makes entry difficult, even dangerous. Yet it calls your attention, at the outset, to the German obstructionist effort which was the overtone of this Mandate from the advent of Hitler to the outbreak of this war.

The Arabs still sail here from Muscat and the hot coasts of Arabia. They come before the rain-laden winds of the east monsoon; they spread the butterfly wings of their ships and sail back before the seasonal winds of the west monsoon. Some of their dhows are over two hundred tons. Some are so primitive that their skippers sail by dead reckoning, sail on the stars, and take thirty-five days for the passage. They bring dates, in jammy masses, and they carry back, as they have been doing for centuries, the trunks of trees, even sawn planks, which they will use for building materials in their arid countries. They no longer carry Africa's first and foremost export—the black slave.

The ancient Arabs brought casuarina trees with them, and, as they did to mark other ports in Africa, they planted them around the harbor entrance, so that Dar es Salaam could be picked up from far out at sea.

And from the sea you espy your first building in Tanganyika, among the towering plumes of casuarina, and the monstrous squat baobabs, with their twenty-foot-thick trunks. It is the long, white, crenellated walls, towers, and onion-shaped arch-ways of a pseudo-Moorish palace, the Governor's residence.

As all homes are rent-free in the British colonial service, when its members are overseas, the cool, spacious rooms of this modern Araby are the goal, the lifelong envy, and the possible zenith for the 820 officials on the Tanganyika staff list.

(Which imposing number, incidentally, accounts for over one-half the adult Englishmen in all Tanganyika.)

This edifice, with all the pomp that it implies, marks the great break in Africa—the break between the ruthless "white civilization" policy of the Union of South Africa, based upon the presence of two million whites against over six million na-tives, and the altruistic English attitude, which, however much it might be prostituted by local traders and big business interests in the various colonies, holds that the black should have at least an equal moral right and chance to get on with the white man. Tanganyika, largest British mandate in Africa, has administered this particular trust so literally that it is the chief and chronic complaint of every white man there, particularly the English settler.

My ship had been built for the China trade. And that meant that although she was only 8,000 tons she carried three funnels. That was "joss"; a Chinaman will never take a two-funnel ship when he can get a three-stacker. Yet even we—because of that scuttled German dock, and how it outraged one to look at it!—had to lie offshore, waiting for the slack water, before we could chance that fierce rip sluicing out between the nodding coconut trees.

Then we ran in, zig-zag through the waving palms, straight-ened up past the old German mission, then into a vista of open water flanked by a settlement of buff bungalows and tree-shaded boulevards, past the high white blocks of the secretariat and high court; and the chain went down in a smooth pool two or

three hundred yards off a drive along which were strolling
hundreds of Hindu women in their rose-colored saris, bearded
Sikhs, gold-turbaned Mohammedans of the Aga Khan's sect,
and more and more hundreds of red-fezzed natives, coal black,
wearing long white gowns that looked like nightshirts.

Behind all this whizzed a steady stream of motorcars (English, for a change), which anyone acquainted with the tropics,
and the hour, knew must hold the *sahibs* on their evening rush
to the club, the ritual game of golf or tennis, and then the welcome sundown drink.

Before us lay the perfect picture of the colonial administrative seat.

From somewhere a bugle called, and a detachment of the
King's African Rifles stepped sharply past. They wore putties,
and had bare feet; black tassels snapped arrogantly from each
correctly slanted red fez. The flow of motorcars ceased. The
Hindu women sat down on the benches, or on the sands under
the coconut palms, and stared at us. Some Arabs hauled on a
creaking block to get their dhow under way. A launch hooked
itself onto our gangway, and a handful of cheery, red-faced
Englishmen, in tropic white, clattered up the steps.

Then, as if unable to withhold its impatience with this scene—
this complacent Englishness, and co-operation of Mohammed
with Whitehall—the clock in the buff German church tower
directly opposite us suddenly struck the hour.

"*Nein! Nein! Nein! NEIN!*" it seemed to whine.

I have struck this German note because I landed in Tanganyika not so very long before the outbreak of this war. Also,
many things I wrote about it then I would not write now. It
does not mean that I have since discovered I was wrong, or that
I have changed my sense of values, or my opinions. I have
merely taken more things into account—say, recent German
demonstrations of character.

It is impossible, for instance, for any thinking man to travel in Africa and not be struck by the high class of the average German settlers, the ability and vigor with which they work their lands, their ability to combine for co-operate effort. By contrast, the British settlers seem slothful, and there are too many "colonels" among them, *not* professional farmers.

There seems always a plethora of British officials. And among these seem too many young man who spend most of their waking moments *being* "gentlemen." The administrations themselves seem to be devoid of any economic initiative, and deaf, dumb and blind to the local settlers' demand for a policy to develop these vast territories.

All this is true. I held and still hold these opinions. And practically everything I saw at Dar es Salaam, and weeks of Tanganyika, and afterwards, helped to reinforce them. But the position of Tanganyika in the world then was different from what it is now. At that time, Tanganyika, still coveted by Germany, was being threatened monthly with an additional menace by the formidable number of German settlers, who, because of the very fairness of the British mandate, had for some time outnumbered the British settlers.

There were more German settlers in Tanganyika at the outbreak of this war than there were men from Britain.

On the eve of this war, the day already seemed over when an intelligent and altruistic administration of the mandate *for the native* would carry much weight in deciding who was to hold Tanganyika. There was no superior court—such as an omnipotent League of Nations—or world opinion, to which to appeal. Tanganyika, regardless of the welfare of its native population, would be held, or lost, by the British, either out of fear, sheer might, or a legitimate desire to placate Germany.

Local Tanganyikans (I am speaking of out-and-out English settlers now, when I say "Tanganyikans") feared this very thing. That is why they, and the English in Kenya, had formed the Tanganyika League, creating a potential Ulster.

"I am an Englishman," declared General Boyd Moss, the

head of the Tanganyika League, to me, "but I am a Tanganyikan first. This is *our* country. And we will fight to the last cartridge before we will allow London to give it away."

They would do it.

Facing such a situation, it was apparent that, unless England wanted to lose Tanganyika out of hand, more English "white roots" were needed in the mandate. The Government (even covertly) should encourage, even subsidize, some form of straight English settlement.

That, it seemed, was the very thing it was not doing—was even discouraging. And, in those menacing days, the local British settlers declared this was sheer madness. I wrote then, for the London *Daily Mail:*

If there is one thing that a trip through the African Mandates should teach anyone, it is that . . . your true colonization spirit needs to be revived. You send out only officials now. And it is beginning to be a question—whether you wish to recognize it or not—if you can afford the altruistic ideal of leaving your African possessions to remain vast, empty laboratories for even the best intentioned experiments in native administration.

It may be held that Tanganyika, as a mandate, escapes this indictment, as it is not rightfully a British possession. But the mandate was not considered "eye-wash" by the officials at Dar es Salaam, and they continually insisted that "native interests are paramount"—these truths may be used as an excuse for the total absence of a Tanganyika "white policy." But that argument is not modern—it is not in line with the realities of today's African developments—and it entirely ignores the fact that the administration at Dar es Salaam was doing nothing at all to prevent some 32,000 Indians and Asiatics from inexorably acquiring practically all the immediate business in Tanganyika which came immediately above the native cultivation of crops.

As I see that other, too pro-British, commentators have always lumped this Indian effort with that of the white Britishers

in Tanganyika, calling the sum of them "British," I think a
brief résumé of the astonishing scope of Indian enterprise might
be useful:

Dar es Salaam, the day my ship dropped anchor in its lovely
harbor, had 1,200 Europeans (African term for whites), 5,000
Indians, and some 25,000 natives.

Among the Europeans were some 120 Germans, a handful of
Greeks, and a slight colony of assorted nationalities. The balance
of the Europeans, say some eight hundred or so, were English.
And over 90 per cent of these were Government officials.

In Dar es Salaam, the Indians owned all the hotels, although
they, adroitly, appointed European managers. (The best one
was a Swiss.) The Indians owned all three of the motion picture
houses, and operated two of them. Along Acacia Avenue, the
main business street of the town, in some nine or ten blocks of
beautifully built office and shop buildings, with their big plate-
glass windows, the Indians owned all but four buildings. (And
they had done practically all the building of them—all that had
not been previously done by the Germans.)

In Tanganyika the Indians were 90 per cent landlords in the
big towns, practically 100 per cent landlords in all the small
towns. They conducted from 70 to 80 per cent of all the retail
business. When you came to a small town, or even a native village, you found that its bazaar, no matter how squalid the shops,
was always a homogeneous hive of Indian traders.

And the Indians were doing at least 40 per cent of all the
wholesale business.

In cotton, going by the ginnery figures, the Indians controlled
70 per cent of the output. In sisal, the most important crop and
leading export of Tanganyika, the Indians were exporting 28
per cent; the British 30; and the Germans, with a few Greek
plantations, were exporting the other 42 per cent.

The biggest importer into Tanganyika happened, quite naturally, to be the Government itself, and this accounted for a
dishearteningly large percentage of all the imports of British

goods. But next came the huge private firm of Karimjee Jivanjee Company—Indian—with its head office in Zanzibar, its own vast sisal plantations in Tanganyika, and its own buyers in Japan. It also maintained the International Motor Mart in Dar es Salaam (with a German manager), in whose spacious showroom you saw that they had the agency for two of the leading American motorcars, the Singer sewing machines, leading English small arms and refrigerators, American radios and air-conditioning machines, and a vast line of German machinery and motor equipment.

Now, while these Indians were astute enough to appoint European managers for the hotels where Europeans were going to put up, and while an occasional German was appointed as manager in their showrooms or motorcar interests, the vast mass of all their employees between manager and lowest laborer was ambitious Indians. In the small villages, of course, just about 100 per cent of the commercial jobs were held by Indians. Not much chance for an educated African clerk there.

Then, too, the British banks were employing Indian clerks; so were the British shops. And the Government itself, so it seemed to me, was employing Indians almost to the exclusion of Africans in all jobs which required any mental qualifications whatever in the civic work of posts, telegraphs, and railways.

This picture is not overdrawn; I have had too many encounters with Indian clerks all over Tanganyika not to know what I am talking about.

Then came the German, as another bar to both native and English development. The next biggest trading company in Tanganyika, after Karimjee Jivanjee, was the Usagara Company. (It was claimed that this was the German Government itself.) This bought the bulk of the Tanganyika coffee shipments that went to Germany, financed the German tea planters and marketed their crops, exported about 13 per cent of Tanganyika's total sisal exports from its own plantations, and held the Tanganyika agency for the most popular American motorcar.

The Germans employed Germans for service in all clerical positions, from the highest down to the lowest, then a few Indians or Greeks. And below all this was the great mass of native labor.

I would rather have all this taken as a broad conception rather than a specific picture (as I know some critic will immediately trot out a few native clerks to confront me); and, as the German bar to both native and English development will probably be done away with, I wish particularly to stress this distinction between Indian and English enterprise in Tanganyika—in all East Africa, in fact.

Statistics could never lie better than to class these two as "British." Such classification misleads English judgment at home as to English progress in Tanganyika; it provides, to some extent, an excuse for Whitehall's almost complete lack of any wide economic scheme for the betterment of even the natives themselves in the various colonies.

The strongest criticism that could be made of the British administration of Tanganyika was that it was fulfilling the conditions of the mandate almost too literally. The Germans, under the impeccably maintained "open-door" policy of the mandate (except where terrified by their own Nazis or in the grip of the Usagara Company, whose ramifications I shall show later on), were living a far freer life than they could have had in the fatherland. Many of them, patriotic as they were, admitted this frankly to me. The Indians, with no class, color, or segregational restrictions against them (and with a business acumen far superior to any European) were, so they anxiously assured me, enjoying a far finer life than they could ever hope to enjoy in India.

Some indication of the Indian's mentality in the mandate, the pride he feels in being a member of it, is vividly illustrated in a letter which U. K. Oza, the editor of the Indian paper *Tanganyika Opinion*, wrote to me:

There were 8,911 Indians in German East Africa in 1914. In 1931 there were 23,000. It is believed the next census will show their number to be 25,000.

The main reason why Indians have selected Tanganyika as their main point of settlement in post-war times is the Mandate. India feels a sense of ownership about it. She possesses rights and privileges in the territory independently as a member of the League of Nations herself. Her nationals possess fully equal economic rights because of the terms of the Covenant of the League and the terms of the Mandate. India knows that she is safe in Tanganyika from the open segregational and other disabling measures to which she is subject in the British colonies.

It was because of this knowledge that the Indians from Zanzibar purchased large areas of ex-enemy (German) agricultural property. H.H. the Aga Khan advised his followers to settle in Tanganyika and open up the deepest recesses of the territory. Hindu capital owners subsequently came and invested money in townships. When non-native settlement began to be permitted in 1926, Indians began to purchase large tracts of land wherever they could.

Indians own about 54,000 acres of agricultural land in Kenya, where, because it is a British colony, the settlers of the British race aim at creating a white dominion and ultimately coalescing with the Union of South Africa; the Highlands is exclusively reserved for white settlement. In Tanganyika because of the security of the Mandate they have 286 holdings covering 278,473 acres of agricultural land. (The British have 436 holdings, covering 775,002 acres; the Germans have 553 holdings, covering 485,257 acres.) If they (the Indians) were guaranteed that the Mandate conditions would be preserved, they would have more, but there has been a setback owing to the agitation commenced by Kenya in favor of declaring the Mandated territory a British Colony, of annexing it to the Empire, of forming an East African Federation and of forcing Tanganyika into a closer postal, customs, railway, and administrative union. If there was a declaration that Tanganyika would remain a mandated territory in the hands of Britain or under an international board of nations, which would not make it a pawn in the world game of regional barter, Indians would establish themselves in larger numbers and start industries.

The influence of British colonial traditions on Indian status in Tanganyika in spite of the mandate has been evil and derogatory to Indian economic and social equality. It is assumed in the British Colonies, even in India, that the Indian standard of living is lower than the European. So the example of Kenya has been followed in Tanganyika, and the salaries, wages, and the profits of Indians are calculated on a lower basis than those of Europeans. The higher posts in the administration are not open to Indians. Trial by jury is not permitted to them. There is also veiled residential segregation. Educational and medical services for the Indians are on a much more inadequate scale than for Europeans.

Contiguity of Kenya, an aggressive colony, retards the economic development of Tanganyika. The customs union annually costs Tanganyika about £16,000. The competition of the Kenya and Uganda Railway and harbors has resulted in the attrition of the ports of Tanga and Dar es Salaam, and the practical bankruptcy of the territorial railways.

Kenya is a colony and the Union (of S.A.) is a dominion. In the Union the Indians suffer from all forms of segregational disabilities. In Kenya the Indians have been debarred from settlement in the Highlands. The Indian community is apprehensive of Tanganyika being annexed by Britain with Kenya in order to promote the formation of a white Central and East African dominion, and of such dominion pursuing the same anti-colored-races policy as the Union of South Africa. If a guarantee that such will not be the case be forthcoming, Indians will develop the territory in every way.

I have quoted this letter in full because Mr. Oza is regarded by the Indians of East Africa as one of their most representative men—he is not anti-British—and because it states the Indian state of mind clearly, honestly and fairly.

This letter shows the urge of the Indians to be allowed to expand in Tanganyika. That raises perhaps the most important East African "question" that will have to be answered in the new world which will have to be formed after this war. I have already shown, by the scope of their activities, what the Indians have already done in developing Tanganyika. I say it is to their credit. And, it seems to me, it is a sad indictment of the white European settler—and of the economic lethargy of Whitehall—that the white man in Africa should feel called upon to complain against this Indian enterprise. The small Indian shop, in the native village, may, perhaps, be considered on too low a scale of life for the European. And it is in such strata that I say the Indian in Africa is probably a dangerous bar across the road of black development; a black man might have run that shop.

But there is no sense whatever in the chronic argument I listened to on the East Coast that a vast and dignified enterprise, such as Karimjee Jivanjee Company, biggest private importer into Tanganyika, has competed unfairly. The company (I am merely taking this firm as an example) has merely shown more business acumen. Also, Mr. Karim, with whom I had many interesting talks, does not live on a scale lower than that of the white man; his conversation, to put it mildly, was slightly superior to that of the average white man I met on the East Coast; his taste demanded a cultivated existence.

Dar es Salaam is demonstration enough that the Indians—given half a fair chance—would commercially develop Tanganyika territory for the British Commonwealth.

But the chief topic of conversation in Dar es Salaam, and throughout the rest of Tanganyika, was neither the Indian nor the German "problem"; it was the chronic contest between the "settlers" and the "official" point of view.

The day after I arrived at Dar es Salaam, eight British settlers gave me a luncheon. They were planters, lawyers, traders, not Government officials. Their intention was, they said frankly, to give me "their" side, before I had my reasoning powers swamped by the official view. And—this also was obvious—they dreaded the effect that official hospitality would have upon me. They knew this, because, in after talks, they told me of the disastrous effects that official notice had had upon themselves. They knew what snobs could do.

"Take the case of So-and-So," they said. "He used to be one of the best men we had; no one could put a case better than So-and-So to the Government. But So-and-So became so much a thorn in their side that the Government took him in; they made him a member of the Legislative Council—and since then So-and-So has shut up."

Usually, they said, it took only invitations to a few meals at Government House to silence the most obstreperous settler. After that he usually went about saying, "But you don't understand H.E.'s (His Excellency's) position!"

The mere fact that there should be this "settlers'" side and an "official" side as to how to run the mandate showed an unstable state of affairs in Tanganyika.

The British have a genius for giving the appearance of self-government, without granting its substance. Tanganyika, like many British colonial possessions, was not run by any elected assembly; it was ruled by the Governor, through the medium of a body called the Legislative Council. A semblance of self-rule is given to a possession by allowing a certain number of seats on this "Leg. Co.," as they call it, to be filled from civilian life. But there are enough official seats, filled by appointment of the Governor, to give the Government always an official majority.

The laws of Tanganyika, for instance, are made by a Governor, with the advice (when he wants to take it) of the Legislative Council. Inaugurated in 1926, it is composed of thirteen official members, appointed because of their political posts in the Administration, and ten *appointed* non-official members. And of the latter three are always Indians. A clergyman is one of the ten nominated members—appointed to represent the 5,000,000 natives of Tanganyika!

The Tanganyika situation seemed to show up the dangers of this form of rule to an alarming extent. Foremost among them was the complacent absence of any economic imagination, either at Dar es Salaam or in the various provinces, and, particularly, from the Colonial Office in Whitehall. The British had had this country for twenty years, yet they had not built as many miles of all-weather roads as the Italians had in Abyssinia in two years. In twenty years they have not even built a road between Dar es Salaam and Tanga, only 120 miles away, and the other important railway port in Tanganyika. When, in the crisis of September, 1938, a detachment of the King's African Rifles had to be rushed up to Tanga, it was found that they had to go by ship!

In all the twenty years, Whitehall had never once produced a Government scheme for the establishment of British settlers. "On the contrary," said a man at the luncheon, "the worst enemy that an English settler could have in this country was a Government official!"

What I am about to voice now is not my own opinions; it is the consensus of the talk at that table and the résumé of talks I had with other settlers, as well as with English officials throughout Tanganyika:

It is this—England does not send out settlers these days; she sends officials. And these officials, although they are almost notoriously honest, are obsolete. These good people still regard an honest, impartial administration over the natives as their foremost, and practically sole, objective. They are not noticeably active in promoting any native economic program. And they do not seem to be even aware of any necessity for a white man's development of the country.

It was not until twenty years after the British had received the Tanganyika mandate that a new Governor (Sir Mark Young) hit on the idea of circulating the settlers with a questionnaire, asking their suggestions for a development scheme.

"But what is the use?" said an up-country settler to me, when he had received it. "It will only be another report. Besides, with the colony simply seething with petitions and complaints, this is a thing which Dar es Salaam should be able to answer itself. But they have no imagination there. Too many 'gentlemen'!"

"Too many 'gentlemen'!"

This, I am well aware, is a topic that must be handled with tact. Yet I am not the first person who loves England to call attention to the danger she runs from class obsessions in filling her Government posts. And while England at home, under the pressure of war—and the example of the totalitarian states—has taken to giving appointments and promotion upon merit, and the actual *need* for brains, the colonies still remain in the dark age of Kipling's day.

I should almost say that the average British colonial official considers it his foremost *duty* to be a "gentleman." At any rate, the whole social structure of any British administration seems to be built upon that assumption. And, with the young and minor officials, this has the result of leaving their minds free for little other work. The minute a Cambridge or Oxford graduate receives his appointment to the Colonial Office, he acts as if he had received the accolade. He is now hallmarked as a "gentleman" in the social scale. And if his post is in Whitehall he will carry a furled umbrella to his work, and wear a black "Foreign Office" hat.

The complacency engendered by this certainty of a career, and a pension, in the Home, Colonial, or any other branch of the great British civil service, frees him from the fear of competition, but it also deprives him of its invigorating effects. In fact, his chief concern seems to be *not* to do anything unusual which might harm a career that otherwise is just as certain as the march of time.

I state this seriously. I think this sahib-complex is one of the most dangerous characteristics of British colonial administration —and, sometimes, at home. It carries with it, this *being* a gentleman, the odious inhibition that, somehow, business men are unclean. And the one thing that Britain must have in Africa is a business attitude, on the part of officials, towards developing her vast territories. That is an obligation. And it must begin at Whitehall.

As I write this, a "new policy for the colonies" has been announced. They are no longer to be considered in the light that they must be self-supporting; Whitehall will now provide funds for development. This has been acclaimed by the majority of the London press as a great advance.

Actually, it does not seem a marked advance in anything except a change of attitude. The "new policy" calls for £5,000,000 a year for ten years, for a colonial development fund. Nearly two million of this will go to the West Indies—possibly to salve recent labor troubles. And Nigeria, I believe, is to get some £75,000. Nigeria has possibly the greatest density of black man power in all Africa—over twenty million natives.

16. Germans in Mufindi

AT Dar es Salaam I bought a Ford V-8, and decided to drive across Africa. I would end up at Duala, in the French Cameroons, on the Gulf of Guinea. Perhaps. The route we selected would take us from the rain forests of southern Tanganyika, up past Kilimanjaro to Nairobi, across Kenya and Uganda, to Lake Victoria. Then we would cross over the high passes in the mountains to Lake Kivu and Lake Edward, up into the Belgian mandate of Ruanda-Urundi; then north past Ruwenzori into the pygmies' forest of Ituri, across the Belgian Congo to Stanleyville on the Congo. Here we would go down the upper Congo itself for some days, then put the car ashore and cut back through the jungle, taking the new road to Aketi, to Bangassou, in French Equatorial Africa.

If luck held, we would drive westward across French Equatorial Africa to Ubangui-Shari, then across Moyen Congo, and the French Cameroons, to the Atlantic Ocean again, at Duala.

The luck held. We reached Duala some four months later. I flew to Accra, where this book ends with an earthquake on the Gold Coast. Eve took a German boat, the *Wadai*, home from the Cameroons, reached Southampton on the eve of this war, and thus narrowly missed being rushed across, a temporary prisoner of the Germans, to Pernambuco, in Brazil.

We did this trip without any servant. There was no room in our car for an indispensable "boy." We lost caste with the natives because of it; they could not understand a white master traveling in such fashion. For most of these last 120 nights we lived on iron rations, cooking our meals on a spirit lamp that cost four shillings, living in native huts, Government rest houses, or wherever we could find a place to swing our mosquito nets and set up our camp beds. It was not too difficult, but it required work, good teamwork. When I came down with malaria on the Gold Coast, and stared dimly at the chaos of my belongings about me, I missed that able partner. Eve, on that trip, had been far better than any man.

I want to say this now because I think, to a great extent, she *made* the trip. It was her love of beauty and adventure (she would insist upon saying that the buffalo looked like barnyard animals) that gave it its tang.

In her eagerness to "get places," she nearly killed me.

Eve had sailed for Africa before I left Durban. One morning her French ship wove in through the palm trees of Dar es Salaam. She was wearing a double felt terai on her head.

I know of no spot in Africa more pleasant than Dar es Salaam to wait for a rendezvous, were it not for the heat. I had been living with a high official. And as bungalows, in the British colonial service, increase in size and pleasantness of location as you go up, we had one of the best. Two stone balconies ran around it. We slept on the upper, in mosquito inclosures. A lemur, in the coconut tree beside my head, often awoke me with the grunts and squeals of his continual lovemaking. Some time around six we got into our dressing gowns and drove down to the beach for a swim. The water was too warm, but we could look back on the green palms of Dar es Salaam, awakening in the morning sun, watch the mists sweep away, and come back to a shower, to wash off the salt, before we sat down to tea and toast. Neither my host nor I ate much for breakfast.

Then he went to the secretariat and I set to work.

Luncheon at the club, or with one of the men in the secretariat, served by barefoot Indian waiters. Then I would vanish into the Indian quarter, talk with some of the German refugees

—Dr. Ehrlich, brother of the famous inventor of "606," had sought refuge in Tanganyika—or spend long hours with the natives.

At five we got into white shorts and undershirts, and, with towels wrapped around our necks, went to the club and played tennis. Then there were sundown drinks.

Another shower. In white dinner jackets, we sat on the veranda of the club, and the red-fezzed Nyasas of the police or military band played the airs. Then somewhere to dinner; bridge, if you wanted it; and then, late at night, an occasional reminiscence.

It was all very easy, and English. And, as I look back on it now, very worthy. For the British empire was not the result of an accident. There may have been, in the eyes of some critics, too many "gentlemen" at Dar es Salaam. But there were some splendid men among them. And the tone of the service was friendship, even love, for the natives under them. Do not minimize that.

"I've often wanted to get out of this blasted country," said a retiring provincial commissioner. "I've thought I was doing it, several times. But after I'd been back in England for a short time I knew I was homesick. When I got out on the dock at Dar es Salaam, I wanted to shake hands with the first black man I met."

One of the "P.C.'s" there had once been a tugboat captain on the Congo. Then he had become a missionary. He went into Tanganyika, with the Belgian army, during the last war. Then he joined the British Colonial Service. It was one of the lessons of Dar es Salaam, to me, to walk with him slowly through the native quarter, watch him put a kindly hand on the shoulder of some old woman, talk to her for a few seconds in her own tongue, and then see her face light up at some humorous remark of his. He always left them shaking their heads, and rocking with laughter.

When he was not in the secretariat, you knew he was down there—alone.

"Too, too many reports," he said to me, sadly, as I passed him one day with an armful of papers, going into his office. "I can't get away from this desk!"

It was a very rare exception indeed when you met a provincial commissioner, or district officer, who was not lugubriously anxious to be out on safari in his district, with *his* natives.

"What," said one to me, at Arusha, "you're going out on the plain to write about the Masai—*my* Masai! How dare you! You won't understand them! You won't do them justice!"

He half meant it.

At Dar es Salaam one day, when I was playing tennis with Englishmen—who always beat me—someone (probably myself) hit me on the shinbone. It was on an old scar. It opened. Two evenings later I caught two flies perching on it. I brushed them off.

Now, this was the time of the "tropical ulcers," when perfectly good people break open in spots, and cannot heal. I was far from fit.

By the time I got to Nairobi, I was dressing my leg twice a day. By the time I reached Stanleyville, on the Congo, the bone was exposed. Yet I reached Accra, on the Gold Coast, without coming down with any infection.

It was three days after I had left the coast of Africa, in a little Italian tramp steamer, with no regular doctor aboard, that I came down with a violent streptococcal infection. They had a man on board, taking him to Teneriffe to die, who had one leg off and the other so black with gangrene that, if you touched it, your finger would sink in.

His misfortune was transferred to me.

I mention this now, because, all over the rest of Africa—in the dispensary of the White Fathers at Kabgai, in Ruanda-

Urundi; in a Russian I found in the employ of the Vici-Congo Transport Compagnie, at Aketi; in French Equatorial Africa, the Cameroons, and in that splendid hospital at Accra on the Gold Coast—I was forever seeking a doctor.

And in that way—not that I wanted it—I got a pretty comprehensive survey of the various medical services throughout equatorial Africa. It gave me an intimate insight into the lives of missionaries, nuns, and natives.

Buying a kit—for Eve of course—was an emotional glut. The Indians of Dar es Salaam had made for me several suits of cream drill that cost only thirty shillings each. They made two pairs of shoes, one suède, one Norwegian brogues, for the same price. For a pound I got a serviceable pair of fawn corduroys. I already had shorts and polo shirts galore. I had two drill safari shirts, in whose patch pockets I could carry almost a camp kit (although they did look like maternity jackets). Eve came with a light, serviceable gaberdine jacket and skirt, made in London, and had the Indians make khaki trousers. I bought shovels, an ax, forty yards of heavy rope, two extra jacks for the car, for this was the beginning of the rainy season. And the betting was that we would not get out of Tanganyika at all.

South African water bags I already had. We bought an aluminum cooking pot and two frying pans, coffee and tea pots, pounds of groceries, and, picking up things as we became aware of our need for them, we soon had a cooking outfit that fitted, one thing inside another, so well that our camp technique became almost automatic at nights. I'd like to have five dollars now for every tin of Vienna sausage that we ate. And while it may sound absurd to say that you can become fond of a frying pan, I hated, when I left the Gold Coast, to give that old iron frying pan away.

It did hold the heat so well!

+

As the rains came down before we could get started, we very nearly never left Dar es Salaam. There is no all-weather road up to Dodoma, a hundred miles back from the coast of Tanganyika. District officers telephoned us that the rivers were in flood; several motor lorries were marooned in the black cotton soil. We shipped the car to Dodoma.

We were going down to Lord Chesham's place, in the southern highlands. From there I was driving across to see the *Führer* of the Germans in Tanganyika, Baron Oenhausen, in the colony of German tea planters on the slopes of the rain forest at Mufindi. In the depths of that dank, green, equatorial forest the Germans had hacked out twenty-four tea shambas (plantations). Lord Chesham had one hundred thousand acres of rolling grasslands and sweeps of blue hills, wide open and still uninhabited, for the sporting British. The Germans were pushing their way in darkness among the trunks of great trees, brushing aside a mass of green, and dangling lianas, with monkeys scampering through the life of the jungle, another life that was being lived a hundred feet above human heads. It was a strange contrast of settings.

With the same thrill that we had felt on many other trips, we knew, as I guided the car off the freight truck at Dodoma, that the breadth of Africa lay before us. From now on we were our own masters. So we thought.

An Indian colonel who was running Lord Chesham's estate said his car would precede us. "These red roads are slippery as butter. If you find yourself going off at the side, the best thing is to stop. Sooner or later, there'll always be some natives coming along. And in the rivers, in one or two places, it might be better for one of you to walk ahead, to see how deep it is. That is, if I get stuck. If I get stuck—don't wait for me!"

We didn't. We went past that gallant colonel, sitting smack in the middle of the red Ruaha River, with the water coming over his floor mats. We stood on the other bank and watched half a native village trying to haul him out of it. The view was exhilarating, with the red river, swinging down through the low, green brush of camel thorn, with a misty blue silhouette of mountains on the western horizon.

Some golden crane were fishing in the rushes above us. They got up, crying, "Down there! Down there!"

It is easy to understand the appeal of this country to retired army officers. It provides just that daily physical contest that they have come to expect from life. Most of them like to do things with their hands, and there is always plenty of that work to do around a farm. The conventional idea of the "colonel" who has come out here to "kill things," is nearly always wrong—in fact, most of the Englishmen who settle in Africa go just the other way. They stop shooting. They give game sanctuary on their farms. Eric, over in South-West Africa, wouldn't let a rifle be fired on his thirty thousand acres. When I had shot my first springbok I announced that it would also be my last; after that I was content to watch them leaping on the plain. And later, along the Mara River in Kenya, I spent days among bounding impala and shaggy waterbuck without firing a shot. It's true, my license only called for one lion, one buffalo, one leopard, and four zebra, if I wanted them, for bait. But I had deliberately not taken a buck license. I got my lion without bait. But that was luck.

The sight of an occasional buck now made up, a little, for the brutal drive. It is a mistake to think that there is an unbroken line of highlands down the east coast of Africa; for about 500 or 600 miles, in Tanganyika, it is low country, unsuitable for a white man, and infuriating to drive across, particularly in the rainy season.

I won't stress the point, but several times in the next weeks it was a very real question whether we would be able to get the car out of the country, with the red, slick soil and the roads turned to butter. That was bad, but get-outable. With the black cotton soil, however, it very often became an impossibility to move. With a white man and three husky natives, loading and unloading, pushing a one-ton motor lorry, I once made just twelve and a half miles in four days. The last half mile took us an entire day. (That, as it happened, was on a side trip, a shooting expedition.) They said to me in Nairobi:

"If you're going down into *that* country, you'd better take some seeds with you and plant 'em, because you won't be back here before autumn."

The procedure of getting bogged in black cotton soil, I shall describe just once, and then forget it—at least, as far as you are concerned. It's this: You suddenly notice that, instead of going ahead, your car is sinking. If you're foolish, you step on the accelerator, hoping to jerk out. Then you realize that your rear end is resting on mud and your driving wheels are spinning in a mess of porridge. You then take an ax, go off into the bush, and cut down thorn trees to make a road. As there is no bottom to this black cotton soil, your road sinks. You can spend a day doing that, a week, a month. And as two-thirds of Tanganyika is tsetse-fly country, you won't find any oxen to pull you out.

But this was all part of the physical exhilaration of the country. Thirty "boys" dug out the car of the colonel, and we went on through the acacia forest. We passed an occasional baobab, a tree whose gray, granite-looking trunk may be anywhere from ten to twenty feet thick. Then there are forests of trees like rhododendrons, and euphorbia, like gigantic green candelabra. The tops of the thorn trees are flat, and give a curious flakelike structure to the scene.

When we reached the escarpment, climbing sharply into the highlands, the steaming hot country lay before us, as flat as a sultry green sea. That night we slept with two blankets on our beds.

Iringa illustrated how the Nazi Government was making life in Africa a hell for the German settlers. There were two hotels here, one English, and the other, the White Horse Inn, was full of Germans. In the first was an English army captain, who represented the Kenya Farmers' Association. He had come there to buy, from the Germans, the pyrethrum that they were afraid to sell to their own Government. And they were also afraid *not* to sell it. They were even afraid to grow it.

The situation was complicated. The biggest importer into Tanganyika, after the Government and one Indian concern, was the Usagara Company. And the Usagara was only a thinly veiled agent of the German Government. The Usagara bought the coffee and sisal grown by the German planters in Tanganyika, and paid for it in aski marks. A German seller to them was given a certain amount of credit at their stores, and only enough cash in Tanganyika currency to cover the bare running expenses of his farm. The rest of the proceeds from his sale remained in Germany.

The tea planters in the rain forest of Mufindi had all failed in an attempt to grow coffee several years before. The Usagara and its subsidiary, the Uhehe Company, gave them credits against their farms. To secure these credits, they had to surrender to the Usagara the title deeds to their farms.

Theoretically, the proceeds of their sales of tea, those aski marks which remained in Germany, were supposed to pay off the indebtedness of their farms. Once this was done, they could get their title deeds back—theoretically. None had ever got them. The statistics of their position were held only in Berlin. None of these settlers, writing to Berlin, could ever get a statement as to where he stood. This was so bad that they had sent a planter of their colony to Berlin. He was to see for himself, and make some new arrangement, in Berlin, with the Usagara. I met this man in Dar es Salaam, the day he got back to Tanganyika. He had brought back such a slave-driving arrangement that even the patriotic German tea planters at Mufindi, all hot Nazis, declined it.

But, while they were lashed to the Nazi chariot for all their tea efforts, they had made no arrangement about pyrethrum. This is a flower, looking like an ordinary field daisy, which, when grown at over seven or eight thousand feet, produces a toxic powder that is the best bedbug powder in the world. There was a boom in bedbug powder at that moment. So Kenya, which sells pyrethrum so scientifically that it is even pushing Japan out of the market, sent down this ex-officer to encourage the Germans to grow it.

The Kenya offer was to pay cash. "Real English pounds!" a German himself said enviously to me. But the Usagara Company (German Government) wasn't having any of that. The situation was, when I came on the scene, that the Kenya Farmers' Association should pay half in cash, direct to the German farmer, and the balance could be turned over to the Usagara. Something like that.

And the German colony at Iringa was sizzling with the affair. Was it, or was it not, unpatriotic to grow pyrethrum? Could they get away with it? What form of retribution might they expect from Berlin? Yet they were all Nazis.

"Nevertheless," this same German said to me, "we have to live, you know."

The Germans, for all their undoubted courage and hardihood, are a susceptible, nervous people. You could see that this situation was a strain on them. They were taut. They are born get-together people; in Iringa they outnumbered the British by about thirty to one and the White Horse Inn was always full of a tense knot of them.

It was into this situation that Eve, exploring the town in a wet slicker the next rainy afternoon, walked, in all innocence. Eve, who was "finished" at Freiburg, speaks pretty good German. The Germans found this out. Eve is not exactly pro-Nazi. The Germans found this out. Then it started.

"I hope," said Eve to me afterwards, "that I haven't done any harm? That I haven't made it impossible for you to talk to them? But they got started on Palestine."

"Yes?" I said.

"Well, matters got to a point where I heard myself saying, 'But, on the other hand, we don't chop people's heads off with an ax.' "

"Yes?"

"Well—they got rather excited about that."

I told her that I had a date that night to play billiards at the White Horse Inn with the English ex-captain, the pyrethrum buyer. "Come along, and we'll see what it is like."

She did. When the three of us came in the door, the Germans jumped out of their chairs. One of them clasped Eve by both hands. "*Ach*, here you are again!" he said.

He went over and laughed, to the English captain, "You know, she said some *terrible* things to us!"

"Serves you right," he said.

It was a friendly, slightly-with-the-guard-up conversation between two sets of people, who, if left alone, would have been excellent friends.

Typical of Indian enterprise, the White Horse Inn was owned by an Indian, and run by a German manager and manageress.

Lord Chesham's place illustrated an interesting phase of British civilization. During the '20's and the '30's of the post-war period, when the Bright Young Things of London were having their fling, it was the custom to deprecate the so-called "hearties," those middle-aged ex-officers who occasionally voiced their desperation that they wanted a life with more action than they could find in the vapid London scene. They were almost "men without a country," for the one they had returned to was not at all the one they had been fighting for—

Lloyd George's "land fit for heroes to live in!" The Bloomsbury "intellectuals" were then holding the chairs of wisdom.

It was considered comic—the spectacle of a man who, in his
cups or not, admitted that he had an urge for "the wide open
spaces." And British colonization, as such, had to suffer from
this superficial sophistication. With four perfectly good mandates to choose from—South-West Africa, Tanganyika, Togoland, and the Cameroons—there were surprisingly few British
(even with the bad times at home) who were anxious to go
out to them. One might have said that the Elizabethan spirit
had died. The English were not "colonizers" any more; they
were content to send out officials.

At the same time England was being penalized by the financiers of the City who were always anxious to get back their
investments in places, say, such as the Argentine, in imports of
chilled beef. So even the agriculture of the English countryside
was being let go by default. The average English workingman
was eating practically nothing that was grown in England; what
meat he had was Argentine beef, Danish bacon, Australian mutton; other items of his diet were Danish eggs, New Zealand
butter and apples, Canadian wheat. The "fat" of England, the
£4,000,000,000 invested capital abroad, was being protected at
the expense of England's own national life—particularly agriculture. It compensated for England's chronic adverse balance
of real trade, but it vitiated the country's stamina. And the proceeds went into the hands of an unjustifiably small number of
people—who could not spend them. British capital is seldom
patriotic!

At the same time, these Bloomsbury "intellectuals," with
their sentimental liberal press, were—so it seemed—interested
in the wrongs of every minority outside of England. Even up
to the September crisis of 1938 a certain paper was raising
£38,000 for Czecho-Slovakia, while there was hardly a word in
its columns about the unemployed miners in Wales and Dur-
ham, and the dead textile mills of the Midlands—there were

nearly two million Englishmen who would never have a chance to do an honest day's work again. "Doped" with the dole.

These unfortunates were finally called, to ease the national conscience, the "special areas," instead of the "distressed areas," and even Parliament, if you can go by the official reports, forgot them. Their case let go by default. Two million Englishmen.

And in these extraordinary circumstances a powerful section of the British press was advocating the surrender of the mandates, because they did not pay. They could have paid, if British financiers had wanted them to. But they were getting better, and quicker, returns on their money elsewhere. It is a matter of record that a rope mill, which was started in Tanganyika to use the vital sisal export, was deliberately closed, because it competed with a rope mill in England!

Therefore, when you arrive at a place like Lord Chesham's, with a hundred thousand acres waiting for British occupants, the question does present itself, Why are there so few Englishmen there?

It must be said that a great deal of the heart had been taken out of English settlement in Tanganyika and Kenya because of the terrific drop in the sisal and coffee prices on which most of the farming was based. I have already shown how practically all the Germans had failed in coffee, lost the title deeds to their farms to the Usagara Company, and were now unable to know where they stood when growing tea. Moreover, those Germans who were still growing coffee in Tanganyika were getting a substantial bonus on their sales to the fatherland, over what the English coffee growers were able to obtain in the open market; and the English coffee growers in Tanganyika were claiming that, at the present prices, they could barely make running expenses for their shambas. Also, in that spring of 1939, the price of sisal on the open market was just exactly what it was costing to grow it. The Germans, even though they were in the hands of the Usagara, were nevertheless being subsidized by the grant they were getting to cover their living and running costs on their farms.

Confronting this situation, the English settler, dependent entirely upon his own efforts, with no Government support, was facing a risky future. One of the most desperate settlers I met in Tanganyika, however, was a German; he had a sisal shamba outside Dar es Salaam. He declared that even with the bonus he was getting from the German buyers the usual allowance he was given left him barely enough money to buy food for himself and his wife. I visited his shamba, which, with its low bungalow among flowers and coconut trees, looked like the Garden of Eden.

"But that only makes it harder to bear," he said grimly, "when we know we have barely enough to eat!"

Settlement, even for the Germans, was not a fat life.

The uncertainty regarding the future of the Tanganyika mandate was unquestionably the greatest bar to English settlement. The German settlers were "sitting pretty" in either case. Under the mandate, as it was being administered so fairly, they were receiving more impartial treatment, and were certainly enjoying a more individual freedom (in spite of local Nazi *Führers*) than they could have found in their own country. If the mandate remained in English hands, they could not have wished for a freer life. If it went back to Germany, then they were Germans again. Which was what they declared they wanted to be above everything else. But recent history had given anyone who was not a German sufficient reason to fear what would happen to himself, his holdings, even his own personal existence, if this territory ever went back to a Nazi Germany.

All in all—up to the very eve of this war—there were more obvious reasons against individual English settlement in Tanganyika than there were for it. But the qualifications of that very statement imply the thing that many Tanganyika English settlers were clamoring for; and that was some Government land-settlement scheme. One of the chief reasons supporting their demand was the desire to plant more English *roots* in the country. There was no doubt, even then, that the large German settlement in Tanganyika was being encouraged and subsidized, from Berlin; a German tea-planter was much more than a tea-planter, he was a political implement.

"But one of the very troubles with a land-settlement scheme in Tanganyika," a far-sighted British settler told me, "is that if we did open a scheme for one thousand farms, we would have 999 German applicants!"

There probably would not be enough English settlers, he continued, "because settlement overseas is not popular in England any more. And that's the bare truth of it!"

The biggest plantation in Tanganyika was, when I was there, Major von Brandies' sisal plantation of 45,000 acres, twenty miles inland from Tanga. Von Brandies, who was chief of staff of the German forces in Tanganyika in 1914-18, and his nineteen German managers were all hot Nazis.

The Germans were understood, at that time, to have thirty full-time Nazi leaders in Tanganyika, all working in constant communication with the German Consul General at Nairobi. They conveyed their communication by motor car, fearing that the British secret service might tamper with their letters!

This weird combination of almost absent imagination with which the British Colonial Office was managing the affairs of the Tanganyika Mandate, and a fairness towards all nationals which could not be matched anywhere in Europe, was the atmosphere in which an inquisitive visitor to that country lived daily.

On Lord Chesham's place you saw an immense horizon that seemed literally "going by default." The natives had been bought off these hundred thousand acres; they had been given a handsome compensation, so there was no troubled conscience about an injustice to them. This was no tsetse-fly country; quite a number of good, blooded stock polo ponies were eating their heads off in the model stables. Neither could it be said that the land was "poisonous" (the tragedy that nearly ruined Lord Delamere in Kenya), because less than twenty minutes' drive from the red-brick clubhouse which Lord Chesham had built as a focus for this estate was a red-headed Australian ex-army captain who had a flourishing and profitable farm.

In appearance the country itself seemed as much a counterpart of the Wiltshire plains as you could find anywhere outside of England. It was a constant astonishment, after the muggy mornings at Dar es Salaam, to wake up in an air as crisp as a Scotch autumn. The long vistas of waving plain, with the short grass glinting in the sun, were edged by silhouettes of cool, blue hills.

And here, you were shown, it was quite possible to live on £400 a year. More than that, you could live a life such as the English squire had enjoyed over a hundred years ago. With an initial outlay of from £2,000 to £3,000, a settler could have enough land, together with the other facilities which Lord Chesham's scheme provided, to have, at the normal price of agricultural produce, a self-supporting farm. Perhaps the foremost problem of colonial farming is not so much to grow things as it is to sell them. If enough settlers accepted Lord Chesham's scheme, then they could live, to a large extent, on one another's fat. A bacon factory had already been started to export bacon and hams. And eating these native products, in the pleasant clubhouse of the Southern Highlands estate, you wondered more and more why so many of the hundred thousand acres were still lying idle.

But there it was—a well conceived, already established, colonial settlement scheme, with shockingly few takers.

+

It is perhaps interesting to point out that, up to the outbreak of this war, there was no income tax in Tanganyika. About a third of the total revenue of the mandate comes from the native poll tax; this, in 1937, amounted to £672,050. The natives pay a poll tax that ranges from four to fifteen shillings, with an equal amount for each extra wife. This is graded according to district and the natives' earning capacity; in some parts of the central province the poll tax of eight shillings a year has taken about half the native's earnings for that year. On the average, the native pays about 10 per cent of his yearly earnings to the Government.

European poll tax in 1937 totaled only £44,000. This was adjudged as follows: Rates for each non-native adult male were, on earnings of

£300 to £400:	£4 per annum
£400 to £500:	£5 " "
£500 to £600:	£7 " "
£600 to £700:	£9 " "
£700 to £800:	£11 " "

In other words, while the native was forced to pay in income tax at least 10 per cent of his earnings, the white man wasn't paying much over one per cent. Some idea of the scale of white man's life in Tanganyika may be gauged from the fact that of the 16,291 non-native persons who paid the above taxes in 1936, 13,551 were returned as having incomes of less than £200, while another 2,247 had incomes between £200 and £600.

I knew a settler with 1,200 acres, mostly paying good profits, who was paying only £2 a year; his white assistant, getting £7 10s. a month, was paying more than he was.

Twenty miles to the east lay the rain forest of Mufindi. Instead of the rolling plains and the distant blue hills of Lord Chesham's country, this was verdant jungle. Here twenty-six tea shambas had been hacked out. Twenty-four of them were owned by Germans; the other two, owned by an Englishman, were being run by a German.

The head of this colony, Baron Oenhausen, was the *Führer* of all the Germans in southern Tanganyika. His wife, a passionate Nazi, was the leader of the German Women's Colonial Guild for all Tanganyika. She, by means of a card-index system which she showed us, was in constant touch with every German woman in the mandate.

The guild (financed by the winter help movement in Germany) sent out a circulating library of the best, selected books to the Germans in Tanganyika. They also sent a surprising number of expensive magazines. They sent, to every German child in the colonies, a toy for Christmas—a very expensive present; one which I saw later in the German settlement of Oldeani was a doll that in England would have cost at least two pounds. If a German himself could not afford it, the guild would bring his child or children back to the fatherland, pay for the passage, and keep them, free of cost, for the duration of their educational lives. And if a mother's health required it she would also be brought back to Germany, free.

The baroness, a typical well-born German woman, was working in her rose garden when our car, after traversing two primitive wood bridges in the valley, climbed up to their house on its hillside. She looked up, brushing back a wave of blond hair with gloved hands. The baron, a lean aristocrat, in shorts and a monocle, returned from where he was at work in his tea garden. Their house, a large, rambling structure, which they had built themselves, had a terrace from which you could look out upon rows and rows of the growing green tea, against its untamed background of dark, clinging jungle. And the house was full of photographs of Hitler, all signed. One was a photograph of Hitler in a *gemütlich* attitude, with Baron Oenhausen himself.

"We are very good friends," said the baron, decidedly.

They were both frankly contemptuous of the English settlers to the west of them.

"The Englishman does not like to do any physical labor himself!" said the baron. "The Englishman likes to live in absolutely open country. He has a car; he has a road; he has his 'sport'!"

He appeared annoyed: "The German likes to *create!* I like it; I like to open up new country; I built this house; I built this road. I think to spend plenty of money, buying a big place —that is nothing. We stay here for working, not for politics. We love this country; we fought for years to hold it; we want it back!"

The baron had been in Africa for thirty years. He had fought for four years under General von Lettow-Vorbeck. Before the war he had owned a thousand acres near Arusha, in northern Tanganyika, on the slopes of Mount Meru. He said it was worth at least £20,000. He had lost his land, as had all the Germans, when their lands were confiscated after the World War. He got 13,000 marks compensation eventually. The first post-war German Governments, he told me, were not sympathetic to Germans resuming oversea colonization. Also, the Germans were not allowed to return to Tanganyika until 1925.

"And by that time," he said angrily, "the Indians and the Greeks had bought nearly all our old holdings. They had been put up for auction, and sold for a song. I still cannot understand how the English allowed these fine properties to fall into alien hands. They missed a tremendous settlement opportunity."

In this, he knew he was putting his finger on one of the sorest spots in Tanganyika. There were plenty of hardy, adventurous Englishmen in Tanganyika in 1923-24, when the bulk of these German lands were being auctioned, but very few had the money to buy them. And then—of all times!—there was no British settlement scheme. The Indians and the Greeks, on the other hand, had both the capital and the foresight. They bought heavily. The Indians bought on so wide a scale that it was asserted they were acting as agents for German buyers.

In 1927, Baron Oenhausen and a band of German settlers went to the rain forest of Mufindi.

"At that time," said the baron, "there was absolutely nothing here, just jungle. The nearest road was sixty miles away, the nearest town was 120 miles. *We hacked this out!*"

His words were challenging and harsh. "*We* built these roads; *we* made these tea gardens! *We* made a life here. And then came the lords—the English lords!"

He rattled off, almost like a Noel Coward refrain, the names of Lord Delamere, Lord Francis Scott, Lord Egerton, Lord Chesham.

"They came," he said, "and they broke their springs. They said, 'Oh, let's build some good roads!' And in 1935, when the Government advanced some money, it was we Germans who built the seventy-mile loop off the Cape-to-Cairo road."

He admitted that the Germans at Mufindi had failed in their attempt to grow coffee, and, to secure loans, had surrendered their title deeds to the Kibwele Tea Company (another arm of the Usagara Company, the Uhehe Company, all thinly veiled instruments of the German Government). The baron, it must be quickly pointed out, did not mention, nor would he have admitted for an instant that the Kibwele Tea Company, at Mufindi, had any connection with the Nazi Government. Instead, continuing his statement of German enterprise, he boasted that the Kibwele was making a large extension of its tea factory at Mufindi. "And they are bringing all the capital and machinery out from Germany!"

It was another, franker, more rebellious German planter at Mufindi who assured me: "We are all under its thumb! Kibwele, Usagara, Uhehe, German Government—we can't get it out of them who It is! Who runs who; that's what we want to know."

It was hoped, that morning, that some slight indication of all this might come out at a mass meeting the Germans of Mufindi were having that afternoon at their "klub." I tried to attend it. The Englishman who owned the two British tea shambas at Mufindi had invited me as his guest. And it was an extraordinary scene!

Not one German in ten at Mufindi could talk any English. Their club was a board structure roughly modeled on a Bavarian mountain lodge. In it were girls in costumes such as you see on Sunday mornings in Munich, when they are going out for a tramp. And there were stiff old gentlemen in gray, green-lapeled jaeger jackets and shorts, who bowed formally from the waist and clicked their heels, as I was presented to them. They were perfunctorily courteous, but—

"I'm sorry," apologized a German who had just returned from Berlin, "but you cannot stay. We are going to wash some dirty linen today, and we don't want to do it in public. I hope you understand?"

I did. He was the man whom the Mufindi planters had sent to Berlin to find where they stood on the title deeds to their properties, and to make some new, more tangible arrangement. And he, I knew, had failed miserably. There was going to be a family fight among the Germans at Mufindi, and Baron Oenhausen, the *Führer*, would be the champion of Nazi Berlin.

When I came up to the baron, he made an attempt to look straight through me. Our conversation that morning had not ended on a *gemütlich* note. On the contrary, when Eve asked the baroness why the Germans thought it their duty to persecute the Jews, the Oenhausens' savagery (from otherwise pleasant and cultured people) had driven me to remark that I had just refused to have one of my books translated in Germany.

"I would not," I said, "sign that non-Aryan clause, stating that I have no Jewish blood in my veins. I don't think I have. Neither do I think it should have anything to do with publishing. But I happen to have a few good friends in Germany, and I didn't want even them to think I'd sign such a clause."

"So!" said the baron, any good will immediately evaporating from his face. But now, aristocrat that he was, he gave me a stiff bow, a quick grasp of the hand, and wished me a pleasant drive—away from the Mufindi Club.

17. Kilimanjaro

FROM Mufindi began the long drive that was to take us from coast to coast across Africa. A hundred and ten days later we came out at Duala, on the Gulf of Guinea, in the French Cameroons. We broke no records. It was not even an unusual drive. In good weather any other person could have done it in a fifth of the time. Our only audacity was to go against the advice of everybody, and set out in the rainy season. We would have taken the same time in either case. Distance bore no relation to the time we took. I don't know how many thousand miles rolled themselves up on our speedometer; we never looked. And then it broke. Our only concern was the attention we paid to our daily mileage (very often an anxious regard) between, say, a transport riders' hotel and the next native village or Government rest house—and, sometimes, just no place at all. For, in large stretches of Africa, the leopards make it inclement to sleep out at night.

In such predicaments we have slept in our car, forced to sit upright, with the windows not too far pulled down. Also, I have a distaste for sleeping out on a road along which elephants are accustomed to travel at night. And I have joyfully greeted the dawn.

We crossed, on our meandering route, hundreds of rivers or their tributaries. The invariable means of transport was a platform, or just some suspicious planks, placed across a set of deep native dugouts. And on these queer rafts the Negroes always sang. Sometimes it was just a ceremony of grunts, with one lazy fellow who seemed to have nothing to do but boastfully beat time by striking the side of his dugout with a wooden block. Once or twice, we felt, there was something insulting to the white man in their grinning chant. But in crossing the broad Ubangui River to get up into French Equatorial Africa, we heard the song of the paddlers as a low, introspective moan, which seemed to hold all the hopes and resentments of Central Africa.

The tempo gets you. You are impatient at first, exasperated. With a definite number of miles to go before you can reach the spot you have selected for the night, and with several more rivers yet to cross, you are infuriated to see twenty natives wait, with their paddles poised, until their leader reaches that particular note, or grunt, which bids them to bend their backs for another stroke. Then, you have the sense to know, you cannot change them. You become accustomed to sitting on the bank of some heavy river, watching the opposite side to see if those dugouts will *ever* move off; some natives are fishing in rapids above you that flash in the sun—and, you suddenly realize, you are content.

Our life was lived, mainly, with natives from then on. Our last look at Mufindi was at natives picking daisies. They were snipping off the heads and drying them on broad burlap mats; for it was there, at 6,000 feet, that some of the finest pyrethrum grows—the bedbug powder that was to liberate the harassed German settlers from the Usagara Company.

There are something like eighty-five distinct native tribes in Tanganyika alone, with fifty-five subtribes. Most of them are Bantus, of the orthodox Negro type. Some are of Arab or Persian descent. And then there are the Nilotic tribes, such as the majestic Masai, who actually regard the white man with contempt. There are twenty-one Christian associations, including several German Protestant sects, with missions. But their converts number only around 600,000. There are 300,000 Mohammedans. The rest of the 5,000,000 natives have gods of their own.

The Masai, whose religion the whites have never yet completely fathomed, have a "laibon," a sort of superior spiritual leader, who must come from a tribe of Masai who live on the mountain of Ngong, in Kenya. But the "laibon" had just died, in the hospital at Arusha, before I got there, convinced that he had been murdered by an evil spirit. (I might say that some of the white men who looked after him there were also convinced of that.)

And that is just the point which makes contact with the African native such a puzzling, interesting, even weird experience. Most of them believe in a supreme being of a sort, a God; but they do not pay much attention to him. Why? Because he is a kindly Person; he will bring no harm to them. What they really fear is that vast reservoir of the dead, the natives who have gone beyond. As a French writer has put it, "The tribe is a community of living and dead where the latter are not the least powerful."

The spirit world, and the use of witch doctors to ward off harmful magic; these are what caused old Chief Muala to be charged with murder over in South-West Africa. And many a "mission native," in his European clothes—sitting, as he might be, at a Government clerk's desk—lives in terror of these things today.

Yet, whatever his belief, these fears do not seem to undermine the native—not until he is certain that someone has put an evil spirit on him. Until that moment he is a recklessly brave man, not afraid to die. You admire him. And the "totos," the little fat-bellied African children—so many of them with umbilical hernias!—are the most lovable live things in Africa. They are a constant pleasure to you.

I could understand, easily, after a few months in Africa, why a disgruntled British settler in Tanganyika should growl to me: "Every man jack in this Government is a Negrophile. They *love* the natives; they resent the white man. They want to keep *us* away."

Then he told me how, when one district officer was clearing a location of tsetse fly, and he discovered that the ground was going to be turned over into white men's hands, he dispersed the concentration of natives, and let the fly come back!

I have heard few greater tributes paid to the paternal rule of the staff officer in Tanganyika over the natives in his care. And, having seen a wide assortment of white settlers, I can easily understand why.

It was amusing, after the tense Germans at Mufindi, to find the three colonels of the Southern Highlands Club holding a bitter post-mortem over their daily nine holes of golf. Sunk in the chintz-covered chairs, each with a glass of whisky in his hand, the flames from a freshly lighted log fire playing on their swarthy faces, they were fighting the game over, stroke for stroke; it might have been St. Andrews.

It seemed incredible that Colonel M. could have lost a ball for every hole. He blamed his "boy"; the damned "boy" had not looked for them properly, or else he had trodden them in under his black toes, and would sell them back to Colonel M. again. Which everyone present knew the "boy" would; because Colonel M., for all his record, was a soft-hearted man. His "boy" was his veteran gun-bearer, and Colonel M. would have faced, empty-handed, a charging elephant, rather than let harm come to that grinning, faithful, artful native.

Colonel M. had three distinctions: He was a "tiger colonel," once the commanding officer of a famous regiment of Indian lancers; and he had the unique distinction of being one of the few men who has been bitten through the shoulder by a wounded tiger, and lived to tell the tale. (Not that he ever told it.) Next, he was nearly always away from the club, shooting elephants in a dangerous patch of country about forty miles off. "And," said the colonel who ran the Southern Highlands

Club, "the silly blighter walks right into the middle of the herd!" Finally, when Colonel M. came around, all the passion fruit on the club's sideboard vanished at once.

He just popped them into his mouth, with a sort of absent-minded innocence that infuriated the other members of the club, who liked passion fruit. Then, having ravaged the sideboard, he would saunter off to dine in his own bungalow, which held, it seemed to me, nothing but a bed and the finest collection of heavy-duty rifles I have ever handled. Although he shot elephants, I think he was subconsciously fond of them and felt lonely away from them.

There are many—perhaps too many—Englishmen like that in Africa these days. But why not? The intelligentsia are fond of referring to them as overgrown children; arrested development. But these men, who have no money urge, have an authentic love of nature, an appreciation of beauty, and a desire for a life of physical contest, that come from some of the finest things in the British character.

The "tiger colonels" may not do much good, but they also do not do much harm to a colony. And their pensions of £400 to £600 a year must be spent to buy things from other settlers, who must grow these things in order to live.

In Tanganyika, of the 493 persons returned in 1936 as having incomes of over £600 a year, no fewer than 334 were Government officials.

As unquestionably a large part of the remaining 159 were well-to-do Indian merchants, two at least were German sisal planters, and a few officials of the Usagara, the social and financial status of the outright British settler can be seen.

The English settlers around the Southern Highlands Club were rather proud of the natives in their region, for they were the famous Wahehe, one of the finest fighting tribes in Africa (with all the good points which that means); it took the Germans from 1892 to 1896 to subdue them. Then, when Iringa fell, the Wahehe chief, Mkawawa, killed himself rather than fall into German hands. They are an aristocratic tribe, and, having made their peace with the Germans, took no part in the Maji-Maji rebellion, which broke out in 1905, in which the Germans killed 125,000, mostly coastal, natives.

The well dressed Wahehe these days carries an umbrella, a long spear, and a muzzle-loading rifle which everyone hopes (for his sake) he won't fire. It is a tawdry piece of "trade" goods, a mere gas pipe, which it seems a crime to sell to a decent native. But it gives him an air of dignity and bearing.

When, in the rain, driving through that weird, cork-like, lichened forest towards Iringa, I tried to take a photo of one of these dignified Wahehe on the road, he merely hopped up on the bank, and raised his hand. His manner was not belligerent or truculent; it merely seemed to say: "No; it is impossible. Sorry. But it is not done."

And I drove on, feeling rather humiliated.

In Iringa, which is a pleasant little town of about a hundred Europeans (where the Germans outnumber the British by 30 to 1, and practically all the trade is done by Indian shops), we listened that night to the news from Europe—and the news was very, very bad. This made things embarrassing, for the hotel is run by a Swede and his wife is a German; aside from ourselves, there were two English civilians there that night— a tipsy planter and the agent for the Kenya Farmers' Association—and then there were the two officers from the King's African Rifles, the K.A.R., stationed at Iringa, with a small detachment of askaris (native soldiers). Because of the large number of German settlers in that district, the rest of the people in the bar were Germans. And the bar itself was a crowded space, some twenty feet long by less than six feet wide; we were all sitting on top of each other.

It was a study in restraint, to watch the faces. The Germans wanted to cheer, but felt they couldn't, in the circumstances. The British wanted to discuss this continual succession of German ruthlessness and diplomatic successes, but knew that that was impossible with all those Germans present. So the two officers of the K.A.R. grinned at the Swede, the obvious neutral, and ordered another whisky.

Everybody felt uncomfortable. And in the few nights that we did spend in hotels on our way up through Tanganyika to Nairobi, I found these evening "prayer meetings,"—as they called them down there, with the semi-circle facing the radio, some of the most taut moments I experienced in Africa. We all felt that the clouds of war were drawing over.

It is about 500 miles from Iringa to Mount Kilimanjaro.

When you drop down from the escarpment of 6,000 feet, you descend to the Ugogo steppe. This is sterile, steaming country, around the 2,000-foot level—not low enough to have the swamps and malarial fevers of the coast, but still an impossible country for a white man to live in; excepting, of course, an occasional district officer. It is in the hands of natives, and there are very few of them.

Two-thirds of Tanganyika is tsetse-fly country. And the natives are well aware of this. If you take a flimsy sheet of paper showing the tsetse-fly country and lay it over a population-density map of Tanganyika, which I have done, you will see that the great congestion of natives is around the lower rim of the great lake, Victoria Nyanza, and on the slopes of the great volcanoes and rock massifs. There are, for example, 25,000 Chaga native coffee plantations on the slopes of Mount Kilimanjaro alone.

Hence, of course, the constant bitterness between the white settlers and the Dar es Salaam British administration, which refuses to push these natives off their fly-free lands to make more room for white colonization. And where the natives are settled, 5,000,000 of them, in such congestion, they have invariably overcultivated the land, with the result that the large native settlement around Kondoa, about mid-way to Kiliman-jaro, is a horror of soil erosion, raw, gaping, red sores in the earth.

The road up through Tanganyika is, therefore, lonely. This is part of the Great North Road which runs from Cape Town to Cairo.

The best way to describe it, as it is in the rainy season, is to say that when you step out of your car you slide. You slip; you slither. And, if you try to right yourself too abruptly, you come down on your behind. The red, buttery mud is as jellified as the bed of an estuary at low tide, a duck marsh. Your feet weigh tons. You drive with chains, to get a grip. And when, in spite of chains, you find yourself sliding inexorably into the drainage ditch, you stop. Then you get out and take an ax, a shovel, and four burlap gunnysacks from out the back of your car. You go into the thorn woods and strike down a tree; you chop off its branches. You return, and, with the shovel, dig out the submerged rear wheels of your car. You lay a small corduroy road of branches before each tire, and over these you lay the burlap bags.

Then you get back into your car, murmur a short prayer, and gradually let the clutch in. If the wheels grip, you're all right (for the moment); you're back on the crown of the road. But, usually, the churning wheels just grind your improvised road into the red mud under you—and you build again.

That is why even the poorest white settler in Africa will never travel without a "boy." And there is no white man too poor to have one.

The slopes of the rain forest, at 6,000 feet, were jungle green, with the huge, gray trunks of tropical trees struggling upwards from the dark undergrowth, dripping with the lianas that were clinging to them and trying to choke them. Down here, on the flats, it was thorn forest, fairly open, with the flat treetops giving a flakelike pattern to the landscape; every now and then a monstrous baobab tree. Gazing down on these flats from the escarpment is like regarding an ocean, with the dark patches of clouds floating across it, and mist blue in the distance, with, perhaps some fifty miles off, a single conical peak rising against the sky.

The sandy spaces of the thorn groves have a profusion of flowers—blue, and white, morning glories, yellow morning glories, with violet heads; wild gladioli, gloxinias, flowering stems like hollyhocks, "red hot pokers," a cactus with its primrose blossom; and then patches of bare country where, among the baobabs, giant euphorbia hold their candelabra arms forty feet above you.

Doves, always in pairs, flit off the road; there was a blackbird, with scarlet gloves on his wings; toucans (actually banana-beaked hornbills) swooped from tree to tree in sagging flight. Orioles. The inevitable golden crane flying over, shouting, "Down there! Down there!" A hawk catches a snake, and we watch it carry it up to a treetop. (In all Africa, I saw only one snake alive.) And in the "drifts," as we were fording them, minute kingfishers, the size of sparrows, shot like arrows of amethyst over the reddened stream.

A few incestuous monkeys scampered through the cork-like forest up on the escarpment, a baby or two clinging to its mother's stomach. Here, an occasional startled buck raised its head, then lightly plunged into the undergrowth. And on the towering rock massifs, along which this irregular road accepted every opportunity for having solid ground, the baboons barked at us from the rocks, the big bull sitting there like a figure carved on the tombs of Egypt, the rest walking disgustedly off, presenting their obscene behinds.

All this in silence. So it seemed. Yet when you were lying under the car, straining with tight lips to take up another link of chain, you became aware of a constant rustle, a buzzing all around you, the humming insects of the jungle. There was no silence.

We reached Dodoma again late that afternoon. It is the junction of the Great North Road and the railway that climbs from the coast to reach Tabora and Ujiji, on the shores of Lake Tanganyika, where Stanley met Livingstone. This was the old slave trail.

Kondoa, where .the old slave traders had a fort, is still strongly under Arab influence; its bazaar is noisy with natives in long white jibbahs, and wearing the red fez. An Arab coffee seller wanders along, his charcoal burner on his back, and clinking his brass cups. But the shops are all Indian. Betel-chewing Asiatics, with their knees up and their backs against the mud walls, selling bolts of Japanese colored cotton prints, German hardware and tin hurricane lamps. On a broad green square, when we got there the next day, the natives were conducting their usual barter market, and their principal offering seemed long sticks of green sugar cane, stacked against a mud wall. They were buzzing like bees with their activity, intent, occupied with their life—unaware that, to us, it was so new and strange.

At Dodoma we found the usual competent German garage, with a blond young Nazi who helped me to reinforce my springs with some added shackles and rope; we filled all the spare tins (which so choked the rear of our car) with extra gasoline for the run to Babati and Arusha. Then we went back to the Railway Hotel (owned by a German and run by a Greek) and found that the road to Arusha was closed. The public works department had declared it impassable. You had to get a permit even to go out on it to emerge from Dodoma. The rest of our afternoon was spent intimidating an insolent Indian clerk, in the P.W.D. department, with an ambiguous letter we had procured at Dar es Salaam. It began: "To all concerned." And its context was that everyone to whom we presented it should give us every assistance within his power. As the white P.W.D. officer was somewhere along the forbidden road, the Indian clerk had no one to fall back on; he succumbed, and signed a pass.

Dodoma lies on that cleft known to geographers as the East African Rift Valley, a great *dischargeless* area, a trough, which, with its soda lakes, and great and small volcanoes, intersects the East African granite plateau from 6 degrees south latitude northwards, and then continues through the Red Sea into the valley of the Dead Sea and Jordan, right to the foot of the Lebanon. It begins an unbelievable part of the world, and people who live along it are not quite normal—especially white men.

It is at about Dodoma that you begin to realize what a vast number of natives in Africa live at altitudes from 3,000 to 8,000 feet; not, as the conventional idea is, in steaming jungle, but in atmospheres which the white man finds cold and rarefied, and which give him what in Kenya is called "East African nerves." From Dodoma you begin to climb gradually, with sharp dips and hard lifts over ridged, rocky escarpments, until you reach those great golden plains, shining in the sun, on which rise the snowcapped cones of Meru and Kilimanjaro.

The red rivers and rivulets were in flood, sluicing down noisily from the blue mountains to the left of us. The previous day we had forded the red Ruaha, a formidable flood. We had taken it gingerly—not too fast, so that the splashing water could not foul our distributor; not too slowly, for fear we would sink in its red sands. It was a tense passage, which we just made. When the Ruaha is really in flood it overflows its banks for miles, and whichever side you happen to be on there you stay.

Today, after the exciting sight of some fresh elephant dung, at the juncture of one of those "walks" which the great beasts make all across Africa, we slid down into a broad, low valley, with a vast red river flowing in abandon through its bottom.

Our hearts sank; we could cheat man to get along this road, but we couldn't outwit nature; we were stopped.

There was a little village of beehive huts on the near side of the swirling red flow, running at great speed; and some natives ran from this village—in fact, the whole village ran towards us —to direct us to where a submerged cement causeway ran to the other side.

We took it.

The river was so high that there was no "curl" where it swept over the off side of the causeway; the red water was splashing against the bottom of our engine case; yet we could feel the good, solid cement under us. It was about a quarter of a mile across, I should judge. And then, when we were almost ready to believe we would reach the opposite bank, we saw a huge thorn tree lodged on the causeway ahead of us. I got out blithely to shift it loose and send it downstream; I got out— and vanished.

Eve said afterwards she had never seen anywhere such an expression of amazement on anyone's face as on mine when I sank into that red, rushing water. I just disappeared. In a few seconds I had been swept under the car and was clinging to the downstream rear wheel. She, who couldn't see me, thought I was gone for good. And I, conscious of the fact that I had an expensive German camera in the pocket of my safari shirt, all our paper money, two letters of credit, and a folder of precious traveler's checks, climbed upright in a fury. What I had been doing was driving on the extreme edge of that submerged causeway, probably all the way from the other bank; it was just a gift from God that I hadn't driven the car overboard.

A naked native rushed from the near bank, and we shifted the thorn tree. I was shocked to watch the speed with which it was swept away. Then, getting the car to dry land, I stripped, regardless of the proprieties, while Eve painted my scratched nakedness with iodine, from head to foot. We spread out the pound notes, the letters of credit, the precious traveler's checks, in the murky sun. My signature on all of them was a bit watery, but still legible enough to permit cashing. Another pair of dry shorts and a safari shirt were exhumed from the back of the car, with some golf stockings. We went on.

That sunset we saw a vision which I shall always remember. We had just dragged our way through the sands of a sudden oasis of ivory-nut palms. We thought the country from now on would be always like that. We went down and up the other side of a thorn valley, from which a herd of bushbuck scattered, like flung shot, at our advent. Then, with the slanting sun gilding some leaves of a tree like laurel, we saw in this frame over the roadway, just a dark blue cone against the lighter blue of the sky. It was some white serrations of snow in its ravines that caught our attention.

"Kilimanjaro!" Eve gasped. "Kilimanjaro!"

For one of her girlhood dreams had been realized. But it wasn't Kilimanjaro; it was Meru—an African Fujiyama, 15,600 feet high—and those white serrations of snow which we saw in its vertical valleys were seldom there.

Animals were feeding placidly in the slanting sun. We came on hundreds of fat-rumped, striped little zebra. Wildebeest, like black bison, regarded us with suspicious immobility. Tiny stembok, like hares, bounced off in the golden grass. Thousands of buck of all sorts looked up from the distance. Behind them was the great blue wall of the Rift. Greater bustard ran for cover. A pair of ostriches turned their hairy necks, then suddenly jolted off. And four huge giraffes, quite near the car, and against a background of mist-blue volcanic mountains, watched us with their inquisitive stare.

It is difficult to remember a more peaceful scene than the herds of game grazing on their golden plains.

The giant cone of Meru turned a deep violet, faded out. And that night, in the darkness, we ran into Arusha, center for perhaps the greatest game country in all Africa.

18. The Egoistic Masai

AT Arusha, I encountered the largest collection of authentic British settlers I found in Tanganyika—although it must be admitted that, if the British Government officials were excepted, the Germans still outnumbered them in the district. They were coffee growers, and the most competent one among them was a Jew from Johannesburg. To talk with him was like getting a breath of fresh air, after listening to the "colonels," or younger settlers of the *pukka sahib* type. He was a professional coffee grower.

Arusha was a hotbed of British settlers' discontent. And while, at their stormy meetings, they seemed unable to agree on many things, there was one point on which they were bitterly unanimous—the fiasco of the mandate. Of any mandate. As one said:

"The mandate has been just one long succession of blunders, a complete fiasco. The very idea of a mandate is wrong. Civilization is built up on pride of race, and when you have a mandate you have no pride of race. A man can live here all his life, a foreigner, and never become a naturalized Englishman. We're all hybrids.

"A man in a mandate is like a mule; he has no pride of ancestry and no hope of posterity!

"But you can't make the people back home see this! Why, the Americans have a far greater knowledge of British colonial Africa than the British have! Whenever I go back to England I'm alarmed about how damned little interest the people there show in their own colonies; and Tanganyika ought to be a British colony! We fought for it, we won it; why the hell don't we take it, instead of going through all the eyewash of this mandate nonsense?"

Munich had frightened every English settler. They were almost certain Chamberlain would, if pressed, give away Tanganyika.

"Damn it all, we're not Czechs! You can't push *us* out of our homes. This is our home; we've got our children here. We don't want compensation; we want to be allowed to live here! If we go, even to England, we find we are strangers. I don't want the money; I don't want *compensation* from the British Government—I want *this* home. *And I'll damned well fight for it!*"

"Native loyalty! That's all eyewash. Native knows he's got to pay his tax, knows he's got to work and get paid, and from which *white man* doesn't make any difference. Food and women; that's all he thinks about. You just let the Germans get Tanganyika, and perhaps they *would* do what they say; they're clever at propaganda. Perhaps, for a time, they *would* only tax the native 5s. instead of 10s. Perhaps they *would* give him higher wages. *And then watch!* You just let those Germans have these 5,000,000 natives in Tanganyika to propagand with, and it wouldn't be a year before the British would be having native uprisings all over Africa!"

"Native liking, or hate, of the white man is independent of *any* nationality! Don't forget that."

"What we need here is a Governor *with full powers;* cut the liaison with London. Break with Whitehall. Fact seems to be, you can't run a colony with the present democratic Government in England."

"We're *unmodern* in colonization—that's what's the matter with England these days."

It is because Tanganyika will be one of the first, and probably the most important colonial problem to be answered in the peace settlements after this present war, that I give these ver-

batim talks there. They are what the British settlers were saying, and saying bitterly—while the British public at home was
thinking (if it did think) that Tanganyika was a proud English
development.

"In 1920, '21, '23, '24, '25," said a representative British settler, "there was any amount of young Englishmen in this country, looking for land. But the Government said, 'No!' Donald
Cameron said, 'No, *no,* NO!' And then the Germans came along
and squatted at Oldeani. Donald Cameron said: 'No!' But the
Germans said, 'We'll stay here—if you try to push us off, we
will take it up to the League of Nations.' They did. Donald
Cameron backed down. Today the Germans out there on the
slope of Ngorongoro crater have a complete unit colony, and
some of the finest coffee country in all Africa.

"And we—mind you, we, the *English*—had been told by our
Government that there simply *was* no more land!"

I will deal with that remarkable German colony out on the
slopes of Ngorongoro crater when I come to the time when I
went out to that country.

I asked most of these settlers what they thought of the new
Government development scheme. They answered in chorus:

"We are so used to 'talk.' We honestly can't believe in the
development scheme. Anyway, it's twenty years too late; as far
as any white policy is concerned, Dar es Salaam and the Colonial Office have not advanced one step from the day when we
took over the country."

"Development scheme!" snorted one English settler who
had been there since the inception of the mandate. "I wouldn't
buy a matchbox on the strength of it!"

It must be admitted that the British settler has good reason
to feel skeptical about Government economic "astuteness" in
Tanganyika. An outstanding example is the railway that runs
today between Moshi and Voi, in Kenya. This was built by the
British during the World War, to get at the Germans around
Moshi. Twenty-five miles of it are in Tanganyika, seventy-five

in Kenya. Governor Horace Byatt, K.C.M.G., tried to have that railway torn up, after the war.

People in Tanganyika claim (a) it was the jealousy of a Tanganyika Governor, who wanted all the mandate's exports from this potentially prosperous region to go out via Tanga, alternative seaport to Dar es Salaam; (b) that Byatt did not want this country to be "opened"; he did not want white settlement around the slopes of Meru and Kilimanjaro.

Whichever is the truth, traffic on the line was suddenly stopped; the settlers were told it was "because of the rains." When they discovered, to their dismay, that the line was going to be torn up they held mass meetings of protest. Lord Delamere happened to be in London at that time. The Tanganyika English settlers appealed to him.

Lord Delamere took his seat, for the first time, in the House of Lords. The movement of the Governor to uproot the railway was stopped. A commission was sent out from London. It discovered that what Governor Byatt had said was true; the Arusha-Voi line was losing money.

But they also discovered that it was losing money at a slower pace than any other railway in Tanganyika!

Today that important little bit of railway feeds Moshi, Arusha, and their important hinterland, and down it goes the important European and native coffee exports—to be shipped from the good dock facilities at Mombasa.

It seems silly not to admit that the early opportunities of Tanganyika have been almost completely let go by default; that there has been no conception whatever of an English settlement policy; that the valuable German holdings in Tanganyika were knocked down to shrewd Indian and Greek buyers for, on the average, one shilling in every pound of their value; and that from the Colonial Office at Whitehall has appeared no initiative whatever, no conception at all, of any broad economic development.

Six months after this present war began, the recommendations of the West Indian Royal Commission have been plain and unpleasant enough to make even the Colonial Office wake up to the fact that there must be some change, initiative, and economic thinking in British colonial administration.

Six months after this war began, Malcolm MacDonald conferred with M. Mandel in Paris. He had the original idea that the French and British should pool their efforts in the colonial field; medical information should be exchanged, for instance.

Lord Snell, in the House of Lords, said that the report of the commission (sent to the islands because of tragic labor upheavals in Jamaica and Trinidad) was a "good deed in a naughty world."

The Marquis of Dufferin and Ava, Parliamentary Under-Secretary for the Colonies, said in the House of Lords that he blushed to have so many bouquets thrown at him.

It seems incredible; he was lucky they weren't bricks!

Surely, the British aren't becoming like Moscow, where, when the program for some great project has been announced, the Bolshies begin to write about it as if it had already been achieved!

Lord Snell's "good deed in a naughty world" is too much like the stock joke which amused us in Moscow during the winter of 1928-29. The office for "The Electrification of all Russia" bore a sign outside its door:

"Please knock, because the bell doesn't ring."

On the other hand, in Tanganyika, both the Colonial Office at Whitehall, as well as the administrators on the spot, combine to see that native interests should be paramount. I do not think that any other natives in Africa have so kindly, just, and thoughtful an administration over them.

The "indirect rule" which Sir Donald Cameron brought over from Nigeria, where it had been instituted by Lord Lugard, probably the greatest of all African administrators, has been carried out unswervingly in the Tanganyika Mandate. This means the reinstatement of hereditary chiefs, or the appointment of others; and through these the British rule the natives. Its intention is to preserve, to as large an extent as is compatible with advancing Africa, the native tribal life and institutions. It also opens up for the advancing native an unobstructed road for his own social self-betterment.

For example, on the slopes of Kilimanjaro there are 25,000 independent native coffee planters. They have their own co-operative, possibly the finest in Africa, which employs an Englishman as secretary to market their coffee for them. The natives, not the Englishman, have the last word; if they think he is not marketing wisely, he has to obey their orders.

These Chaga, who are possibly the most intelligent (and unpleasant) tribe of natives in all Africa, have their own courts and appeal courts, sitting under their native chiefs. The final appeal, of course, still rests with the local British provincial commissioner or the Governor, but the great mass of everyday cases (and how a native loves litigation!) are disposed of in these native tribunals. I have sat in one of these courts, watching its proceedings (it was a breach-of-promise case); and I believe that once you have been able to rid yourself of the idea that the native must be stupid because he is black, you will recognize a considerable amount of "native" wisdom in these still self-conscious and overserious proceedings. They often chuck law—and go for fairness!

The natives try themselves. And the British relegate all the power that they can back to them. It is good. And it is an honest program, not "eyewash."

Not that the natives always appreciate this. A few years ago, when the Chaga thought that the British were interfering too much with their liberty, they became so furious that they burned *their own* co-operative stores. The British held firm. And the Chaga had the mocking humiliation of having to build their own society stores again.

I think that much of the love which the British administrators almost invariably come to feel for the natives under their charge is not reciprocated. The native, except in faithfulness to an individual master, I would not class as a grateful person.

Kilimanjaro, with its two vast peaks, 19,720 and 17,570 feet high, topped by eternal snow, covers an area of 1,300 square miles. On those levels where coffee is grown the density of native population is about 450 to the square mile. "One reason," said the provincial commissioner, drily, to me, at Arusha, "why we claim there isn't any more room for Europeans in this district." In spite of the insistent clamor of the white settlers, mostly British, in that region, the administration resolutely refuses to evict the Chaga from their land. It is said: "On the mountain masses of Kilimanjaro and Meru, and in certain parts of the Mbulu district, the native possesses a natural heritage unsurpassed, if equaled, anywhere in Africa."

There are twenty-one chiefs on Kilimanjaro, ruling over a population of some 156,000 Chaga. There are about 46,000 taxpayers. The native poll tax on the mountain is 12 shillings a year, from which a rebate is allowed for the roads, which the Chaga build themselves, their construction and maintenance of hospitals, and the expenses of their own schools. The Kilimanjaro Natives' Co-operative Union is the largest co-operative in Africa, combining 25,700 planters. Its program calls for much more than merely the co-operative growing and marketing of coffee, however; it plans for the establishment of communal cattle plots (at the present moment most of the Chaga keep their cattle continually in sheds, like pit ponies, always in the dark); the co-operative is erecting its own butcher shops; it is installing village milling machinery. And the time is already within sight when the Kilimanjaro Natives' Co-operative Union *could* be the most powerful machine for propaganda in the province for measures designed for native welfare.

The Chaga are experts in the handling of water, and their irrigation canals, running for miles around the slopes of Kilimanjaro, are flowing cheerily wherever you go up to 5,000 feet. In this respect the Chaga equal in skill the Andorran peasants in their mountain republic of the Spanish Pyrenees.

The Chaga are also expert iron and steel workers, and used to make the long, slender spears for the Masai warriors; the price of one spear was an ox. They seem to have a genius for craftsmanship.

Nevertheless, the Chaga are probably among the most irritating natives in Africa. They are enough to break any district officer's heart. The reason is that all this amazing development is post-war effort; the Germans had alienated these lands. There are German missions on the slope now, which rent their freehold land to the Chaga—land which the Chaga, ironically enough, use for crops with which to make native beer. (There is also an American mission, holding some of the finest freehold land, which complacently rents its land to the Chaga at £2 per acre per year, a very high price.) And these industrious natives, cultivating on one to one and a half acre plots, produced, in 1938, 1,900 tons of "parchment" coffee, for which they received £58,425.

As there are some 25,723 members of the co-operative, this works out at an average of £2 5s. per native cultivator for the year. Not much, judged by European standards, but each one of these little Chaga shambas had its own banana plantation, and, presumably, a few head of half-blind cattle. By African standards, they were rich. (An Indian cannot rent land on Kilimanjaro without the consent of the Chaga chiefs.)

The rapid development, since 1920, has meant that the Chaga have learned to run before they could walk; politically, they are suffering from "growing pains." The co-operative may not be able to provide openings for all the young talent, but it does provide a forum for free speech, of which the Chaga have made full use. This is abetted by a slick firm of Indian advocates in Dar es Salaam, who invariably send a legal adviser up to Kilimanjaro at awkward moments.

The young Chaga, with a revolt mentality somewhat similar to that of the university students of Europe, felt that they had progressed so fast that they were ahead of British "indirect administration"; they wanted to take the bit in their teeth. There was the ancient dissension between chief and chief. And various recalcitrant members of the Kilimanjaro Native Planters' Association, as the co-operative was at first called, felt they could do better by marketing their coffee on their own.

The very geography of Kilimanjaro played an important part in this, particularly in the rivalry between chiefs. Kilimanjaro is serrated, ravaged, by deep gorges and wooded ravines. In some places it is still impossible to cross on foot from side to side. People live in the clefts of deep valleys. Some tribes, which can see each others' beehive huts on the ridges, and the light splash of their banana plantations, have been split in two from time immemorial. The chiefs of some of the more inaccessible tribes have an outlook that is deeply parochial. Others assume they can do anything they please. In June, 1938, Chief Ngatuni of the Khokoma was deposed for murdering his brother—the outcome of a royal feud dating back to the earliest days of Tanganyika.

Dissension constantly comes out at the meetings of the Chaga council, where personal interests and petty jealousies are always foremost; and, then, there is the disrespectful attitude of the young, advancing Chaga towards their hereditary rulers. In an official report, sent to Dar es Salaam (not for publication), which I was privileged to read and quote, I found this:

The chiefs, who are aware of the "progress taking place around them," have discharged their responsibilities in a satisfactory manner for the present year. . . . But they are by no means the revered autocrats they are made out to be. . . . People regard them as the "instrument of will" . . . but the Chaga are not the type of people to suffer oppression.

"The Chaga," as the provincial commissioner put it to me, "are an energetic, progressive people, and, therefore, need handling with wisdom, firmness—*and* tact."

In 1937, when the British tried to put a stop to the Chaga dissensions, provide for plant sanitation and grading, and persuade the dissenting Chaga it was more efficient to sell their entire crop by acting as a communal unit, the Chaga revolted. They rioted. In their indignation they even burned down four of their own native "godowns" and attempted to wreck the masonry built co-operative union office. Their contention was that "anything savoring of compulsion in a measure relating to cooperation was out of place."

Nobody was killed. But 200 police were brought in; to overawe the Chaga, two planes of the Royal Air Force were flown around the disaffected area on Kilimanjaro (which planes the progressive Chaga cheered!); and the acting Governor of Tanganyika himself flew up and made a very sensible speech. He said:

Now, what is it that has made the Chaga people on this mountain rich? Coffee. . . . Coffee of the Kilimanjaro Natives' Cooperative Union is known amongst those who drink coffee overseas and who buy it; they do not know it as the coffee of this one, or that one, or the other one; they know it as K.N.C.U. coffee, and if it were not for this mark, now well known overseas, it would not be bought by these people. . . .

We cannot control here; we cannot say here what the price of anything will be. The people who say what the price will be are the people who buy at the other end. It depends upon how many people want a thing; if only a few want it, the price goes down; if many want it, then the price goes up. . . .

The K.N.C.U. is your organization; it is not the Government's. The Government supports you; but it is yours; you can do what you like with it; you can keep it or you can break it. But if it is broken the Government must protect the wise people who understand the wisdom of selling their coffee in large quantities and through one channel. If the K.N.C.U. goes, the Government will step in and take control itself to insure that the coffee goes through one channel to whoever is buying it at the other end. . . .

I have said some hard words today, but I think that the Chaga people are wise enough to like to hear straight words, and not too many words tied up in other words so that no one can understand; I have spoken these straight words out of what is in my heart. . . .

The chiefs are placed here to rule this mountain, and so long as they are doing it well the Government will stand behind them. Those who plan against the chiefs—those who do not speak their words openly but behind shut doors, and whisper and plot and hope that others will do the same thing—are known to my officers here. . . . If my officers can bring me evidence against this man or that man that he speaks his grievances secretly to disturb men, instead of speaking openly, I shall send him to a far country until he has learned wisdom.

I give rather lengthy excerpts from this speech, because it is so beautiful an exposition of "straight talk" to the natives—a perfect combination of wisdom, firmness, and tact; the British administration in action! After this elementary lesson in economics the acting Governor had four of these agitators deported. One, sent down to Iringa, did not own even one coffee tree, it was found. The provincial commissioner made a swift night descent upon the headquarters of the malcontents at Moshi, and left the minor agitators up on the slopes of Kilimanjaro leaderless. The revolt was over.

But in 1938, when everything seemed quiet, two Hindu lawyers from the firm of advocates in Dar es Salaam, seeing a legal point, came up to the mountain, and there was another riot. This time a witless amateur newspaper correspondent at Moshi cabled London that the R.A.F. planes had dropped bombs on the Chaga, and there were "questions asked in Parliament"; the Labor Party got all hot and bothered.

When you know the inside story of some of these African "troubles" (I confine this remark almost exclusively to Tanganyika, however), you begin to feel a real sympathy and admiration for the local provincial commissioner and district officer, for his unbelievable patience.

One of the things which caused the late riots was that the Chaga learned that the Germans in the district were getting £50 a ton for their coffee, f.o.b. Moshi, whereas all the Chaga were able to get was £35. But £35 per ton, as it happened, was the world price; it was all that the British settlers were getting. The Usagara Company (the German Government) was simply paying a bonus, from £15 to £20 a ton, for coffee grown by their own nationals, as the German settlers were accepting the bulk of the payment in "aski marks." The money remained in Germany.

Now, here are some interesting points about the coffee situation in Tanganyika, and the British settlers' chronic complaint (a groundless one) that German competition is ruining their coffee market:

Ninety per cent of the highest priced coffee in Tanganyika is grown on the slopes of the three huge volcanoes, Kilimanjaro, Meru, and Ngorongoro crater. The natives export about 35 per cent; the Germans 40 per cent; the Greeks one-half of the remainder, and the rest is between the Swiss and British. The other 10 per cent of high-grade coffee is exported by Germans from other districts.

In 1938 Germany bought only £53,932 worth of Tanganyika's £385,576 coffee exports, slightly more than one-seventh. England took about £13,000. The rest of it was nearly all shipped through Kenya, out through Mombasa; it was native grown, mostly low-grade "robusta" coffee. It went to Holland, Marseilles, Canada, and New York.

One-seventh of the coffee export (which the British didn't even grow) could not wreck the British Tanganyika coffee growers. If the Germans took roughly £53,000 worth and the British market wanted only £13,000, and the German Government paid a bonus to their nationals in Tanganyika, then, it seems to me, the British settlers' complaint is (a) not against the Germans, but against their home Government for not patriotically taking more Tanganyika coffee (even at preference prices); (b) for responsible lack of organization in their own growing, grading, and marketing endeavor.

"But," complained one of those *pukka-sahib*-type British settlers to me, "the Germans here are using that bonus to pay higher prices for labor!"

This is nonsense. It is not for lack of labor that the British are not better coffee growers; the South African Jew I have mentioned has no difficulty marketing *his* scientifically grown coffee crop. His shamba is a model for even the Germans to regard. There is also at Arusha an Australian woman, handsome and intelligent, debonnaire in her corduroy slacks and felt terai, who runs her own paw-paw plantation and manages an Englishman's shamba for him, where she can grow high-grade coffee against anybody. Finally, more candid, seasoned British settlers themselves admitted to me that this Germans-paying-higher-wages-because-of-the-bonus lamentation is a weak and shameful excuse.

Yet it was to get a definite statement from the German planters on this that I again went "up the mountain" to see Herr Troost, *Führer for all the Germans in Tanganyika.*

"On the mountain." "Up the mountain." "Trouble on the mountain."

It was amusing, when living on the gentle slope of Kilimanjaro, to hear these phrases, used so constantly about "the mountain" (with its turmoil of local politics); and then to think that back in Europe and America the average person thought of Kilimanjaro as some remote, mythical, *perhaps* snowcrested shape that rose out of the African jungle. Which is precisely the same way in which I envisaged Kilimanjaro when I was living at Dar es Salaam. Even now, living on it, I had no conception of its shape; and it was days before I saw its snows, for its two peaks, with their glistening saddleback, are nearly always wreathed in clouds.

It is said that it was fifty years after the first white man saw and reported the three glaciers on Ruwenzori that another white man saw them. I shall never forget my glimpse of them —sunset, with the hippos blowing like whales around me on the marshy shores of Lake Edward.

When Krapf and Rebmann, two German explorers, returned from a trip into the interior of Africa in 1849, a dangerous adventure to where Arusha now thrives, and talked of snowcapped peaks on the equator, they were simply laughed at by an incredulous world.

You cannot know the shape of a mountain when you are on it. In 1929, when I was riding horseback over the Caucasus, my first sight of Elbruz was from sixty miles away on the steppe. Its twin nipples are a mile apart; at sixty miles' distance they seemed one. Then it was three weeks, after riding across the lower ranges, before I ever saw Elbruz again. This was at midnight. I had crawled out of the "kosh," the stone igloo in which I was sheltering in a long-forgotten pass, when I saw something glistening in the moonlight. I thought, at first, that it must be some peculiar form of cloud. Then—and it made me gasp—I knew I was looking at the snows of the Caucasus.

It was the same with Kilimanjaro. We had been having dinner with the district officer at Moshi. He was a South African, and one of the most pleasant, tolerant, and informative administrators I met in Africa. And along about midnight I went out on the lawn.

"There it is," he said casually.

And there, above the shadowy trees in his garden, glistened the cocked hat of Kibo (19,720 ft.), then a long field of blazing white, and the rise of Mawensi (17,570 feet), first climbed by Dr. Hans Meyer in 1889.

I stood in the stillness of that garden, and satiated myself with the sight. I wanted to become familiar with it, contemptuous of it, so that it should never plague me again. I wanted to have my fill of it. For I knew that in a few days I should be passing on, and I did not want to have any residue of regret in my memory. I wanted to be able to command that sight always.

Kibo is not an imposing mountain; its slope is too casual. You can walk up it; you do not need to climb. The Australian woman whom I have mentioned would, of course, have walked up this mountain. And, odd coincidence, the best climber of Kilimanjaro today is a Russian priest, a Cossack. And he came from the very place where I first saw Elbruz—the Don steppe.

The Chaga are wonderful road builders, and, as you wind your way up Kilimanjaro, you ascend through a mist forest of dark, deep-leaved green trees, dripping with gray moss. You double around the tip of some deep ravine, and the tinkle of falling water comes from the labyrinth below you. Four Chaga trot past, barefooted, carrying an old woman in a plaited hammock made from reeds. She is being taken to hospital. You pass the dark green rows of coffee trees, with their lighter background; the splash of banana leaves. You reach an alpine meadow, and there, under a little thatched shelter of banana fronds, sits a Negro, a Chaga, in khaki trousers, white shirt, and straw hat, industriously pedaling a Singer sewing machine; he gazes at you blandly; then off to the blinding white snows of Kilimanjaro. They are appearing behind fast drifting clouds today.

From 5,000 to 6,000 feet up Kilimanjaro is a deep forest reserve, in which no one may live. The Chaga are allowed in there to cut an occasional tree, to collect wild honey, and to shoot rock rabbits. This deep forest extends from 6,000 to 10,000 feet; then come pines. Then the bronze uplands above the timber line. And a range of giant lobelias, 15 feet high. And standing there, in the crisp air coming down from the snows, you can see across a vast empty space—Lake Jipe, half of which lies in Kenya, the blue mountains fifty miles away, and the dark green belt of a sisal plantation just inside the Kenya border.

Herr Troost, the *Führer* for all the Germans in Tanganyika, was sitting in a dark green house, in the shadows of the shade trees over the regimented lines of coffee plants on the Usagara plantation. The Usagara Company itself (German Government) exports 350 tons of coffee from the slopes of Kilimanjaro.

He was a baldish, unspectacular little man, with spectacles; cool, concise, and, apparently, candid. He made you think of a German watchmaker. In 1905 Troost was the manager and part owner of a Greek sisal plantation. Then he bought a small holding at Moshi. He lost that, presumably after the last war, when all the German holdings were confiscated. Now he was manager for the Usagara's Kilimanjaro coffee plantations. He said:

"The authorities [British] are absolutely correct. I myself can say they are not only absolutely correct, but they discuss matters in a friendly manner.

"There is no reason why we should not be good friends, because politics will be settled in Europe.

"We have always forbidden members of our own community to discuss the question of the colonies *among themselves*.

"What could we do in event of war? Futile!

"In that case every German here, however, would want to be in Germany and fight for his country!

"There are natives here who understand German. Therefore I have forbidden even members of our own community to discuss the colonial question among themselves. I am the head of the Nazi party in Tanganyika!

"The Germans do *not* pay higher wages to the natives than do the British. Why should we? If I heard of a case I would try to expose it, use all my influence to prevent it—but I have never heard of a case here."

Then, as if unable to control his bottled-up indignation at the British occupation any longer, he suddenly said:

"Karl Peters, in England, would have been a Cecil Rhodes!"

You liked Herr Troost—chiefly because he was a competent, even dangerous, man. There was nothing smarmy about him. And a lot of what he was saying was coldly accurate; instructions *had* been sent out from Berlin for the Germans not to play politics with the natives—not for the moment. But it is an important factor to make clear: There were more natives in Tanganyika in touch with German employers (and in intimate touch) than there were with British employers—simple reason being, there were more authentic German settlers. There were, of course, the British Government officials; but British colonial administrators do not go about "talking politics" with the natives; they have a prudish code of honor on that subject—and a wise code.

Whether Herr Troost was aware of it or not, there were German agents talking to the natives in Moshi at that moment; the British agents reported what they were saying; and there was not a German settler in the northern or southern highlands, or on the hot sisal shambas along the steaming coast (or in the Dar es Salaam offices of the Usagara Company) who was not telling the natives: "You will find things much, much better when the Germans come. You will be taxed less. You will have a better life." They told the natives that, when the Germans wanted to do so, it would be easy for them to retake Tanganyika. And as evidence, with the more intelligent natives—the clerks, for example—they merely showed them that very good newspaper, the *Tanganyika Standard*, or the London *Times*, full of the news of recent German successes.

Also, as every one of the higher British officials in Tanganyika knew, the Germans had an organization *already* appointed, among the Nazis in the territory, to take over within twenty-four hours. "And I don't blame them," said one of the leading members of the Tanganyika League, to me. "Why shouldn't they be able to take over at twenty-four hours' notice? *They're organized!* They could do it properly."

It was one of the dinner-table jokes among the British administrators at Arusha and Moshi that a certain Herr Zitzloff, a competent and one-time likable German coffee planter in the district, was furious because he had not been designated as the future district *Gauleiter!*

These German Nazis were even indulging in jealousies among themselves about the distinctions *which were to be conferred.*

It must be admitted that British propaganda among the natives has always been rather a hopeless mess. To an Australian friend of mine, who owned a farm in German East Africa, was given some propaganda to disseminate among the natives in his locality during the last war. This propaganda was chiefly about how the Germans were raping the women of Belgium.

"Imagine that!" he said. "Why, it was just the one thing to make the blacks, who are afraid of the Germans, admire them; make them certain the Germans *must* be top-dog in Europe, if they could go about raping our women like that!

"So I changed it; *I* told the natives how we were raping the women of Germany. The Germans just couldn't stop it; they were too weak. And that went down like Christmas pie!"

I have good reasons for believing that the allegedly native demonstrations at Mombasa and Dar es Salaam, during the September, 1938, crisis, were organized. They were not spontaneous. Natives don't go in for things like that, particularly not the detribalized mixture of clerks and heavy laborers of the coast. And in the interior, to the native a white man is a white man. They will follow any white man who is manly and can command respect.

For example, look at the 4,000 or 5,000 native soldiers who stuck to that gallant German commander, Paul von Lettow-Vorbeck, through four years of losing war in German East Africa. They fought for him and died for him in swamps and jungle. They knew he was losing, because he was always dodging about, retreating, making swift attacks upon the overwhelming British forces against him, whose number was around 114,000.

And at the end, when he was still undefeated in Northern Rhodesia and was preparing to march again into Portuguese West Africa, he surrendered on November 23, twelve days after the war was over. At that time his force had dwindled to 30 officers, 125 other whites, 1,165 native soldiers, and 2,900 other natives, including nearly one thousand native refugee women.

Moore Ritchie, in his excellent book, *The Unfinished War*, says: "Thus ended a four years' feat of arms by this Marshal Ney of the tropics, a man whose conduct, both as a soldier and chivalrous foe, won the admiration of the world."

Ritchie fought against von Lettow as commanding officer of a flying column in East Africa; and it is the men who fought against von Lettow—and *with* him—who understand why his men stuck to him.

Why didn't they desert him? They were taking a terrible punishment. Why didn't the natives of Tanganyika, who didn't know the difference between a German and an Englishman (or a Tibetan) desert en masse to the invading British?

Don't take those "mass demonstrations" of natives in East Africa—allegedly against the Germans—too seriously. They were organized as a publicity stunt to get space in the London newspapers, to awake, shake, focus a lethargic British public opinion on the danger of losing East Africa. And, as such, they were perfectly legitimate; they were even necessary.

The British public needed some awakening.

But *if the Chaga heard that the Germans were coming back* you would hear a spontaneous howl that would shake Kilimanjaro!

For the Chaga, that most intelligent and irritating race, know that their remarkable advancement, since the last war, would go by the board. The Germans would simply alienate once again this valuable coffee country on the slopes of the mountain; and the Chaga would become "black diamonds," laborers.

The British Tanganyika administration has given to the Chaga—even against the loud protests of British nationals—an open road for "African" development such as that great Negro American educator, Booker T. Washington, would have wanted.

The Chaga have nothing to lose but their own political agitators—and the Indian parasites. But even here the Chaga have shown that, when the Indian is not about, the native can run his own stores and shops. You will see, on the slopes of Kilimanjaro, a thing which you will see hardly anywhere else in East Africa—native communities in which there is not one Indian shop.

The Chaga represent advancing Africa.

Around Arusha, that pleasant, tree-shaded townlet, and Moshi, you will find the greatest density of authentic British settlers anywhere in Tanganyika. On the British sisal plantations of the coast—sisal, at over £2,000,000 yearly, is customarily over 41 per cent of the mandate's exports—on these steaming shambas, as on the tea gardens of Ceylon or Darjeeling, you will find that they are only too often being run by paid managers in the employ of London moneyed interests. This can, in no sense of the word, be called colonization. It is exploitation.

But, even so, this settlement in the great northern province of Tanganyika (31,514 square miles) is on a small scale, a scale shockingly weighted in the balance for foreigners. There are four districts, Arusha, Moshi, Masai, Mbulu. And when you consider their composition, the unbelievable mixture of nationalities to which the administration must give equal opportunity; when you realize the overwhelming number of ubiquitous Indians; when you see the vast numbers of the native population, and realize that *"native interests must be paramount"*—then you will have some grasp of the complexities in the Tanganyika Mandate.

It is not "British" at all.

Arusha, for example, had, on the eve of this war, 150 adult males; 21 were British officials; 30 can be said to have been British planters; then there were 71 Germans, who were either storekeepers or planters; and the rest, after a comparatively large colony of Greek coffee planters, were one American coffee planter and three missionaries; then Swiss, Danish, Italian and Norwegian planters; then some 200 South African Dutch, "irreconcilables" from the Boer War, who had come into this region in German time, to escape British rule.

In addition, chiefly in the bazaar, there were 500 Indians.

And, in a district of only 1,172 square miles, there were 48,-000 natives.

Some grasp of the small-scale English settlement in Tanganyika may be gained by pointing out that Arusha holds the only English school of any consequence in Tanganyika. It is run by a mission, of course, the Church Missionary Society, and, with 60 pupils, it is rated as "overcrowded." It keeps children there until the age of fifteen, when they can go up to Kenya, or, if their parents have the money, to the much coveted schools of England.

(I wish it could be the English policy, as it was with the Nazis, to pay for the voyage and bring all children home to be educated in the home country; free, if their parents could not afford it. These children, forced to hang on out there, where the climate or altitude is deadly for them between the ages of six and nineteen, make you think there is something very rotten in that phrase, "outposts of empire." They deserve a better chance.)

In Moshi, which was virtually a Nazi stronghold, the cards were even more stacked against the British settler. Moshi had 46 English officials and 43 English planters, but there were 174 Germans, most of them scorching Nazis. There were 14 Americans, all missionaries and harmless. There were 80 Greeks, nearly all industrious coffee planters. Then Persians, a Roumanian, two Polish women, and the usual mixture of Swiss, Swedish, and Portuguese planters.

In Moshi there were 826 of the inevitable Indians.

In an area of less than 2,158 square miles there were 175,600 natives, mostly the difficult Chaga.

And, in Moshi, the administration considered things sufficiently dangerous to maintain a battalion of the King's African Rifles.

On the great Masai plains, where the Tanganyika Government is doing its utmost to preserve one of the finest fighting tribes in Africa, there are 37,000 Masai herdsmen in an area of over 22,508 square miles; a density of about one and a half Masai per mile. There are only seven British out here—four officials and three settlers. And there is only one missionary, a German.

The British administration at Dar es Salaam is obdurately protecting this vast Masai country from the British settlers, who would like to have some of this land thrown open for them. Anthropologists, and neutral observers such as I, of course hope that the administration can hold out.

The British, who are leaving the Masai as much to themselves as possible, have given them a far greater range to graze their cattle than this splendid race had in German times.

Then comes Mbulu, with 5 British officials and 21 non-officials, with 85 German settlers, 30 Greeks, 4 French; then one each of American, Dane, Norwegian, and Swede.

In Mbulu there are only 160 Indians.

But there are 123,800 natives in its cramped 5,675 square miles.

All of this white settlement—and much that is native, it should be recognized—is on the immense slopes of these three extinct volcanoes—carbuncle shaped Kilimanjaro, the highest mountain in Africa, forever capped with snows; cone shaped Meru; and then that majestic volcanic upheaval, Ngorongoro, an extinct volcano that is only 8,000 feet high but has a crater that is ten miles in diameter.

It is on Ngorongoro's crater that the Germans have their completely self-contained colony of coffee planters, at Oldeani; a settlement made in 1927, against the feeble protest of the Tanganyika Government, which tried to oust them; a settlement "cut out of the blue," into whose untouched forests the arrogant, adventurous Germans cut the first road, penetrating the elephant, rhino, and buffalo country, as late as 1927; a bevy of modern pioneers who hacked out a new life; and, up to the outbreak of this present war, owned some of the finest coffee land in all Africa.

The "boma" at Arusha, the Government headquarters, is an old German fort, white walled, with a moat around it, very much on the Beau Geste model. Inside it sits the provincial commissioner, a South African, who, one might say, has "borne the heat of the day," for he was captured by the Germans in the South-West African campaign, and was a prisoner in Fort

Namutoni. When he was liberated by Botha he came over and fought in British East Africa. Then he joined the colonial service.

In his interest and understanding of the native, he reminded me of Major Hahn, the Native Commissioner, with whom I lived several useful weeks in Ovamboland, in remote South-West Africa. The natives would have followed him.

Behind him, in another room of the fort, sat the district officer; an Irishman, witty, balky as a horse at any display of sentimentalism, yet the man who said to me:

"You! You are going down to see *my* Masai! How dare you! You don't know them. You won't be able to do them justice!"

As I have said before, I suspected that he half meant it; he was very keen on *his* Masai. Yet he was a sophisticated man (he had been aide-de-camp to a former Governor); and he telephoned in my presence to the District Officer over the Masai, and, after suitable warnings about my menace, officially requested that District Officer to make Eve and me his guests.

The Masai are cattle raisers. Their life, under the open African sky, is just cattle. They are blood drinkers. They insert a tube in the neck of a living animal and drink its warm blood. And the animal goes on living. They are not Negroes. They are Nilotic. And their warriors are the most beautifully built men in Africa, perhaps in all the world.

I have never seen such men elsewhere!

The Masai and the Zulus have never met in battle, although they have come close to it. And it is still a question among anthropologists as to which side would have won. The Zulus had a saying, "He who goes forward into battle *may* die; he who retreats *will* die!" The Masai have precisely the same battle psychology. Today, when the "moran," their warriors, cannot blood their spears, they feel that life holds no purpose any longer. So they take to cattle stealing, then battles among themselves, between the senior and the junior "morans."

This, it must be stated, is to impress their women.

And it was into one of these battle scenes that we walked—that, and a female circumcision dance.

But before we meet the Masai, those strong warriors, see a few paragraphs from the provincial commissioner's "notebook," the year's report. With a bad case of flu and a handkerchief pressed to his nose, he was writing it for Dar es Salaam. It shows so delightfully his own ironic mind, the still existent bloodthirstiness of the natives under him, and what some of these natives thought of the Masai:

. . . East of the Rift, Masai thieving has stopped. But at Lolindoo and Ngorongoro they are not so good. There were two large-scale cattle raids, and, in December, a 40-cattle raid. This was done by the youths to prove their manhood. . . .

The laibon Mbeiya, the "spiritual head" of the Masai, died in October in the Arusha hospital. Mbeiya suffered from an acute complaint of the liver . . . but there are grounds for believing he thought himself bewitched. . . .

"He might have been," said the P.C. to me, drily. Then:

In 1938 a Masai killed a Sonjo, a "honey-hunter," presumably on the point of stealing. Four Sonjo warriors, thereupon, 36 hours later, murdered in cold blood three Masai herdsmen. War was expected. . . .

The Sonjos hid their women and stock and manned the defenses of their villages.

A party of 50-60 Loita "moran," from Kenya, set out to attack the Sonjos. They were prevented by the Masai elders.

The Sonjos hastened to pay over 450 goats—while the case is being investigated.

This is the first *known* case of Sonjo killing Masai.

This shows how protection from the Masai has given arrogance to the Sonjo. This is perhaps not quite the result at which "Pax Britannica" is usually aimed.

The provincial commissioner removed his damp handkerchief from his streaming nose, for a second.

"About that laibon," he said; "the members of the Engidon clan, from which the laibon is always chosen, are credited by the tribes with powers above those of ordinary mortals. They might be right." I read:

Mbugwe: These charming, but almost incurable sluggards, merely picked enough cotton this year to meet their tax—and left the rest to rot on the ground. It is hoped that, in 1939, under continuous European supervision, matters will improve . . .

Barabig: A murderers' tribe. The chief has been having trouble with his young men . . . only one Barabig was committed for trial on the charge of murder at the local Mbulu court. . . .

Chief Mikael Akho of Iraqw . . . continues to devote himself to the needs of his people . . . constantly on safari, in lorry, or on foot. . . .

Chief Gejar of the Barabig, having seen the benefit of an artificial lake . . . dug another branch furrow to create another artificial lake. . . .

One tribe did not want to drain a swamp as they regarded it as a natural protection from the Masai . . . and they still proudly point to where some one hundred Masai met a muddy death. . . .

"Blast these reports!" sneezed the sick commissioner. "Let's go and have tea."

But what vivid little vignettes these were of native life. And of the commissioner!

The District Officer over the Masai was a Welshman, a blond, bulldoggy little man, an Oxford graduate, who was just as touchy over *his* beloved Masai as was the Irishman back in Arusha over his men. Nevertheless, he was trying four of them the next morning on a charge which might give them two years in prison. "Although I don't like that," he said; "the Masai are inclined to die when you lock them up. About ten per cent kick out." He scratched his en brosse tow head: "I shall have to think of something else."

The red-roofed bungalow of the district officer lay on the crescent of a knoll surrounded by huge shade trees. I do not know their names. But, unlike the bare trunks of the jungle, which will rear up two hundred feet before they put out a branch to gasp for air, these trees have great extending branches beginning close to the earth. And their leaves were a vivid, living green. Directly facing the white stairs of his residence was a flame tree, flaring with the life of its scarlet candelabra. And on the lawn, which the wife of many a D.O. had improved with flower beds to give interest to her idle hours, a dozen "boys," with long, crook-shaped knives, which they switched back and forth from an upright position, were cutting the grass.

We had finished our breakfast of paw-paw, excellent bacon and eggs; and, after a second large cup of coffee, and a last regretful glance at the latest *Times*, which I had brought out to him, the D.O. put on his topee and we crossed the lawn. On the way we passed a smiling Bantu "boy" who was wheeling the D.O.'s first-born, a baby of one year, along the red drive around the crescent.

The "boy" had been humming something, but whether it was for his own consolation or the baby's amusement, I could not tell. A tall, white flagstaff stood on the lawn before the Government "boma," with the Union Jack hanging limply from its tip. Seated along the low cement veranda of the "boma" were some natives to be arraigned. They were from an inferior tribe, the Bantu, living in the jungle of the mountain behind us. They were not Masai. When the D.O. stepped upon the veranda a native policeman snapped out an imperative order to these natives, and they all stood up. The sergeant, dressed in shorts and a blue jersey, with a black pill-box hat, brought up his arm in quivering salute. Then I saw, for the first time, the four red-painted Masai, standing contemptuously apart in a group by the flagstaff.

They were junior "moran"; you could tell this because their eight-foot slender spears, nearly all steel, had a little six-inch middle haft of brown wood. With the senior "moran" this small section of wooden shaft is ebony black. Their hair was daubed red with ocher, and was dressed on their slender, flat-cheeked heads in the shape of a Roman helmet. They had long, thread-bound pigtails (the warrior's mark) hanging down their backs. And their sole bit of clothing was a blanket of soft, red skin, pinned over one shoulder. The other red shoulder was insolently bare. You could see their private parts when they turned sharply around.

They stood with the tips of their painted buffalo shields resting upon the lawn. Blue, white, and red; the designs of these beechnut shaped shields had the heraldic significance, bespeaking ancestry and prowess, of an English nobleman's crest.

"Good-looking lot, aren't they?" muttered the D.O., unruffled by the cool, painstaking unawareness with which the Masai made known their complete indifference to what he was about to do to them. "They always make me think of the centurions."

You must be an actor to handle natives. And the histrionic abilities of my host made me blush with shame. Such a deliberate pose, a Machiavellian use of "theater"! The D.O. put on a performance that was better than John Barrymore. I hung my head.

I had noticed, with the primitive Ovambas in South-West Africa, with the Masai here, and, later, among the tribes along the northern rim of Victoria Nyanza, that the chief native contribution, when he is talking with, or being talked to by a white man, is the interjection: "Ah!" or "A-a-a-a-h!"

And unlike Katharine Hepburn, of whom the acid Dorothy Parker said, in a review of her acting, she ran the emotional gamut from A to B, these black men, with their "Ah's," can express every emotion of the white or black man—and then beyond. Because they *imply* things; they have the quality of perfect art; they arouse emotions you cannot put into words.

When the D.O. sat down at his desk and opened his "case book," his good-humored face assumed an expression of acute concern. "A-a-a-h!" he said.

"A-a-a-h!" said the Masai interpreter, standing by his side. The Masai are not literate, and how this grizzled one had learned to read and write is immaterial—other than that it showed some terrific feat of will. In khaki slacks and tunic, with buttons bright, he stood reverently beside the young D.O., much as an elder statesman would wait upon the Mikado. He was a sage.

The first case stood before them.

This was a trivial affair; a "boy," appointed by an Arab as a cook, claimed he was not being paid his wages. The Arab, from Zanzibar, was sewing in one of the shops in the little Bantu village below the "boma." The D.O. merely said, "Ah!," with no inflection, and sent a "boma" clerk back with the "boy" to confirm his evidence.

The "boy" was dressed in blue corduroy shorts and a black-and-red striped football sweater.

Case No. 2, dressed in a white shirt, European coat and skirt—showing the ancient Arab influence—had a complaint against a white settler. He had wanted to borrow two shillings from the white man; and, so the white settler said in his letter to the D.O., "the 'boy' intends to skip his contract. I engaged him for a month, and he has only done two weeks."

"A-a-h!" said the D.O. He stared thoughtfully at the "boy." He frowned. The "boy" shifted uncomfortably from one bare foot to the other. "A-a-a-h!" said the D.O.

"Do you know," he said to the "boy" in Swahili, "that you can be put in jail if you don't finish the term of work you contracted for on your card?"

"Ah!" exclaimed the alarmed "boy."

"U-u-unh?" said the D.O., expectantly.

"Oh, it's all right," rapidly answered the "boy," in Swahili; "I'll go back and finish it. It doesn't make any difference to me, anyway."

The policeman led him out; the D.O. gave the settler's typewritten letter to the "boma" clerk to be answered. Then there was an interruption; a native secretary brought in the "cash book" of a native tribe up on the mountain; nearly all tribes in Tanganyika have these "cash books" and have to balance them. They can draw their own checks, but the D.O. must countersign them. The D.O., looking like a professional accountant this time, quickly surveyed the plus and minus on the book, saw that there was a remainder in hand, and countersigned the check which the tribe wished to draw. He then looked, sternly, at his "case book," for Case No. 3.

These were two Masai. They had red and purple beads around their slender necks, and terrific, dangling loops in their ears, from which hung heavy copper pendants like miniature pestles. They wanted permission to move from where they were stationed, at the Rift Wall, to thirty or forty miles out on the plains, where, they declared, their cattle would find better grazing. West of the Rift Wall there was no Government control for bovine malaria; the Masai impose their own quarantine. And that district, the D.O. knew, had rinderpest now.

"A-a-a-a-h!" he said, with deep concern—for the Masai. He explained to them that he did not see how they could move their cattle from this rinderpest area out on the plains. It would probably infect the healthy cattle of the other Masai. This was a case that needed going into. He sent for the book in which, apparently, are registered the names of all the taxpaying Masai. It was then disclosed that one of these men had not paid his poll tax for two years and the other, when he was challenged, now admitted that he had never paid one.

"A-a-a-a-a-a-h!!!" said the disillusioned D.O.
"Ah!" said the Masai, miserably.
This case was held over.

"If you tear a man's ear-flap," said the D.O. to me, while we were waiting for another case, "it's worse than rape or murder. Those chaps put in big spools of heavy soapstone to make their flaps longer. But—imagine it!—*never* paid any tax."

It is rare that quarrels among the Masai are brought up for a white man to settle; most intratribal troubles are adjusted among themselves, usually by compromises. This is done before a debating council in which the whole tribe takes part. When a dispute arises between a Masai and an alien, they let the case go to the D.O. And it is said that among themselves the Masai are extraordinarily just.

The telephone rang. It was from Arusha. Would the D.O. please send his assistant D.O. out into such-and-such a district, to enlist the help of the Wanderobo (a very primitive tribe of native hunters) in the search for a young German who had just come out to Tanganyika? He had been shooting in the bush with his companion, got lost—it was two days now—and his German companion feared he had been killed and eaten by lions.
(He had been.)
The D.O. got on the telephone to his assistant D.O., told him to take a lorry, and "Get going!"

"Silly ass!" said the D.O., when he put back the receiver. "Apparently he sent back the boy his pal had sent out to accompany him. Joy-through-health complex, or something like that. D.O. at Arusha says the Germans at Moshi are already 'darkly hinting' that it was his own German boy friend who killed him; apparently the one who came back was *not* a hot Nazi. Leave it to the Germans, to get politics even into a thing like this! Next case."

These were the four Masai junior warriors who had been standing so contemptuously out on the lawn. They left their spears stuck in the ground, with the shields leaning against them. These would, they knew, be quite untouched by any of this rabble parked outside on the "boma" steps. They filed in silently. I noticed that their slender legs were painted red with ocher up to their knees, as if they were wearing stockings.

Their case held hot interest. They belonged to "the party of the left hand," the "junior moran." They had been feeling their oats, flagrantly disobeying the orders of the "senior moran," who apparently bored them. Eight of these juniors had resolved to have a fight with the seniors. To do this, they wanted to separate a couple of "right-hand moran" from their senior colleagues, so they had invented a lion.

Four of them had rushed into the Masai "boma" (made of thorns), shouting that a lion was attacking their cattle. Two of the "senior moran," being handy, seized their spears and dashed out. (The Masai hunt and kill the lion with spears.) Then, when they were out on the steppe, beyond sight of the "boma," the junior warriors threw themselves on these two "senior moran."

"The trouble with this case," said the D.O. to me, "is that we've got only the accused here. One of their victims was taken to Arusha, where he is lying in hospital with, among other dents, a broken leg they gave him. The other refuses to come and testify against them; he's lying in the Masai 'boma,' getting well, getting ready to get his own back—and then there'll be another row!

"A hell of a row!" he added.

Then he turned to stare at the Masai. His bulldog face was set like a rock. This was no funny business. "A-a-a-a-a-ah!"

he said, without taking his eyes off them. The Masai stared back at him; their almond shaped eyes, with the staring pupil directly in the center, were like those enameled eyes you find in the tombs along the Nile, from the banks of which the ancestors of these beautiful men once came. Their noses were aquiline and their curling lips were sensitive, sarcastic. Then one of them held out a slender, aristocratic hand, and spoke softly:

The trouble was, he explained, that these two "senior moran" had attacked his sister. He pointed to his own bandaged head, where, he said, a "senior moran" had wounded him. It was the senior, the "right-hand moran," who had begun the attack. They . . .

"Ha!" snorted my host, contemptuously. "Ha!"

That was all. But I have never heard a man better called a liar to his face. The "moran" started, then stepped back. The D.O. looked at me and said: "Huh!" Then he shook his head and stared, as if completely disillusioned with *all* Masai by such deception. He shook his tow head gravely; then he gave a low, melodramatic moan, "A-a-a-a-a-a-h!"

What these staring "junior moran" did not know was that, carefully folded in the D.O.'s "case book," was a letter from the headman of their clan (he must have got some Sikh letter writer to do it for him); and it read, after giving the true story of their crime:

I'm fed up with these young men. I can't do anything with them. Will you please fine each of them 150s., or give them two years in jail.

When I point out that the Masai are not literate, perhaps I should also make it clear that they cannot count. They may not know how *many* cattle they have—there are 300,000 on their plains—but each owner knows every one of his cattle individually—he can instantly tell if one is not there!

"Tell them," the D.O. said with dramatic resignation to his

interpreter, "to speak straight words. The Masai do not lie. Don't these young 'moran' know that? Tell them they ought to be ashamed of themselves—they are not true Masai! They're degenerated!"

The old Masai, who would have been an elder, a headman, if he had stayed with his clan, knew how to squeeze the grapes of wrath over these young upstarts' heads.

Whatever he added to the D.O.'s withering words was affecting the four young warriors before us as if they were being flayed alive. They were in consternation. Not at all about what was going to happen to them; but that they—Masai!— should be talked to like that. Quickly the one with the bandaged head, their obvious ringleader, held up a protesting hand.

His manner had changed now. His words were no longer gentle. He stared straight at the D.O. and poured out every circumstance of the true story, even adding details that their headman evidently did not know. They were bored with the conceit of the "senior moran," said this young warrior, and they had given them what was coming to them. So what?

He stepped back against the wall. And the four stood silently, regarding a framed photograph that was above the D.O.'s head. It was a photo of four "right-hand" Masai, in full war paint.

"You know," said the D.O. to me, with what seemed shocking irrelevance, "when a Masai looks at a photograph he can *see* something; he knows what it means. Whereas the usual primitive Bantu will often hold it upside down; it doesn't convey as much impression to him as a dog gets facing its own image in a mirror. This is going to be a very hard case. Good-looking chaps, aren't they? I'll hold this one over."

And so ended a district officer's morning.

Once, in India, I went out into the Punjab with the district police officer, who was searching for a murderer. He held court in the various mud villages through which we passed, trying cases under the overhanging peipal trees, with the raucous peacocks screaming and swooping through their branches. I was impressed by the primitive justice with which he tried each case —very often, as he confessed to me, breaking the solemn regulations of the statutes book. "For," he said, "these people have their own particular code of ethics—sometimes quite horrible— but essential justice itself can only be administered when you can make *them* believe they have been doing wrong. For that reason, I very often have to make a compromise with our own code. For, as Pilate asked, 'What is truth?'"

I could see this same yeast working in the mind of the African district officer as we walked back across his pleasant lawn to luncheon. There were, he said, tribes around Meru who organized fights between themselves "just the way we would arrange a football match between Wales and England. They mean no harm by it; they are just expressing a vital instinct—the joy of battle. And these 'senior morans,' in some of these clans, must be intolerable! They take all the pretty girls. The 'morans,' you know, can take any of the young girls to live with them in their 'barracks,' so long as they don't put them in the family way. These Masai are an unfathomable race; we don't know half enough about them yet. And when I punish these four young wasters—which I shall do—I want them to *know* that they have done wrong.

"It presents a problem, doesn't it?" he concluded, as we sank down in the long chairs on his veranda. Eve and his attractive, black-haired Welsh wife were walking among the rose bushes in the garden. They were discussing, we learned afterwards, the different, changing style of ocher with the Masai; this year's tone had nearly ruined a Bantu tribe upon the mountain who previously had thrived upon their ocher mine. This year's tone was more subdued, and could only be obtained from a mine fifty miles away. The Bantu "boy" had put the tiny baby to bed, and was hanging up diapers on the line as he chatted with the house "boy" through the kitchen door. Miles away,

across the Masai plains, was a nebulous range of misty volcanic mountains.

"That blasted German!" said the D.O. "I suppose all they'll
find now is his hat."

The circumcision of females practiced by the Masai seems to
be carried out when a girl is around fourteen or fifteen. It is
something more thorough than a mere vulvectomy. And it
must hurt like hell. It is done by the old women of the clan,
with, nowadays, rusty safety razor blades. On the west coast of
Africa, where it is done with a sharp shell, it must be an even
worse agony. But the girls are not supposed to make even a
moan during it. In some clans of Masai, I am told, a cow pat is
placed upon each upraised knee of the girl while the operation is
going on; and if she flinches enough to shake one of them off
she loses face—so to speak.

I have talked with both men and women who have witnessed
the rite. They said they'd never heard a girl make a sound. And
in the Belgian Congo an *Administrateur* and his pretty young
wife showed us an album of photos they had made during this
dreadful ceremony. "*Bon; n'est-ce-pas?*" said the Belgian official. I told him that if he had them enlarged to post-card size,
he could make a fortune by standing in the Place Vendôme,
Paris. That pleased him greatly; he said he had often wondered what he should do, when he retired, to augment his
pension.

The Kikuyu, in Kenya, are even more savage in the extent
to which they carry out this operation. It maims some of their
women for life; it causes death in childbirth for others. And
when the Scotch mission, several years ago, tried forcibly to put
a stop to this practice, there was a furore that created a political
crisis of first magnitude between the natives and the Government at Nairobi. The missionaries were called off, officially.

At that time a mission girl, an advanced Kikuyu maiden who
refused to be circumcised, was waylaid by her father and some

Kikuyu men on the outskirts of the mission, taken to a hidden spot, and so brutally circumcised by two old women that she nearly died. She lay for months between life and death in the mission hospital. Then, when she got well, she sued her father.

She won £750 damages.

This was the first, and possibly the last, case of its kind ever to be brought before a court. And this female circumcision, so intimately interwoven with all the rites of tribal life, is a custom with which the Portuguese, French, Belgian, and British Governments interfere very gingerly. That is, when they say anything at all against it.

All over Africa, when you see these dusky débutantes going about with their faces painted white you know that it is only a question of hours now before they will willingly, proudly, undergo this horrible mutilation.

When I strolled along the coral strand of Mozambique Island I saw a half dozen girls washing themselves in its emerald surf, presumably preparing themselves for this important day in their life.

The aristocratic Masai do not invite witnesses.

A Masai "boma" is just a circle of thorns, inside which is a cluster of mud-and-dung huts, like igloos, less than shoulder high. You have to bend over, almost crawl, to get into them, and they are blue with acrid smoke which bites your eyes. Inside is usually a young calf, or so. The "boma" is about a hundred yards across. If it has been there any time to make it, there is a floor of cow dung as squishy as mud.

The beauty of the Masai, compared with the filth in which they live and have lived since anyone has known them, seems incomprehensible.

The "morans," the warriors, are not allowed to marry. "Junior moran" are from the age of about nineteen to twenty-four; "senior" from around twenty-four to thirty. When they reach thirty they cut off their pigtails, put away their spears, and become married men. The wiser and richer among them become elders; and one, of course, is destined to become head-man. They do not have a chief.

They elect the headmen at a tribal council, and when they see that an elder's "gray matter" is waning they chuck him out. Lembelikeli, the headman of the "boma" we were coming to, was reputed to be one of the most influential men among all the Masai.

He came out of the "boma" to receive us. A strip of dark Indian cloth was slung over one shoulder, and he was carrying his sign of office, a black baton, in his hand. He had the bearing of a Roman senator. A pear-shaped gourd of milk was pro-duced; the milk was smoked, and had an acrid tang that was very appetizing. After the D.O. had drunk, and said: "Aa-a-a-a-a-ah!"—as if he had never enjoyed anything so much in his life, that shameless actor!—Eve and I did likewise. We have, in our time (on the puszta of Hungary), eaten even chickens' eyes, for politeness' sake.

We also said, "Aa-a-a-a-ah!" with, we hoped, equal con-vincingness.

The incidence of syphilis is rather high among the Masai.

The Masai have a strange odor—aromatic, spicy, like the smell of a wild animal. It is not unpleasant. Eve had her nose pressed against the flank of a Masai warrior when he was being taken on the running board of our car out to where he had spotted three elephants in a swamp. She said she rather liked the odor.

And Eve, who has more moral courage in these things than I have, asked the headman if we could not see the two girls who had just been circumcised. His wise brown eyes regarded her thoughtfully.

"Why not?" was his considered reply. "You are not savages."

"Pretty good!" said the D.O. to us, sotto voce. "The old boy was saying we are not an inferior tribe, like the Bantus. Rather encouraging, that."

In some tribes the girls are made to sit in a stream all night before circumcision, so that the cold water will partially anesthetize them. In other tribes, with a nocturnal pandemonium of chants, drumbeats, and the sight of men leaping around fires, the girls can acquire a fervor, a dervish-like frenzy, which makes them almost ignore pain. But these girls had not had that.

The hut in which they lay became like the stock scene in the days of the old silent movies—the Ford which, when its door is opened, emits a stream of about a hundred people. From this low mud hut emerged, it seemed to us, about twenty warriors, some grinning old women with yards of copper telephone wire around their necks, and a handful of small children.

When we crawled in we met a young calf and two kids. It was almost completely dark, except for the light which came from a small hole in the wall. A rancid fire was burning. Both girls were, obviously, completely knocked out. But they were also completely silent. One sat upright, with her mother beside her in silent commiseration—or was it pride? And the other lay on her back, staring up with blank eyes.

I was glad to get out.

A band of visiting Masai came, with their graceful, loping stride, across the grassy steppe to the "boma." The local clan lined up with their shields and spears to meet them, and stood ceremoniously in a long row, each with his shield resting on the ground before him. The visitors passed in line, reaching out long, ocher-reddened hands just to press their palms against those of the local Masai, then they wandered about, arm in arm, or holding each other's hands, like girls. Their slenderness accentuated this feminine mannerism.

The dance was preceded by the Masai "moran" hopping up

into the air, without, it seemed to me, even bending their knees to jump. It was as unbelievable as levitation. Then the girls, from the smallest virgin in the tribe (and there was hardly a female there who had not been tampered with) formed in long lines on each side of the warriors. "A-hunh-hunh-hunh!" With a rhythmic moan, a soughing sound like that of surf, they moved step by step forward.

In Kenya they have taken away the heraldic shields of the Masai. It is claimed that the "moran" go mad, at times, when they see the shields. This is true. Today two or three Masai in the dance suddenly had a frenzy strangely like epileptic fits. They commenced to groan and cough and make noises like a wild animal. Their mouths frothed. They have been known, in these fits, to sling a spear at the nearest person handy, or else whip out the strange little flat sword they carry and—this was an actual case—almost cut him in half.

But they do not carry, in this dance, spears or shields, which are stuck into the ground at a convenient distance. And the Masai who had not become so worked up flung themselves on the others and held them until their moaning and heaving ceased.

This is all very authentic. And, I think, pathetic. "The sight of the shields!" That this can invoke in the Masai such a tempest of emotions, all concerned with a life that is forever dead, brings sad reflection.

When Eve, the D.O., and I were standing there, a figure, almost legendary, stalked across the plain. It was a "junior moran," completely reddened, striding with staring eyes and open lips towards the dancers. As he strode past he saw the D.O., turned quickly, and came up. He thrust out his slender arm to press his palm against the D.O.'s. Then he smiled.

I think he was, perhaps, the most beautiful, yet insolent, man I have ever looked at. The D.O. was immensely pleased.

"Rogue of all rogues!" he said in an awed whisper as the

painted warrior strode off. "He comes up and shakes hands with *me!* He wants to show there's no ill will. That fellow's the most daring cattle thief among these Masai. Last week I fined him £15, which is a lot of money, and which his clan will have to pay. And the rogue comes and shakes hands with me. What a sport!"

When the Masai hunt the lion, with spears, they surround it, closing in with provocative shouts. The lion, switching his tail with anger, glares from one approaching figure to another. Finally he charges, in great pounces, like a cat. The Masai who sees the charge coming towards him kneels down on the ground, spear ready, and *takes* the charge on his shield.

He usually gets in his thrust, and, the next instant, the lion is a pincushion of trembling Masai spears. But the Masai who takes the charge is nearly always mauled, and in many cases he is killed.

The D.O. in Arusha, who said, "How dare you write about *my* Masai!" had lived five years with them. When he first attended one of these lion hunts, he could not stand the sight of just one slender Masai, crouching under the shield, waiting for the lion to jump on him. He shot the lion.

"You!" The Masai were outraged. "Here you go! We invite you to come and see a lion hunt—and then you go and spoil it!"

"It took a long time," said the D.O., "before I ever lived that down!"

The Masai idea is that the Masai are "the salt of the earth." All the rest, including Europeans, are beneath them. They are the perfect egoists.

19. Night on a Crater

WEST and north of Ngorongoro crater graze some of the greatest game herds left in Africa. You doubt, as you watch them, if they ever could have been any larger. For some species, I don't think they have. I have stood on the running board of my car and looked across a single herd of wildebeest, and their backs glinted in the sun as far as I could see. These Serengetti plains, waiting for the rains, stretched out in vast sweeps of unbroken distance, lying low under the accumulating clouds. With pastel intangibility a few blue mounds of hills rose at an infinite distance. And on these, among the glinting boulders, the leopards lie and yawn in the midday sun. These immense plains are crossed by a few wooded rivers. And here, among the acacias and thickets of thorn, prowls the greatest lion population in all Africa. Their favorite food, the zebra, is so plentiful on these grassy spaces that after a time even those pleasant, fat-rumped little creatures begin to pall on you. Tommies and Grant's gazelles stand and stare in herds of hundreds. Then they take it into their pretty heads that they simply *must* cross the plain before your car. Their russet flanks with black stripes stretch out; in great jack-knife leaps they bound beside the car, quickening their pace, until the leaders, swift as arrows, shoot through the air before you. Then they stop, stare incredulously, and twitch their ridiculous little tails.

You slow down, of course, for you do not break this peace by "racing" the herds. You try to allow them to settle. And then, with a great thunder of hoofs and rising dust, a mighty herd of wildebeest will begin the same silly game all over again.

In the night, crossing Etosha Pan, in South-West Africa, I have been aware of the black wildebeest racing beside me like frenzied spirits on a haunted moor; bullfrogs big as pug dogs staring at my lights in rapidly nearing mudpuddles; the scintillating pink of the klipspringer's eyes, bounding up and down as their jumps led them towards the challenge of my two glowing lamps; and then the roar and splash and flying of manes as three huge, black, rocking wildebeest shot across directly in front of me. The violence of this charge, often less than ten yards ahead of you, is a startling experience.

These Serengetti plains are so untroubled by man, particularly on the eve of the disastrous rainy season, that you frequently come upon hyena in broad day. I drove to within less than twenty feet of two of them in a mudhole. They emerged angrily, staring at me as malevolently as only a hyena can, over their dirty sloping backs.

The distance plays tricks, and a figure that we had taken to be a Masai shepherd in a white cloak (an impossibility) turned out to be a greater bustard with its wings spread out. Investigating a thorn thicket, we put up a lioness and watched her pad off with a sullen dignity which, in everything but words, said, "I simply will not be hurried."

At Lion Hill, which we reached with five of the thirteen leaves of my front springs unbroken, we had the sudden shock of having a leopard drop directly out of a thorn tree just ahead of us. It had been lying up there, stretched almost invisible along a branch, and obviously waiting for a buck to pass. And it dropped in what seemed nothing less than a stream of spots.

We had intended to drive across these roadless plains, and then on, finally to reach Musoma, on Victoria Nyanza. From there we had planned to ship the car up to Entebbe, in Uganda. Bad weather, by good luck, prevented us. We should have been lost, mired, on the Serengetti, for months, and aeroplanes would probably have been sent out to drop food to us—as had been done for a foolhardy party the previous rainy season. Instead, we were forced to do what had been really in our hearts, and that was to drive up into Kenya, then cross-country to Uganda, where we arrived at Entebbe a month or so late on our already timeless schedule.

There were two things I had resolved to do before I left Africa—or else never leave Africa. They were to get one lion and one buffalo. I did not want to shoot any of the beautiful buck, or any other animal, nor did I wish to commit that monstrous crime (for a passer-by), destroy an elephant. I did not know until much later, when I was shooting in Kenya, that the elephant will probably be the last of the big game to vanish from Africa.

I could not shoot out on the Serengetti, for that is now a game sanctuary. And the enterprising proprietor of Arusha's "English" hotel (the other one is run for Germans) has turned the lions of the Serengetti into a debased form of trick circus. American tourists who wish to see "the majestic lion in his native habitat" are taken out onto the Serengetti in luxurious safaris, in limousines, with trucks carrying their camp kit, and there they see lions, (a) playing tug-of-war with a dead buck or piece of meat being towed behind a truck; (b) lions actually jumping into the back of a truck for some meat that has been placed there; (c) a lion actually entering a tent and taking out a piece of meat, while a score of frightened bystanders look on. Lions are fed by the safari manager, close enough for photographs to be taken of both lions and the jolly tourists having their luncheon.

The photographs taken on these expeditions, for the tourists to take back to New York or Iowa, are absolutely authentic. There is one thing which must be said about the proprietor of that hotel: he fakes nothing. And you more than get your full money's worth. But there are two things to be said against it: First, it debases the lion; next, what about some poor soul who doesn't know about these frolics? When he gets out to fix a tire, will he be annoyed when a lion walks up and jumps into the back of his lorry? The lion will, if he doesn't find any meat. He will very likely maul the man. For this reason, because the lions have been taught to *expect* food when they see a motor-car coming (a sort of conditional reflex, as in Pavlov's experiments) the lions come up when they see you! It's dinner time. And, for this reason, the lion, which is the most fearless (and therefore safe) animal in Africa, becomes dangerous.

You are told, when you go out on the Serengetti alone, that under no condition must you get out of your car. A ridiculous injunction! On the Serengetti plains I spent more time out and under my car than I did in it. We had two punctures on our way out to Lion Hill.

Eve and I welcomed our departure from that comfortable Arusha hotel, with its eight huge buffalo heads, staring at us from their eyeless sockets as they hung in a prehistoric frieze on the dining-room walls.

"On your way," said a little, gray, English colonel, "you might stop at my place and have a filthy meal."

His home, a damp little bungalow lost in creepers, lay in the gloom of dark cypress, silver oak, and a wet mire of decaying banana stalks. But encircling it, as if in a desire to forbid him to live in such shadows, were great, white banks of open moonflowers. "Cheerful plants," he said with his deprecating air; "would you like to look at my ghastly coffee?"

The shade trees had been allowed to cut off the proper amount of sun from his berries. His banana plants had run riot in a jungle of their own. There was no order, and he said: "I haven't been able to eat a banana from my place for years. Natives always come in here at night and steal them before I get ready to eat. So this year I've had my 'boys' pick a few bunches for me while they're still green. Ripening them inside my house. S'pose my house 'boy' will eat them. A lion chased my cat around the house last night."

The luncheon was, as he had promised, filthy. He chuckled as he told us he had cooked each course himself. "Here's my *spécialité de la maison*," he said grimly, when he put down the sweet. "Ghastly!"

It was. It was nothing less than a suet roly-poly over which he had poured Italian vermouth!

"I've got some wretched little cattle outside," he said. "If you could bear the sight of them."

The cattle did look rather mingy, and I asked him what he did with them. He replied:

"I watch 'em die. Rinderpest. East Coast fever. Gall fever. Natives drive all their cattle across my land, you know. So they all get it."

"But what about your wire fence?"

"Oh, they stole all my wire, every beastly foot, from the entire estate. Make it into armlets for the Masai girls. You can bet your life a Masai never *buys* a foot of wire in his life."

"But what about your 'boys'?"

"I keep a hundred of them—that's what I mean to the country—but they're too lazy to move."

"How many cattle have you got?"

"Don't know. Haven't counted them lately. 'Bout eight hundred, I should think. Half of them get born or die before their time."

When he called a "boy," we saw the "boy" sneaking off to hide in the bushes.

"What's the meaning of that?" I asked.

"Oh, he's afraid if he comes up to me that I shall give him a job of work. Like to see some giraffes?"

I do not know how many hundred, or thousands, of acres he had. (I'm not certain he did, either.) But after ten or twenty minutes' drive through a wilderness of scrub, which had never been touched, he pointed ahead. There was a huge male giraffe, almost black, staring at us from over a thorn tree.

There was a herd of giraffe, a line of forty-eight inquisitive, long-eared heads, all watching us curiously from above the thorn forest. Behind, so far away, and so faint that its blue cone was almost figmentary against the lighter sky, rose a volcanic mountain.

"Are these giraffes always here?" I asked, in astonishment.

"I don't know. When I came out here to shoot a lion the other day—he had been annoying my beastly cattle—I found them. Pretty things, aren't they? And *so* inquisitive!"

The old bull, who was getting a bit gray around the top, like the colonel, flicked his ears, fixed his eyebrows in concentration, then began to rock—ker-lump, ker-lump, ker-lump! The huge herd of living towers rocked off. It was as if their legs had no joints in them. And their great hoofs beat a subdued thunder. In Kenya, along the Mara, I have cursed these beautiful animals, for when they become alarmed their heavy-sounding beat stampedes all the game on the plain. I spent the better part of a day trying to get within shot of a herd of buffalo, only to have giraffe stampede the herd again and again.

But this herd of giraffes was remarkable. They had probably been free guests of the colonel for years. He, of all men, would not bother them. And now, as time and again we crept up to within twenty or thirty feet of them, he, Eve and I, hidden, squatted there in silent delight as we watched their well fed spotted flanks glistening in the African sun. There were seven calves among them, much lighter in color. With frisky tails. I whispered to the colonel how, over in South-West Africa, old "Mooie" had assured me that giraffes make the best whips; but, I added, I didn't see how even a Boer could bear to shoot one.

"I'd *much* rather shoot a man," said the colonel.

We thanked him for his "odious luncheon," which pleased him immensely, then we drove towards the blue wall of the Great Rift.

"But he has charm," said Eve, after we had been driving for some time in silence. We had just passed the long shamba, with its regimented coffee plants, of the South African Jew, who alone ships 400 tons of the 750 tons of coffee that go out to the world from around Arusha. His place was as meticulously run as a vineyard in Burgundy; I'm sure he even knew the number of *berries* he had!

"Yes, charm," I nodded, for I knew Eve was still thinking about the gray little colonel. "I've just been wondering what it is that *stimulates* him; he's bubbling like a fresh bottle of soda!"

"I think it's the giraffes," said Eve.

"Or things like that?"

I pointed to where, on our right, the blue wall of the Great Rift lay like a painted band along the lighter sky. It was some forty miles off, and we knew that we should have a zigzag climb of two thousand feet to get up its escarpment. And on the left, in a prehistoric skyline, stretched the long panorama of volcano cones.

"Yes; he doesn't fuss about life. He just loves living *here*."

"A true settler? He does not need the world any longer."

"Of course. What business is it of anybody's if he doesn't make as much money as he should from his coffee? What if he does pig it—if he's contented? He's happy. I'd much rather have his life than X's!"

X was an Italian settler. A modern Italian. Tall and—if you can imagine it—a very masculine actor type; he was a good six feet three, all bone and muscle and Fascist arrogance. He was a great friend of the late Marshal Balbo, who, he was quick to tell me, had been sent to Libya not because of the Duce's fears of having a high head of corn in the field, but to make a real colony. And it was obvious that he thought someone like Marshal Balbo was needed to pull Tanganyika into shape. (This was before Balbo's death.)

Otherwise he was a charming Italian of noble family, happy with a beautiful and wealthy Dutch wife. They already had three children; and everything on the place at the moment— wife, tenants, cats, dogs, a tame deer—seemed in the family way. "Which," he said, "ought to please Mussolini."

His stone veranda, built upon the slope of a mountain, looked out into fifty miles of space across the Great Rift. The level floor of the Rift was so far below us that it looked like a smooth carpet of patterned greens. We watched the shadows of the clouds drift across it. In the distance humps of blue volcanic mountains lay under the gathering thunder of these clouds. It was an eagle's perch, an aerie upon which it would be almost impossible for a man to sit and not dream great dreams. And certainly X was troubled with them.

"The Governor of a colony," he said sternly, "must be a complete dictator, a demagogue. Lesser men should not be allowed to interfere with him, especially people back home— politicians who don't know what a colony is! Grandi and Balbo, for instance, can't stand each other. Grandi is the perfect diplomat; he will fit into the scheme of things. Balbo won't; he will *make* the scheme of things; he will demand 100 per cent responsibility. That's why the Duce gave him Libya."

I was dead wrong, he asserted, when I supposed the Italians were populating Libya from the overcrowded, starving peasants of southern Italy. "Just the contrary," he said; "we are sending good, well-to-do peasants from the north. We are making a *real* colony of Libya. It is no makeshift affair; our Italian idea of colonies is not to make them human dumping grounds."

He liked the English, and was quite obviously of the manly, sporting type of Latin whom the English would like and understand. But he said:

"England hasn't the settlers to come here. That's the real trouble with English 'colonization' these days. And if a country has not the settlers to send out, she has no right to keep a colony, as a sports ground in which to shoot and kill things!

"Look at Kenya! It's pathetic! Twenty-five years—and look at the 'settlers'! *Speculation!* The big men secured land through influence, then they sold it to the suckers who came out.

"Royal Commission! Eyewash! Eyewash! You can't go on forever throwing dust into the eyes of the settlers. Where and what *is* England's Tanganyika policy?

"My dear friend, England is always talking about this famous 'up the sleeve.' They've always got 'something up their sleeve'!" He grunted, and sneered down his own tweed cuff.

"There is *nothing* up that sleeve! If we, or the Germans, had Tanganyika, we'd have 50,000 settlers here!"

"But what about the natives?" I asked meekly. "Where would they live?"

"They would work on our farms," he said, haughtily.

And that was just it!

For Africa, the British lack of initiative was probably the kindest thing. Don't harry the old black continent, let it yawn and emerge from its primeval sleep without hurry. Yes, I concluded in my thoughts, if England can be strong enough to hold Tanganyika against all comers, if the people at home ever realize, once England has come here, that the natives cannot be passed about any longer among white men like slices of cake. Yes, if—

Mussolini had been particularly outrageous on the radio the previous night: "Too long a period of peace is bad for civilization. . . . We will have more ships, guns . . . even if we have to famish civilian life. . . ."

I pointed out to Eve how even Bismarck, when the Congo Basin treaties were being formed, tried to get the European powers to agree that no war of their own should ever be carried to the African continent. But with men like this modern

Italian settler and the Nazis, no peace seemed in sight for emerging Africa.

The great explorers, the great administrators, the great men, white or black, even the great days, were gone, and now the African natives faced the cheerful prospect of being "civilized" by second-rate men being sent out from a Europe which had returned to barbarism itself.

As I have said repeatedly, the colonial administrators have, strictly as individuals, risen above European standards in their effort to establish a decent progressive life for the natives entrusted to them. This was true of most Native Affairs officials, even in the Union of South Africa. But whenever you read in your London or New York paper that a big commercial company has been formed in London, or an existing one has just embarked upon a program *"which will be best for the native,"* you may look up the definition of just one word in the dictionary: "Hypocrisy."

You will never know, unless you happen to be on the spot, just what such hypocrisy can mean. But from the days when the Matabele War was fought (for the benefit of the Chartered Company) to the latest combination of the cocoa-buying interests in London against the native growers of the Gold Coast, the heart of the London business man in London City is unchanged. It is not capable of contemplating such charity as would diminish one tithe of its profits—not these choleric-cheeked, cigar-smoking "gentlemen" in London. (Any more than they wanted to change living conditions in London itself, where, up to this war, at least one of the biggest department stores, always boasting of its welfare manager, was paying its girl clerks £1 a week, and forcing them to live in.)

Why should we Englishmen and Americans, when we are aware of so much skulduggery and meanness going on at home, think that we should suddenly become such pure-minded altruists in our business overseas and in colonial administration? It seems such a buffoonery of conceit.

Therefore, as opposed to all the "efficiency" that German colonization would bring in, and the regimentation of colonization, such as X, the Italian, would like—a ruthless Balbo for Tanganyika—the sprawling, shabby shamba of the little gray colonel seemed to be doing less *harm* to Africa. It is practically certain that by bringing the white man's scientific inventions to Africa we shall destroy or devitalize the Africans as we have ruined the American Indians.

God knows, although the rest of us seem loath to admit it, that we are being destroyed by our own inventions ourselves!

A holiday from "progress" seems needed for the world; for Africa, particularly. In fact, what most white men are striving for in Africa seems to me nothing less than catastrophic for the natives.

An ascent of 2,000 feet does not mean very much in a European's life, or to his ability to exist; in Africa it usually means the difference between hell and a grateful freedom from physical misery. I would not say heaven. The plaque of Lake Manyara hit our eyes like the blazing sun itself as we drove towards the blue mistiness behind it that was the Great Rift wall, rocking in the heat haze. I envied the hippos wallowing in the waters. There was a great emptiness around us on the yellow plain; we stampeded a few herds of wildebeest and zebra. We passed castellated gray anthills that were higher than my head. We passed into gray volcanic dust which we ground through in second gear. And once or twice, for no reason at all, we were bogged. An Indian motor lorry, full of shouting Sikhs, halted while its turbaned occupants warned us not to continue on the road tracks we were following. They had been bogged all morning—eight lusty Sikhs—and they told us, very kindly, that they had put some thorns across the road, to block it, where they had rejoined it after their detour.

"Where is your 'boy'?" they asked.

"We have none."

"Where are you going?"

"The Serengetti."

"Ho, no, sahib!" their driver laughed. "You're not going there!"

"Why not?"

"You see!" they said. Then they drove on, all laughing.

At the foot of the Rift Wall itself was a native village, a few mud walls, thatched with banana leaves, on each side of the road, and a planked gasoline station. Its men were asleep in the sun. Those of its women who were awake were putting plaits into each other's kinky hair. They laughed, and made a few indecent jokes among themselves, as they stared at Eve and me. We should have trouble, the Indian said, getting up the escarpment; rains had washed away a good deal of the road; we had better take plenty of extra water, as our radiator would boil over. Beyond the village was one of the most peculiar, poisonous looking growths of jungle I have seen. In outline, it was strikingly similar to a dense beech woods. But not only were its leaves a vivid green—every trunk, every branch looked as if it had been sprayed with moss-green paint. It had beauty. And yet it was a frightening thing to look at.

Another Indian truck coming down, its locked wheels failing to hold their grip among the avalanche of small, sliding shale, nearly pushed us off into space. When I saw the Indians deliberately charging down upon us—for I saw that they made no attempt to brake until nearly on top of us—I deliberately took the inside of the road, against the cliff, and let them take their bullying chances. They slid by with about a foot to spare between them and a 1,000-foot drop. And they went on (I judged by our exchange of curses) more moderate Indians.

If you have ever met an Indian lorry driver, coming down the middle and taking the whole of the road on *any* road in East Africa, you will understand.

+

On top of the Rift we came into open, rolling grasslands. They were amazingly like prairies. The grass had been burnt yellow this late in the year, and the few thorn trees might easily have been a scattered orchard. A buck or so occasionally got up from under one of them, stared at us placidly, then bounded off easily. A more somber note was the sudden ascent of fluttering yellow butterflies from off a fresh ball of elephant dung in the road. The red sun sank in a notched and rolling line of mountains. From the brush the eyes of many animals glowed as they stared. We dropped down a ridge into the spring-shattering bed of a dry red river, and, then, climbing up its steep bank, saw the upright, oblong light of a door across the space of another ravine. This was the German store at Oldeani.

By now our car and its modest equipment had taken on a definite personality. It was not much more than twenty minutes after we had reached a place before we were "settled in." Burlap bags, with our camp beds inside them, were first taken out of the rear locker; then, as I set up these and stretched a rope for the mosquito nets, Eve began cooking dinner.

This was always on the little four-shilling alcohol stove. It lasted us across Africa. It was limited, but sufficient; for the same water that had been heated to warm a tin of mulligatawny soup was now brought into immediate action to cook a tin of Vienna sausages. Small sections of meat or birds—and, when we could get them, bacon and eggs—were cooked and kept warm in our heavy iron frying pan. An aluminum tin of coffee came to a boil while we ate. Then, if the flies or gnats weren't too unbearable, we read, or I wrote, until we were tired.

That night, before I turned in, I took a short stroll around the little mound on which stood a neat Government rest house. In the misty moonlight I saw that some of the clouds were even below me in the valleys. The dark wall of Ngorongoro crater rose above us. A native policeman stamped his bare feet, saluted, and said we should sleep with our windows closed. "There are robber men about!" And I cocked my finger at him in playful imitation of a revolver.

He seemed to blanch, even under the moon: "No, master; don't shoot!"

I explained to him carefully and gently that I never carried a revolver. A man would be foolish to do such a thing. He saluted and, smiling, left me.

The next morning we found out that the huge native, with a pronounced squint, to whom had been given our dishes to wash, was a convict out on long parole.

The story of the German self-contained settlement at Oldeani, with its own hospital, school and store—and not one Englishman about—is a pretty good example, in a quiet way, of the reckless determination in German character; yet at the same time it shows how the British, by adhering scrupulously to the ethics of the mandate, have even penalized their own nationals rather than infringe the trust of their mandate for Tanganyika.

It shows a law-abiding toleration strangely similar to that which the British exercised for seven months during this war towards the German violation of all international law.

As I have said, all the German holdings in Tanganyika were confiscated after the last war. The proceeds of their sale were credited to the reparations account, and it was left to the good will of the German Government to compensate its own nationals for the holdings they had lost.

But in 1925 the Germans were allowed to come back into Tanganyika, to settle on an equal basis with the British or any other settlers. An Englishman setting out from Southampton with £100, and a German sailing from Hamburg with the same amount of money, or trade goods, had equal chances. However, the British at this time considered that unless the Germans, or whoever else wanted fresh land, could buy some land from a present European holder, no more land could be taken away from the natives for European settlement.

In Tanganyika, a country larger than France, only something over 1½ per cent of the land had been alienated for Europeans. Two-thirds of Tanganyika belonged to the tsetse fly. The rest was being held in trust for the natives.

No more land was to be opened. Yet in 1927 an adventurous band of Germans trekked westwards from Arusha and squatted, at around 6,000 feet, in the virgin rain forest on the sides of Ngorongoro crater. With them came quite a number of Boers.

The German storekeeper at Oldeani told me they trekked on foot the 111 miles, and he himself had seventy native porters, each carrying the maximum head-load of 60 pounds. For six months he lived in a tent, with his German wife. And when this store was built it was only a native mud-and-wattle house, with a thatched grass roof. Meanwhile, the adventurous Germans were hacking out clearings in the dense elephant- and rhino-infested forest, to make way for some of the finest coffee planting in East Africa.

When the British Government at Dar es Salaam awoke to what was going on, it ordered the settlers to vacate. This land was being held in trust for the natives. The Dutch-Boer settlers obeyed. The Germans refused. They said they would take the matter up with the League of Nations. Dar es Salaam (probably under pressure from Whitehall) backed down. The Germans were allowed to stay. And a new land report was then made, which said that now there just wasn't any more land available for European occupation.

This was called the Bagshaw Report. All British settlers in the mandate will tell you that it has done more to harm British settlement than anything else done in Tanganyika.

That, of course, is the settlers' point of view. The natives' would be precisely the opposite.

The head of the German colony at Oldeani was, up to this war, a certain Herr Buxell. He was an aristocrat, an ex-naval officer of the Kaiser's fleet, who went to Dar es Salaam in 1907.

"I fell so in love with the country," he told me as we stood looking over his coffee estate, "that I left the imperial navy and bought a farm on the slope of Kilimanjaro. When the war of 1914 broke out my place was worth about £50,000. I lost it."

He fought for three years under von Lettow-Vorbeck. He was bayoneted, left in the bush for dead, discovered, and nursed to health by a British doctor; then he was sent to be imprisoned in India.

After the war, these things then happened to Herr Buxell: His estate was lost in Tanganyika—a Greek had bought it for £1,000; the crash of the mark left him penniless.

He went to Sumatra, where for fifteen years he was the manager of a Dutch plantation. In 1933, hearing of this German settlement at Oldeani, he wrote to an old friend, a German professional elephant hunter, and asked whether he could buy the lease on these very acres on which we were standing.

"You see," he said to me with a smile, "I fought over this very place in the war. I always remembered it—it was so beautiful!"

The white hunter bought it at auction for him—300 acres, on a 99-year leasehold of sixpence an acre to the State.

When I walked with this ex-German naval officer, a man who had been in more bayonet charges in the African jungle than he liked to remember, he showed me the coffee trees he had planted year by year. Below us lay a 35-mile-wide valley full of rhino and buffalo. Towards the sun we saw the waters of 100-mile-long Lake Eyasi glinting in the setting rays. He told me how he had built his strong but pleasant home 6,000 feet up the mountain, of mud, rocks, bamboos, and mortar, in three months.

"It's all here," he said with an understandable pride, as we looked down over his terraced coffee plantation. "I have got started again!"

Since 1933, when he first came, he had become the president of the German coffee planters at Oldeani; he was on the board of the mixed British and German planters for the Meru and

Kilimanjaro districts; he was also a member of the Government's coffee board.

This year, he said, he would get his first crop. With typical German thoroughness he showed me how, after all expenses had been paid, he would have about £1,000 a year clear from his present 100 acres under coffee.

"That will allow me to educate my children in the way I want them brought up. And every three years or so the whole family will meet in the fatherland. I shall have enough money to travel, and live in Germany in the manner I am accustomed to. I have a good life!"

He was a man of good type, as were so many others of the officers of the Kaiser's navy, as has been shown by the rapidity of his rise in position during the six years he had been back in Tanganyika. We had a big German five-o'clock coffee with him and his good-natured wife and the three tow-headed children. He had made himself one of those circular table trays which spin, allowing you to bring opposite you the jars of wild honey, the homemade blackberry jam, the whipped cream, in a game which kept the children clutching eagerly until they were "ssshed!" by their mother.

"But the news," he said, eyeing me intently; "it is not so nice; yes?"

"No." I shook my head.

His wife's eyes left the children and looked to my wife. "No," said Eve; "it is very bad."

The German settler and his wife looked at each other across the table, for just one unguarded moment.

There was one thought, we all knew, that was in the minds of all of us, all except the children. It was: What a pity to get started, and then lose all this again!

He never got that first crop.

When you are actually on its slope you are not able to grasp the immensities of Ngorongoro crater. The fact that in some prehistoric age this was a volcano which blew off a top that was over ten miles in diameter just will not present itself to you. You never get an image of Ngorongoro in your mind's eye. Up to 8,000 feet its mountainous slopes are deep with dense, virgin jungle. In the mysterious, dark depths of this forest roam herds of elephants. One of the German planters on Ngorongoro told me that he had counted 250 elephants on his place the previous year. Herr Buxell told me that his nearest neighbor had been killed on his shamba by a female elephant three years before. And the largest tusker on record was killed by an Arab, in a similar rain forest on the slopes of Kilimanjaro, in 1889. Its tusks weighed, respectively, 230 and 235 pounds. They were sold in Zanzibar for £1,000. He shot it with an old-fashioned, muzzle-loading rifle. It might be interesting to note here that the average weight of all tusks imported into Zanzibar does not exceed, probably, 30 to 40 pounds. When I drove up along the mountain road that Herr Buxell had cut to get to his coffee shamba, I saw, on a narrow bit of road, two fresh balls of elephant dung. I thought about them most of the afternoon while I was talking with Buxell; I did not want to have to face the challenge of an elephant in possession of that road, on my way back.

To picture the tangled complexity of a rain forest you must deal with emotions rather than attempt a description of vegetation. To reach the lip of Ngorongoro crater, which is only 8,000 feet high, there is a road that is nine and a half miles long. Covering that distance took me from around nine o'clock in the morning until just this side of sunset. And a heavy lorry, from the game department, making a last desperate dash out on the Serengetti before the great rains came, started just after me and did not reach the camp until nearly midnight. My own purpose, to spend the night on Ngorongoro crater and then get as far out on the plains as I dared, before the rains, required some relief plans before I chanced it. The plan was that, if I did not return to the German store at Oldeani within three days, a big motor lorry was to be sent out to look for me.

"But the blan is unbractical!" said the storekeeper. "You get stuck, den someone comes to look for you, and he gets stuck! So what?"

"Send along another lorry."

"You are joking!"

I told him that we were serious. Then he said:

"I gannot promise that anyone here will want to do it. And it vill cost you a lot of money!"

I looked at the clouds. They were hanging low over the rain forest. Then I asked him for spare tins, which we filled with extra gasoline and water, and with a car stripped of everything but camp beds, blankets and a light cooking kit, we set out.

"Py Jof," said the storekeeper, when I paid him for the fuel, "I wish I was going with you! I haf never seen the Serengetti."

The emotion of entering a rain forest near the equator is that you pass from rolling scrub country, where the scattered thorns are seldom over twenty feet high, into a dense mass of jungle which at once shuts off most of your light and air. You see the smooth trunks rising like pillars from the mass of undergrowth, and, falling from them, a great network of lianas drops into the jungle again. You become aware that life is being lived on two different levels. One sign of this is a sinister stirring and waving of the bush tops in the dense undergrowth, and you wait, hoping that you won't see an elephant, with outspread, angry ears, emerging upon you. Above, flinging themselves along the upper life of the forest, a train of shrieking monkeys hurls itself across the bending branches. You may catch an occasional glimpse of a white-rimmed, "human" face staring down at you. You may even see an inexpert monkey fall, his four hands grasping wildly, until he hits with a swish in a lower level of branch tips. But, for the most part, you will see just nothing—merely those mysterious shakings of the bushes.

And on the road on which your car is climbing, nearly all the time in first or second gear, the roar of your approach has driven everything to take cover. There is nothing exotic in this vegetation except its unbelievable luxuriance and shape. There is only one colored flower, a rare bit of flaming scarlet. And you never see a bird.

At least, that has been my experience.

The circumference of Ngorongoro crater is nearly forty miles. We reached the lip at a narrow spot where we could look down on either side. Behind us lay the dense, dark jungle forest. On the other side lay an immensity which it took a considerable time to bring into focus. Some 2,000 feet directly below us lay the smooth floor of the crater. From this height it appeared to be as smooth and green as a lawn. In its sump lay the brown mud and shrinking plaque of a saline lake. Some eight or nine miles away was a dark patch of green, which we knew must be another forest. Then the green floor rose upward in an unbroken sweep to meet a low-lying bank of clouds, level —and just ten miles across the open space between us.

In this crater lives an unkillable herd of game. An Englishman who had a farm there, until he was killed by a rogue elephant, estimated that there were some 50,000 head of zebra and wildebeest alone; they are inseparable companions of the plains. There are grass, water, shade, and shelter—everything that a wild animal requires; the place is a miniature Africa, all in itself; but, although we scanned every inch of the sward below us that sunset, and next day sat on the lip for over an hour to watch the dawn, we did not see a single animal.

We watched the cloud flakes, along its rim, flame up with the orange of sunrise, the shadows withdraw across its plain. And then, discovering that we had already broken two leaves of our front spring in climbing, we circled gingerly around the rutted road of the rim to get out and down again to the Serengetti plains.

Suddenly, without any warning, we found ourselves staring out into a space that left us gasping. Miles to the north, an unbelievable number of miles, rose some blue gossamer mountains that we knew must be up in Kenya. The vast sweep of steppe ahead of us was painted in pastel. The smoky blue of the peaks along the low skyline; the darker patches of blue where some clouds were floating between the sun and the unbroken plain; then, immediately below us, a vivid bowl of green in which some Masai were grazing their spotted cattle and their goats. From our height we could see an occasional glint of sun on the short lion spears that the Masai were carrying.

In the last patch of thorn scrub before we entered the bushless plain, a herd of beautiful impala leaped in their aimless fashion, colliding in mid-air, as we passed them. Some kongoni stared from the green slopes ahead. In another moment there was a crash, the wheel was jerked out of my hands, and our car nearly rolled down the mountainside. We had struck a patch of volcanic dust, liquefied into a stew by some trapped falling rain, and the thing that had saved us from going any farther in any direction was that both our engine case and rear end were resting on soft earth.

The huge trucks that go on the Serengetti up to the game ranger's place at Banagi Hill dig ruts so deep that the ordinary passenger car gets trapped in them.

It is usually an hour's hard work to dig yourself out, if you do get out. And down on the plains, where the volcanic dust of ages had been settling, this ash, between the rainy seasons, is so powdery that you sink in it up to your wheel hubs; you are constantly grinding along in second gear; and your radiator cap threatens to blow off constantly.

We were forced to laugh ironically when we thought that we had once intended to drive across this nightmare to try to reach real ground, and then the shores of Victoria Nyanza.

Successive crashes threatened to break the car's frame. Two punctures. The spring shackles slipped down and clattered alarmingly against the end bolts. I lay under the car, screwed them back, lashed them with rope. And in this fashion, with the hood red with radiator-water rust, we reached Lion Hill where—lions or no lions—we lay under the comparative shade of a thorn tree and gratefully ate two tins of sardines with some bread, over which, in lieu of butter, we poured the oil from the tins. We were perched there, watching the great herds of game grazing so peacefully on the plains, when a drop of rain the size of a quarter plunked down on my solar topee. Then, for a few minutes, a gray veil swept over us.

"The rains!" said Eve.

"And now," said I, snatching up our things, "we face the pleasant prospect of getting back to Ngorongoro—and, if we *do* get there, going down the side of that blasted volcano tonight."

The game stood as if stunned by the rain. We reached the side of the crater just at sunset. To avoid falling off the mountain where we had been trapped before, I took the inside; there was a crash when we were hurled into the bank, and my entire left wing was folded back. I pried that loose from the tire. The rains had already filled the rutted roads going around the crater; twice, with Eve holding the torch, I had to cut brush to fill the ruts, in order to get out. A leopard that had been coming up the road suddenly turned and darted ahead of us. In my foolish eagerness to have a close look at him, I ran the car hard into the bank again. For some reason, it suddenly had not answered my steering. Sometime around midnight we did finally get to the broad, lower slope of the mountain, out of the jungle. Thinking that all trouble lay behind us, and wanting a bed and something hot to drink, I stepped on the accelerator as we passed the signboard of a side road leading up to a German's plantation. The next instant the car had taken the bank, and we came to rest in the middle of his field.

By now I knew that it must be something more than the corrugations of the melting road which was making our car take these crazy dives. Brushing aside the dense grass in which my axles were buried, I flashed the torch and took a look. There, staring at me, were most of the points of my front springs, all that had not fallen out. Those that remained looked like a hand of cards spread in a crescent upon a table.

At the rate of about one mile an hour we limped into the three-house settlement of Oldeani; the silent shop, the rickety board garage, and the district officer's rest house. We climbed through a window into that. I collected wood from its shed. In a few minutes we had a roaring fire going. Outside thundered the rain, rasping like a steel brush on the roof, tossing the jungle on the slopes of Ngorongoro, turning the plains of the Serengetti into flooded mire—but not with us out on them.

The next morning I bought a complete, new front spring from a German planter at Oldeani (he always kept one in reserve, he told me; to find that spring there was a miracle—and there's no use enlarging upon it). The next day we cut back early to drop into the Great Rift, took the road going west up past Kilimanjaro, and raced the rains to Kenya.

I am far enough away from that German now for him never to be identified, and have him, or his family, visited with Nazi vengeance. But this is the picture of the one German settler I met in Tanganyika who, not a refugee, was openly, courageously not a Nazi! He was a nobleman and bore a familiar title. Yet I have never seen a man so wrecked and ravaged by his own countrymen in a supposedly free land. What first impelled him, unless it were some strain of independence in his character, to go against the Nazis in Tanganyika, I did not have the heart to ask. But, since 1933, when Hitler came to power in Germany, the Usagara Company, the Uhehe, none other of the German organizations in Tanganyika would buy his produce or give him any credit. And, as he lived in a colony of Germans, he could not find access to any British buyers. He did not even have a lorry to take his goods to market.

It was an Englishman, an agricultural expert, who told me to see him. "Because," he said, "that man knows more about the *politics* of being a coffee planter than anyone else. He ought to!"

"Yes," he said to me wearily, when I went to see him; "I have tried everything. I even washed gold in the Lupa gold fields for a time. Without any 'boy.' I tried ivory. But after one season, when I broke about even, I did not have the money to buy another license to shoot elephants. I have prospected for diamonds. I walked down to Rhodesia in search of a job. I've walked all the way across Tanganyika up to Victoria Nyanza. In the heat of the sun. Yes; and in bare feet. I have a family to keep, you understand?"

He had a heavy-boned face, putty-colored now, sunken both with fever and disaster. And (perhaps it was indicative of the spirit that still flamed inside his heavy body) he had an astonishing crest of orange hair that was only now turning gray. He jabbed his calloused hand through this mane. "Come in," he said; "I grow coffee; anyway, I can give you some of that. Nobody will buy it! And my wife makes excellent jam from the berries that we grow. We're not so badly off, after all; I think we can manage to live as long as Hitler does."

He laughed as he led me into his low, "roundable" bungalow, with zebra skins in patterns along the walls and a center rug of leopard skins on its cement floor.

"I have brought you company," he said to two girls who were cutting out a dress on the floor.

They jumped up, and thrust away the cheap cloth and paper pattern. One was very, very blond. The other was brunette. Both were shy. It was obvious that company was not customary, and the sight of a stranger plainly alarmed them. It was hard to believe that for some six years, since when they were twelve and thirteen, these two pretty girls had been living in the position of exiles from even the German community around them. But it was obvious that the tired old man had more than made it up to them for that. They laughed when he told them the joke about the coffee, and now added to us, "And I hope you don't take too much sugar."

"Oh, you fibber!" they cried.

Later, just as I was leaving Tanganyika, I met an English

planter in a town where I had never thought to find one. He was a bit mysterious about it at first, then, after a drink or two, he said:

"You want to know what I'm doing here? Well, old chap, I'm getting a marriage license—if I can raise the money."

"Well—congratulations!"

"You know her," he said, with a slow smile; "old So-and-So's daughter—you know, the blond one."

"Then I double those congratulations."

"But what about the other one," said Eve, "the dark one?"

"Ha!" The English settler ordered another whisky. "Make it a double." Then, to us: "The dark one—what? Dark one obviously needs a dark horse—what? Good idea, that. Must tell 'im. For, you see, there *is* a dark horse. 'Member that chap in the agricultural department, fellow who told you it would be a good idea to talk to old So-and-So, what a decent old chap the German was? Well, he's getting a license to marry the other one."

I must have shown my disbelief, for the Englishman said (he had his drink now): "But *his* marriage, I'm afraid, must hang fire for a bit. You see, he's in the service, and, what with all this hell Hitler is raising in Europe, young men in the Tanganyika service aren't encouraged to take unto themselves a German wife—pretty, and as anti-Nazi as she happens to be. Bad luck—what?"

We wished him good-by and good luck. "Oh, I'm all right," he said; "my marriage is going to go through right bang off! I'm lucky. If any woman can make an honest man out of me, it's she! I'm damned lucky!"

We knew he was. But I'm thinking now of that little white-walled, thatched hut among its bed of red cannas. Who was still sitting there on the afternoon of September 4, 1939?

20. Kenya Colony

KENYA should no longer be known as "a place in the sun for shady people."

It is true that there are still any amount of people out there who have earned for the colony the right to ask the question: "Are you married, or do you live in Kenya?" And in Nairobi, I must say, I ran into the grandest assortment of "types" that I have encountered in any capital. Still, everyone there will tell you:

"Oh, *this* isn't Kenya!"

What Kenya is, I can't say; I never could bring that colony into focus. I think it is a state of mind more than anything else. But these things can be said about it: It is the only British colony, protectorate, or mandate in Africa where the white settlers can stand up against the Official Point of View, and usually ride roughshod over it. It is "A White Man's Country," as is called a book by one of its pretty and most versatile inhabitants—no nonsense about "native interests being paramount"—not in Kenya! Its 19,000 white inhabitants, nearly all of whom live above 6,000 feet, seem slightly daft from the altitude, and less than 2,000 of them are registered as owning land, as real farmers. They have a "white highlands policy" which refuses to let any Asiatic settle in the glorious alpine regions, from which they have dispossessed the natives, a policy which gives old Mother India homicidal mania whenever she thinks of it, and causes continual eruptions in the vicious circle of Nairobi, Delhi, India-Office-Whitehall-to-Cabinet-to-Colonial Office, then back to Nairobi again. The Kenya white settlers always refuse to bow the knee to all of London's frantic efforts to placate Indian home opinion. It has among its inhabitants the greatest proportion of ex-soldiers, generals, colonels, majors, of any country in the world. It contains a goodly number of names that are in Burke's Peerage—and some quite terrific specimens in the flesh. And it is probably the only country in the world without a public opinion on the question of unmarried love.

I love Kenya.

"But *that* isn't Kenya!" said one of its most attractive inhabitants, when I read to her this absolutely accurate résumé. So where are you?

In 1923 the Kenya white settlers planned to kidnap the colony's Governor. This was a serious affair, in a potential African Ulster. The reason for the Kenya white settlers' indignation, this time, was that it looked as if Whitehall—to appease the Indian Government—was going to give equal voting rights to the Indians in Kenya, there being in Kenya today some 46,000 Asiatics, 13,660 Arabs, and 3,200,000 natives, as against only 19,000 whites.

In 1921, when the Indian Nationalists in India began agitating for equal franchise for Indians in Kenya (this, you must remember, was during one of the sentimental phases of Whitehall politics) the Kenya whites formed a vigilance committee to keep Indians out of the white highlands—if necessary, by force. Plans were even prepared to take over the Government by a sudden, armed uprising. As I said, Kenya has more ex-officers, in proportion to the total number of whites, than any other territory in the world. These were intensely patriotic Britishers (as were the Ulster gun runners). Their motto was, "For King and Kenya." The armed revolt was to be only against a misguided King's minister, and the settlers' secret meetings always ended with "God Save the King!"

Symptomatic of the schoolboy mentality with which the hereditary British statesman class often plays its game of gentle politics, efforts were made by Whitehall to keep secret the Wood-Winterton agreement which was intended to give to the Indians in Kenya full ballot-box equality with the whites; unrestricted Indian immigration into Kenya; complete abolition of the Whites' segregation policy directed towards the Kenya Indians.

This bit of polite skulduggery was a complete reversal of the promises the settlers had obtained from Winston Churchill only nine months before; this was now the end of 1922.

The Kenya viligance committee now (a) took stock of its rifles and ammunition; (b) plans were laid, and people appointed, to seize the railway and telegraph systems; (c) detailed plans were perfected to seize *all the Indians in Kenya* at a given signal, pack them on trains, and send them to Mombasa, then put them on ships to be sent back to India—42,000 of them!

(This was all, mind you, to be done in the teeth of the Government at Nairobi, the battalions of King's African Rifles stationed in Kenya, and the weight, power and edicts of Parliament, Whitehall, and, very possibly, an unsympathetic English public opinion at home.)

This, perhaps, is the most important thing to keep in mind about Kenya's white settlers: They are not impressed by the Foreign Office black hat and the furled umbrella. A large portion of Kenya's leading settlers come from a social stratum which is not awed by British politicians; they are aristocrats themselves. And a vast percentage of the remainder, the active service generals, colonels, etc., have been realists, men of action, all their lives, and, in final analysis they can be dangerous men, if put to it. The Elizabethan breed.

There is something of this in the air of Kenya, this exhilarating land which so many people think of lightly as an escapists' paradise.

The Governor of Kenya was to be kidnapped and kept hidden on a farm sixty miles from Nairobi.

✦

About the officers of the King's African Rifles?

It will perhaps be remembered that there was considerable speculation in the clubs of London on whether the English officers on the Curragh, the military camp in Ireland, would march north to fight against their brothers in Northern Ireland, if Ulster refused to obey London's edict to give way and merge with Southern Ireland—speculation, in fact, whether a British officer would do such a thing. British generals and colonels, as civilians, were running guns into County Down. It was the same in Kenya.

The white settlers understood that the King's African Rifles might take a similar stand on this Kenya revolt; many, they thought, would resign their commissions and join them.

It is always exhilarating to watch what happens when Englishman meets Englishman. The Governor, and Lord Delamere who represented the settlers, rushed to London. An Indian delegation rushed to India, hoping to see Mahatma Gandhi.

The Wood-Winterton agreement had been accepted by the British cabinet. The Government of India, and the Viceroy, were trying to push the thing through. If this were done, the white settlers in Kenya declared, the colony would rapidly become a second India; twenty years' labor would be lost.

In London, Lord Delamere pointed out that it was Indians who had originally financed many of the slave raids into East Africa—an objection sure to appeal to a large section of the English mind—and he also pointed out a thing which seems not yet clearly understood in England, that the Indians were retarding black development in Africa.* Lord Delamere tried to make a sentimental, but lethargic, complacent and grossly underinformed British public see that the mere presence of so many Indians meant that the blacks simply could not get into the positions they might hold.

(A great truth. Still not recognized in quarters where it should be.)

* See my remarks about this in Tanganyika, p. 170 et seq.

So, with apparent good grace—but really because of this stout threat of a Kenya settlers' revolt—Whitehall backed down. A white paper was published. (What amazing documents these white papers always are!) It was published in 1923; it was rejected by the Indians until 1931.

This white paper upheld Lord Elgin's policy that the white highlands should be reserved for Europeans; more Indian members were added to the Legislative Council, to give them "a measure of advance." Whitehall saved its face, which was buried in the sands. And the Kenya white settlers got just 100 per cent of what they, rifle in hand, had set out to get.

Nothing less than this rifle in hand would have got it for them. Bear this in mind when thinking of much maligned Kenya. Kenya is often more British than the British (Whitehall chair sitters) would like it to be.

Another fact not sufficiently widely known about Kenya is that about some 600 members of the 950 in its progressive Kenya Farmers' Association are men who have to depend upon their farms for their livelihood. They are not "check-book" farmers. And the K.F.A., as it is known in Africa, is considered by most people there to be possibly the most efficient buying and selling whites' co-operative on the continent.

We arrived at Nairobi on Good Friday, and faced the cheerful prospect of having nothing to do for four days. Nairobi is the Paris of the East African coast, of all Africa below Cairo. It continues its rebellious attitude towards the conventions of the mother country by going in for cafés that are positively continental in their gaiety. They are vast; they are packed; they buzz with excitement any time after eleven in the morning.

Who are these people?

That is one thing which will completely baffle you while you are in the colony. For, as I have just mentioned, everyone present at any of these gatherings will be quick to tell you, "Oh, *this* isn't Kenya!"

Outwardly, these persons appear to be gentlemen farmers. Delamere Avenue is lined with their safari cars. These have box bodies, of the station-wagon model, whose open sides are often protected by wire nettings; the more impressive of this species have glinting patch pockets made of aluminum along their exterior. These cars speak, without words, of expeditions into the bush, of charging lions, and (to those who know their owners best) of charging creditors; for nearly every farmer in Kenya is in debt to the bank. Particularly this type of agriculturist whose safari car you find parked in Delamere Avenue at eleven.

These cars always contain at least one dozing "boy." When you wake him he will tell you that the *Bwana Makuba*, the Big Master, is shopping. You know what that means, and you enter the nearest café. There sits the *Bwana Makuba*, having a gin-and-It.

His *memsahib*—as he will probably call her—is really out shopping. For along Delamere Avenue, with its pleasant central spine of grassy islands, and along the other main street (for the Europeans) that runs at right angles to Delamere, there are shops, with immense plate-glass windows that not only look like Fifth Avenue, or Piccadilly—they *are* that! Not only do they contain practically the same range of goods that you find in London, with a little touch of Paris thrown in—it is not without meaning that the only chic restaurant in Nairobi is called *Chez Gaby*—but the people strolling along the sidewalks and either arrogantly or with a faint distinction fingering the goods on display, *are* the people you would ordinarily meet on a morning's walk which took you into the fashionable New York or London shopping districts.

It costs money to become a successful farmer in Kenya—at least £2,000 to £3,000 is essential for a start—which is the one bit of proof I will put forth to sustain my picture of Nairobi's shoppers. They nearly all come from a respectably well off, or pensioned, middle class—with, of course, a garnishment of spectacular lords above them, like walnuts on the cake.

"My dear boy!" said a splendid old retired general I had known in Egypt during the World War, with whom I had stayed in India, and whom I again found among his rose bushes on the mountain of Ngong, outside Nairobi. "Don't," he said, as he let his blue eyes rest for a moment (unpleasing to him) on the old young men and elderly youngsters, dressed in shorts and safari shirts, having their gin-and-Its, "go off with the impression that *this* is Kenya!"

He was lending me his twin .400 to shoot a lion.

"You will shoot it on the ground, won't you? I've often wondered, when I've heard of you darting off to this place or the other around the world, if one day you and I wouldn't have a shoot together. But you've come too late; I couldn't even stand the weight of my rifle now. So all I can do is lend it to you, and let you tell me about it when you come back."

We went across to the gunsmith's (German), where, very fortunately for me, I bought some fresh ammunition, a few hard- and some soft-nosed bullets. Two days later, two hours before dawn, another white hunter and I, with three Kikuyus, in a one-ton motor lorry, took the road for the Great Rift and the Masai plains, and headed for the Mara.

If you have seen the sun rise over the Great Rift you will, at least, have come to the door of feeling what Kenya really is. You will know then why the English who live there speak of Kenya with such unashamed tenderness. Kenya possesses them. And they are unlike Englishmen in any other part of the world; the country calls from them open avowals of affection. You know now why they are so prone to tell you about everyone, every scene, "Oh, *this* isn't Kenya." For Kenya is a mode of life, lived in a landscape of such grandeur that man himself—any man—is dwarfed by it. Kenya can awe the most truculent soul, stir mean ones to resent its majesty—and it can mean the very poetry of life to the appreciative few who can respond to its splendor.

I was lucky; Downey, the white hunter I went down with, was a man perfectly in tune with his setting. He loved animals; he did not want to see them shot out; he had made it his life's work to study their mentality; yet the technique of the chase—say, a stalk—made him tremble like a pointer. He was the perfect hunter.

Kenya has, without doubt, some of the vilest, most unpardonable roads in Africa. A few miles out of Nairobi you leave the paved highway and rumble along a red, rutted horror. In the darkness I knew that coffee shambas stretched in green serrations of the rolling hills around us—for I had been out twice before to the Great Rift—then I knew that all trees must have ceased, and we were crossing the bare, mournful hills of the Kikuyu Reserve. In the half-light before dawn itself we made out the wretched huts of thatch and wattle, each emitting the feeble blue smoke that meant at least some attempt at breakfast. Your heart sinks when you consider the plight of the dispossessed, herded people. Then, with the ball of sun behind us, we came to the edge of the Rift.

It was filled with clouds which seemed to flow like a great river below us. I could sense the space, and get some idea of the descent by the pitch of the gradient that lay ahead of us. Our aneroid here registered 7,000 feet. We were taking this instrument along because the country we were going to shoot in had never been shot over until 1928, and Downey wanted to map some of the rivers and ridges in it. It was characteristic of him that he should have spent a couple of years planning how to get into that country, and that, having found, or made, a drift across several rivers to get into it, he should keep it to himself. He asked me to do likewise. At first I thought his attitude rather precious. But now, having seen the unmolested game in that inaccessible triangle, I feel as anxious as he for its preservation; I shall merely call the place where we began to hunt "a river in Kenya."

We waited for a few minutes on the rim of the Rift for the sun to dispel the mists that choked the road going down. It was as if the sun blew out his cheeks and blew the clouds like smoke before him. Green unrolled itself below us, the patch of eucalyptus trees around a plantation; then the great, yellow plains came bare and shining in the sun. Far off arose a sharp volcano, blue, in those glistening mists, as a kingfisher's wing. Then it began to shade into bronze.

"How far do you think it is?" asked Downey.

I tried to focus my eyes. "Oh, I don't know—about fourteen miles."

He smiled slowly. "It's exactly forty. We're going down, just around that one, today."

The Masai plains are great sweeps of rolling hill lands, bare as a Russian steppe under the vast, cloud-hung sky, with only here and there, in the ruts of river beds, a thicket of whistling or fever thorn. These last seem poisonously green. The Masai wander across this windy space with their spotted herds, their tall spears, their women with their babies tied to their backs, and little donkeys carrying all their household equipment. Strangely enough, for so warlike a race, the Masai do not hunt wild animals for food. There is a Somali store several hours away, down along the bed of the Rift, and there the Masai headman asked us if we wouldn't stop the night and shoot a couple of lions which had been eating their cattle. I was all for it, but Downey was now already trembling at the thought of returning once again to his promised land.

The great herds of Thomson's and Grant's gazelles stood in splotches of light yellow across the rain-welcoming plains. For we could sense that the animals were coming now—Kongoni, wildebeest, zebra. And here, late in the day, we came on a scene that I think was one of the most senseless, prodigal, murderous wastes I have ever witnessed. It was the camp of a professional wildebeest and zebra killer—not a hunter, a *killer!* He was being employed by the game department to rid the plains of these animals. He was to kill about a thousand or so of them. Reason: the Masai had complained to the Government that the wildebeest and zebra were eating so much grass that there was not enough left for their cattle. Therefore, as there was no more land available to give to the Masai (there could have been, if the Government had wanted to spend some more money in clearing up some tsetse-fly country), these peaceful herds of wildebeest and fat little zebra were to be exterminated.

The killer's arms were red with blood. The "boys" around his big camp were drying tons of wildebeest meat on sticks around a fire. There were piles and piles of dripping black wildebeest and striped zebra skins. These were the pay that he was to get for his work. I don't know what a wildebeest is worth dead. But a zebra skin may be bought in Nairobi for five shillings. The killer was, he told us, having a good thing.

And all around on the plains, for miles, glared the hacked-off skulls of fallen wildebeest.

I think one of the most torturing things I have ever seen was one lone wildebeest, standing as if stupefied among those skulls of his fallen comrades—with terror so strong in him that we could almost *feel* it from a hundred yards away. The animal was so bewildered, so forlorn, that it seemed unable to move.

For the first time I began to admire the tsetse fly, for it is he, and he alone, who protects the African game. He does not harm them;—in fact, they usually carry him—but he is certain death to cattle, horses, and, in some species, to man.

The country where we were going to shoot was thick with tsetse fly.

The shadows began to deepen along the bronze walls of the Rift. Beyond them, across the high barrier, lie Lake Naivasha and the blue mountains about which Rider Haggard wrote in

She and *King Solomon's Mines*. We ourselves were following the old gold-fields trail. We crossed, on a raised road, through one belt of thick, leafy jungle, full of unseen buffalo; and then, about an hour before dark, we turned off into a belt of fever thorn.

Here we came on four lionesses sitting around a topi they had just killed.

They were much lighter, and infinitely less afraid, than I had expected—in fact, one, which had its back towards us, looked leisurely over its shoulder and snarled. Then one arose, stared at us speculatively, and slowly walked off. The others followed.

We watched them go. There was no hurry, no sign of any uneasiness in their gait. They were not afraid of anything; nothing in their lives had ever taught them to be. They were just annoyed that something had interrupted their dinner. But when we got down to examine it, we found that a large part of the topi had already been eaten. There was the usual packed-down circle around it, covered with manure, where the lions had ripped out its entrails and kicked them away in the grass. The carcass reeked of their power.

That sunset, after a grueling, zigzag grind through thorn forests, mud, and water, we came to the dense jungle along the banks of a steep river. The water looked black and ugly, flowing through that glistening mud. A crocodile slid into it. We put a stake where it would show how much the river had risen by morning. The "boys" had pitched our two camp beds under a tarpaulin stretched out from one side of the truck.

The rains came. The white ants rose by millions, danced their brief ecstasy of winged life, and fell into our coffee cups. The natives make quite a good porridge out of them; I have seen natives in the Congo, at night, tapping on the ground outside the anthills to bring them out and trap them in a pit. In their aerial stage they have four wings, quite detachable, that easily become mixed up with your tinned fruit compote. I loathe them.

Trickles came through the tarpaulin and tapped our heads. A curtain of falling water poured unceasingly from the edge. The river, which we hoped to ford the next morning, became audible. The dark jungle that hid the steep banks gave out peculiar rustlings. From some tree in it an anvil bird banged out his infuriating note. The deep, heavy grunts of lions came from across the bank. We traced one making a semi-circle around our camp. "*Ungh!—ungh!—ungh!*" Low, heavy grunts. There was the harsh, saw-like "*Aaaagh; aaaagh!*", the cough of a hunting leopard. Then there was a terrific "*Huroosh!*" in the brush, thrashing less than forty yards from where we lay.

"Master," said one of the "boys" to Downey, "the elephants are here!"

Through all this we lay, smoking in the murky light of our hurricane lamp. With unloaded rifles. And with great expectations.

But in about three days I began to be fed up with Downey for being such a stickler about not shooting a lioness. When we had awakened that first morning, we found that we were trapped. The tall stick we had stuck in the mud bank, to mark the rising of the water, had vanished. The place where we had hoped to ford the river on the little stone drift Downey had spent months in building was about seventeen feet deep in water. I have met few things which have impressed me as being more ominous than one of these deep, slowly swirling African rivers concealed in its sheath of jungle. If there were any "crocs" watching us, we did not see them, although on the previous trip Downey had shot at this spot a fifteen-footer which he had come on dragging a water buck under by its nose.

The hair trigger—a nasty gadget, anyway—of my own Mannlicher had become stuck; this required taking out the lock. While we were doing that I saw troops of baboons emerge from the woods opposite and come out into an open glade of short grass.

A big bull sat there and eyed us with an idol-like insolence. We let them be.

When we had finished with the Mannlicher we slid down the sinister bank again, only to find that the water had risen another foot or so to meet us.

We turned inland to find a way out. Here, under some tall trees that rose and then branched out like stalks of cauliflower, we ran into a herd of water buck—beautiful, sturdy, little animals, mouse-gray, which looked as if they were wearing black socks. Their rugged charge through the brush left waves of glistening spray in the intermittent sun. That way was blocked.

The rains were already dispersing the game. They were making for the open plains. The lions come out of the bush when it rains. But it was too wet and slippery for us to shoot a zebra for bait and tow it, to make a drag with our truck. The wheels could not have got a grip to pull its body. And we watched the zebra going.

We were bogged for hours in one small patch of black-cotton soil. In there we started up a herd of glistening, reddish impala. They leaped with such abandon, so foolishly, that we could have hit them with a stone. We were surrounded by leaping antelope, which looked as though they were dancing. A topi, with slanting back and rear thighs looking as if he had lain down in cigar ash, stood and "huffed" at us—a perfect picture of indecisive curiosity. He could not make up his mind whether we spelled danger to him or not.

He could not have known it, but we did not mean danger to any buck. Only to a few, for bait. To save myself from an inherited instinct to hunt any and everything, I had deliberately refrained from taking out a buck license. After three or four days without firing a shot, I began to regret this bitterly. But then I became aware that I had saved myself from the anxiety I otherwise would have felt upon the appearance of so much game, the desire to stalk a big head; and I know now that I was able to do that rare thing—look at African game with open eyes, tranquilly, taking in every aspect of their beauty and their habits, without being fevered with a desire to point a rifle at them.

You lose a lot of Africa if you hunt with either a rifle or a camera. In the first case you are seeing them only through the sights. With the other you are losing everything while you fuss and fiddle with your camera apertures, distances, exposures. No; it is better just to stand, or hide, and watch them. Take your fill of them.

I took a few photographs during this time, usually when the game simply stood and invited us to do so. And I took over a dozen of two lionesses up a tree—at less than twenty feet distance—simply because some people will try to tell you that lions do not climb trees. I took some giraffes, so close that I could have hit them with a marble shot from my thumb. But other days, while watching the impala, the most beautiful small buck in Africa, leaping about me, I could do nothing other than stand and gape at them.

But those days will always remain with me.

One evening we counted up the animals we had seen that day —nearly all at close quarters. Buffalo, lioness, leopard, eland, zebra, wildebeest, kongoni, topi, Grant's and Thomson's gazelles, bush buck, reed buck, duiker, stem buck, water buck, hyena, jackal, monkeys, giraffe, lynx, serval cat, bat-eared fox, impala, baboons, the black-faced monkey, wart hog; also ostriches. In one day! These, and *flotillas* of wild boars! All running with tails erect, the little ones scampering after their mothers.

By the most uncanny set of misfortunes, I never saw a rhino in Africa, although I have come on the spoor several times only a few minutes after one had passed. Neither, along this "river in Kenya," did I see an elephant, although there was a herd of them within forty yards that first night. We crossed any number of the big swaths of beaten-down grass they had just made, and we came into patch after patch of thorn forests which they had ripped up, butted over with their heads—just as if they had been angered by that particular bit of scenery and had destroyed it!

Yet I had already had a bad scare from four elephants I saw all too much of down along the Tanganyika border. I shall always stir (and tremble a little) when I recall the sight of those four trunks, suddenly lifted above the swamp grass, *smelling me out!* And in the Belgian Congo an elephant was to make me— with a crippled leg!—do something which I thought I had not been able to do for over twenty years; he made me do a hundred-yard dash in something less than eleven seconds!

I distrust elephants.

But what did terrify me, with the ever present idea of snakes in my mind when swamp wading, was a small incident five days after we had found ourselves trapped in the triangle of rushing rivers down in southern Kenya. We had worked back, intending to reach the high bank where we had spent the first night. But it was all under water. Even the open glades, where the baboons had sat, were flooded. Fearing that a crocodile might grab us at any moment, we waded about a quarter of a mile to reach a patch that seemed out of water. And here, in a grove of camel thorn, something—*several things!*—moiled the water at my feet where it was less than knee-deep! I suppose I—and the "boys"— all rose in the air about four feet.

Then one of the "boys" gave a laugh, and started feeling around in the mud with his naked feet. He gave a grunt, dived down his hands, and held up, laughing, a mudfish. It had been lying there in this previously hard ground for we didn't know how long, certainly many months, possibly years. The boys unearthed a half dozen of them, which they baked, impaled on stakes, over our rain-sputtering fire. I think they are the most unpleasant fish I have ever tasted.

+

Vultures circled high in the sky. We watched them particularly; they might give us sign of a lion's kill. Storks, cranes, rose from the drenched wilderness. We were mired.

The only thing to do was find a spot of land which looked as if it would remain unsubmerged, and pitch our tent upon it. We found a slope with a crest of camel thorn and some candle-like euphorbias, and camped by an old wallow. Below us lay the treacherous river hidden in its belt of jungle. Beyond stretched the great green plains and the blue hills of Africa.

It was a pleasant spot.

There is a sense of languor about a camp that is far more restful than the same feeling in a ship. You have no one to bother you. The sun blazed out at midday, steaming the earth, and we were grateful for the big fly under which our small tent rested. This place had been so little shot over that the buck on the plain came close and stared at us through the thin grove of thorn. There was no underbrush. This cost a plump little Thomson's gazelle its life. For we had not brought much in the way of food with us—I was doing this expedition on little money. And the chops from a "tommy" are very succulent. So is its liver!

When Downey dropped it, Juma, our Mohammedan man of all work, raced out to cut its throat before it died, as is laid down in the Koran.

Juma was just about the most hopeless, lovable black man I have ever encountered. He was so ugly that he had charm. When I did shoot a lion and we cleaned the head, Juma, when he held it up, convinced us that there was not much to choose between them. He had no teeth; his blubbery lips bulged out far beyond his flat nose; his face was shrunken, and drooped in heavy dewlaps. And he never smiled, for fear the other two "boys" would laugh at him.

Juma would never leap out of the motor lorry when it was moving, as the rest of us had to, so that we could get to pushing before it lost momentum and stuck. No; Juma just sat there until the lorry stopped because we were stuck. Then Juma descended.

Then, when we did get it started, Downey leaped in to seize the wheel and keep up momentum, while I and the two other "boys" raced along and slung ourselves aboard whenever the chance offered. But not Juma. He couldn't run, he said. So, often, on what appeared a dubious bit of ground, we had to slow down for Juma, almost to a stop. Then, when he had seated himself, we found we were stuck again.

"Oh, Juma; *Juma*, JUMA!"

I can still hear Downey's despairing exhortations to that faithful, unperturbed, unteachable old Mohammedan, whom he loved so much.

On the other hand, Karithe, our Kikuyu "acting cook," could not be defeated by any set of evil circumstances. When the downpour reached such a fury that it seemed about to float our firewood off the ground, I watched Karithe cook a meal while he lay under a leaning tree, like a worm under a stone. But, like all natives, he was always late in wet weather. Karithe, like our lorry, required a considerable amount of cranking to get him started.

The finest "boy," a huge Kikuyu, bigger than either Downey or I, I never did know by name. Perhaps that was because he was always with Downey and me; he was a rabid hunter. And his eyes, unaided, were almost as good as ours with binoculars.

His duty, when we were lurching along in the lorry, or proceeding on foot, was to do nothing but look. From an indentation, or some pressed-down grass, he could tell instantly which animals had passed, and to within an hour, perhaps minutes, how long since they had passed. "Two elephants, master. They just come by." The flattened grass had not yet begun to show the discoloration from being bruised.

"Master, plenty buffalo! Plenty! They make for river, over there." He pointed to a high ridge to the west along which, we knew, the game was emptying itself out on the harder plains. As might be imagined, these aftermaths did not add to my good spirits.

That afternoon we shot three topi, tied a rope around their horns, dragged them for hundreds of yards across a sloping hill, and hung them in trees. We had placed them in advantageous spots, to which we could crawl, with the hope of bagging a lion or a leopard.

The next dawn, after the most stealthy approaches, we found two of them untouched. The third had had its legs bitten off by hyenas which had jumped up in the air and hung there, their bone-breaking jaws locked like traps. I felt sorry we had shot the topi.

There was something distinctly unpleasant about shooting these innocent buck for bait. I did not like it. Neither did Downey. You could see that he had a distaste for the job. And the next day, when we shot another, to put on the edge of a little wood, Downey had a fit of remorse because he did not drop it cleanly, and it managed to elude us for a time, on three legs. "Oh, my God, my God!" he said, running after it through the thorn thickets. We wasted the whole precious hour before sunset until we found that topi and Downey put it out of its misery. He looked positively ill.

We found a baby Thomson's gazelle that had actually been beaten to the earth by the driving rains. Downey and I stood there, debating whether to kill it or try to revive it. While we were talking, it died.

As I said, Downey was a real hunter. To him, life could hold out nothing better than the life he was living. It was romance. And at night, with the rain splashing the muddying plains around us, he talked of the great hunters—Selous, Pretorius. The lion, said Downey, would be the first of the big game to be killed out of Africa, because everybody was after him. If it wasn't sportsmen who wanted to kill lions, then it was the farmers or natives who wanted them wiped out as vermin.

The buffalo and the eland might be next, if they had a bad go of rinderpest. In 1912 the buffalo, eland, and one or two other species of buck in Kenya were almost exterminated by the disease. They suffer most from it. So do the kudu. Giraffes get it. But the elephant, hippos, rhino, wildebeest and water buck seem exempt.

The elephant, Downey insisted, would be the last to go. The chief reason for his staying on is because people don't shoot small tuskers any more; they have time to breed. Then, the elephant cow is crown game, not to be shot, as is also the cow giraffe. They don't shoot a Kenya elephant whose tusks are judged to be below 70 pounds—not any more. A 70-pound tusker would be from 80 to 100 years old; old enough to have done plenty of breeding. An elephant may live up to 150 years, but he is not considered mature until he is 40.

Downey felt that when all the rest had gone, these great animals would be solemnly plodding along their "walks," which criss-cross all of equatorial Africa.

"But the poor old rhino, he's in for it. Definitely! The Chinese will pay any price for his horn. Aphrodisiac. And," added Downey, "I wonder if it really works?"

The country was so park-like that once the tent was pegged I felt immediately at home. After a few hours the sight of a buck staring at us through the thorn scrub no longer seemed unusual. Nor, it seemed, did we appear that way to them. Between the cloudbursts there were some amazing light effects. The wet jungle along the river became an unbelievable green; every one of its wet leaves became a sun reflector. Then there were lemon-colored sunsets, in which the far plains suddenly glowed with flame as the jungles in their crotches became absorbed in the gathering mists. It seemed to bring the plains nearer, somehow, until we found ourselves watching things at an incredible distance. Then, sharp at six, night dropped like a hood.

We hung around our bait for a few days, and then decided to give up. We heard lions every night, and during one of them we listened to two lions "talking" to each other for hours. But their deep, booming tones we knew came from across the river.

We decided to go in for buffalo.

Downey knew of a deep, grassy valley, over a far ridge, which usually held a big herd. We started some time before dawn and spent the better part of the morning getting there. The last three hundred yards was a stalk so careful that I separated the .400 cartridges in my pockets so that they should not clink.

But this was the day of the giraffe. We got right into the middle of a herd before either they or we knew it. Then the most amazing things happened. One old, old buck—he seemed almost frosted on top—swayed his head from the tips of a twenty-foot-high thorn tree he had been nibbling, and stared at us. Two others, lighter and younger, swayed and walked up. We stood motionless.

It was like a fairy scene, the way these lovely creatures stood in a silent ring around us. Then there was a roar like thunder. The earth trembled. The whole herd—God knows how many of them—fled as if the devil were after them. We saw flash after flash of their spotted bodies among the trees.

"And that," said Downey, "will stampede anything!"

When we came to look down, our valley was empty.

We ran onto these or other giraffes all the afternoon getting back to camp. By pure chance we had one of the best bits of luck I had in Africa. We came on two lionesses standing up in the branches of a tree. About forty yards away, lying in the crotch of another tree, was a cub, with its paws crossed.

Getting close to the lionesses to get a few good photographs, we came so near that I found myself looking up into the amber eyes of one. I could see its vertical slits of pupil open and widen.

And that story about looking a lion in the eye—that, I can tell you, is buncombe. When I found myself staring eye to eye with that lioness it was I who shivered.

With the grace of a cat—which a lion is—the bigger lioness dropped from the tree to the ground. She seemed to float down. Then, disregarding us completely, she walked past us to the cub. The lioness gave a few flicks of her tail, to show that she was annoyed. And, from the postures of the cub, a conversation then took place which must have been something like this:

"Come on! Get down!"

"Why?"

"Because I say so."

"But why?"

"Do you hear me? You come down out of that tree—at once!"

"But it's nice here. You were up a tree yourself. I'm only doing what you do. You told me to copy you."

"Do you hear what I say? If you don't—"

The lioness, stiffening, slowly advanced to the tree. The cub gave an alarmed start, and jumped. It was a clumsy flop. Then, the cub following its mother, the two walked directly past us and sat down at the edge of a deep wood. The mother gave a sulky shrug and stretched out on the ground, her head, watching us, lying along her front legs. The cub, bored, sat upright. Meanwhile, the lioness on our left had dropped out of the thorn tree—again the same silent stream of yellow. Now, with an effortless leap, she jumped up into the fork of the branches again; she walked along one, and turned to watch us.

"I've known this family for several years," said Downey. "I have sort of an idea they know me. It's a bit of a tragedy; they had a fine male with them, with a beautiful mane; and I'd made up my mind not to kill him. But a partner of mine took an Indian prince down here; he didn't know it was this particular lion. And one morning, on a zebra they were using for bait, the Indian shot him. That little cub's her grandson."

"So she's not still a widow?"

Downey smiled, and pointed to the cub. "Not entirely," he said.

We shot a topi on the far side of the plain and dragged it out into the open. Then we withdrew behind a knoll and watched. There seemed nothing in the blue sky. Then a speck materialized. It was a vulture, seeing the little rivulet of blood on the buck's side. In curves, the vulture planed down. Then, with horrid, outspread wings, and with its wicked, naked old head craned down, it swooped low over the dead topi. The glide of its pinioned wings carried it to a thorn tree, into which it dropped with a jerk. Five, ten, fifteen, twenty vultures performed this cautious survey. Always ending in trees. Then one, flying near, dropped by the buck. And, like the evil spirits they are, there were soon some forty or fifty of them on the ground. One came near, aimed its head at the smear of coagulating red, and drove its beak into the flesh. It tugged. . . .

The three lions had been watching this, of course. Through the glasses we saw them all sitting upright. Then the younger lioness slowly walked out towards the buck. As it came near, the vultures drew away in an angry group. Then the cub came across. It came up and sniffed the buck. The loathsome-necked vultures withdrew further, and kept humping their wings. Then the big lioness strolled across. She lay down on her elbows, without ever coming near the buck. The little cub, then, did not know just what to do.

It came near its mother, and she rolled it over, with one huge tolerant paw. The cub lay on its back, staring happily up at the blue sky. Then it reached up a chubby paw and cuffed its mother's chin. The mother rolled it over again. This was delicious. The cub bounced back. Then it stood on its hind legs, and put both paws on its mother's nose. This was too boring; with a flick of her mighty head the lioness sent the cub rolling over and over.

Then the cub stood up, stared from the lionesses to the buck, and then to the vultures. "I know what!" it said by its attitude. "I'll charge them!"

The vultures were furious. I don't know what chance the cub would have had with them, if left alone—not much, I suppose. But with those two formidable lionesses in the background, he was lord of it all. He knew this, even if the reason did not occur to him, and he walked back with pride to show his mother how brave he was. If you have ever watched cats at play, then you have this domestic scene in equatorial Africa.

"It's hard," said Downey, "to shoot lions, after that."

But, then, the Nairobi graveyard is full of men who have shot lions and not finished them off, and who have met their death in pitting themselves against these great cats. It is by no means a one-sided affair. So the chase goes on; man trusting to his eye to put into the lion a shot that will kill him, or waiting, with nerves as steady as he can keep them, to meet their pouncing charge—and not daring to waste a shot.

These lions had obviously killed and eaten the previous night. They sat on this kill more to keep the vultures away than for any other reason. We left them.

In hunting lions, the one thing that you must do is watch the other game on the plain. When a lion is present, every buck in the vicinity will stand still and face it. He will never take his eyes off the lion. You may drive right behind him with a lorry, and he will never turn around. Therefore, when we were hunting we always watched for the attitude of the game.

The next morning, making a long tramp over the hills, for buffalo, we saw three hyenas trotting towards us. As they went past at about sixty yards, we saw them suddenly look up into a tree and dash on.

"Leopard!" said Downey.

We had not seen the leopard. It was the action of the hyenas which put us on to him. For a minute or so it was still impossible for us to spot him. Then we saw his spotted body lying close along a branch. As I threw up my rifle he vanished, quickly as you could snap your fingers. We ran towards the tree. "He's going down on the other side of it!" said Downey.

Then for an instant we saw its head, some forty yards away in the high grass. It was making for a thorn-choked gully. Three hundred yards away it appeared again. This time it was sitting up, watching us. I sat down, rested an elbow on a knee, and drew a bead. It covered the whole leopard at that distance. Then, just as I was carefully squeezing the trigger, I realized there was no leopard. It had gone. There was a dense wood at the end of the gully. We knew it would be waste of time to hunt a leopard which had once been caught out in midday.

A honey bird came and, perching on a tree, distracted us. "Cut-cut-cut!" it went. "Cut-cut-cut!" It looked towards us. And then, as though it were leading us on, it flew to another thorn tree and clapped its wings. "Cut-cut-cut!"

"Yes, master," said the black hunter; "he will lead you to the honey. He knows where it is. And he wants you to help him get it. But you must leave some for *him!*"

"What would happen if we didn't?"

The Kikuyu grinned. "Next time, master, the honey bird will lead you on to a sleeping rhino."

Even that, I replied, might be welcome.

In the wet dusk which settled over us, Downey took to talking with the natives around their fire. They discussed all sorts of African beliefs, taboos, and problems. Juma claimed that there were snakes a hundred feet long and two feet thick. There was another snake that had hair on it like a man's head. But to see this one, he claimed, you must have a man with you who can cast a spell on it.

"*Shuri Ya Mungu!*" said one of the blacks. "It is an affair of God's."

Karithe, the Kikuyu cook, was annoyed that a lesser bustard we had shot had gone bad. He said that a Kikuyu could eat pigeons until he was circumcised; after that he could never eat one. But a woman, he said—implying they did not count—could eat pigeons all the time. This was when, to augment our pot, I suggested knocking over some doves.

The huge king vultures, I learned, were absolutely useless to us in the hunt; their appearance did not signify anything. But on a wet, gloomy dusk they made an ominous sight, flapping off towards the dark forest.

There are twenty-one members of the Kenya White Hunters' Association. They are almost a monastic order. They range from a foreign nobleman, and generals, to men of any station of life who hunt for the sheer romance of the bush. But only seven of them were hunting at the beginning of this war. The others had retired or else they had been crippled by leopards or lions. One caused a first-class scandal in London by marrying the daughter of a peer he had taken out on safari. But it caused no scandal in Kenya, for the hunter was a man whom most people liked if they did not have him as a competitor—and the peer was not of the blood.

The man who most of the white hunters themselves admit is the best hunter in Kenya is an American. He does not belong to the association. In fact, he has frequently offered to knock their blocks off. And he outraged the association by sending a circular to rich sportsmen in the United States, saying:

"YOU WANT LIONS—WE HAVE THEM."

Some rich sportsmen take out safaris that cost them at least £200 to £300 a month. Actually, a trip that was costing £100 a month would be doing it "on the cheap." The Aga Khan had his own brass bed and portable toilets, heading a retinue of lorries and limousines. Another Indian potentate, in an open car, fired away with his revolver at everything he could see. He brought back one mingy little lion—so small, so out of condition that the two white hunters who had taken him out had to hang their heads in shame before their comrades in Nairobi. They had tried to prevent him firing at it.

Then they are still telling the story of the two Americans—one of them very, very rich, the other a very, very good shot. Jovial chaps, they set off with a safari carrying good food and whisky and loaded with comfortable tents and tables. The rich man expected Africa to treat him as all the rest of the world had done—bow, and offer him the biggest and best of everything. "But then, he couldn't hit a barn door!"

Acrimonious discussions began to take place every night, over the day's bag. The poor man claimed he could not help it if his aim was straight. "That there leopard was just asking to be shot!" But the rich man was not pleased.

Then one day the rich man did shoot a lion. It was quite a good lion. He went back at once to camp and when the poor man came in met him with an outstretched hand and a whisky and soda.

"Ever see a lion?" he said, pointing to the salted skin. "What about *that* one?"

The white hunter who had been with the poor man had stood all he could. He liked the poor man, who, he said to me, was a first-rate sportsman. "Couldn't ask for a better man to have with you in a tight spot!" So he grinned at the rich man, and jerked his head towards the rear of the light truck he was driving.

"What about *that* one?" he asked.

Inside lay one of the biggest lions ever killed in that part of Africa.

The safari broke up that night, and returned to Nairobi. The rich man complained that his friend, who had been accepting his hospitality, was just "hogging" everything! "He'd be gol-darned if he would stand it!"

So they returned to America on different steamers. Friends no longer.

Then, take the African side of those mighty movies which have thrilled America. Tame or even "wild" animals, some of which have even been brought to Africa for the occasion. A leopard and a python kept in two separate enclosures, without food, until they were almost mad from starvation. Then the barrier between them is removed. A FIGHT TO THE DEATH! then takes place. The animals try to eat each other. "AFRICA!" comes the hushed voice of the commentator: "THE LAW OF THE JUNGLE!"

And so the world goes round.

At Ninia, in the Belgian Congo, a Frenchman managing a transport riders' hotel—a veritable Ritz in the jungle—asked me whether I knew a certain Italian "explorer" who had just passed by. I told him, "No; and I don't want to." "Why?" smiled the Frenchman. "Well, you ought to know; you've met him," I said. Then I added, "I've just read a story of his about the place I've just come from; it filled me with horror; the story, I mean, not the place." The Frenchman laughed outright:

"*M'sieu*, we had a tame baby leopard here. He asked us whether he could borrow it. We saw him and his men staging a leopard hunt. It is all, you know, merely a question of perspec-tive—if you don't know leopards. That movie ought to be quite a hit in New York."

"And in Paris?" I retorted.

"*La même chose*. We are all fools."

One of the books I had taken with me in my rucksack was Evelyn Waugh's *Vile Bodies*. I began to read it for the second time; its snottiness about all mankind appealed to me, and its title seemed so apposite. I'm afraid Downey did not find me very good company on these nights.

We were already on our way out, trying to escape from the mud, get back upon the old gold fields road, and try to make Nairobi. "Although," said Downey, as another cloudburst threatened to crush our tarpaulin on our heads, "the Masai plains will probably be about nine feet deep in water." (They were.)

"I don't care," I said.

That day we had made only half a mile. And—this *would* happen—when we walked down to a stream ahead, to see when and where we might be able to ford it, we met two buffalo. No rifles in our hands. They had been lying there, hiding, within a hundred yards, for at least the last three hours.

"Well, that's that!" I said, and returned to *Vile Bodies.*

The soles of my shoes had come off; my corduroys were sodden as sponges; I had only one dry flannel shirt and a damp safari jacket. But that night, when I went to bed, I placed a dry pair of gray flannel bags on the chair, and in my hat I placed a handful of hard- and soft-nosed .400 cartridges. Our rifles lay across the table, to keep them dry.

"Ungh! ungh! UNGH!"

The last grunt sounded almost in my ear. I was sitting bolt upright. It was just dawn. I thought I had been dreaming. Then—"UNGH!"

"My God," I said to Downey, "he's right *here!*"

No firemen ever got into their clothes more quickly.

"Master! master! Big one, big one!"

The black hunter was looking under the tarpaulin.

Now here is where the benefit of the presence of a seasoned white hunter comes in. A real one. Like Downey.

He just stood there, waiting. He waited until there was another grunt, and then another.

"Quick!" he whispered. "He's circling us. Making for the river. We've got to cut him off."

Downey wore rubber-soled canvas American basketball shoes, to hunt in; they were silent as moccasins. I felt I was making an awful clatter with my heavy, flapping boots. We hurried, zigzagging behind every tree, to get up to the lion without him seeing us. It was a stalk in broad daylight.

It was the rain which killed him. The noise he was making with his own heavy pugs drowned the sound of our approach. We caught glimpses of him, heavy with food, plodding along majestically for the river jungle where he intended to lie up. Big, heavy, black mane and shoulders. The epitome of dauntlessness.

Then he saw us.

He turned his head, and, for an instant, I saw that noble, unafraid face. I fired—and missed him with both barrels.

Then, in a split second, all the big fish I had lost, all the misfortunes of shooting, swept over me; all the good things that I just hadn't got! Miss this one, I said bitterly to myself, then shoot yourself! You'll never get over it! (Of course, these were immediate flashes, like the swift thoughts in an aeroplane crash.)

I'd known there wasn't even time to load both barrels. I slipped a soft-nose into the right, took careful aim at his shoulder, fired.

There was no lion!

"Good shot, massa! God damn, God damn!" The black hunter had seized and was wringing my hand. It was the first I knew I'd knocked the lion over.

The lion is a sensitive creature. He will, unlike a buffalo, go down under the impact of a shot. For a moment his nervous system is thrown out of gear. Then he will get up and charge you. So I lost no time in slipping in two more cartridges. And we walked gingerly towards him.

The first shots, when we paced them out afterwards, were at

a distance of 120 yards. Now, when we were within 30 yards from him, he tried to rise on his front legs. It was a last gallant effort. And I put a bullet into him quickly. He lay down.

He was dead. And suddenly all the reaction of it hit me. I won't say that I felt ashamed, because I was tremendously satisfied. But I knew then, when I looked at that noble face, that I would never want to kill another lion. Nor would I ever want to see one killed. And Downey, who was standing there, rubbing his chin, said sadly:

"Yes—yes—he was the king of beasts!"

*

21. Home-Life in Nairobi

EVE and I "did" Nairobi for a few days, before we pushed on for the papyrus swamps of Uganda and the steaming Congo. From now on it was to be Eve, more than I, who was to take over the daily "home life" of our car. I was left to worry about times and distances and to battle feebly with Eve about which routes we took (Eve exhibiting her usual passion to take side roads, even in Africa!); and I appointed her, with relief, commissariat officer.

We drove out to Ngong, where my old friend, the general, had built his stone bungalow, to return his beloved twin .400, and tell him about the lion. He was delighted to find I had got it the one way that every hunter hopes he will get his lion in Africa—a fair stalk in daylight. He seemed lonely, tired. The arsenic cure for the malaria he had contracted while he was game warden of Tanganyika had been overdone; his hair and his fingernails had once dropped out; he was about half his normal size—and this was a man who, as a young subaltern, had killed his Pathan in a sword-to-sword fight in the Khyber Pass, and who had won the D.S.O. the same day for carrying a wounded sepoy out of action after he had received a bullet through the stomach himself.

I am always astonished at the peaceful, commonplace end of so many of England's adventurers. By going to Kenya he had escaped the obligation to read the service in some ivied village church. He was not obliged to address either the Boy Scouts or the Girl Guides, or become a justice of the peace.

But he could not escape the retired warrior's inevitable garden.

He had regimented his. Lines of plants, rows of trees, hundreds of yards of hedges, all dead straight, stood on parade.

My leg was so swollen, with the bone showing (it had not been bettered by this lion-shooting expedition under the cloud-bursts of southern Kenya), that I had to remove the bandages and loosen everything, while we were dining with him. "I've always thought you were a bit of an idiot," he said; "but you are simply mad to go into the Congo—with *that!*" Then we said good-by, probably the last of them. The first was said in the summer days of 1918, when he and I stealthily slipped out of Ras el Tin Hospital to sail Egyptian feluccas around the ships behind Alexandria's breakwater.

We were invited to lunch at Government House, with the Governor, Air Chief Marshal Sir Robert Brooke-Popham, G.C.V.O., etc. The same pleasant, easy, yet formal ceremony, with the attendant A.D.C.s, to a varying degree, that I had experienced at Simla, lunching at Vice-Regal Lodge when Lord Irwin was Viceroy, and which I had just enjoyed in that Moorish fantasy inhabited by Sir Mark Young, Governor of Tanganyika.

The room was spacious. Its cream-colored walls were hung with the portraits of former governors. The servants wore scarlet, gold-embroidered jackets, and blue puggrees. The food, strangely enough, was excellent. There were some splendid alligator pears. The conversation was such as it was expected to be; not witty or dull or overserious on any topic. And through it all Sir Robert Brooke-Popham sat with that courteous attention which a gentleman in his position is expected to display through hundreds and hundreds of such meals which must have bored him to death.

They must be the heaviest penance for taking a governorship.

We had luncheon at "Hoppy" Marshall's with a young Englishman, a mere boy, who had just installed himself upon a plot of land in Kenya, hoping to get in on the momentary pyrethrum boom. He offered me a bongo—incontestably the most impossible animal to stalk, in its own bamboo forest, of all wild game. Theodore Roosevelt actually did stalk his bongo on foot. "But I've got dogs," said this callow young Etonian. (He was, we could see, taking the wrong road in Kenya.)

I ran into my penniless friend again. Over several gins, he implored me to go diamond prospecting with him up around Lake Rudolph.

"But," I asked, "has anyone ever heard of any diamondiferous land in that locality? Have you any reason whatever for thinking there *might* be diamonds around Rudolph Lake?"

"No," he said; "but the fishing's marvelous!"

We dined with Lady Delamere, Nairobi's mayor, in her stone house, with its furniture, on a hill that we found somewhere in the night. The house seemed all veranda, and to get from one room to another you went out on the porch. She spoke almost entirely about her late husband, that great eccentric whose name still heads all Kenya's personages—and what a picturesque lot they were! We dined with Cavendish-Bentinck, who told us how the Tanganyika League, which he had formed, would never allow England to give Tanganyika back to Germany. He looked like De Valera and talked like Lord Craigavon.

And we attended a circus of luncheons, teas, and dinners which, now that we look back upon them, were like the Mad Hatter's tea parties. At one dinner an outrageously good-looking bit of precocity, at seventeen, with a chestnut poodle-bang six inches high, told me how two distinguished Nairobi bachelors had shot themselves because of her. Both within the past year.

"I never, in *all* my life, got myself into so many tight spots as I have right here in *Nairobi!*"

"You!" I said. "You seem all right. It never occurred to any of these young men to shoot you, did it?"

"No. But it's so *embarrassing*, to have people going around *shooting* themselves!"

"Must be."

"And then, mamma gets mad as hell at some of the young men that come here, for leaving their cigarettes to burn themselves out on the piano."

I looked at that ebony baby grand. It had been branded, right enough.

"Now that *is* embarrassing," I said.

"It's just HELL!" she cried.

22. Lunch on the Equator

"SHE was only a settler's daughter—but she lost her Native Reserve!"

We sat on the lawn at Njoro, toying with a refrain that might fit Elspeth Huxley's geste. Eight interrelated dachshunds rolled gloriously in the sun. This was at 8,000 feet, and before us the Aberdare Range rose another five thousand through the thunder of the sun-filled clouds. I was reminiscing on the evil beauty of the two soda lakes below us—stagnant plaques, which, when I passed them, were rimmed with pink flamingoes, like islands of lilies, along their margins. And then, Lake Naivasha below them, with the white yachts sailing and the hippos blowing like whales in the shallows—and then the blue distances of the Great Rift, with its bronze volcanoes! That day I had driven around a volcano into which the groove of an old Phoenician trail disappeared, and began on the other side. Which proved, said my hostess, that the volcano had erupted since the Phoenicians had worn that trail in the search for gold.

"Ah! this is Kenya. *This* is Kenya!" she said challengingly, patting the cool lawn with her firm, sunburnt hands. "How dare you?"

I had told her again that I still could not bring this enchanted, or bewitched, colony into focus. And I was still resentful over what she had done to me the previous day. Without the slightest attempt to find out whether the person we were going to see was home or not, she had shoved me into a station-body Ford and driven me 100 miles! Of course, he was not at home.

He was Peter Kornange, the son of the senior chief of the Kikuyu. He had been to Columbia University; then he had had a year of Cambridge; then he had gone to the London School of Economics. When he returned to Kenya they offered him a teacher's post, at half the white teacher's salary. Peter refused to take it. He said, "My tuition charges were not cut in half because of my color!" So he had opened a native school to teach teachers himself; he already had six hundred pupils.

We went there, and found most of them, little tots up to the sixth grade, as puzzled about the sudden disappearance of Peter Kornange as we were. We learned that he had received that morning an urgent telephone call to go into Nairobi. I have nothing but my own instincts and suspicions to go by—but it was known that I was going to see Peter Kornange, and I feel perfectly certain that was the reason why Peter Kornange was not there.

I was obliged to spend the day listening to a colonial official. At that moment the Kikuyus were upset because the white settlers were forcibly ejecting the "squatters" from their farms; these were Kikuyu natives who, in return for the permission to live on these lands, gave the white owners a certain amount of free labor in exchange. Some of these Kikuyus had been living on the same land for several generations. It had been accepted in their simple minds that they had some claim to it, something slightly more than a moral dual ownership. But their cattle had been getting in the way of the settlers' cattle, and so they were told to move—evicted, in fact.

As the places selected for them were some 30 to 85 miles further out from Nairobi, the Kikuyus claimed that this would ruin them; they would not be able to get their stuff to the Nairobi market. And I now give you verbatim (because from their talk you may know them!) the "sporty" way in which this official answered these desperate Kikuyus:

"I said to them, 'Oh, but you blokes must remember this is *our* market—what? We built Nairobi. If we chaps hadn't built Nairobi, what would you blokes have done then—what?'"

Amazing, I know; but this conversation is accurate. I stopped the car and made notes as soon as I escaped from him.

There was at that time a row, just subsiding, with the Wakamba, a stout-hearted tribe of natives, over the destocking of their cattle. The whites were right; the Wakamba, who regard cattle as tokens of wealth and social position, had thousands more than they could use, sell, or care for. They had so many that the cattle ate all the grass; then erosion took place, and there was no grass. The Government issued an order that the Wakamba had to sell a large number of their cattle.

It was unfortunate (and no accident) that the representatives of a big London packing company appeared in Kenya, coincidently with this order, and erected a packing plant. This plant had to have at least 4,000 cattle a month to make it profitable. When the first batch of Wakamba cattle was forcibly auctioned there were no buyers—no one, except the packing company. It got the Wakamba cattle for a song.

Then there was hell to pay. A large body of Wakamba marched into Nairobi, and refused to leave. They demanded to see the Governor. He did not see them then (pity!); but later, when they had been persuaded to leave, he made a firm speech to them; they must obey the law. Then it was discovered that, legally, the Government could not force the Wakamba to sell their cattle!

The company then packed up. It announced publicly that it had been promised 4,000 cattle a month.

To all questions on topics like this, this complacent official (he was a "military fellah") replied: "Oh, those blokes are *agitators*! Mustn't listen to stuff like that. These blokes here [the Kikuyus], they're getting politically minded, too. No end of trouble. When these natives learn the error of their ways—."

When I asked him whether it wasn't true (as a Government agricultural expert had told me) that the Wakamba problem could have been solved if the Government had supplied water to

their country, instead of taking the easier, destocking way out—
this good man said, "Oh, you've been listening to somebody!"

When we turned around to drop down into the Great Rift
again, begin the 100-mile return trip, and forget the futile day
in the majestic vistas of Kenya, my hostess was silent for about
forty miles. Then she turned to me:

"I know it's bad," she said. "But you must remember one
thing: We British are the only race who would feel *worried*
about such things. We do not do them with an easy conscience.
That's something to be said."

I admitted that it was something—to feel remorse when you
have done someone a wrong. "But you will never forgive the
natives," I said, "for having made you do it."

That night we dined with an American who went out to
Kenya with Lord Delamere. After lurching, in the darkness,
about a mile across his place—mostly through water—we entered his house, whose interior might have been on Fifth Avenue. There was everything; all the latest American magazines
carefully shingled along the drawing-room table, the pseudo-
baronial fireplace—even the false model of a sailing ship.

Cocktails and dinner, ending with a candied float, were
served by his two Chinese. He paid these men once every five
years; then they took a year's refresher back in China. He spent
that year on the Riviera.

"But it's quite a blow," he gasped, petulantly, "when the
five years' pay day rolls along—what a ghastly amount I have
to cough up!"

He wore a mauve velvet dinner jacket.

The agricultural expert at Nakuru told me a good story.
He said he had been down arguing with some of the Wakamba
about not keeping their old or diseased cattle. Then one of
the old Wakamba said to him:

"Listen, master; here are two pound notes. One is old and

wrinkled and ready to tear; one is a new one. But they're both worth a pound, aren't they?"

He nodded.

"Well, it's the same way with our cows," explained the Wakamba. "They are both cows."

I've said enough about the retired-colonel type of settler, to give you the refreshing story of "the Etonian Who Made Good."

Eve and I left the charming little house, with its eight dachshunds and its real Goya over the modest fireplace, and its air of rich intelligence (for it was a remarkable woman who owned that lovely place at Njoro) and set out west over the mountains to the Kakamega gold fields and the papyrus swamps of Uganda.

That day we ate luncheon by the road directly on the equator, at 9,300 feet. There is a road sign there which is most exhilarating:

THE EQUATOR

| Southern | Northern |
| Hemisphere | Hemisphere |

The country around us was like an English landscape, with its light-green pasture land shining in the sun, and little stands of trees, like oaks. The lightness which you felt at that altitude gave you a constant exhilaration. The green was a vivid Irish green, on good, rich, red earth. It was easy to understand why the Kenyaites always feel so tenderly about their country. It is a lovely land.

That night we ran into the gold-mining town of Kakamega, mostly streets of unpainted, corrugated-iron shops, and felt for a second we were back in the American wild west.

The man I had gone to see was the one who had discovered this rich section of the Kakamega reef. He went down from Oxford in 1925. From 1925 to 1930 he was growing coffee in Kenya, and failed in the slump. Then he took a public-works job, building minor road bridges (reading how to, and getting the mechanical formulas out of books). Then, with £24 left, he set off into the bush.

For something like a year he and his "boy" prospected the rivers around Kakamega, where he felt sure there was gold. He lived on 50 cents' worth of native meat a week—and kept the key of his "chop box" in his pocket, so that his "boy" should not eat the groceries.

"Because, sometimes, we were very hungry," he told me.

He found plenty of "color" in the streams—but you may find that anywhere in the streams of this part of Africa. He concentrated his prospecting in a narrow area. Rivals came in, intrigued by his actions, and they staked claims practically all around him. He did not want to waste his precious chance for a claim. Finally he staked his claim—after a few weeks of intense reasoning with himself—and hit the main reef dead on the nose.

He went to Switzerland that winter, met an American girl, also there for the skiing, and married her. When Eve and I stayed with them they were living in the same papyrus-lined hut that he and his "boy" had built. He had not had enough money to work the claim by himself; so, in London, he enlisted three other men. This year they were installing a cyanide plant, and they had netted £10,000.

And that, the £10,000, was the peculiarly interesting part of his story; he and his partners did not expect the mine to make much more than that. They had decided that if they raised more capital in London, installed heavy, productive machinery, and sank big shafts, they might lose everything, or they might find themselves working just for the machinery. So they deliberately decided to keep the mine small. I watched them erecting the three new cyanide tanks in the jungle. But the shaft was just a square hole in the forest, down which the grinning natives disappeared, to send the stuff up in buckets. From £10,000 to a possible £20,000 a year was what these four men decided to net

each year. And this man, the discoverer and field superintendent, got one-quarter of it.

"It won't be a fortune," he said, with his unemotional, quiet
smile, "but it won't be precarious. We are not running any
stock-exchange racket here. I don't know how long it will last,
but if I get £2,000 or £3,000 a year, I can save half of it. And
that's enough for any man."

He and his pretty young American wife were planning to go
again to Switzerland to ski that winter—but that was in 1939!

They weren't going to enlarge their house, as she liked the
buff reeds of the papyrus lining their walls. They had gone in
for the luxury of bringing out an Austrian girl to nurse their
baby. "We live simply," she laughed, as the cocktails were
served, "but I find that our drink bill is one and a half times
our household accounts!"

I had never realized that a *gold* mine could be tamed to become so domestic an affair. I thought the precious metal would
either make you a millionaire or drive you mad. It's true that
down in Johannesburg, at the request of the Rand *Daily Mail*,
I had unearthed and interviewed old George Honeyball, the
first man who walked along the great Rand Reef and knew he
was walking on it. He warned his aunt not to sell her farm, as
there was gold underneath it. But he never made a penny of it
himself. He was a wheelwright and contented to remain one,
and he told me the largest sum of money he ever made in one
day was for tiring four wagon wheels. "I think it was £2 10s."
The largest sum he ever held in his hands was £400, which he
was carrying from one man to another. And the largest amount
he ever possessed at one time was £100, which the late Sir Abe
Bailey gave him a few years ago, when his existence and whereabouts were discovered.

When I sat with him and his little black dog, as he faltered
and tugged at his long, white beard, as if tugging at memories,
he was getting a pension of £15 a month from the Johannesburg
mine owners.

"But it is quite enough," he said, patting his fat, black little dog. "She hates Kaffirs," he said, irrelevantly. "Good day, sir."

George Honeyball had gone the way of most discoverers. But here in Kenya was a young Englishman, entitled to wear the "old school tie" if ever a man was, who had set himself to find a reef, found it—and hung on to it. His good sense was almost unbelievable.

"But what on earth ever gave you the original idea of turning prospector?" I asked. "Did you know anything about gold?"

"Only in sovereigns," he said. "But I could not think of anything *else* to do. You see, I was just about broke. And I had made up my mind that nothing—nothing—was going to be allowed to squeeze me out of Kenya!"

It was a fitting farewell to that colony which, unquestionably, holds more "personalities" to the square mile than any other section of the British Commonwealth. It was also significant. For Kenya, the days of the gin swillers and the remittance men are over; it will be men like this gold miner who will make it. And it holds quite a number of them.

The next day we dropped down into Uganda. It became hotter and hotter. Soon we were in the deep papyrus swamps. Those tufted stalks, with the black water gurgling beside the road, and the cranes, made you think of Egypt. We passed a frontier police post. The native roads were narrow, winding, but made of surprisingly good red earth. Soon they became flanked with banana plantations.

Then the earth seemed to fall off short!

This was Victoria Nyanza, the same color as the blue sky. A huge, white-sailed dhow was just standing out across it towards a faint line across the world where this inland sea and sky met. This was at Jinga, near the source of the Nile.

The historic Ripon Falls are only some sixty yards across, with a drop of less than twenty feet. There is a rocky islet in the center, bearing some fresh green trees, which splits the smoothly bending overflow. Below, in a narrow, deep gorge, the river twists and turns in sparkling whirlpools. Usually, in a cove here, you can see the hippos standing on the bottom, feeding.

"The Germans have a queer idea," a man on the hotel veranda told us. "You know what scientific chaps they are? Well, one of their geologists has discovered that Lake Tanganyika lies 1,200 feet below shallow Lake Victoria; you know, this lake is never more than 250 deep at any place. Well, this is the German's idea: The barrier of flats between the two lakes is only inconsiderable. It would only require a slight change to *drain* Lake Victoria. Just a few blasts of dynamite—and bang! goes Lake Victoria!"

"What do you think would happen to Egypt then?" he ruminated. "Wake up some morning, the poor 'Gippies,' and find there just *was* no Nile! No Nile in Egypt! Grandiose idea, isn't it?"

He took another suck at his pipe. "The hell of it is, that German geologist was right; it *could* be done. In 1926 the Egyptian Government sent some archaeologists to Tanganyika, who confirmed this."

That night we drew up before the glittering lights of the Hotel Imperial, at Kampala. We had left the last "white man's country" in Africa.

23. Uganda Politics

"YOU'LL find the roads good in Uganda," said an English-man in Kenya; "the natives build them."

This strikes the note. Kenya has the worst roads in Africa—and the most important one, the one down from Nairobi to Mombasa on the coast, has been deliberately let go to waste, so it is said, because it competed with the unprofitable railroad; the Indians had developed a cheap freight service by motor lorries.

Uganda, on the other hand, is not a "white man's country." Practically all the cultivation is done by the natives on their own plantations. Almost the sole export is cotton. And to get out the cotton the natives have constructed this fine spider web of narrow, red roads which allow you to get almost everywhere in the country—particularly in the kingdom of Buganda.

Uganda, if it were not for the climate, would be the British colonial official's paradise. There are roughly 3,700,000 natives, 17,300 Indians, 2,100 white men. The natives grow all the crops; the Indians do all the middle-man work in selling them; 76 per cent of the European community, the "whites," are Colonial Office officials, missionaries, or their families. The 1936 census showed that, of the remainder, 282, including 57 occupied in clerical tasks, were engaged in industry and commerce, and only 103 were in agriculture.

The territory known as the Protectorate of Uganda is commonly supposed to be a native kingdom. Actually, it is divided into four sections: Buganda, Toro, Ankole and Bunyoro. In the agreements which the British made with the natives in 1900,

Buganda was considered to have an "established government," and it was conceded that all the "occupied land" was in the gift of the Kabaka, the native king. Consequently, 9,003 surveyed square miles out of 18,600 were reserved for the Kabaka of Buganda and his 3,700 native chiefs. Today a Kabaka rules at Kampala, with three native ministers and his own native assembly, the Lukiko. He is "advised" only slightly by a British Resident. It is probably the nearest thing to an independent native kingship left in Africa.

Ankole is ruled by a Mugabe. Toro has a slightly less powerful native ruler.

Today, out of the total area of 80,371 square miles in Uganda, excluding open water, only 9,627 square miles represent the areas *actually* left with the chiefs (at their disposition); yet, of the total area of Uganda, less than 500 square miles are in non-native hands. Only in Buganda is there recognized private ownership of lands.

This gives you a rough image of the scene: The Kabaka, with his small pomp (and salute of nine guns), behind the rush palisades of his palace at Kampala, with his own prime minister, minister of finance (a very intelligent man, whom I met), and a chief justice empowered to give death sentences, subject to approval by the British Governor. The last Kabaka drank himself to death.

The kingdom of Buganda is governed by the Kabaka, his native parliament, and a highly organized (and not altogether altruistic) system of chiefs and subchiefs. In the Ankile and Toro territories the officials of the British Colonial Service have their district officers, and carry on their usual colonial administration. There are eleven British officials in Buganda itself.

And these British colonial officials in Uganda, working in a purely native state and unimpeded by white settlers' demands, have an administrative laboratory in which they have made their work a model for the rest of Africa.

It is encouraging to watch the way in which the English are

administering this "protectorate," living up to the spirit of the word itself, governing this land of natives *for* the natives as much as they can *by* the natives; in short, living up to their promises to "protect" the black man from the white.

Compared to Kenya, Uganda is also a paradise for the natives. It was the Kabaka of Buganda, who, when the commission for a closer union in East Africa met in Whitehall, refused with all his might to be forced into this white settlers' dream of a fusion of Kenya, Tanganyika, and Uganda. His minister (the intelligent finance minister I have just mentioned) said:

"Uganda does not wish to become a horse in the Kenya stables."

There is in Uganda a dizzy confusion of nomenclature, quite unpardonable, which prevents the outside world from discovering who is who and what is what. It seems to be the chief pride of the local white inhabitants—a priggish pedantry, quite mid-Victorian—to remind you about this unnecessary madness of words.

For example, the protectorate is known as *Uganda*. But its chief division is called *Buganda*, its people are the *Baganda*, an individual person is a *Muganda*, and its language is known as *Luganda*. In Ankole, the people are known as Munyankole or Banyankole, the language is Lunyankole; the adjective is Kinyankole, and—I am a bit confused by now—the cattle adjective, I believe, is Ensagala. I think I'm right when I say that Ensagala are cattle of Ankole—anyway, it doesn't matter.

But it is a part of the exasperating backward-thinking of many complacent Government servants in Uganda that they stress these distinctions, to demonstrate the superiority of their intelligence over an eager newcomer's, and it makes understanding what anything in Uganda *is*, the greatest difficulty.

But, as in Tanganyika, there is one thing that the British have a right to be proud of in Uganda; that is the justness of their administration.

You feel that at Entebbe, the British capital. Here is a domain that has never known the heavy German touch or the rapacity of the average white settler. Here is administration undefiled by Big Business interests. It is as if, freed from these pressures, the dream of a colonial officer's home had come to being on the riffled shores of Lake Victoria. Here on a high promontory jutting out into the lake is a colonial seat that has been planned and has not grown by accident. With remarkable foresight, the British have tampered as little as possible with its original landscape. Mangoes have been introduced to give shady drives; there are lawns, lawns, lawns everywhere. Each bungalow has its garden. And the center of it all is a vast, green, open space, giving everyone a wide view over the limitless horizon of Lake Victoria, full of happy hippos!

The atmosphere of Entebbe is one of altruistic administration. It speaks of unhurried research. You feel, suddenly, that this is the way things *ought* to be in Africa. This is a native country, left as native by the British as possible, yet still held in fief as a British protectorate. If there is any oppression, it is the oppression of one native over another—which is not altogether unknown in Africa. And if the Kabaka of Buganda and the Mugabe of Ankole and the Mukama of Toro are not *absolutely* independent rulers, you will have to admit, when you know the arbitrary despotism of other native chiefs, that such a state of white control is probably the best for the rest of Uganda's black inhabitants; also that the Kabaka is the highest example of an independent native king left in Africa.

Entebbe provokes novel thoughts in your attitude towards Africa. It disturbs some hereditary white man's prejudices. In Tanganyika, the natural thing for a white man to think is: Why don't the British develop this vast territory for the natives, as well as for England? In Kenya, your paramount feeling (if you have any feelings) is one of pity for the natives who have been driven out of their highlands; this feeling being always accompanied by the question, Why, after fifty years' settlement, have the whites done so little with the land they pre-empted that today there are still less than 2,000 white settlers there, settled on the land, and most of them are in debt to the banks?

At Entebbe one of the hereditary suppositions that you drop is that Africa is destined, all morality being unavailing, to be exploited by the white man. Also, that turning it into a factory to supply European requirements is not necessarily advancing the steps of civilization. In short, when you see this example of British control, you begin to wish heartily that the whites had used the same restraint in the rest of Africa.

The British found a high native civilization when they went to Uganda—the Bunyoros and the Baganda had dynasties of kings—and the British have taken a pride in preserving as much of the native independence of this part of Africa as possible.

"Independence" is always a term which demands strict definition. What is the independence of the Kabaka? And how much? How far do the British, or would the Germans, or will the Italians let a native ruler exist, undisturbed, in changing Africa? In Uganda the British have already given their answer to the last question.

When the British explorers, Speke and Grant, went to Uganda, in 1862, they were astonished to find an African kingdom with an already highly developed political organization, and comparatively civilized life. At its top, the governing class were the Bahima, the Hamitic tribes which swept over Bantu, negroid Uganda, in the seventeenth century. They were ruled by a Kabaka (king), with his ministers, and a Lukiko, a native parliament which was responsible for legislation and was the final judicial authority. The Kabaka, even in those days, was somewhat like the King of England today, leaving the work of governing his country to his cabinet and Parliament.

Also, as in England, Buganda was divided into counties, each under the rule of what is known as a *saza* chief; under him were lesser or *gombolola* chiefs.

This essential structure the British took over, and confirmed in the 1900 agreement, which recognized the ruling Kabaka as the "native ruler of the province of Uganda under His British Majesty's *protection and overrule.*"

Subject to the veto of the Governor, the power of the Kabaka is large, if limited, today; it might be compared to the liberty enjoyed by some of the smaller native states in India.

For example, the court of the Lukiko can pronounce the death sentence, although it must be consented to by the Governor, and a final appeal can be made to the Privy Council in England. The *saza* chiefs have criminal powers up to one year's imprisonment and twenty-four strokes. The *gombolola* chiefs can sentence up to three months or ten strokes. Prisoners are confined in native prisons in Buganda, though convicts with over two years' sentence are usually transferred to the Protectorate jails. These native prisons can be inspected by British officers.

The Lukiko (native parliament) has, subject to the veto of the Governor, the right to pass laws for internal legislation in Buganda, such as the right to evict peasants who are on Buganda-owned lands; the right to impose a tax on land, and the right to define native custom in regard to succession anywhere on the 9,003 square miles "left within the gift of the Kabaka" by the 1900 British-Buganda agreement. Of course, the native courts cannot try any white man or any African who is not a Baganda.

Now, although the names of the prime minister, the chief justice, and the minister of finance must be submitted to the British Governor (who has the right to reject them), the Lukiko itself is constituted on oligarchic rather than popular lines. It consists of the three above ministers, the county chiefs, three notables nominated by the Kabaka from each of the counties, and six other notables appointed by the Kabaka from the country at large.

It is not a House of Commons, an elected assembly. There is no form of election. It is a native House of Lords.

And the Baganda—the people, that is—would like to change

it. Buganda, with its system of private ownership of land, has a leisured class. These are native landowners, many living on their rents, like English lords. But this leisured class has bred its own destroyers—the Baganda intelligentsia.

And it is between these two factions—the "ruling families" and the intelligentsia, which may come from either the Buhima aristocratic class or the Bantu working class—that the British Government at Entebbe must act as referees, often uncomfortable.

The Kabaka, his ministers, his *saza* and *gombolola* chiefs receive 25 per cent of the poll tax in Buganda; this, in 1938, amounted to £30,880.

Furthermore, there are revenues controlled by the Kabaka's government, such as commutation for obligatory labor for state purposes, land tax, fees and fines from the judicial courts, market dues and licenses, etc., which in 1935 amounted to £128,638.

Apart from the 25 per cent remitted by the British from the total poll tax, the whole of these other revenues may be said to have been imposed by the Lukiko, and the Buganda budget (subject to approval by the British Governor) is made out by the Lukiko itself.

It is felt at Entebbe that too large a part of this native budget is spent on personal emoluments, establishment, and "overhead charges."

The Buganda budget does not *have* to provide items for either education or medical activities, although an annual grant is made of £1,600 to the Protectorate Government for medical stores, and in 1937 there was a nonrecurring item in the Buganda budget of £5,000 for the erection and maintenance of dispensaries and maternity centers. (These last have been very popular, by the way.)

So there you have it, the independence of the Kabaka of Uganda. Similar but more restricted liberties are allowed to the Mugabe of Ankole and the Mukama of Toro. There are some eleven British administrative officers serving under the British

Commissioner in Buganda, theoretically to control tax assessment and supervise the subordinate courts. In practice they are often not only "advisers" but take a direct part in the Buganda administration.

This last has been questioned by Lord Haily, in his tremendous, authoritative work, *An African Survey*. He says the present system may not be taking "full advantage of the opportunities offered by the Buganda *as a training ground in administrative responsibilities.*"

There it is. There are something like 3,700,000 natives in Uganda, of which the Buganda alone number 877,000. I have given you a brief outline of the administration. You can imagine for yourselves what it would be under the Germans or Italians. It is not a static state; the Protectorate of Uganda is still "in the making." If the British administration thinks that the Kabaka and his chiefs are being too oppressive with the minor peasantry, it forces a new agreement with the Kabaka. If the Kabaka's parliament thinks that a British "suggestion" for a contribution to education is too steep, it may refuse it—and has already done so.

"I often wish," sighed a British official to me, "that we had a small unofficial minority in our deliberations at Entebbe. Some of us get tired of having our duty to our 'little black brethren' shoved down our throats all day long by our own staff!"

Here it may be interesting to note that practically every Baganda in public life is nominally a Christian.

But if you wish to get the real flavor of this unique native kingdom in Africa you must go to Kampala, the native capital and the commercial center. Entebbe is such a garden of bureaucrats that there is not even a hotel. It is a park of English civil servants. Kampala has a hotel with plaster columns, floors of polished stone, and a foyer which is part of the dining room that is Moorish in its use of height and space. It is owned by an Armenian, who owns the only European newspaper, among other things, and whose operations are so broad and powerful that he is known as "the uncrowned King of Uganda." Kampala is a Baganda cosmopolis—in which the English are shop or bank employees.

Entebbe, practically on the equator, is hot and muggy, despite the fact that the waters of Lake Victoria are nearly 4,000 feet above sea level. Kampala, a confusing town, is built on seven hills. Along its main cement street—with the three inevitable British banks, the post office, a branch of the Scotch druggist shops which you see throughout East Africa—stroll tall Baganda women, all looking as if they were dressed for a ball. The male native population, dressed in white trousers and European tweed jackets, threatens to run you down with bicycles which flash by like shoals of flying fish.

Over most of Africa the women seem content with a bunch of leaves fore and aft, or aprons of beaten bark or softened leather, or a loose winding of printed cotton that will sometimes bear quotations (I saw one, in Uganda, which said: "O.K. I love you"). In some parts, such as South Africa and parts of the Belgian Congo, the missionaries and white man's prudery have forced these beautiful, bronze bodies into disgusting Mother Hubbards. But Baganda girls seem always going to a ball!

The fabrics are silk or taffeta. The favorite color is primrose or cerise. The rustling skirt, showing an incongruous bare foot, sweeps the ground, and there is always a sash of the same material around the waist. These women, the wives and daughters of *saza* or *gombolola* chiefs, or comparatively rich Uganda cotton growers, are the best dressed women in Africa—often better than the white.

The silk dresses are gathered tightly over budding and what seem always firm breasts. They have shoulder straps. In broad daylight you see soft, satiny shoulders gleaming in the sun.

The European shops and banks account for only a meager

minority of the buildings along the strange street. The majority are wooden native emporiums; each with a Singer sewing machine being busily pedaled on their street-level verandas, and all being watched by these beautiful, tall, bronze women to see what models are being sewn.

Kampala is only twenty-five miles north of the equator. The sun here can kill a white man easily, but these kinky-haired women all go about without hats. And their well-shaped heads, above the lovely shoulders, all look as if they had just had the latest thing in European crops. To a white man, sweating along under a sun helmet, his eyes perpetually squinted to protect his optic nerves against the white heat, these ballroom figures make him suspect, if he is new to the town, that this time he really *has* got the D.T.'s!

Owing to the Mohammedan influence, many of the men are dressed in the long white robe that is so much like a nightgown.

On Kasubi Hill, amidst the flame trees, is the tomb of Mutesa, who was Kabaka when the British came. His anti-Christian son often used the hill for human sacrifices. The present tomb, a richly carved hall, still sees each morning the descendants of this brilliant African monarch. They are the hereditary guardians of his grave.

Below the main street, looking down into a valley always filled with the red haze of constant building and excavations, is a hillside of Hindus and Sikhs. Thousands upon thousands! These ant-like Asiatics do over 90 per cent of the business in all Uganda. They are rich, therefore insolent, and some of the worst artificers I have ever met. When one of them ruined my valuable camera by trying to *twist* it apart!—I found that all my fine phrases of European cursing were wasted upon him. He sat there—bearded, full of explanations, impervious. Until I had a brain wave:

"By God," said I, "you're a bloody disgrace to the Aga Khan!"

Then his four comrades fell upon him, and, verbally, fairly eviscerated him. That Aga Khan!

I hung around hot Kampala several days trying to see the Kabaka. I was told by the British Resident, with a frown, and looking as if he intended to protect the Kabaka from me, "The Kabaka, these days, never sees anyone." I was told that His Majesty was ill—the usual diplomatic chill, I suppose; and then an official in the lounge of the hotel probably gave me the real reason:

"You won't see the Kabaka, old boy, because he's always suffering from a hang-over. It's ruined his looks, so he won't let anybody see him. What you ought to do is get next to the finance minister—there's the lad for you! He's just about ten times quicker on the uptake than any Government wallah in the district. Always gives the Resident a headache. What say, Snaffles?"

Snaffles, who was an oil man, tossed back his second whisky. "See 'im," he said, "an' tell him what I think of him, lettin' all these damn Hindus come in here and run all his country for him! Have y'ever tried to do business with one of these 'Wogs'?"

(In case you don't know it, "Wog" means Wily Oriental Gentlemen; it's a word not unknown among the English in India.) Suffering from my camera trouble, I was inclined to agree with him. "I know," I said; "I've been listening to Indian trouble all the way up from Durban; but how do they do it?"

"Human chain," said the official. "One Indian gets in, pulls a whole string of other Indians along after him."

"Yes," said the oil man, "and the natives don't seem to know how to organize, whereas the Indian's a whiz at it." Then he turned to me:

"And you can imagine the Indians claiming that *we* impose upon *them*! No wonder we people in Kenya won't let 'em settle in the white highlands! Bloody locusts—that's what they are!

Here, in Uganda, they're eating up every job that a native could take. Three cheers for the Aga Khan!"

"Well, I don't know," said the other. "If we really mean what we say, that we're going to help our little black Uganda brothers along the rocky road of progress, then I think it's up to us, the Government fellows here, to use some initiative in working out a plan to help the Baganda market their cotton crop—use some wits—don't let the Indians have such a middle-man monopoly. Some sort of Government plan."

"Government plan, my foot! You know what that means—miles of official reports on 'What's the Incidence of Left-handedness among the Baganda Cotton Pickers,' and bilge like that.

"Look here, how do you account for this? I've been working on some specifications. Now, tell me this: Why is it that you can buy the same gauge and quality of corrugated iron from an Indian agent in Kampala—ordered from England, mind you—at the price the public works department says they pay for it? The P.W.D. doesn't have to pay the 15 per cent import duty; they get rebates on railway and shipping rates. Yet they say the stuff doesn't cost them a penny less than they could buy it from a private Indian trader here—*the same make of goods, mind you!*

"We're supposed to have a crown agent purchasing for the colonies, aren't we? Is he just plain stupid—doesn't know how to buy corrugated iron in England—or is there a crown agent's graft?"

"Scandalous, these Government contracts," smiled the official.

"Well, I can tell you one thing—the Government spends £2,000 to put up a bungalow for one of the wallahs over at Entebbe that a private builder could put up for £600! Just check up on that!"

"Don't want to. My trade's just as easy as selling postage stamps. All we have to do is persuade millions more natives and Chinese to get the nicotine habit. Civilize 'em with a cigarette."

" 'Boy!' " shouted the oil man, and clapped his hands. A barefooted native materialized. "Same thing again," ordered the oil man. Then, to me: "Speaking of civilization," he said, "when you're talking to these Baganda chaps keep some of our own cabinet in mind! See the whole blinking cabinet, if you can." And so it was arranged.

I have spoken of hereditary prejudices, and certainly one of them is the belief that a convocation of black politicians is, somehow, funny; in other words, it's rather apelike or backwards in its deliberations. It would be merely priggish to deny that we think so. Otherwise, why (aside from land grabbing) should we be always trying to justify our "educational mission" in Africa, presumptuously teaching the natives how to live, how to govern themselves, bringing the word of God to them, and all that? More than half of it we cannot do (govern ourselves properly, run our own economics) or don't believe (religion) at home. So if you let the humor of that situation prowl about in your mind as you face a native council, you will have some novel fun.

I was received by the prime minister, the chief justice, and some twenty *saza* and *gombolola* chiefs. They were all dressed in European jackets, worn over the white native robe which reaches to the feet. They were kindly, inquisitive, with very intelligent minds. One or two faces bore the stamp of nobility of character.

I was received in the cabinet chamber adjoining the rush palisade which surrounds the Kabaka's late-Victorian "palace." This is on a red hill, up which I had driven along a broad avenue of flame trees, and I made a fairly agreeable contact with the three ministers, and the chiefs, by saying that in the rear locker of my car rested the verbatim report of the Parliamentary Committee for Closer Union in East Africa; of the proceedings in which the finance minister had said, of the British effort to merge Uganda with Kenya and Tanganyika:

"His Highness, the Kabaka, says he does not want to be a horse in Kenya's stables!

"We should like things to remain the way they are. . . . Are we not in all fairness entitled to oppose a scheme which will literally rob us of our birthright and substitute therefor a mess of pottage which in all possibility will have acquired a bad taste, but which we know will be the means of introducing discontent where heretofore has been almost perfect harmony? . . . Honorable members, we are a small community, comparatively, but we ask for fair play, we ask for a continuance of the redemption of the promise given us, we ask for that justice. . . . It would be worth while to put it down on paper in black and white . . . we should like whatever is going out to be printed out exactly in that paper. . . . We get promises; we do not doubt those promises, but when an official paper comes out there is nothing mentioned with regard to the position of the Buganda Kingdom. . . ."

Question: "Is it the unknown that you are afraid of?" Answer: "It is strange to us, and we cannot express an opinion unless the whole thing is put down on paper, so that we can understand after considering and digesting it properly."

Q: "But a scheme which is put forward, *with very general powers to a High Commissioner* [my italics], you are afraid of. That has been published?" A: "We are afraid of the whole white paper as it stands at the present time, and, as I said in my statement, *we would rather be left alone where we are now.*" [Again my italics.]

Please explain! Please leave us alone! Please put it in writing —*where the public can read it!*

(You see this intelligent finance minister of Buganda appearing before the British Joint Select Committee on *Closer Union in East Africa,* trying to get the English "to speak straight words.")

Big Ben tolls the hours overhead; for days the proceedings are persisted in; the British, without saying so in so many words, are mentally encircling the African delegates, trying to get them to agree to a merging of Uganda with Tanganyika and Kenya; then they try to get acquiescence in a process which, by inevitable steps, will inexorably lead to the same thing. This smiling minister before me here at Kampala shows a mental adroitness which refuses to be trapped; he won't agree or admit anything that is not put in plain words. With apparently innocent suggestions, and by devious approach, the best brains in England try to "establish statements" in the record. The finance minister has a hereditary awareness; this is like being chased about by assassins in the darkness among the huts of a village! He keeps on his toes mentally.

The committee before which he is appearing consists of an earl, a viscount, nine barons, two knights, and seven, as yet, undecorated others. Sometimes, as you read the words (page 546, etc.) you begin to suspect that these Englishmen are not always intentionally confusing; they just don't know their own language well enough to ask a simple question in plain English.

"Chairman: Lord Phillimore, I think you will get better satisfaction if you put your questions perhaps with less exordium and more directly, if I may suggest it." (Page 558.)

But outstanding appears the fact that the noble lords are incapable of asking direct questions because (a) they have not read the testimony submitted by the Africans to this committee; (b) they know nothing about the background of Uganda which forms the basis of these reports; (c) they are mentally incapable of grasping the subjects; and, from their side, they do not wish to make their motives plain.

Finally, these peculiar proceedings begin to give off a bad odor in the British press. The proceedings are dropped. That report, from H.M. Stationery Office, will cost you £1 10s. 0d. It is a weighty tome, worth the price!

One of the questions that the finance minister was forced to answer was (Paragraph 5633): "Anyhow, you do not want a central legislature set up [for Kenya, Tanganyika and Uganda] that might start with a very small degree of power, but might extend its power later on?"

Serwano Kulubya, finance minister and representative of His Highness, the Kabaka of Buganda, answered, "No."

"Why?" I asked him, as we sat in Kampala.

"Because such a commissioner, beginning with the fusion of railways and economic services—as the British suggest—would have the power of legislating for these services. With the power to legislate, degrees of political fusion would be inevitable. We prefer to remain by our agreement with the British of 1900."

On the committee in London sat Lord Lugard, who had made the original British agreement with the Baganda. I believe that if the natives had been left to deal with that grand old African administrator alone, many useful things might have emerged from the London talks. There, at least, was a white man who talked their talk!

The frantic desire of the Bagandas to be left alone to develop their own Africanism was the paramount impression I carried away from this discussion in Kampala. Some of their wishes were paradoxical; for example—I think it was the prime minister who said this—"We want more of our own engineers, professional men able to hold higher positions now filled by the British service. We think the kingdom ought to take over its own medical services and supply them. But most of all we want more primary schools; we want to raise the general level of education."

Therefore, when the Resident, and the Government at Entebbe, had asked the Baganda to give £5,000 in their budget —just once, in the year 1938—towards the expenses of the new Makerere University at Kampala (a most advanced African training school) the Baganda refused.

"We gave £1,000 to Makerere and £4,000 to the lower

schools," said the minister. "We want all our children to be able to read and write."

This struck the note of haste, and of apprehension on the part of the Africans—you see this all over Africa—that the best defense of the native population against encroaching demands of the white man is *education*. It was as if they feared the white man wished to create a native *élite* which would be nearer to the white man than their own people—an *élite* which would do away with the old tribal traditions.

The three ministers are paid by the native parliament £800 a year each. The Kabaka gets an official payment from the Buganda budget of £5,692. There is apparently more, besides. And the *saza* and *gombolola* chiefs around me each controlled on the average 7,000 people. The *saza* for the Kampala county had administration over 165,000 people on 1,638 square miles, and had 14 *gombolola* chiefs under him. Salaries for the *saza* and the *gombolola* chiefs amounted yearly to £14,000 for the 20 *saza* chiefs, and £46,000 for the 170 *gombolola* chiefs. Out of this, these chiefs paid their own retainers, native police, etc. It seemed an imposing and well paid bureaucracy.

All this money, you must understand clearly, came from the native Bagandas themselves. No contribution is made to them by the British colonial service; in fact, the service, by taking 80 per cent of the poll tax, pays for itself without getting any grants from England. Uganda is a self-supporting show.

"Economically, there is no reason whatever why the Kingdom of Buganda should not be completely self-contained," said the finance minister. And he pointed out that of the £5,700,000 Uganda exports in 1937, over £4,269,000 had come from cotton, nearly every boll grown on native plots, averaging one acre out of their five-acre farms. "A very good example, if you want it," he said smilingly, "of *native* industry!"

The ministers all added that if left entirely alone Uganda could look after itself. Nevertheless, they said—though not in so many words—the British Protectorate was a *fait accompli;*

they accepted the Governor's right to final veto, and, with a few minor changes, *they would be perfectly happy to go on with things the way they are, along the lines of their present agreement with the British; they have been very fair!*

(Again the italics are mine.) The opinion emphasizes a pleasant situation in Africa.

British white papers are not the Bibles they once were. Before this war is over they will be rated less and less—until they will take a sharp upward curve again. I do not think that such an exhibition of hypocrisy will ever again be permitted by the British people as the so-called naval disarmament conference of 1930 (where disarmament as such was killed in St. James's Palace); nor do I think there will ever again be so questionable a performance as that sitting of the Parliamentary Select Committee for Closer Union in East Africa, in Westminster, in 1931. In the vast and vital change of social values which will take place during this war the power of titled incompetents such as Lord Dumbell is bound to diminish. Something like realism and truth will be demanded by the public.

My prediction is that the Kingdom of Buganda is only on the threshold of its career; that is, if Great Britain wins.

We sat there most of the morning. I submitted to considerable questioning from the *saza* chiefs, who had not seen so much of the world as Serwano Kulubya. The last act in leaving, as I was getting into my car, was from an old *saza* aristocrat. He clasped my hand and said: "We were afraid to talk to you, when we heard you were a man from the United States, when we heard you came from the United States, because of the way you treat Negroes in the United States."

He still held my hand, and looked at me questioningly. The other *saza* and *gombolola* chiefs drew nearer. Obviously, some explanation was demanded. But I couldn't give it.

"It's too long a question," I said. "I've been asking you

questions all morning. I wish you had begun to ask me this question earlier."

Then I hastily drove off. Into my eyes came the image of Coffee Bluffs, with its tattered shanties, outside Savannah. My God, what would I have been able to tell them, if they had asked me that question? *We*, who had robbed the African of his dignity!

24. Lake Victoria

"YOU could put all Ireland into the middle of that lake, an'
still not be able to see it from the shore. I've sometimes
thought of trying it!" he said dreamily.

The Veterinary Man (who was an Irishman himself) waved
his arms towards the blue distances of Victoria Nyanza. There
was a chill dawn wind, so that the water near us was slaty and
melancholy. On the horizon, some islands, the Seses, rose up,
green, with here and there a red cliff. And the white sail of a
native dhow moved between them.

"The equator runs right through that one," he said.

On the previous day I had been shooting crocodiles among
the rushes around that half submerged vegetation—or, rather,
shooting *at* "crocs." "Old Charley Croc, he's pretty quick! I've
never got *one*," said the assistant in the Research Department.
"Hits galore—seen them thrash the water—but then they go
down! How long can they stay under water? Why, I've waited
around *all morning!* Waiting for one to come up—a 'croc' I'd
shot, I mean. He was looking at me all the time, with just his
eyes sticking out. Then he went in among the rushes."

I had been fishing with the natives, in a thirty-foot canoe,
made from four slabs of tree sewn together. I mentioned my
wonder at the millions of birds which lived on this low island
opposite us, the one which the equator ran through. These
green islands, resting on the slaty inland sea—sometimes so
calm that they seem to be floating in mid-air—have a nimbus
of birds nesting, or perched on their spidery branches. The
white of egrets, the constant movement of cormorants, the dives

of snake-birds. And there is hardly a rush which does not hold one of the little bell-like nests of the weaver birds, into which these vivid flits of yellow climb from underneath.

There is an ambatch tree, growing out of the water with orange flowers, its branches splashed with white guano. The lake has long channels and water barriers. I had brought my shotgun along to shoot a goose (the native fishermen I was with had reported seeing some around the island), but all I could come on were millions of coots, jerkily darting, like wound-up toys, into the hidden places. Resting in a channel among the rushes, I had been staring at a crocodile for fully a minute before I knew he was a "croc." He wasn't thirty yards from me, just his eyes showing.

The *silent* "croc"! There he was, like a bit of log!

When I shot, thousands of cormorants dropped from the ambatch trees, striking the water so that they could take flight. White egrets rose like feathers blown into the air by the explosion. Small terns zigzagged and squeaked around me. Black-and-white kingfishers shot past on a dash for safety. But Charley Croc did not show his face again.

This northern end of Lake Victoria is subject to terrific electric storms. One hit us now. It was both terrifying and delicately beautiful. The wind was terrific, but under that gunpowder sky the sea was silvered by the wind and rain. Frosted. This dark little island near us, with its jungle center and shores covered with hippo dung, was uninhabited, said the natives, because the tsetse fly which had once entirely depopulated the Sese islands still lived there. Anyway, the natives still believed it did, and wouldn't live there. None of us wanted to push through that tangle of water reeds and steaming undergrowth, so we hauled our canoe up on a granite ledge and lay there, watching another canoe fighting its way to the same sanctuary against waves and wind. It was extraordinary, lying directly across the equator (with possibly, for all we knew, our heads in the Northern Hemisphere and our legs in the Southern) to be so cold.

Yet the broad waters of Lake Victoria lie 4,000 feet above sea level, where the Nile begins—at 3,792 ft., to be precise. Even when drenched on some Scottish loch in April, Eve and I never felt such a shivering. I had not got the malaria, yet, but the hot, lower country had already drained the blood out of us.

We had just finished going along our net, which was over a mile long. It took us two hours. And we got six fish of about 1½ pounds each, and three crabs. The fish were ngege, the only kind worth eating in this district, and, as an Irishman would say, "along the lines of a perch." The Baganda are not troubled by any generic word for fish; they are simply "the things in the lake."

Still, you are grateful for the firm-fleshed ngege in this land where everything seems pulpy and without flavor—including humans. While we were lying with the rain lashing at us, the fisherman told me there were some taboos on the islands. There were some places where a woman could not go; there were some where no sheep could be brought; there were some, he said, with opening eyes, that were inhabited by nothing except pythons. Then, he said, there were islands where the sitatunga, the web-footed deer, lived.

All of these islands, of course, abounded with crocodiles and had hippos around them. When we paddled back across a leaden sea to the veterinary station (where a lovely sitatunga happily roams its paddock), we hauled up our canoe through a margin of purple and white lotus and beached it where the Roman Catholic fathers first landed when they came up this vast inland sea from the shores of Tanganyika.

"Yasoni," said Dick, my host, "get everything ready—beds, mosquito nets, pots, pans—three people. Understand?"

"Eh-h-h!" said Yasoni.

"Ah!" said Dick.

In this simple fashion we prepared our own camp equipment for a cruise around the Sese islands, hitherto not much more tangible than a mirage. By the grace of the Governor we had found ourselves in possession of a Government launch and three black "boys" dressed in nautical sweaters with red lettering, and having, it was asserted, a knowledge of the lake. Yasoni was Dick's "house boy." He had been with his master in parts so remote in Uganda that the rule of Kabaka, Mugabe, Mukama, and all the *saza* and *gombolola* chiefs was unknown —in land where the chief rain maker, or the best hunter, was the top dog of the native clan. So Yasoni seldom forgot anything—except the very thing that you wanted.

But, with the possible exception of a red carpet, I can't think of anything he omitted on this trip. I took my Mannlicher, and Dick brought along a .350 Rigby Magnum. "For Charley Croc," he grinned.

I'm taking quotations of description and appreciation from Eve, as I describe this weird picnic on a lake 225 miles long, covering 26,828 square miles in the heart of Africa. For if a cruise among the Seses is exhilarating for man, their beauty will drive a woman mad. They are enchanted. And, then, you must remember how "recent" all this country is for the white man. Speke discovered the southern shore of Victoria Nyanza in 1858, but the first visit to it from the east was made by Joseph Thomson in 1883.

These Sese islands to which we were going had been decimated by the sleeping sickness which swept the northern shore of Victoria in the 1900's, killing a quarter of a million persons. Until sometime after the last war there was not a solitary living person on the Seses.

Stanley knocked about the northern end of the lake in 1875. Part of the strange story tells of his giving his services to Mutesa, the Kabaka near Kampala, and offering to lead a canoe expedition against the warlike Sese island warriors. (Stanley is supposed to have brought the sleeping sickness with him from

West Africa; this contaminated the tsetse fly, which has since killed natives and Europeans by the thousands upon thousands, and is still killing them.) The tale is still told there of Stanley's leading a naval expedition of Baganda from the mainland—until the Baganda saw the war canoes of the Seses heading out to give battle—then the whole Baganda flotilla fled for shore again. They did not think, they said, that they were quite such good "canoe fighters" as the Sese islanders.

(Mutesa wrote a letter to Queen Victoria which got Gordon held up in Bunyoro. Gordon was planning the conquest of the whole country. Then the wily Mutesa combined *with* the British to defeat the Bunyoro, and as a result added to his own kingdom a considerable slice of what had once been the ruling dynasty's in what is now called Uganda. Later, I talked to the King [the Mugabe] of the Bunyoro, who had been thus disinherited!)

The charm of the Seses, of all this country around the lake, lies in these recent ties with the past; so many memories still reach back to the days before the British were here. In a thatched hut on one of the biggest islands a native had just died who claimed to be ninety-nine years old, and his widow took me to a "coffee" tree which, she said, the dead man's grandfather had planted. This island, I was told, has a special taboo; no pig may set foot on it, or it will bring disaster.

With the picture of Stanley, and the big war canoes, Speke, and the missionaries coming up the big lake, the constant thought in your mind is how they must have gasped at the beauty they found here.

It was a windy, bright day when we started. The blue sky was full of flying clouds, and the lake whipped itself up into flakes of azure. For six hours we approached an island that rose high out of the water, with a great red smear of cliff at its highest point. As our launch drew near we could see the sandy beaches of Bugala, with the canoes pulled up and the brooding, tangled wall of the forest behind, with bright red splashes of dying banana fronds, and ropes of liana with red, poinsettia-like flowers climbing up them.

Thousands of cormorants were nesting in the skeleton bushes along the water's edge, and suddenly two hippos popped up beside the boat; their large, amiable faces were covered with pink spots like vast freckles.

It would be nonsense to go through (in words) the tom-foolery that Dick and I did in action, trying to bag a crocodile among the islands that windy afternoon. I leaped ashore at one island, crawled across a sandy spit, and put a soft-nosed bullet smack into the head of a "croc." It did not, apparently, even feaze him.

This was not mere juvenile fun, or unthinking cruelty—to destroy the "crocs"; far from it. When you realize the terror the natives live in caused by these murderous, waiting, silent deaths along their shores, you realize why they shout with joy when you hit a "croc"—even if you don't get him!

The crocodiles are ghost-like in their stealth. With their half-moon eyes and snout barely above the water, they can lie within twenty feet without your seeing them. This is particularly easy for them when there is a slight riffle on the water. And we shot three in a lagoon that day, two of which we think we hit badly, and saw them appear and reappear hundreds of yards away.

Eve, who expected me to produce crocodile bags and traveling cases out of Nyanza, was most annoyed! Enough of "crocs." Old Charley Croc, I'm beginning to like you!

About 5 o'clock we put in at Kalangala, the chief village on the island of Bugala, where two askaris (native policemen) and a *saza* chief, awaited us. Behind was a great mass of smiling natives. We ran in beside a rickety little wooden pier surrounded by giant water lilies and stars of lotus. The scene made you stare. Sweeping upwards was a great, sun-drenched hill of green, on top of which glistened the white walls of the Government "rest house." The road up to it was the steepest I ever remember. It went up, apparently vertically, for one thousand feet!

When we got there (and how my weary heart hammered!) we found that the "rest house" was only the usual daub-and-wattle, with walls that were only a few feet high and a clay floor. The remaining space to the thatched roof was open, so there was a considerable amount of publicity. But it was clean, and with that surprising tact (which we found only among the Sese island chiefs, and which Sir Harry Johnston stressed) the *saza*, the Kwebe of Bugala, waved an arm that banished all the *totos*—for a moment. He smiled to show us that he well understood the wish for privacy. He looked like a fat, prosperous New York Negro—wearing a nightgown under his business jacket.

Yasoni was already there, putting up camp beds, slinging mosquito nets, arranging washstands, setting up camp tables; and then, with an army of too-willing natives, he erected on the plateau outside something that looked like a bridal cage—an enormous, square box made of nothing but mosquito netting. This was our first contact with an African dining net (for I must call it that). I will let Eve tell the rest of the story.

"Meanwhile," she says, "the two chiefs, *saza* and *gombolola*, had been sitting near by with most of the population of Bugala, watching everything. Here, obviously something was expected of us. We invited the two chiefs to tea and some rather limp biscuits, and resigned ourselves to an hour's uphill work conversationally.

"The *saza* chief spoke some English (he spoke a lot), but the *gombolola* chief none, and we had to fall back upon the series of 'Eh-h-h's' and 'Ah-h-h's' and long grunts that are always such a feature of East African conversation. After this somewhat meager entertainment, the chiefs beckoned to a procession of people waiting near by, who then advanced. They were carrying attractive flat, woven baskets, filled with presents for us. Eggs, oranges, bananas, pots of milk, live chickens, and lumps of manioc or tapioca root for Yasoni and the crew.

"It was in some ways rather a mortifying episode, but we accepted the gifts, to the accompaniment of much presenting of arms by the two askaris, which gave the affair a feudal flourish, and I proceeded surreptitiously to unloosen the bonds of the wretchedly trussed chickens, which thereupon ran away and were seen no more." (Eve was always doing things like that.)

"It was late but not dark, as an incredibly full moon floated over the islands. After an unconscionable time, the two chiefs withdrew. Our black audience was doubtless still there, but had melted into the shadows. The lake lay so far below us that even the frogs' chorus was faint and soothing. Yasoni had put up Dick's dining tent, and inside it we ate soup, Frankfurter sausages and a fruit salad, in perfect peace.

"The breeze blew cold at 5,000 feet, and yet, directly beneath us, vibrated the invisible, magic line of the equator."

The mornings were cool and dewy. We awoke to the crazy flapping of the widow bird, clapping its wings over its back in the sky; the anvil bird began his hideous clangor. I woke to see an almost naked lady kneeling in the opening of our tent and talking her head off. Feeling startled and sleepy, we could only stare at her. Her hands were pressed together in supplication. She was a good-looking old girl, with a slim head and a pompadour of gray hair that any society dowager would have envied. Finally, two men came and removed her, still talking.

"She must think I'm the district officer," I said to Eve, "and was bringing some complaint. How disappointed she must be that I didn't answer!"

Later the two men came back and told us she was the island's madwoman. They seemed a little afraid of her.

The incense tree and the violet tree, and green starlings with white eyes, and old Charley Croc, lying like a bit of log in the rushes below us, with the hippos wallowing and puffing like exhaust valves—we wandered among things like these in the islands. Some were still uninhabited, with only the white egrets flashing from out the mystery of their dense green shores; on some the people made the women kneel as we passed them. One island seemed far more advanced than the mainland in civilization.

There were two daub-and-wattle schools, a boys' and a girls', where we saw the pupils writing in exercise books with a neatness that would put to shame my own twelve-year-old son at school in England. You never cease being astonished in every African school at the excellence of these black children's writing; it is as if they thought there was something cabbalistic about the rite, a black magic which demanded that a line be drawn just so. The girls' school gave an odd effect, owing to the fact that several of the pupils had babies strapped on their backs, who slept peacefully while their mothers (as Eve would have it) went on with their lessons.

The schoolmaster, who looked hardly more than fourteen himself, was a serious Nyasa, who spoke good English and continually kept drawing Eve aside to ask questions about European politics which Eve felt quite unfit to answer.

"Madam, who will be the next Prime Minister after Mr. Chamberlain?" "Madam, is there going to be a war?"

He followed us with the two chiefs and their island entourage through groves of bananas, bananas, bananas, splashes of green fronds; plantations of papaya, that insipid, pulpy fruit, so full of pepsin, that sits as a reproachful pick-me-up on every British breakfast table in the tropics; coffee bushes, "maniako," and maize which covered the slopes of the island in a waving sea. As ever, all the work seemed to be done by women.

There was a herd of long-horned Nilotic cattle, six or seven feet between their horn tips, who answered to a flat-headed Buhima who had been imported to look after them. Some of them were Maltese-cat-colored, especially about the muzzles; and it is the only place in the world where I have seen a man "talk" to cattle; they came to a full stop at a word from him.

After we had done the honors by asking to be taken into the

house of the chief, a European bungalow with a tin roof and a lithograph of King George V in its horsehair furnished parlor, as our launch was chugging out through the rushes and lotus the schoolmaster's voice came faintly over the water,

"Madam, what is Hitler going to do next?"

Eve thus describes the next two days: "All that day and the next we wandered among these enchanted islands, Dick and my husband keeping up a desultory fusillade at—to me—invisible crocodiles, to an accompaniment of: 'Good shot, old man!' 'I know I got that one!' 'Oh, I clearly saw one hit.' 'Oh, bad luck, old boy!' "

But we did get five Egyptian geese.

On the island of Bukasa we came on a very pleasant sight, a band of islanders intent on making a 40-foot ceremonial canoe for their chief. The huge tree trunk had been hollowed out by hand to make its keel; four 40-foot slabs of tree were being sewn together with bamboo lacing to make a dead-rise canoe. A native was making the bamboo lacing by drawing rough strands through grooves in a mussel shell; like drawing steel wire. Not a nail would be used. The job, they said, would take them two years. Time was cheap, and soon passed.

Ours had already run out. When we got back to Entebbe at sunset, all along the harbor there seemed to be dense clouds of yellow steam obscuring the shore line. It was immense clouds of lake flies, in solid pillars and blocks, which settled on us disgustingly, choking us as we landed. They are notorious, with reason. If they stung there would be no white men today around Lake Victoria.

That evening a cicada sang warningly as we sat in our mosquito-cage veranda. A violent storm came up. As we looked out over the lake, the lashing tropic rain seemed to have washed the Sese islands away.

25. Buffalo Hunting

"NEVERTHELESS," said the Governor, "big-game shooting is a tonic. Good for the nerves."

He was drinking his pick-me-up after his ritual evening gallop. He was dressed in white whipcord breeks, boots, and a heavy blue navy sweater. And this was in Entebbe, mind you, whose atmosphere is always that of a steam laundry, despite its cool, green lawns stretching down to Victoria Nyanza. We had been discussing the various ways in which a man can get himself killed buffalo shooting (all of which seemed too easy to suit me); and if my comments on the Governor's state of rude health seem irrelevant, they are not.

In a Government seat full of real sahibs whose complacency was painful; in a stifling setting like this (which you, and the natives, must endure around the globe wherever it is painted red) it was stimulating to encounter once again one of those "characters" in the British overseas service who are the vertebrae of its unbreakable backbone—men, usually at the top, who keep themselves physically and therefore mentally fit, and are, consequently, several mental jumps ahead of the class-obsessed "gentlemen" under them. Governor Sir Philip Euen Mitchell, K.C.M.G., M.C., was like this.

"The place you've picked out"—he lifted a lovely looking whisky and soda to his firm face—"around Fort Portal, Ruwenzori country—why, you might as well shoot yourself now and save the gasoline."

"Why?"

"Grass is too high. The buffalo never gives you a fair chance.

I know the man—salt of the earth—clearing tsetse fly up around Mbarara. He'd be delighted to have you get a big buff; they carry the fly."

Then, in an action characteristic of this vigorous man, the Governor leaped to his feet, went to the phone; and I heard him talking to someone two hundred miles away in Uganda. "Fixed up," he said.

In that way I met Kennedy.

Kennedy was another of those exceptional beings whom Africa seems to make. He was a mosquito-bitten Scot, lean as a greyhound, with a Scot's racial hatred of all blah.

Two days later, after a 200-mile drive through the papyrus swamps, and savannah country and rolling green hills, we found lanky Kennedy in shorts and with a safari car, the car parked outside the district officer's office at Mbarara, where some Bunyoro "boys" with lawn mowers were shaving a lawn as smooth as any golf green. The tsetse-fly camp, said Kennedy, was down on the banks of the Ruizi River, about twenty miles farther on.

"I hope you won't find it too barbaric," said Kennedy. "I've got the food, and some new phonograph records. Are there any special condiments that you fancy?"

I grinned.

"Ah, well," said Kennedy, with the faintest smile in return; "perhaps you'll take a fancy to buffalo brains?"

"Are they good?" asked Eve, nervously.

"Ah, well," said Kennedy slowly; "they tell me they are."

(Everyone, of course, knew that Kennedy had been knocking over buffalo for the past thirty years.)

Kennedy was the Uganda Government's tsetse fly officer. The way into the country he was trying to clear—by periodic burning or poisoning of trees, for the fly must have shade to breed—was another bit of Africa that makes you think you are back in England. I suppose the altitude was between 6,000 and 7,000 feet. As we were directly on the equator, this meant that we would find in this open savannah country great hill-lands covered with knee-high grass, thick (but low) forests of hard-wood and thorn; and, although the sight of them brought a gasp of unexpected pleasure, mountain ranges whose slopes were a vivid apple-green. Where Kennedy had been "burning," the isolated thorn trees that were left were scattered about like an apple orchard; and it was delightful, as we drove, to see some water buck rise and stare at us from under the shadow of the trees, and then a long line of eland, their horns laid back along their flat backs, along the skyline.

Kennedy was enough moved by this to stop his car and come back to ours. He didn't say anything except "You notice those eland, eh? Grand beasts."

Then, when he saw that we were enchanted by the vision: "I'm keeping this place as a sanctuary of sorts; we'll shoot nothing in here, except buff. And baboons. I *hate* baboons!"

"I don't," said Eve.

"Ye know nothing about them," said Kennedy.

Then he went back to his car and drove on. We followed. "Taciturn chap," I said to Eve.

I had a pretty strong suspicion of what a grand man Kennedy could be when he let himself go. But I was quite taken aback by the "gorgeous" conversations we had on those nights, when he and I, alone, in pajamas and bathrobes, sat before the big fire kept burning inside the "boma," and he let his mind wander along, loud, easily. The Scots, as we all know, are poets and romantics and all that, but what forty years of Africa had meant to Kennedy staggered me. There were, most of them, nebulous things that took a lot of thinking, on my part, to get my teeth into; but when I did bits of Africa moved into focus, so that images I had never imagined formed in my mind. It was deep Africa that I got from Kennedy.

The Governor knew his man.

+

This "boma" on the banks of the Ruizi River was an oval
stockade of stakes and thorn brush about ten feet high and a
hundred yards long. The stockade was made of weathered,
pointed logs stuck upright and dead thorn brush piled high, to
keep lions from jumping over it. For this was thick lion country (we heard them grunting around us all night); and the
"boma" held about a hundred natives with their wives and
"totos," those lovable black children.

They lived in beehive huts at the end, and at our end was
a thatched pavilion under which Kennedy had pitched a tent
for us, shaded by the deep thatch to protect us from the heat,
while he, without mentioning the sacrifice, had his green tent
pitched under a tall camel thorn. The yellow weaverbirds woke
us at dawn with their chattering. We ate in a shady little arbor
made of thatch. For a year Kennedy had lived here, clearing
the "fly." There was within the compound a latrine with a dome
of mud, and a hole in its center, which always gave me jitters
for fear that it would collapse under me and let me fall into
the pit.

At this distance from the natives, under the thorn trees, we
lived at least a vice-regal life. The "boys" came up and salaamed
to Kennedy for orders. One could write, the rest were the usual
intelligent natives, but two were not one step above the aborig-
inal. And the river, the ominous Ruizi, flowed along like a
bronze snake in the inevitable cloak of jungle.

"But a lion," I said to Kennedy, "could easily jump those
thorns."

"Aye," said Kennedy, sucking an empty pipe; "but it's what
you might call a symbol—to the natives, ye ken. That's why
I have two men who have nothing to do but keep that fire
going all night."

I think the thing that won him out of his reserve was that
he discovered I had been fishing, the previous autumn, not ten
miles from his old home in Kirkcudbright.

"I'll be fishing there myself next September. Did you meet the young provost, Brown?"

When Eve told him I had been partridge shooting with Brown (who got all the partridges) our affinity was established.

The best way to describe the atmosphere of the "boma" is to tell you that all the time I was there, with the natives buzzing around, I felt that I must be in an old slave traders' camp. Its portal was an immense gate of sharpened stakes which took some six men to swing back. We had not got out of our cars before the headman rushed up to Kennedy and said that, not an hour before, two big bull buffalo had crossed the green hill just beyond us. So while Eve unpacked her toilet articles and so forth, spreading them out on the neat tables that were ordinarily Kennedy's, the Scot and I, rifles in hand, walked towards the sunset and a deep wilderness of thorn.

Here we came on the herd. It was a peculiar sensation, being so close to them; for we lay in the brush and watched these big, black bodies move unconcernedly about in the patches of open thorn not thirty yards from us. They were feeding. We saw several big cows, but not a bull. It would have been almost too much to hope for, to get a big bull my first night. Probably an anticlimax. I walked back, not saddened, as the darkness dropped down.

It was a picturesque cortège. For, while there was still light, the "boys" with tiny butterfly nets, made of fine mosquito net, kept flicking flies off each other's backs. This was all part of the tsetse fly curriculum, for they were perpetually catching flies to "make a count." These flies were totted up afterwards—so many male, so many females, and so many females that were about to have a fly. For the tsetse fly only has one baby at a time. A larva, not an egg, is deposited in the soft earth under some log. All of which I learned as Kennedy went over the headman's "fly book" when we got back; the "counts" of several weeks.

"It's a dispiriting effort," remarked Kennedy. "You burn an area; you think you've got it clean—and then you get this!" He showed me an area marked in the book, a section which had once been marked clear; and here were the flies back in it again. "So kill all the buffalo you like," he said; "they spread the pest."

He found *Laguna* among the phonograph records, and played it twice to cheer himself. "I dare say you've heard that one? Old favorite of mine." Then he put on another.

"What was that show like?" he asked.

It was Noel Coward's *Bitter Sweet*. We told him what the show had been like. Then, as we went through his records, we found some tunes from other shows, and told him about those. "It's about all *I'll* ever see or hear of them," said Kennedy.

"Miss them?" I asked.

"I don't know. Never can make up my mind, exactly, whether I've gained or lost a lot by sticking out here. Anyway, I've made a living of it.

"What in the devil are they all so upset about in Europe?" asked Kennedy. "The poor human race!"

"Whenever we burn the brush," said Kennedy, "it upsets me if we kill any game. But I'm always glad when we fry those damned baboons!"

"But why?"

"I hate the brutes—they're so damned *insolent!*"

One of Kennedy's gems before the fire that night was about "success" in the African colonial service. It was occasioned by a fat-kneed district officer we both knew, down in Kenya, who, I said, looked as if he were continually suffering from sex starvation. He was an old Cambridge "blue."

"Aye," mused the Scot. "Either wanting a woman, or trying

to get rid of one. That's the trouble with a lot of the sahibs out here"—he put a slight drop of acid on "sahib"—"but you can't rise in the service unless you're regarded as *sound*. Evidence of being that is to have a *wife*."

"Why for?" I asked.

"Ye blither!" laughed Kennedy. "To show that you're not after *somebody else's* wife!"

"So that's soundness?"

"Aye. And so it is."

The night fire was a chest-high heap of logs, stacked pyramid fashion, beginning ten at the bottom. And it was lighted in the middle. This way it was always a blazing canyon of pointed edges which the two natives on guard silently shoved towards each other. It painted everything in the "boma" with its flamingo glow.

"What do *you* think of a black man's ability to think?" I asked Kennedy.

"A lot. Though I'll be damned if I think I ever know *what* he's thinking about. There's a lot of great things going on in these black heads. Take the different minds I've got to contend with in this 'boma,' for instance. Or the Mugabe's!"

That afternoon, before we left Mbarara, Kennedy had taken us over to meet the Mugabe of the Bunyoro natives and see their sacred drums. The African King, Edward Suliman Kahaya, weighed 350 pounds, and was six feet seven.

"Whether it's thyroid, or just majesty, I cannot say," said Kennedy.

The Mugabe had some 60,000 taxpayers under him, from whom he received slight tithes, and he was being paid £2,000 a year by the British Government. His "palace" was a long, rambling bungalow, painted battleship gray, inside a large official "boma" of plaited rushes. A Ford "10," the Mugabe's, stood in this sandy compound. Black ministers, wearing European coats over white native "jibbas," awaited us at the front door and conducted us to the royal presence.

The Mugabe was wearing a brown and black striped business suit. He held a scepter in his black, ham-like hand. He wore, on his lapel, a British "Mutt-and-Jeff"—the two service ribbons from the last war. And behind the Mugabe was a lithograph showing him in khaki uniform and clasping a rifle. We asked some polite questions of state, to which the Mugabe returned answers as if some monstrous idol were speaking (we were seated below his throne). Then I asked him:

"Did you see Lord Lugard?"

"The Englishman?"

It is a confused, romantic, full-of-heroes story, of Victorian imperialism, which you may read in the histories—of the time when, under Baker, General Gordon, and Emin Pasha, the Egyptian flag flew over the Nile districts of Uganda from 1874 to 1889, and when in 1862 Speke and Grant, coming from the south, were the first white men to reach the capital of Mutesa, on the shores of Lake Victoria (its later name), they found an organized and comparatively civilized people already established in what is now called Buganda.

Stanley, already known for his relief of Livingstone, visited Uganda in 1875. He came out and told the Christian world of the opening for missionary enterprise in Mutesa's dominions. The first English Protestant missionaries arrived in 1878, and were followed in 1879 by French Roman Catholics. Then the "fun" began.

Mutesa died in 1884 and was succeeded by his unstable son Mwanga. "Christianity," naïvely says one account, "had made much quiet headway, but Mwanga showed his true colors by compassing the murder of the English Bishop Hannington (an authentic hero, by the way) in Busoga; and for his father's (Mutesa's) tolerance he substituted persecution and even massacre of the missionaries' adherents."

This black patriot, failing to free his land from the encroaching whites, had to flee before native Christians to lower Lake

Victoria; then the Arab slave dealers and native Mohammedans gained the upper hand and drove out all the missionaries
and native "Christians." Mwanga became reconciled with his
exiled Christian subjects, and regained his throne. Then the
Christians broke out into war between themselves; Protestants
(English) versus Catholics (French).

It was when this civil war was imminent that that incredible
English empire builder, Captain (now Lord) Lugard arrived
at Kampala, December, 1890.

It all seems comparatively recent. European agreements—
Brussels of 1876, Berlin, 1885, the Anglo-German agreement
of 1890—these had confirmed British "influence" as extending
over Kenya and Uganda. In 1888 the British turned over, by
royal charter, to the Imperial British East Africa Company the
whole of Uganda—all that Lugard could include in treaties
with the chiefs.

Lugard made a treaty with Mwanga, and led remnants of
Emin Pasha's troops into western Uganda; war broke out
between the Protestants and the Catholics; Mwanga fled; he
was restored; the company failed; in 1893 London annexed
Uganda as a "protectorate"; and the Union Jack replaced the
company's flag on Kampala Hill.

The British then co-operated with the Baganda tribe to drive
out the Bunyoro. And so, 178 miles from Kampala, today sits
the Mugabe of the Bunyoro, Edward Suliman Kahaya, with a
Ford "10" in his front yard, £2,000 a year from the British,
and the two sacred drums which have been in his dynasty for
over 150 years.

"Yes," said the Mugabe; "I saw the Englishman, Lugard.
I made a treaty with him. But I don't remember what he said."

Then, obviously anxious to get rid of us, he clapped his
hands. A palace minister appeared and salaamed before him.
Then he handed Eve, at the Mugabe's command, a native
wooden quiver, beautifully carved. And to me he presented a

leopard skin. Too beautifully marked to put on any floor, it hangs over the back of this chair in which I am sitting in London today.

Kennedy, who had maintained an impressive air of official dignity when we were in the royal presence, gave a slight chuckle as we were bowed out. "Of course the Mugabe couldn't tell you what Lugard looked like or what he said; his ministers did all the treaty making for him. The Mugabe was only five years old."

The two sacred drums had their own house which is as holy (to the Bunyoro) as is the shrine which used to cover the Vladimir Virgin in Moscow. They were black from age and handling, and a victorious enemy tribe once contemptuously slit their heads. They were guarded by their own hereditary priests, three always on duty, and they were tapped just once in the lifetime of the ruling king. At his coronation. This he did by softly rubbing his hand once across each drumhead.

After that they were silent.

They had a personality so strong that it hushed you as you faced them. They lay on their sides, and their irregular heads had a sinister shape; for they were not round; they were like two huge, black-belted kidney beans. And now I knew the origin of the strangely shaped gold badges on the askaris' black, pillbox hats; they were shaped like the sacred drums of the Bunyoro.

The drums, like a Russian ikon, were protected by a barrier —in this case just a white, wooden balustrade. Watched by the three hereditary priests.

"What would happen," I asked Kennedy, "if some fool took it into his head ever to beat those drums?"

Even the Scot looked shocked. I had awakened him from some reverie. He had an expression of actual enmity towards the image of such a man I brought to mind.

"Well, in the old days, he'd never have got out of this hut.

Today, if it was a native, he wouldn't last long—poison, or a spear. And if some white wag did it—well, I'd like to shoot the fool myself!"

We walked on towards a low, white, stone building where a native judge was trying some cases. One was that of the usual triangle; a pretty Bunyoro girl was showing her bruised face to the court, the black husband with grim lips was waiting to give evidence of how he had been made a cuckold, and a smart but thoroughly frightened young libertine was attesting that the whole affair had been merely platonic.

"But he won't get away with that," said Kennedy. "In the old days, among the Bunyoro, the punishment for adultery was death. We British have lowered the dire penalty for that!"

The charge was assault, against the husband, and the case was being tried by one of the native chiefs under the Mugabe. He looked a very intelligent person (he was a direct descendant of the Hamites who swept over what is now Uganda in the seventeenth century, giving it its ruling class), and was dressed in a European suit of spotless white. He might have been a young professor at any advanced American Negro university. Anyone in the audience was entitled to speak if he felt there was a point he could call attention to or elucidate. This constituted an informal jury, whose consensus of opinion or moral indignation (not that it was obligatory for the judge to accept it) usually influenced the verdict.

"About as sensible expression of public opinion as I have ever seen," I said to Kennedy.

"Aye," he smiled; "and did you notice that there are no lawyers in this court, particularly not one of those plausible Indians? They don't allow lawyers. *That's* an advance over our system, isn't it?"

The Bunyoros, who were the paramount race in what is now Uganda until the British combined with the "more reasonable" Baganda to drive them out, have their own parliamentary system. It is also run on direct lines.

"It's seasoned stuff," mused Kennedy. "When you consider that this man we've just left, the Mugabe, is alleged to be the thirty-ninth of the direct descent in his dynasty. Lot more than most European royal families can say—what?"

"Think? Do they *think?*" gasped Kennedy, struck by an example suddenly, as we sat before the campfire that night. "Well, listen to this: We British put the Baganda on a money economy; the growing of cotton. And the worst oppressor of the African in Africa, you must remember, is the African. The poor class, the Bantus among these Banyankoli here, go for seasonal work in the Baganda cotton fields. And now the Baganda have petitioned the British; they say *the Banyankoli are getting too civilized!*

"They've actually asked us if we wouldn't find them another tribe, good workers but too stupid to demand much pay!

"Does that answer your question about the native mind?" asked Kennedy, getting up.

It was still dark when Kennedy stood in our tent, a hurricane lamp lighting up his lean checks, saying:

"We'll just have time for a bite of breakfast, if you hurry. The 'boys' have come back and say there's some buffalo on the hill."

I was shooting a Rigby, Magnum, which holds three cartridges. The buffalo were supposed to be up the rush-lined valley we had walked to the previous night. To get up on them, we had to climb over the mountain between. It was a mount of only a thousand feet or so, which we did by zigzags, but on its top I felt dead beat. The morning wind, however, was blowing cold, and before us stretched one of the most stirring sights in Africa, the apple-green mountains of Uganda.

We were well into May, in the penumbra of the rains. Hazy mists lay between the outlines of the hills. From the height on which we stood the thorn trees looked wet black. Streams con-

verging here and there brought down with them each its sheath
of jungle. Then the green hills rolled on and on like the bil-
lows of an emerald sea.

Sometimes, through a rift in the clouds, beneath a ray of
sunshine, a patch of marsh ground would light up so that we
could see its lake of rushes and ring of billowing shrubbery.
We searched these with our glasses.

Then, miles away, we saw the herd of buffaloes going up a
green slope. They looked like black maggots. And we watched
them cross over a high ridge.

"My God," sighed Kennedy; "it'd take a day to come up
with them!"

It is painful even now to recount the agony of that morning.
It was an everlasting succession of descents and climbs, with
infuriating intervals when we had to tear our way through the
dense undergrowth of the river bottoms. We had about twelve
natives with us, of whom three were sent off posthaste to try
to find the other "watchers" who were supposed to be trailing
the buffalo. The rest, with their spears, tried to rip a way
through the growth for us.

I walked directly behind Kennedy. When he came to a pit-
fall in our path he slapped his leg and pointed down without
looking back. We were going fast in our attempt to make contact, and in such fashion did Kennedy, a hundred times, save
Eve and me from wrenching our legs. The mists blew away.
At precisely 1.15, Eve, Kennedy, and I, with two natives, lay
sprawled on a grassy hill. A dozen natives had either lost
themselves, or were still pursuing some quest in the clumps of
forest. Below us, directly under our feet, was a patch of thick
swamp with a central patch of river forest.

Then, two miles off, we saw two dots. They were natives.
And through his glasses Kennedy saw that they were trying
to attract our attention; they were pointing to the swamp below
us.

"Well," said Kennedy, slowly, "they seem to be telling us the buffaloes are in that."

Then the lost natives—I did not bother to question then how they maintained contact with each other—appeared at different spots on the green mountain slope opposite us, and converged swiftly on the swamp.

"Ah!" said Kennedy.

We left Eve where she was (after a battle with her), and went down to the edge of the swamp. Here we selected a red anthill, about five feet high, and Kennedy suggested I should sprawl myself across that. "But we must keep the back door open," he said, professionally.

And we ripped all the impeding branches off two trees behind us, so, if we needed to do so, we could quickly scramble up. I put a hard-nosed cartridge (to break the shoulder) into my rifle, then two soft-nosed cartridges.

I have always seen much to admire in the Africans' fearlessness in tackling dangerous game. But this day I think they excelled themselves. They were a bit frightened, of course, about going into that swamp after the buffalo. They beat on the trees as they went, and, shouting, made a terrifying din. "Well," I said to Kennedy, rolling over on the anthill, "they aren't there. The natives are just about to come out."

And, just as I said it, the bushes before me began to lunge like a sea in storm, and out came five buffalo. The biggest, a huge bull, had a green haycock of branches still stuck on his horns. I raised my rifle.

"Don't shoot!" whispered Kennedy. "If you wound him, he'll go back and charge the natives!"

The bull took a quick run forward—then stopped. It was a weird pose, with his nose stuck straight out. And I put the hard-nose bullet *plunk* into his shoulder. They were off!

The five buffalo charged as one over the ridge of a ravine before us. We thought we had lost them for good. Then they came back, charging at us! Kennedy, obstructed by a tree before him, jumped aside and fired one chance shot. By this time they were thundering past within twenty-five feet of us. The bull leading—

Shooting beside Kennedy, I put a shot into the bull *that made him wince!* I could see him hump his massive shoulders. I was appalled that he didn't drop. But I was more amazed that he didn't turn and charge us right then—he wasn't twenty feet from us! His momentum carried him on. Then they appeared again, racing through an open patch between the thorns, and I fired the third shot. (This, we found afterwards, was too far ahead; I knocked a hole right through his upper jaw.) Then we saw nothing more until one of the boys spied the small herd galloping up the far side of the opposite mountain.

It was a pretty (if discouraging) sight to watch them. We could see now that two little calves were running beside their mothers. It was astonishing to see the swift pace at which they went up that steep mountainside.

"Well, that's that!" said Kennedy. "They've gone!"

I was troubled by a thought. Were there only five at the beginning? Had we, in that comparatively tall swamp grass, seen the calves? Wasn't there another buffalo somewhere? I had been convinced that a wounded buffalo always leaves the herd. And after the smack I had given that big bull—the blow that made him wince—I didn't see how he or any other animal would have either the strength or the guts to face that mountainside. Kennedy, when I remarked all this, nodded and said: "He's badly hit, all right. And if he is, he'll go down along this river."

There in the swamp grass we found bloodstains. There were bubbles among them. "You got him in the lungs," said Kennedy. "He'll be dead before sundown."

I shall not bore the reader with the details of that five hours' pursuit. It was a thoroughly scary performance. And we made Eve, despite all her protests, keep out of the deep grass.

"It makes me go all hot and cold all over," shuddered Kennedy, "when your *memsahib* is along. When there's just the two of us we can look out for ourselves—but not for a third person!"

Eve refused to be convinced; she said we were cheating her. But when we came to one solitary island of elephant grass, and the boys could find no bloodstains leading out of it, we just made her go a short distance up the hill.

As most people should know—particularly if they are going to hunt buffalo, usually considered the most dangerous beast in Africa—a wounded buffalo will backtrack and stalk *you!*

We spent an hour throwing brush into that patch of grass. One of the "boys," a frantic huntsman, even offered to go into it to stir up the animal; the buffalo was probably lying in there —dead, he said. But we didn't permit that. Then a roving "boy" came on the bloodstains again. They were dry, but full of white areas where the bubbles had burst.

"I've put fifteen shots in one, and still had him go on," said Kennedy. "This 'un's a tough one!"

The sun was sinking. It's an unwritten law of the bush that you must not leave a wounded animal; he may kill somebody else. We were beginning to be worried as to how we should break off the chase, and begin it again.

"Probably find him dead tomorrow morning," said Kennedy. (Pause.) "Then, again, we might not."

Then we came to another one of those dark, round patches of jungle in the river bottom. A half-hour search all around it showed no bloodstains leading out, no beaten down reeds, whatever. He was in there.

"It looks rather inclement," said Kennedy.

I felt my breath catch a little; I did not want to go into that tangle. Still—

"No," said Kennedy; " 'twould be sheer suicide. The grass here is way over our heads—and *he* knows that. That's what *he's* going to count on. What he'll do is try to sneak down in the bed of this deep elephant grass, if the boys make enough din on this side."

So we took up positions on each side at the lower end of the jungle patch. The vegetation there was about ten feet high. One or the other of us would probably have just one snap shot as he went between us down the river bed. Then the screams and the beating of the "boys" arose.

We had spent five hours following this wounded animal through the high grass. I felt something implacable about the whole affair now. I had loaded with a hard cartridge and two softs. And he was going to get all three of them. There was no waiting; the brush was storming in my direction almost before I knew it. Again and again I held on a point, still unable to see the buffalo because of the high grass.

And then, absolutely fresh and full of fight, he broke cover and charged at right angles out of the river bottom. Nose held straight out, going like hell—

It was the supreme thrill I have had of all my shooting. I had to wait for an instant until he passed between me and a startled native. Then I took a quick but deliberate shot at the base of his neck. I broke it. All the driving power of the great beast was automatically cut off. But the momentum carried him on; he slid suddenly, on bent knees, into the reeds. I jerked in another cartridge, and watched. The great head slowly turned over until a hooked horn came to dead rest, glistening in the setting sun. Still, I mounted an adjacent anthill, and watched him.

Kennedy came through the high grass. "Dead?" he asked. "Well," I said, keeping my eye on the buffalo, "he looks pretty dead to me." "You never can tell," said Kennedy, as he climbed the anthill; "don't walk up."

He grinned and rubbed his stubbled jaw. "Well, I'd give him one more wee shot, just for luck."

I did. But it was into obviously so much dead meat. The

ebony horn still gleamed in the setting sun. There was no answer.

For a moment I felt regret. That wet, blue muzzle would never again smell the night mist under a Uganda moon. Running with his nose stretched out—that is the way I shall always remember him.

Then the boys began to shout. They closed in, running, and ripping off their spear blades to use as knives.

And Kennedy said: "Well, aside from the bones, it's about 1,500 pounds of lovely meat for them!"

The mathematics of the thing never struck me before. But this dead animal meant smoked meat for a month for over a hundred persons. Nor had I realized the vast size of the dead buffalo; it took the whole dozen natives to turn him over. When I tried, I could not even shift the head. I found the three shoulder shots so close together that you could have covered them with a dinner plate. Any one of them, it seemed, would have killed any other beast—but not the great buffalo.

I had no compunction about killing him; in fact, I felt a great sense of relief. I had been lucky; his was about as good a head as you can get in the Uganda region. I had had the thrill of being more or less taut and frightened for five hours in the thorns and dangerous grass. It had been the complete picture.

"Boys" had already been racing, hard as they could go, to the "boma" to fetch others to carry the meat. Of course, any we left would be eaten by the lions before morning. And I could almost hear the crunching and snapping of the bones as the hyenas cracked them that night. What a treat!

Also, Kennedy and I had to stay, with our rifles, to protect the safari of "boys," each one of whom would be carrying 50 pounds of fresh, tempting meat on his head. An irresistible invitation to a lion—and there were two patches of river jungle that we had to pass through after nightfall.

"Hurry!" Kennedy ordered.

The "boys" were like a lot of noisy vultures around the bloody carcass. The hide—it seemed to me an inch thick—would have been worth £7 in the days when the Kavirondo were allowed to carry shields. Now it would make thick sandals for the "boys." They were already quarreling over it, how it would be divided. Kennedy, of course, would take care of that. I was idly smoking, contented, when a movement on the far ridge of mountain caught my eye. It was eland. A long, buff line of them was passing along in single file, their horns laid back, their tawny coats burnished by the setting sun.

It was a reproachful token, this passing of the largest antelope in Africa—some stand six feet at the shoulder and are larger than a horse—and I watched them go with moody thoughts. I had reloaded my rifle again, but this was because we might need it on the way home, if the lions became too ravenous. But otherwise I would never fire it again in Africa.

It would only be the little Mannlicher now, when needed, perhaps, against a chance leopard in the Belgian Congo, as I crossed French Equatorial Africa, or in the Cameroons.

One lion, and one buffalo; I had got what I wanted. I felt peaceful now. I took Kennedy's glasses and watched the eland, heraldic on their green ridge.

It was a long walk back, dangerous for me (with my injured leg) in that brush. The boys chanted. The night fire in the "boma" was casting its flame into the thorn trees of the enclosure as we marched through the great gates. They were closed as the last head-load of meat was carried in. Some immediate meat was doled out. The skin was pegged out on the ground. Silhouettes of the blacks were already forming around their cooking fires as they watched dozens of sticks holding lumps of buffalo meat before the glowing embers. We heard the high laughter of the women, their shrill sounds of joy. And little fat "totos" waddled around the fires. The headman came and salaamed to Kennedy.

"We only want the tidbits," said Kennedy to his own "boy"; "some blood, marrow, and then the brains and tongue."

"Ah!" said the native. "Aye!" said Kennedy—both in that manner between white man and black, in these parts, to show that an order had been given and understood. Kennedy further instructed that aside from the three pounds of meat on each of the forty sticks before the fire, the main mass of the buffalo meat must remain untouched until he should supervise the division the next morning. The four hunters who had originally located the buffalo were to get double shares, and so were several "boys" he named, who had shown themselves particularly brave that afternoon in the high grass.

Our dinner was buffalo-blood soup, fried tongue, brains and marrow (on toast); then some ghastly mashed plantain—the last named to take the place of mashed potato. It didn't.

The buffalo's brains, fried, tasted like sweetbreads. They must have been excellent. But, because I had shot the beast—and I could still picture his black, dusty hide; that immense mass of meat with its lolling tongue—I could not enjoy them.

Kennedy was a man who, I would say, had an immense amount of that precious thing, interior solitude. This afternoon had, obviously, recalled to his mind a host of images of his previous years in Africa. I let him play with them; I was too tired to talk. We smoked in silence before the fire. It was one of the most satisfying hours I knew in Africa. Finally, I heard him rapping out his pipe on the leg of the camp chair, a signal that he thought it was time we went to bed. He coughed, a bit awkwardly, and spoke:

"Up and down, we did seventeen miles today."

26. Into Belgian Congo

IN London, when I was asked how I thought I was going to get across from Uganda over into the Belgian Congo, I took a pencil and drew an east-to-west line between Lake Kivu and Lake Edward. "There," I said—and I hoped it was. It was not a contour map. I had visions (disquieting ones) of being bogged, or short of gasoline, on some track which had just been cut through the African jungle. That part of Africa looked to me as if it must be deep and steaming. But by the time Eve and I said good-by to Kennedy, on the banks of the Ruizi, we knew that an 8,000-foot pass lay ahead of us.

Even so, we were not prepared for the bizarre experience of looking down into the craters of hundreds of extinct volcanoes. This incredible road, completed in 1934, soars through a landscape of nightmare beauty.

The great lakes of Africa lie along the spine of a great mountain range—not, as one would expect, in the low country. And to get the feel of Africa, to have some consciousness of what it is really like, you must see this great hump of mountains and volcanoes that runs down, holding the great lakes like pools of water between the spines of a lizard's back. The air is cool here, rarefied, and in the perpetual mist of the rain forests the vegetation is abnormal and primeval.

This, the great gorilla and elephant country, is a world you will find nowhere else on earth.

That night we slept at Kabale—slept under three blankets, almost directly on the equator, after dining on a mushroom omelette and strawberries and cream—after two golden cranes had dropped down from the sky to do a gawky love dance on a grass lawn green as any in Ireland. Green, green, green! We had left the rolling blue-green hills of Uganda and were now climbing into the volcanic mountains. There were lakes up here at about 7,000 feet, lying in the clouds. Some were in the craters of volcanoes. This side of the range was now swept with rain, and at one breathless ledge, where there was a straight drop of 1,600 feet—the Kinaba Gap—Lake Bunyoni lay below us, steel-blue as if cloaked in a Scotch mist. Then, at 8,000 feet, we made the pass, and we stopped the car here to enjoy the silence of a deep green bamboo forest. Feeling the cool mist on my face, I sat outside on the running board to let my senses subside. This whole scene was too tremendous to encounter without giving your emotions a chance to re-orient themselves.

It is well that we did, for on the far side of this beautiful pass there was no rain—there was just space. We found ourselves looking across a great rift, with hundreds and hundreds of volcanic cones rising from its floor. These, too, were of an unbelievable green. And along the skyline, mist-blue, rose the greater cones of the volcanoes over in the Belgian Congo.

We slid down. An hour or so later we were passing through the tufted reeds of deep papyrus swamps, with black water running swiftly through them. Clouds floated over the yellow-green uplands around us. The heat began again.

At 1 P.M. we came to a corrugated iron shed with the notice

BULWANT SINGH
CUSTOMS OFFICER

and made this dozing Sikh wake long enough to stamp our passports and give our car its exit visa from British East Africa. We lurched across several miles of no man's land, where there was no road, just a horrible track of volcanic cinders; then we swung around a mountain-toe drenched with deep and dank vegetation, dripping with lianas. This we knew was the beginning of the gorilla country when a black man, looking alarmingly like a gorilla himself—except that he had a rifle in his hand and was in uniform—stood on the road that began there. We were in the Belgian Congo.

On the customs house veranda, while we waited for the Belgian officials to be aroused from their long afternoon siesta (for travelers are few in this part of the world), we examined some elephant tusks we found nonchalantly propped against the wall. They were small, and looked as though they had been taken from dead elephants who had lain for a long time in the jungle, for they were stained and their tips had been gnawed in deep, criss-cross gullies by rats. These elephants had not been shot by hunters. From the small size of the tusks, you knew at once that all these elephants had died young—say, before forty, which is about their age of puberty.

We were looking for Colonel Hoier, a Dane, and Commandant Hubert, a Belgian, who were the chief and assistant in charge of the great *Parcs Nationaux du Congo Belge*—the Albert Park, in particular, which is not a park (a term the Belgians took from the United States) but a vast, unmolested stretch of Africa in which all living things (except human, I am tempted to say) are preserved. No firearms are allowed, and you may bring no flower or seed or introduce anything that is not of the indigenous flora. You may not even carry a weapon to defend yourself.

Preservation of a biological nucleus in its primitive state, by the elimination of all human influence.

That is the definition which King Leopold III gave of this internationally controlled section of original Africa, in his speech in London, November, 1935. It was the late Carl Akeley, the American naturalist (who probably knew more about gorillas than any other man then living), who conceived the idea of these sanctuaries, after he had led an expedition to Lake Kivu in 1925. He is buried in the park.

At Rutshuru, with our eyes still dazed from sight of the hundreds of volcanoes we had come through and from the white heat of the sun slashed down through the green trees and scarlet flowers, we were told that Le Commandant Hubert had "the fever"—malaria.

Colonel Hoier? Well, he was somewhere around Lake Kivu. With this precise information—for Africa—we turned the car around, drove back towards Uganda, and then took one of those amazingly good, red roads that the Belgians have built throughout the Congo.

The natives here look horribly like gorillas—enough, you would think, to convince even a Scotch parson that Darwin must be right; these people seem to have taken hardly a step away from their original ancestors. Working among them, and building a new rest house, we found the gray-haired Danish colonel.

He gave us his own favorite rest house ("my retreat," this strange and deep man called it) to sleep in that night. And as we reached it in darkness, guided only by an inarticulate native, we had no idea what it looked like, except that it was a board shack on the slope of a volcano. The volcano (14,600 feet) was not active, but the lava was still boiling in it, or in one of these earth pots immediately about us. Looking upward that night, along the huge cone, we saw the convolutions of the clouds above us lighted at intervals in colors of flaming rose. Then they resumed a blood-red glow.

If I am not mistaken, Akeley died of malaria, and lay in the lichened, moss-dripping forest just above us. He had been alone, too weak to get down, and they had buried him there on the volcano. What a perfect end for a man like Akeley!

Hoier, that good man, had no more worldly or material needs than the average saint. One look at that rugged, unrepressed face was enough to show you that here was a man who had found happiness. His shack looked like it. It reeked with disdain of soft, personal comfort. Every homemade, slung-together object in it spoke of a man who was consumed with delight in the country around him—and in nothing else! Morning revealed, behind my bed, a roll of skins of squirrels or flying foxes, the tusks of a tiny elephant, a pile of dusty phonograph records, several scrolls of maps of the *Parc Albert National* or plots of the volcanic region, a ball of twine, two dirty soup plates, and a tin of boot polish.

The hut was made of native-hewn clapboards. Its windows were made of glazed paper stretched over a cloth netting, and wouldn't open. In one corner lay a pile of enormous bulbs, and a cluster of dry immortelles hung from a native arrow. These flowers grew on the cone above us, at altitudes above 13,000 feet. I found two mouse traps.

Looking out into a dew-drenched morning, I discovered we were in a perfect little paradise! Colonel Hoier's garden sparkled in the sun. Roses, violets, an abandon of white lilies, and about a half acre of ripe strawberries. There were white climbing roses, fresh with dew, around the unpainted door (there was, in fact, not a daub of paint anywhere; of course, it would have ruined this charm!); and, walking around the hut, I found peach trees in an orchard. Over all this slowly passed the shadows of the clouds hanging over the tips of each of the three volcanoes. The sun rose, and the cloud shadows retreated upwards over the dense mist forest above us.

I know no other scene which has ever given me such a pang from its sheer beauty. But perhaps it was only the associations of the hut, that a modern man should have the wisdom to live like this. For Colonel Hoier was no long-haired recluse; he was a professional soldier who had fought with the Belgians against the Germans.

All this weird country lay in the Albertine Rift, that huge trench holding a series of great African lakes, along the eastern frontier of the Congo. It runs from the Zambesi to the Nile. The trench of this central African rift, along whose flank lie the glaciers of Ruwenzori, is usually about thirty miles wide, with an escarpment on either side about three thousand feet high, and, along this particular region we were in, the eastern barrier was a chain of volcanoes. One of these had been continuously active, with violent explosions in 1938 which cut off the settlement of Sake, and a flow of lava twenty-five miles long was still sluggishly overflowing its crater to hiss and steam and coagulate with sullen *bulps* into the Mediterranean-blue water of Lake Kivu.

I have gone down the volcanoes of the Andes—and I suppose that inner New Guinea still holds some unknown plateaus that are like Conan Doyle's *Lost World* (as all those who have not seen them say)—but I doubt that there *could* be any more fantastic region than this volcanic African range: Mikeno, 14,600 feet; Karisimbi, 14,800; Visoke, 12,200; Sabinyo, 11,500; Gahinga, 11,400; Muhavura, 13,000, and hundreds of other volcanic cones which seem too unimpressive among these giants to be worth naming.

Lake Kivu, which is the highest lake in Africa, was not known to the white man until 1894. It is a feather of brightest kingfisher-blue, dropped into prehistoric vegetation, like the plants before the coal age. And on Ruwenzori, whose glistening snows were not confirmed until fifty years after they were first sighted by an appalled white man—on this mountain, elephants, buffalo, lions and leopards roam up to 13,000 feet, and man, a pygmy, stands under lobelias that are twenty feet high.

There are also pygmies in these mist-drenched forests who live where few white men can penetrate, and they trap and kill the strange, striped okapi, a horse-like animal which has the stud horns of a giraffe. Its coat is the color of a burnished horse chestnut.

And among these cloud-capped volcanoes, tearing their way through the mist forest, live the last gorillas left on earth.

The good Colonel Hoier was so obsessed with the joy of carpentry (what fun, building huts among volcanoes and gorillas!) that we did not have the heart to present a letter to him from the previous Governor of the Belgian Congo. Anyway, he had forgotten Europe. Give him a week, he said, clasping a bubble gauge, and he pointed the level towards Lake Edward.

No doubt, he said, *le brave Commandant* Hubert would be over the fever. (I had been warned about Hubert ever since Tanganyika. "He will kill you!" said the game warden down there. "He throws chunks of mud at elephants!" And in Kenya they said: "Don't let him lead you to destruction—the man doesn't know what fear is—he's mad! One of our wardens came back from there, from a stay with him, looking ten years older.")

"Is—is Commandant Hubert's 'fever' very bad?" I asked Hoier.

"*Non!*" he grunted.

I felt like saying, "Too bad!"

The path down from the volcano, disclosed by morning, was through native maize fields; the "good red road" soon turned into slabs of sharp lava; I could *feel* it cutting into our precious tires. We dropped into a torrid jungle full of mahogany trees and hordes of baboons. We passed the hut of a chief behind its ceremonial palisade of plaited rushes. More baboon-like natives stepped off the road and stared at us. Some, with a little feathered crown around their heads, carried bows. These were usually cross-bred pygmies. And occasionally an aristocratic individual strolled along, wrapped in a robe of imperial yellow, who was seven feet high. These were the Watusi, the African giants, into whose alpine land we were proceeding. But the greater part of this continuous procession (although there were a few female beasts of burden wearing nothing but leather flaps) were rather impudent African Negroes in puce sleeveless jumpers and dirty shorts, with their women who wore the inevitable yards of Belgian colored cotton print.

(I gasped, about a year later, in London, when I watched a movie on this part of Africa—a very good film—which showed an expedition "penetrating" into this Watusi country, scaling breath-taking volcanic slopes—when they could just as easily have taken this road. I've come to the conclusion that Africa's greatest export is gaudy buncombe.)

Lava in flow proceeds along under a hardened crust. It will usually hold your weight. There will be hissing, sulphur-coated grottoes, broken blisters, with fiery breath and sounds of flames and dull explosions somewhere below you. You may sit before this open furnace door, if you like—so long as you don't sit there too long and become asphyxiated. And you can even cross lava where it is still so hot that it will melt rubber soles. You may do all of these things again and again, with the odds all in your favor. But you must not cross a field of active lava *when rain is falling!*

This is just about the last thing that would occur to you or to an "ignorant" native. Eve and I found a Watusi who had been cooked in this lava field. He was an El Greco figure, supernaturally attenuated, most of his flesh that artist's favorite green, and one gaunt arm, looking as if it had been embalmed, was clasping a skull which was ivory white. All the flesh had dropped off it.

The natives, who ran across this blistering bit of field, ran, I think, because of the horror of this sight—of the spirit of this man—more than they did for fear of the same thing happening to them. I know that when Eve and I were standing there, staring at him, our two natives ran off to an upper curl of the lava and looked down at us. A French commercial traveler zipped past, his "boy" trotting behind with the Frenchman's big sample case on his woolly head, and the Frenchman, seeing what we were looking at, gasped *"Horrible!"* and raced on.

Five hundred yards back, he said, beyond a granite island which rose above the lava, and on which were some dead trees, we would strike a particularly dangerous bit.

"I would advise you," he called back, "to hurry when you come to that. It looked thin, to me."

There were four natives, like this, cooked in the lava—all killed by rain. What happens is that the rain water seeps down through the crevices of the hard lava, strikes the molten flow, and shoots up again in poison-gas steam. The lava crosser loses his way in that and falls beside one of these poisonous grottoes, or is just killed by the steam itself.

The flow, coming down from the volcano twenty-five miles away, is about a mile and a half wide as it nears the lake. In various areas long lines of smoky fumes arise from it—smoke, the shudders of subterranean bubbles bursting. Some of these fiery, open grottoes are like the inside of broken pebbles which have crystals inside them. Their coloring is fascinating. The lava itself is like burnt-black bread-dough. Split open, it reveals a soft, reddish, ready-to-powder earth below. It solidifies like coils of rope, in long, jammed convolutions like charred bundles of sheets that have been rinsed and not unwound again, like the waves of a tar sea that, heavy and slow-rolling, have suddenly stopped.

All along the lake front, geysers of steam shot up as fresh lava, molten treacle, met the turquoise-blue water. This scene, set against vivid, green mountains that rise in broken silhouette against a white-hot sky, jolts you. To a normal man it is the discovery of all discoveries—that his planet has not finished forming. A Negro preacher might claim that here was hell "bustin' right in my face!"

But the thing that impressed me most in that semi-inferno was the sight of a green triangle of brush, already beginning the growth that would one day cover this flow of molten earth.

Disconcerting, but not an altogether irrelevant sight, we saw two natives who hurried past us, carrying on a pole over their shoulders a trussed, squalling pig. He was destined for the Greek who runs the isolated, filthy hotel in cut-off Sake. This Greek, living in his splendid isolation, was cashing in on this

volcano; he charged for a meal that I would not give my dachshund (indeed not!) five shillings. And when I made a feeble
protest he waved his hairy arms, and cried:

"But look! Look, mister—look at all dat lava! Looka dis
hotel! Look"—he pointed a thumb towards the pig—"how
much you t'ink it cost me to get him? Jesa Christ, I hottas-
hell!"

On the way back we found that new lava is far kinder than
old. We got across a patch of country that, at least, I can guarantee will be safe forever from onmoving man. As we wanted
to see what molten lava actually looked like in action, we took
a canoe and paddled along where it was seeping into the lake.
There was about a mile of muffled explosions and steam jets.
They created, by various wind suctions, their own surf. And it
was boiling. About the molten lava itself, Eve and I saw two
different things: She wrote it was like molten glass, almost
crimson; I said, except that we knew it was not *entirely* liquid,
that it looked like boiling blood. Mine was the more melodramatic description (I have yet to see boiling blood); so the
glass has it.

There was something peculiar, some smolder of menace
gained by staring that red lava straight in the face, that evoked
a sensation which I cannot name—but it was too much like staring The Beginning of Things in the eye.

Deceived by a shore of green rushes, and only lukewarm
water, Eve and I left the canoeists and told them we would take
a short cut across the lava field back to our car. One of them,
a gentleman, instantly began to shout, *"Non! Non! Non!"* But
the others, being just as smart business men as the Greek, shut
him up, took our money, and paddled off. They left us.

After about an hour it looked as if we were to stay there for
the night. What had happened was that we had gone ashore on
the lava of 1912. It was covered by a low growth of saplings
now; this frequently concealed grottoes that were forty feet deep

beneath our feet. There were, across some of these broken blisters in the earth, natural bridges that were thick enough to look trustworthy. There were others that we were afraid to chance. And there was one that we did chance—and fell through. All this tumbled lava was a pumice that had edges sharp as knives. And then there was a horror of lava blocks coated with a strange moss that powdered as we touched it. In this mess we were likely to break an ankle at any step. There was a nice brimstone smell, wafted over from the smoking lava of 1938. In a fury at our foolishness, we made our way over this silver-mossed moraine, looking like spectral coral, across more pie-crust domes that cracked under our feet, until we reached some deep ravines of broken bubbles, which stopped us entirely. Along these the new lava from the volcano was just solidifying; it simmered with heat waves as does the lid of a stove. And we went up along this, until it cooled, and, in a grotesque sunset which turned these colorless heat irradiations into waving flame, we found four of the primitive gorilla-faced natives, all clutching their semi-circular bows, timidly admiring our car.

They dashed off as we came up. And that night, with a full moon over Lake Kivu, we ate a full Belgian supper under the table lights on the cement veranda of *L'Hôtel des Volcans*.

"*Un peu de fromage, Monsieur?*" said a black man whom the proprietor had "trained."

"Odd, to hear *him* talking French," said Eve.

Odd, to hear him talking anything, I thought. I was thinking of an article I had read a few months before. It was written by a well known Italian "explorer," a bombastic man who is, unfortunately, not well enough known. He described his "discovery" of the African giants, the Watusi, the overlords of this black population. He pictured the sky-reaching volcanoes. War-dances, drum beats. But he had never thought to mention this excellent little hostelry, *L'Hôtel des Volcans*.

The contrast between his verbal bilge and the practical everyday work of the Belgians in this district made me laugh. "I have an idea," I said to Eve, "that you and I are going to find the Belgian Congo one of the best run parts of Africa."

"Not too well run, I hope," sighed Eve.

We looked at each other. The greater part of our married life had been spent in trying to get as far as we could from the alleged human race. But a forest fire had destroyed one paradise we had lived in for two aloof years in British Columbia; Thomas Cook & Son had discovered a wooden hotel we had found in the Slovenian alps and were selling tourist tickets direct to it the next season. "It's owned by a religious order, you know! *Very* primitive, board floors and all that, but very clean and comfortable; just the stuff to catch them!"

"And the Belgians will be running buses here, next," said Eve.

"But just think!" I exclaimed, "of the 3,300 square miles that are forever consecrated to the gorillas—and of Colonel Hoier!"

"I'm thinking," said Eve, "of a good, hot bath. We haven't had one since Entebbe. You're getting a bit whiffy!"

27. White Fathers

I NEVER approached a White Father in Africa, even with the intention of writing about him, without the most intense personal curiosity about his personal life. Was he happy? I never left one without the feeling that he had genuine happiness and not merely a bullock form of peace. I often had the suspicion that these celibate men had known greater moments of ecstasy than I had ever experienced. Belgian, Hollander, Frenchman or Pole, they were of course internationalized by their faith and God and their strict religious order, but, as I saw more of them, I became aware that they were united by a continuous experience which, if less spiritual, gave a daily joy to their work. It was their belief in the usefulness of their mission.

They made me suspect that belief can be made the greatest of all experiences.

We drove for two days up into Ruanda-Urundi, that African Switzerland, to stay with the White Fathers at Kabgaye. The mission there is probably the most important in central Africa. For it was to this high plateau in the volcanoes that Monsignor Classe, then just a bold young White Father, led two other priests on a 107 days' walk up from the Indian Ocean at Dar es Salaam. This was in 1892. They had 300 head-porters. They advanced into a completely unknown country where the witch doctors still ruled supreme, where the then discovered African giants, the Watusi, had had the same royal family for 400 years, and where the frightened giants thought these peaceful white men were fantastic monsters.

"We had a mule," smiled old Father Classe, who still heads

the mission, "whose ears never stopped. The natives had never seen a mule. When the mule began to bray, the natives ran for miles. They felt certain that someone would have to die on the opposite hill that night!"

A few months later, when the natives had overcome their first superstitions, they attacked the little group of three white men. "We had to fire," said the White Father. "Our order allows us to carry weapons to defend ourselves. After several nights, we beat off the attack."

Monsignor Classe and his two White Fathers were attacked as late as 1901. In 1910, when the present mandate lay in the disputed territory between German East Africa and the Belgian Congo, the mission actually flew two flags. During the war of 1914-18, the three White Sisters there nursed wounded Germans when the Germans occupied the mission, and nursed wounded Belgians when the Germans were driven out. Today the mission has a vast, red-brick cathedral built in this wilderness by the Watusi and the White Fathers (who are all ardent house builders), a long cloister, a large native hospital, and a set of boarding and day schools in which 2,000 children sit down at their benches every day. Every brick was laid by the natives and the White Fathers. The whole is strikingly like one of those majestic church strongholds you find in the mountains of Spain.

Such dates and statistics are essential here, for this first White Father mission in Ruanda-Urundi is a remarkable example of the civilizing force in that inseparable trio—government, big business, church—and Ruanda-Urundi, recently the most backward of regions, is now fast becoming one of the best examples of "planned development" in Africa. A few years ago it was noted for just three things, locusts, rinderpest, and famine.

In the 1929 famine, 20,000 natives died in Ruanda and 15,-000 over on the British side of the line, in Tanganyika—and they died beside rivers and lakes full of fish; they would not eat their sheep or cattle; and they refused to cultivate their lands more than once a year, because, they said, it was their custom.

"So, you see how unpardonably slow our progress was!" sighed the gray-haired White Father. "Traditional stupidity takes a long time to change."

There are 3,000,000 natives in this tiny mandate, and the density of population is so great, in an area of only 21,230 square miles, that they grow their crops right up to the very tops of the volcanoes. They have cultivated their towering mountains until they are practically devoid of trees, so that it was necessary to plant eucalyptus and wattle. And under the strict Belgian administration, every adult male in Ruanda-Urundi had one and a quarter acres a year under cultivation *all the time*, and at least a third of this had to be under tapioca and sweet potatoes. They must sow twice a year. They must irrigate and cultivate the swamps during the rainy season. In the reforestation campaign, every taxpayer must plant at least a fifth of an acre in trees. And some of these trees must belong to a communal plot.

It was an old native custom that each man must work a certain number of days every year for his chief. The Belgians conscripted such labor for building roads. Road building in Africa was a high point in Belgian colonization. They, far more than the British, realized its vital importance in developing a territory. In four years the Belgians built 2,000 miles of roads in Ruanda-Urundi, using native labor. And they are roads whose engineering feats and perfect upkeep made those of Kenya and Tanganyika look like cowpaths.

Yet, in spite of all this regulated, swift progress, and the recent opening of gold and other mines in the mandate, anywhere from 50,000 to 70,000 natives have to migrate every year from the mandate over into Uganda to work from two to six months in the rich Uganda natives' coffee plantations and cotton fields.

✦

Ruanda-Urundi is one of the strangest countries in the world. The natives live at altitudes of 8,000, 9,000, 10,000 feet. The working class, the plebeians, are Bantus, and some are the most primitive natives you will find in Africa. Yet it has a ruling aristocracy more advanced than most Negroes in the United States. I am not speaking now of merely the Watusi royal family; I refer to the general level of these dignified African giants whom you see among the towering mountains and volcanoes. They are giants; you seldom see an adult Watusi, man or woman, who is not well over six feet, and a man six feet six would not look tall among them. They are as slender as deer. They have long, tapering fingers, V-shaped heads, with slender chins and enormous squirrel-like eyes. A baby Watusi, with his huge brown eyes and sharp little face, looks exactly like a squirrel. These are descendants of the Hamites who are supposed to have swept over Uganda 300 years ago. Their king can show a direct descent of thirty-seven in his line, and can trace his dynasty back for 400 years.

Like the Masai and the Banyankoli, who come from the same stock, they are a cattle-raising aristocracy, inclined to be insolent, and contemptuous of the white man. But, unlike the Masai, they take a pride in their literacy, and at Astrida the Belgian Government supports a school run by the White Fathers, for the sons of the Watusi chiefs. It trains them in medicine, clerkship, typing, and for the lower subordinate administrative services.

The Belgians, who showed great practicality and good sense, combined with continental cynicism, in administering the Congo, approved of the existence of the royal family, as a token for Watusi pride. In a manner *slightly* like the British, they administered Ruanda-Urundi through the native Watusi chiefs, but, like the French, they had no hesitation in removing them. In 1935, the records show, they dismissed twenty-eight chiefs in Ruanda and fifty-two in Urundi.

Ruanda-Urundi was governed by the Belgian colonial service with a staff considerably more commercially minded than the

British. For 3,000,000 natives they had a *commissaire de province*, to visit every district in his territory at least once a year, and send in semi-annual reports on it. There were also 2 residents, 22 administrators, and 25 agents. An *Administrateur* in the Belgian service had to be out on safari in his district, in camp or being carried about in a "chair," or racing along these good, red roads on a motorcycle *twenty-one days out of every month*.

There were only 1,076 white men in all Ruanda-Urundi when we were there. Of these 331 were missionaries and 158 were Government administrative officials. There were 328 civilians working as managers in the mines, shopkeepers, etc., and there were no white settlers. The Belgian Government did not encourage the individual white settler, either as storekeeper or farmer, in the Congo.

The ubiquitous Indian is here, but only 286, and existing on durance. Sixty-eight had just been thrown into prison for illicit gold buying, and the Belgians had taken them over to Costermansville, in the Belgian Congo proper—in order, it was being said, to get them beyond the laws of the mandate (subject to inspection from Geneva) and to soak them proper!

I have never seen Indians anywhere so depressed as those wretched creatures hanging on in Ruanda-Urundi; they were beyond the pale. Some swaggering Arabs still followed the trails of their ancestors to trade with the natives. The 23 Germans and the 42 Englishmen in Ruanda-Urundi were practically all missionaries.

All cultivation was native.

Now, here you see 3,000,000 natives being hustled along the road of progress, and the Roman Catholic mission at Kabgaye was the seed from which it all grew.

Driving into the upper mountains, we often came to long stretches where the side of the road had been planted with red roses. There were other stretches, in steep valleys, where the rivers rushed down like those of Austria, and where for miles we drove between hedges of white moonflowers. The Belgians had caused the natives to plant eucalyptus along nearly all the roads, just as the French plant poplars and sycamores along the roads of Normandy or Provence.

Along one river, up which we drove all one afternoon, the valley steps were waving with green rushes from which we put up hundreds of golden crane. "Down there! Down there!" they screamed as we disturbed their gawky stalk for frogs. We came on one rose-red mission where two White Fathers, their white cassocks tucked into their leather belts, were captaining two violent native soccer teams. The Watusi kicked with the bare foot; the Fathers wore knee-high leather boots, and as they raced against the deer-swift Watusi their beards dripped with sweat.

The river thundered in rapids, swift and white; then it poured over ledges in a deep bottle-green, falling, falling to send up continuous spray from a frothing pool hundreds of feet below. You pass no native villages; the natives live in kraals, stockaded compounds on the slopes of green hills, built at such an angle that you can nearly always look into them. And their patchwork fields of maize and waving banana fronds fringe the mountains' edge.

It is said that the Belgians have made the natives put down 60,000,000 coffee trees. In 1938, these Africans exported 1,800 tons of coffee. In 1939 they hoped to export 4,000 tons. Everywhere you look you see the Belgian effort, Government directed, to make these people safe against their own hereditary superstitions which lead periodically to famine and poverty. "Until," a Belgian *Administrateur* told me, "we can open a door into the Congo for this congested population." From the Belgian side, he was anxious to point out, this must not be mistaken for mere philanthropy.

"They are a valuable labor supply," he stated.

He sent for the son of a local chief, a six-foot-six young man, and made him jump over his head. Then, when the native failed to clear a bar that was about 6 feet 6 inches from the ground, the

Administrateur turned on him angrily. "You're not trying!" he said.

These amazing Watusi giants jump feet first, a technique which was just coming into recognition when I was at my university. And this was "Darkest Africa"!

This intelligent young *Administrateur*, who came from one of the "ruling families" in Belgium, had a chip on his shoulder about the British. The scandals of "red" rubber which shocked the world under old King Leopold's administration of the Congo were, he said, based on a tissue of lies. The English had sent Sir Roger Casement in there to make a "case" against Leopold. Later they shot Casement!

He had some rather definite ideas about how to handle natives. Abolish flogging, he said, and all Europeans would have to leave the Congo. But it would be better to see that the local chiefs ordered the flogging.

"You must always keep the local chief under your thumb," he said. "For example, take a chief who governs 8,000 men, of whom, say, 4,000 are working in the mines, or over in the Congo on European plantations. These men get ahead of their chief; if the chief does not progress, the natives become detribalized. That's the worst thing that could happen to them; they cut loose from their old traditions before they've any conception of how to lead the new life. Therefore we Belgians have to see that the chiefs progress. We can't afford to bolster up the old type of fat, lazy, stupid potentate, so we fire 'em. That's sensible, isn't it?

"People at home howl when they hear that we *make* a native grow an acre of coffee or cotton. That's slavery, they say. Well, I'd like to ask you: What alternative could they propose in the circumstances? Let 'em die, I suppose. These sentimentalists in Europe make me vomit!

"Things that appear *drastic* in Europe are *not*—in Africa. For example, in the towns, a native must carry an 'identity book.' We have a curfew of 10 P.M. in all towns; but the native can get a pass card, and he can circulate with a *light*. We have reasons for not wishing native snooping around white habitations when our eyes are closed! But what difference is that between his old and new ways? An ordinary native always goes to bed about sundown, or is dancing in his kraal, and few want to stay up later than 9 P.M. Now what great injustice have we inflicted by that?

"Again, a European may fine a native one-fifth of his pay, or one-third if he is giving the native food. If the native had the 'good old days' back, with an arbitrary chief, he'd more than likely have his hand cut off for the same offense.

"We make them grow coffee. We make them submit to vaccination. All the cattle in Ruanda-Urundi have been vaccinated, 600,000 to 700,000 of them, all 'proofed' against rinderpest and most against anthrax. Every man, woman, and child in Ruanda-Urundi must appear before a doctor; we have eight Government hospitals in Ruanda alone. I'll admit that the white man brought venereal disease to Ruanda-Urundi—I think it was the German noncommissioned officers—but we're fast curing them of that; that's one of the reasons why we insist upon examination—and we give them injections, treat them for yaws, operate upon their various horrible tropical diseases and malformations, and force them to take pills to bring down their malaria. All free.

"Look, if you please, at the living alternative! He is Musinga, the Watusi king, whom we exiled. This horrible king will go down for a thousand years, in Watusi legends, as a hero. Yet he was a usurper; he killed his brother to get to the throne. He is fifty, ugly, full of vice—he went to bed with his son!

"But he hasn't got the drums! We took them away from him and gave them to his son. This son now rules, with the queen mother. And the queen mother rules everything!"

(Here again, as with the Banyoro over in Uganda, the sign of kingship was not a crown or a scepter; it was the sacred drums.)

"Now, to put things concisely," he said, "we have a poll tax, and a cattle tax on the natives; we have income tax from the mines—we *tax the Europeans* here and in the Congo!—it is not all run on native money. And these contributions *almost* meet all running expenses. We respect and uphold the two kings in Ruanda and Urundi, we bolster up their chiefs and subchiefs, and we *make* each native grow certain stipulated food or export crops. The *Administrateur's* direct contact with the individual native *must* come through the chief; therefore, you see why we deliberately train chiefs and their sons to be able to hold their positions and dismiss them ruthlessly when they can't.

"And with all this," he added, finally—it was he who insisted I must see that great White Father, Monsignor Classe—"we work hand in hand with the church."

When we finally got out of our car in the huge clay square that is made by the red-brick cathedral, the long lines of school barracks, and the palm-shaded cloisters of Kabgaye, we found the three White Fathers high over our heads, working, cigar in mouth, among the sagging trusses of a new cubist church they had just built.

Its roof was sagging.

"Nay," said a bearded Belgian White Father who received us; "if my brother walks out any further on that scaffolding it will collapse! Let's stand outside."

This little Belgian was smoking a cigar so frugally, so close to his teeth, that it had blackened the under tip of his nose. The brother he referred to was a huge Pole who, with cassock wrapped around his belt, was standing on a beam some seventy feet above our heads. Natives, clinging like limpets to ladders and rickety scaffolding which had been placed against the interior walls of this "advanced" church, passed various tools up to him. Imagination had had full play in the designing of this latest model of churches; its tower was a square campanile; its Christ might have been carved by Mestrovic; its "atmosphere" would have delighted Epstein. But it was so new that the Fathers had lost their hold on the amazing technique with which they had erected the vast original cathedral, and the recalcitrant roof was coming down on them as a consequence of such profanity.

I mentioned this to the little Belgian White Father, and he gave an amused chuckle. "To progress is always dangerous," he said.

We had a room in the cloister (those ascetic rope beds!), clean, stark and agreeably commodious. It pleased the Fathers to have visitors; they fussed a little as they looked after us. They smiled bashfully, and asked Eve whether she had everything she wanted. They bustled off, laughing, jolly; and we knew that we should have several jokes with them. They would chaff. I looked forward to the first dinner. The old monsignor was taking his afternoon nap, they apologized; he would soon appear.

(The thought came: 1892—1939! All these years. Being a White Father, he could have gone back to his home in France just once in all that time; then, by the rules of his order, he had returned to Africa forever. And here—the long afternoons. The priest trekking up from Dar es Salaam. The priest fighting. The priest building. The years pass. And now in the peace of the afternoon, the monsignor, his white beard on his chest, the ecclesiastical ring on his finger. Sleeping.)

"For heaven's sake, don't wake him!" I said.

The three younger priests smiled. How naïve of us! As if they would awake the beloved Father! That was all in the good-natured grin with which the youngest of them, a Frenchman with the first fuzz of hairs on his chin, left us to ourselves.

We two sat in a bare room. "You ask me," smiled Monsignor Classe, the old Father in white, with his silver crucifix hanging below his white beard, "how do you say it?—'I go about' converting. Well, I can tell you, it is very difficult. And"—he sighed—"slow."

This was all in French. But I give the old gentleman's whimsy. He was cultured, immensely man of the world, who kept himself in day-to-day touch, by radio, with the horrible mess that was being brewed in Europe, yet he had that penetrating simplicity, that almost uncanny ability to come direct to the point, which, it seems, can be developed by people only who have lived their lives where they have been completely free to form their own individualities. He had insight.

"It always takes us a long time to convert—four years, at least. We always begin with medicinal help. We begin with a *quid pro quo* in the language question; we use a little bit of theirs, they are imperceptibly taught some of ours. In the beginning, when we first came here, we found it took us about a year and a half before we could make ourselves understood at all. We began with twenty-five children; now we have two thousand. I would say that the converting process can be compared to weaning; you must not do it abruptly.

"Not," he added with care, "if you wish it to be *firm*." He said frankly that today he had some 30,000 Christian natives in the mountains around Kabgaye. "But there are about 110,000 non-Christians, pagans. And many of them are polygamous.

"The pagans believe in Imana." (Our God is called by them Mungu.) "Imana is altogether good; he doesn't even *punish*." (The monsignor, probably thinking of our own hell-and-damnation religious heredity, smiled sweetly.) "Imana does not punish evil; and that makes him a formidable competitor. Yes?"

I smiled.

"They give Imana all the attributes that we give our Christian God. These people never knew cannibalism. They have no fetishes; that makes them laugh. But Imana is so good that nobody has any fear of Him. There are no prayers, only continuous evocations. They even parallel our expressions, these pagans; they say: 'Kumanu,' 'To God.' We say 'Adieu,' 'To

God.' It is like that, you see. We have almost forgotten what 'Adieu' means, strictly." He sighed again.

"But there are the spirits of the dead! These they do fear! These spirits, when it wills them, can be favorable or unfavorable—and it is these latter spirits that these pagans propitiate. They sacrifice bulls and goats, which, they believe, are the most desirable things they can offer. The spirits of the dead *remain* in the country, but they can't be seen! Famine or sickness; an evil spirit is at work. It cannot be *seen*. But these natives each build a tiny little hut outside their own—sometimes it is only a few sticks—and every day they put in it a few kernels of grain, a few drops of beer." He waved his pale hands. "And so it goes. "'*Indaro ya bazimu!*' they whisper. 'There go the sorcerers!' And they believe in them. When there is a famine and people starve; when a child is ill and they fear it will die, they go to the witch doctors."

He shook his head.

"I have talked with many of these witch doctors here; I have even converted one of them. They are not really a bad lot; there is no 'smelling out' here, you know, no ordering an innocent person to be destroyed. I find that there is a psychological basis of soundness in a lot of their work. And they even have one or two useful purgatives. They have certain forms of bloodletting which are not far removed from European cupping. So we meet them squarely, as man to man."

Changing Gods, said the monsignor, was a tricky business. "*C'est très compliqué. Tout doucement!*"

The wise old man said that much more was needed than to get a native to say he *accepted* Christianity. "You must convert the *mind*. The native doesn't think it strange for God to lie or be tricky; you must inculcate these new values. But, to do that, you must first free them from the illusions of ignorance.

"We begin by intimating to the natives that they should keep what is good in their own Imana. It is a slow transformation in which, of course, the most important thing is the example of the White Father's *own* life. We must live so that they come to respect us. Then we begin to make profit of the witch doctor's mistakes. We point out where his prophecies fail. We say to him: 'Why do your own children become sick? Why do you let them die? Why do *your* crops fail, if you have all these powers?' "

"They find that difficult to answer?"

"Very," he said; "considering the fact that our persistent questions, asked as often as we can before the other natives, begin to have a cumulative effect. You see, he really hasn't much to say in return. Then, his tariff is always extortionate; he always gets a pot of beer, then he will demand a hoe, often a steer."

The monsignor added: "I have even had a hard-pressed witch doctor offer to split his fees with me! So like our own medicos!"

The twinkle again came into the Frenchman's blue eye. "The sorcerer's strongest evidence," he said, "is one which he does not know the distinction of, and that is, he is sometimes completely sincere. They *believe,* these sincere ones, in their 'medicines'; I, for myself, would also be surprised if I saw the effect of some of these purges. They administer juice of a cactus, for example, so dangerous that we would class it as poison. It has terrific results! But most of them must be aware they are quacks, like many of those we have in Europe. They work on a complete theory of auto-suggestion; the sorcerer is consulted by everybody, and everybody reacts."

"Did they ever try to poison you, monsignor?"

"Oh, yes; when we first came. That was only to be expected. One tribe here uses the poisoned arrow today, but only for game."

He repeated, to emphasize the laboriousness of the struggle, that, after forty-seven years, he could claim only a quarter of the natives around him as having been truly converted to Christ.

His candor made him invincible.

✛

The laws of the White Fathers do not allow them to build a fort, but (and how beautiful this is!) they may build a wall. It was behind such a barricade that the White Fathers lived for several years in this country, sleeping in huts of straw, until the natives began to approach them with friendly and not warlike intentions. They finally persuaded the natives to help them build a house to sleep in. (They could easily have built this by themselves!) They worked beside each other. Their comradeship began to be felt in this mutual toil. The natives expressed curiosity at some of their ways, their utensils, their firearms. Finally, one spirit became a friend. And so the seed was planted.

Dinner, in a plain, whitewashed room with nothing in it but the long table and chairs, was eaten in the subdued light of an old-fashioned oil lamp. Though I wished that these White Fathers had upheld the reputation of the early monks by doing themselves well, there was sausage of a sort and some sweet potatoes; but it was obvious that the Fathers had long since lost their taste for decent food, knowing that they couldn't get any.

The talk was more interesting. It was plain that each one of these Fathers had an interior solitude in which he did most of his living. And, with the Pole, you imagined that this must amount to a resentment held in check, for, with his muscular, healthy body, he gave out an air of moroseness; he let you know that he worked, with his hands, all the day, and he forced upon you the impression of a man who was flinging himself into physical toil in order to reach exhaustion and forgetfulness. This sullenness was very strong from his end of the table.

The young French priest was buoyant with vitality and expectations, had just finished his training at the Maison Carrée, the school of the White Fathers in Algiers, and it would be some years yet before he made his first (and last trip) home. Monsignor occasionally gazed at him paternally—this young man must be made happy in his work—and the old White Father joined in gaily in an argument the young Father was having with Eve.

My French is too atrocious to risk any quips in conversation, so the little Belgian priest fell to me. And he, I knew at once, was the born bachelor who would be happy anywhere, as long as he had a hobby. The present one was church building. But I learned that he and the Pole had built a palace for the queen mother of the Watusi. "You will find its style interesting," said this little Belgian; "it is entirely my own."

Then I heard the monsignor telling Eve that there were three White Sisters at the mission.

"We do not eat together. We meet only at work. Otherwise, the natives would not understand."

And the next morning we watched these three White Sisters at work. The previous night we had seen a woman being trotted across the clay common, slung in a matted hammock which was carried on bamboo poles on the shoulders of four running Bantus. They seemed in a great hurry—and with reason. She had a baby ten minutes after she was put to bed in the maternity ward. She was a Watusi princess. Looking at us with her round squirrel eyes, the center of an admiring coterie of her kinsmen, she made it plain that although the White Sister had asked her to see us, it was distinctly bad mannered of us.

There was a white surgeon there, not connected with the White Fathers, who showed me two lepers, some yawning cases of yaws, a bad case of Marula foot. It would be amputated, he said, and I, who had had the same pain, felt a keen interest in the number of natives whose legs I saw split open to cure osteo-myelitis of the tibia.

All these patients showed that mute, fatalistic patience with which all Africans meet affliction.

But there was a Dutch White Sister who held me. She had the broad face of the Low Countries, with eyes like bits of the Holland sky, and a laugh that said that if she ever had had troubles or disappointments she had left them all behind her.

She had failed to do the one thing she wanted. She had wanted to be a doctor. Her father thought it was not the work

for a lady. She left her home, and went to the school in Belgium
which was preparing men and women for tropical work in the
Congo. There she was studying medicine. "But the call came,"
she said, smiling to explain how impossible it had been for her
to ignore it. "People said that more help was needed *at once*
in Africa! And so I came."

This was before 1910, because she had been in this same spot
when the cloisters flew two flags, the Belgian and the German.
She had drawn no distinction between wounded men. And now
she still made no exceptions; they were just men. She had a
book in which she checked off each name of a native as he came
up to her. If it was for malaria, she made him take the pill on
his tongue and swallow it before her. "Otherwise," she said,
"they will throw it in the bushes!" And two native dispensary
assistants stood beside her, wrapping up powders, counting out
pills to be taken away, giving an occasional injection, when she
ordered it.

The line held about two hundred.

"I do this every morning," she said, proudly.

It was rainy that dawn. I got up for the first Mass and watched
that strange sight of hundreds of little African "totos" creep in,
kneel, and pray with clasped hands. I saw a dying native brought
in in a hammock. Here, the young French Father took his
rosary, knelt down, and pronounced a benediction. After Mass
this young Frenchman hauled up his cassock, jumped aboard a
motorcycle, and hummed off into the rainy mountains. There
were other cases he must visit up there. And the gloomy Pole
climbed his scaffold.

Our audience with the Watusi queen mother? Yes—the palace, as the Belgian Father had said, was unique. It was built of
orange-red brick, had two circular towers with pointed tips, and
was surrounded by a fort-like wall. It was a reversed illustration
of *Gulliver's Travels*, for we were the Lilliputians.

A slender creature in an orange and blue robe of silk met us. She was backed by a crescent of bearded ancients who were obviously the elder statesmen of Ruanda. With silent gestures they led us into a "European" room where the furniture, all made of local wood, was of the orthodox bourgeois pattern. The ancients left. The slender woman sat down opposite us and smiled.

Except for that smile, which became horrible after repetitions, we were utterly unable to get one thought across to her.

We sat there half an hour. An interpreter from the mission was supposed to be riding over to us on his bicycle. He did not come. Eve became impatient.

"When *will* the queen come?" she asked me.

"This *is* the queen!" I said.

The woman before us smiled. I stood up and bowed our leave. The elders held their robes around their beards as we climbed into our car, for this was a cold morning. The queen (for it was she!) waved a slender hand.

I was crushed by the thought of what fools these well bred Watusis must think us!

28. Elephant Hunting

IN their desire not to upset the "balance of nature" in those reserves which the Belgians have consecrated to the preservation of life in Africa they have made one cardinal mistake; they have removed man from the scales.

By giving the natives other lands to live on outside these special areas they have taken away a vital element. African life must include the native. A certain number of natives, living their traditional lives, automatically insures the preservation of other animals. That sounds queer, doesn't it? But a man versed in African wild lore has probably already guessed the reason; the natives burn the grassy plains at certain seasons to enrich the earth, and make way for a fresh, green growth. If this plain isn't burned the jungle brush will gradually spread across it. If the green grass disappears, so do the gazelle and the antelope. As these become fewer the indents of the lions upon them make deeper ravages. For lions must eat buck and zebra and wildebeest, to live. Finally, one by one, and usually by species, the buck disappear from the plains.

That, in part, was the story of the golden Rwindi plains, when Eve and I went there. They were rapidly passing from open grassland to dense brush and savannah. The buck were noticeably decreasing in number. The elephants and the buffalo, which were enjoying this more wooded habitat, were increasing rapidly. And the lions, leopards, jackals, hunting dogs, were taking advantage of this growing cover to stalk the antelope, cobs, and topi.

We found Colonel Hoier and Commandant Hubert breaking the laws of the *Parcs Nationaux,* defiantly trying to adjust the "balance of nature." They had started several extensive bush fires that morning on the grasslands of the Rwindi plains. The blue curtains of smoke hid the long horizon of volcanoes. And they came in black-handed from the job.

Brussels was a long way off, we were made to feel. And the institute wasn't always right in holding that nature automatically adjusted the balance by firing the plains herself every three years. Nature couldn't be trusted.

Hubert, a diminutive man, light on his feet as a Jap tumbler, wore a toothbrush mustache, a Montana felt hat, and bell-like shorts. He had commanded a detachment of Belgian sharp-shooters in the last World War, and looked every inch the reckless man that everyone had warned us against. His smile was charming.

We drove down along the Rutshuru River with him the next morning to get some close-up photos I wanted to take of lion, elephant and hippo. We got them, all right. And I got two of the shocks of my life. *Hubert did throw chunks of mud at animals!*

Remember, these animals are not used to the sight of man; the Belgian reserves are kept as free from company as possible. An ordinary visitor would not even be allowed to dismount from his car; he is absolutely prohibited from going off a few main roads. In some areas no man whatever may set foot. The animals are left completely alone.

The previous year a Swede had been killed just beside Rwindi camp because he insisted upon getting out of his car to photo-graph a bull elephant. The elephant knelt upon him and then pushed his tusks, once or twice, through him; and, then, as if ashamed of what it had done, the elephant went about tearing up bushes with his trunk and covered his flattened victim.

The beginning of which was reported by a native hunter who had been supposed to guide the Swede. It took Hubert and the native an hour to find the body. And later, after Hubert had written to Brussels for permission to kill the elephant (which Hubert thereupon did), he found an old round ball from a native's muzzle-loader in the elephant's brain.

"He might have got that a hundred years ago," said Hubert; "anyway, it must have annoyed him and made him dangerous. Therefore he was a rogue elephant."

" 'An elephant never forgets,' " I quoted.

Hubert looked at me. *"C'est vrai!"* he said.

Well, there were Hubert, Eve and I, all jammed on the front seat of my Ford, with a native outside on the running board. The native jabbered something and pointed with his spear.

"Lion!" said Hubert. "Proceed!"

I proceeded. It was a lion, all right. A big and fat one. His stomach fairly bulged with a buck he had been eating. Walking along with his head down (he was obviously going home to lie up), he made me think of a city magnate who had been out on a spree and was wondering what new alibi he could find to give his wife this gray dawn. Now, remember once again—this was not the Kruger National Park in South Africa, where lions are used to humans. This is way up in Central Africa, where the animals are supposed to live in privacy. This one, for all we knew, had never seen a white man.

"Proceed," said Hubert. "Closer, closer." I did. We were going along, parallel to the lion, some fifty feet from him, over the tussocked plain. He did not look at us. He was the king of beasts; he feared nothing; he was lost in thought. "We will now dismount," said Commandant Hubert.

We thereupon did. He got out one side, I the other. So did Eve. Between us that time we got at least a dozen fine close-ups —without a telephoto lens, which I do not possess. As the lion came directly opposite us he was not more than thirty feet away. You can see, from the photo I got then, the lion's utter unconcern and a terrified buck in the distance keeping his eyes on the lion. Then, not without haste (I am speaking for myself, anyway), we popped back into the car again. "You see," said Hubert. "Quite simple."

"Yah!" yelled the native, sticking a terrified face into our car. The lion had stopped and was staring at us, giving every indication of a charge. "Yah, yah!"

"Hurry," said Hubert, "for the native's sake!"

So much for that episode. The native glared at me reproachfully when we were back on the road. *We* were all safe, inside the car, but what about *him?* he imputed. In that bulky, tussocked grass, we never could have outpaced the lion; he would have caught up to us in five bounds.

"And then I am just cat's meat!" the native's expression said.

"But the lion had just eaten," said Hubert, "and wasn't hungry. The native is nervous."

I knew that *this* native was. Consequently, when we came on some giant hippos feeding on the dewy grass far back from the Rutshuru River, I protested when Hubert suggested we dismount again, and get behind some bushes between them and the river. "Now," I said to him, petulantly, "the one thing I've been told all over Africa *not* to do is to get between a hippo and his water!"

"That is not important."

"To me, it is."

"But, m'sieu, even the streets of New York are dangerous!"

"I know. But what the hell—"

I might say that by this time we *were* behind the beastly little bushes, all crouched; and I—in the lead, if you please—quickly adjusted my camera to the aperture and time which would "catch" the hippo at anywhere from about a meter to infinity. I took one peek.

"He approaches!" whispered Hubert.

I looked around the bush. *And there were the hippo's slobbery lips within five feet of mine!*

I have never seen such a look of surprise on any animal's face!

It is on record that I took the photo. I also took two others when the hippo, bewildered from surprise, jumped off a few feet from us. We stared that way. "Hunh!" said the hippo. He lowered his head, and frowned. "Now," I thought, "we're in for it!"

Then something bounced off the hippo. Hubert was hurling cakes of clay at him. Hubert told me afterwards he had been collecting them while we were crouched there. "Yaaah!" shouted Hubert.

To me it was the most suicidal performance I have ever taken part in. But it worked. The hippo stalked off. He stopped once or twice, as if to make up his mind whether he would charge us or not. Then he shook his head, and plodded down to the river.

"You see," said Hubert. "Quite simple!"

"Have you ever been charged?" I retorted.

"Yes; once. A lion."

"And what did you do?"

"I threw up my hand and shouted, 'Stop!'"

"And the lion?"

"He stopped."

After that I knew it was hopeless. Eve and I were in the same predicament as the game warden from Kenya, the one who came back from a visit to Hubert looking five years older. If an elephant had my name written on his tusk—well, it was written on his tusk. And that question, I knew, was soon to be answered. For, said Hubert:

"This deep grass by the river is *full* of elephants. Lots of them are coming into the *parc* now from other parts of Africa."

And there was one!

He was a big tusker—he seemed to me about forty feet high— out on the open plain, with a patch of waving elephant grass between us. He was making for the grass. Hubert signaled that I should do that also.

I glared at him; at Hubert, I mean. Was he completely crazy? "Proceed! Proceed!" he whispered, eagerly, for we were near enough to the elephant for a whisper. The Ford was not a noisy motor; I drove to the very end of the elephant grass, and stopped.

The next thing I knew was an enormous black pall hanging over me. The great convex head of the African elephant. Two ears flapped like the wings of a nightmare bat! "Wheeee!" went the elephant. He reared back on his hind legs, came down with his forefeet in a diagonal direction, and rocked past us.

"Whew!" I said.

"Wait! He will try to charge us again," ordered Hubert.

"*What?*"

"Of a certainty. See, he is getting ready!"

The elephant was rocking back and forth on his feet. "Wheee!" he squealed, peevishly. "Wheeee!" He ripped up some bushes and tossed them into the air. His great ears came forward. Now I knew what those ears looked like; they were sails! "*Now!*" said Hubert.

Hubert had said that as soon as the elephant came near us I should race my motor; that would drive him off. The elephant would not understand *that*. "But my horn?" I asked. "No good," said Hubert; "use the motor."

Now, my motor had been ticking over so silently. I noticed it was stopped. As the elephant charged us, I jerked my hand forward to press the self-starter. Hubert seized my hand; he thought I was reaching for the gear shift, to get away! "Don't, you idiot!" I hissed.

I just managed to get my hand on the self-starter and press down on the accelerator. "Rummmph! Rummph!" roared our gallant Ford. It also could make "Wheeee's!"

The elephant stopped, fetching up short. Then he backed off, screwed up his courage, and began to make "Wheeee's" again. We stopped him, mid-way in another charge, by racing the motor.

But what if he got used to it?

"*Non!*" said Hubert. "I know. The horn? Yes, that is not always certain. The motor, they are afraid of that. M'sieu, even the streets of New York are dangerous!"

The Rutshuru is clear and swift. It has great, sandy beaches in the bends, where the hippos lie. Behind the bends are deep banks of luscious vegetation, decked with palms. The hippos lie there in the sun—huge, enormous hippos, with little, fat babies. The babies look like pork sausages on four sticks. Some of the hippos' sides are scored, for they are terrible fighters at nighttime, ripping slabs out of each other with their two lower teeth. Some yawned, opening a pink chasm ringed with teeth. Some lay in the water with only their muzzles out. And some, for the sheer joy of the thing, bouncing up and down as the cool water swept them along, came past us.

"Paaaaaaah!"

It came from directly under our feet. Even Hubert had a conditional reflex that lifted him off the ground a foot or two. I found myself staring straight down into a hippo's inside. "H-a-a-a-a-ah!" it said.

"*Attendez!*" gasped Hubert. "He is coming out!"

"Let him come," I said. "He'll be all by himself!"

But he wasn't. With the grace of a cat he had mounted the bank and was now walking directly past us. I don't think he ever saw us. If Hubert had thrown a clod then—

"You see?" said Hubert. "Even aeroplanes—"

"Are dangerous," I said. "So are you. I'm off."

I don't know which front Commandant Hubert fought on. But I know that if they ordered him to dent the German line he would at least make a hole in it. The man *was* fearless. And (perhaps Eve was right) he was a lot more than that. He was able to approach animals so casually and calmly that they did not take a fright on seeing him. "Always walk toward them *diago-*

nally," he instructed me. He was like an American "Trader Horn" I met in Durban, a famous character, like old fabricator Horn, who said, "One thing not to do, pardner, when you've got a black mamba in your hand—*never squeeze it!*"

He added: "Just let it run through smooth-like."

Hubert was no bluff. He did not have that type of brain. He was the straight stuff, the real McCoy, as they say in Texas. And that night, as we were running through his startling photos, he showed me the actual one of the lion charging him.

There it was, incontestably, in full pounce.

"It's slightly out of focus," said Hubert. "I didn't have time to set it."

"Hmmm; pity," I said. Then, unable to be humorous, "Why, this is the most *incredible* photo I have ever seen!"

"What do you think of this one?" said Hubert.

He handed me one taken by young Count Lippens, son of a former Governor of the Belgian Congo—at least, it was a photo of Count Lippens taking a photo of an elephant; Lippens crouched behind a bush, with a big bull elephant *staring straight down at him.*

I said I was glad Count Lippens was not there with Commandant Hubert.

"*Voilà! Mes buffles!*"

Hubert pointed to a herd of buffalo. They were grazing in the low grass among some euphorbia trees. There must have been about twenty of them.

"*Diagonally!*" whispered Hubert, as he forced me to get out. The buffalo stopped eating. They held up their heads. One or two took several paces forward, and stared.

"I think this is far enough," I said, hoarsely, to Hubert.

"Ssssh! *Diagonally!*"

Honor demanded it. So I got some extraordinary buffalo photos. All without a telephoto lens!

But afterwards I blew up: "You're so damn *sure* of everything! Now suppose that elephant, the one that scared the life out of me this morning, had been that rogue elephant which killed the Swede? What then?"

"Ah, but that is different!"

At that moment a black "boy" dashed out of the darkness and shouted excitedly in Hubert's face. Hubert ran off for his car. I saw his lights racing along the Rwindi plain, then vanish when they came to where a narrow bridge crossed through the jungle of the Rwindi River. He returned in an hour.

"What's up?" I asked.

"A 'ippo. 'E was lying across the road. 'E was blocking the bridge for Colonel Hoier, so—"

"You threw stones at the hippo, I suppose?"

"*Oui, oui,*" said Hubert.

Hoier had lived side by side with Hubert for several years. *He* had no such foolish ideas about *mes buffles!* He distrusted buffalo. He said you could take it for certain that an elephant would charge the instant he got your wind. He said that a rhino would charge anything that he saw moving. And, he declared testily, a man was a plain damned fool to take chances with any of them.

He said: "There will always come a day when—" He never finished that sentence. Yet, he said, when the wind was blowing strongly from an elephant *towards* you, you could do anything. He would prove that to us.

Accordingly, my mind was full of unfinished sentences when we drove down to Lake Edward the next day. But once we got down there I forgot them; I could well understand, now, Hubert's abandon with the animals. For both him and them this must have been the Garden of Eden. A large part of the road down ran through a tricky, savannah swamp, with the tall, green grass waving above our heads, then through groves of acacias and thorn, with numerous elephants ambling in this happy grazing ground; and this was this part of Africa such as it was first seen by an early white explorer. The lake country is said to shelter more wild life than almost any other place in the world.

There the lake lay, with a gentle riffle making its near waters lap the shore, sparkling in the sun, coated with low skimming pelicans. And its far waters bent over the curve of the world where earth and sky seemed one. About a hundred hippos were puffing and diving in the little bay near where we left the cars.

We knew that for the scores we could see at any one time there were hundreds of others, walking around on the bottom of the lake. The lake has a nice, hard, sandy bottom, and some of these playful hippos lay half down, with just their eyes and snouts out of water, snoozing in the warm sun.

Edward lies in the floor of the Central African Rift. To our left lay the boundary range of green mountains, some parts of the range 10,000 feet high. And in the far distance rose the blue mass, in the lighter sky, that we knew was Ruwenzori. Its cloud cap did not draw away from its three glaciers until just before sunset. Of the far side of the lake, the east, we could see nothing at all.

In the forest above us we knew there were gorillas, which are found in no other parts of Africa. Up there was again the strange, prehistoric vegetation. Down here were the candlelike euphorbia thorns and the fanlike borassus palms. Sitting on the edge of the low rushes, I watched pelicans sailing to and fro. Off the coast of Peru and Chile I had often watched them play their tireless game of "follow-the-leader," skimming the waves. They were at it again here. Little tern wheeled and screamed like dry pulleys around my head. A reddish Egyptian goose came down right beside me and walked up on the shore to eat. Diving birds made small white explosions as they dropped into the water before me. And then I realized that a strange apparition I had been puzzling over for some time was a buffalo, lying up to his neck in water.

"That's an interesting sight," said Hoier. "It is sheer mimicry. There are two buffaloes here who do that. I have watched them for several years. They are copying the hippos. Sometimes, when I have been observing the birds here, I have seen those buffalo lying up to their necks in water all day. But one of them died."

"But there are two there now," I said.

He reached out his neck and then drew his head back, smiling. "Then the other must have found a mate. No, that couldn't be; the two original ones were both bachelors. They were big bulls which had been driven off by their herds. I think that is why they came to the lake; to lie in the peaceful sun all day. They probably knew they were going to die."

I felt that I would not mind such an end for myself. Here, on the peaceful shores of Lake Edward. The sun poured down, and I basked, and the mate of the Egyptian drake alighted, her feet shoved out, and waddled ashore past me as I lay in silence. Looking sideways as I lay, I saw three elephant, feeding in the acacia woods at the foot of the first mountain behind us. A swift flight of ducks passed overhead, and I watched the sun flashing on their underwings.

We were waiting for a particularly unpleasant person, who called himself an engineer, to start the motor of a steel pontoon which the Belgians had brought up in sections and put together on the lake. No boats are allowed on Lake Edward except this official craft, which hardly ever moved, and a few fishing canoes in the Tanganyika territory, some sixty miles away. The "engineer," who was terrified of the hippos, had to be made to go out to the anchored pontoon. I laughed as I watched him being poled out by natives in a long, dugout canoe, for, several times, great hippos floated up like blimp balloons and broke surface almost under the canoe. He clutched the gunwales, and, I know, cursed me and Eve to hell and back.

The native who was Hoier's shadow held up some dry sand and let it fall softly from his hand. "He," said Hoier, "says that whatever wind there is, is blowing from the elephants to us. Shall we walk up to them?"

He awoke me from a reverie of goose shooting down in Curri-
tuck Sound, with the icy rollers of the Atlantic thundering, to
break and rush with a swish up Carolina's golden sands. The
Egyptian geese made me think of that. But this was the equator
—this was Hoier—and there was Eve.

I think that in the long run Eve would have frightened both
the Dane and the Belgian, for she had a grand insouciance with
lions. Buffalo, she said, looked too much like barnyard animals.
And she was avid wherever a Tembo showed up. There was no
mountain of Africa but that she did not want to climb it; no
river along whose banks she did not want to linger for hours,
watching the birds; no village into whose precincts she did not
want to wander, beginning adroitly, as did the White Fathers,
by converting suspicious mothers by her squatting down and
"converting" the babies. And with the pygmies in the Ituri
forest Eve had a grand success; for some reason, they seemed
to feel that she meant well by them.

Now I knew that she was having Tembo-trouble again. She
would walk way beyond the bounds of discretion towards those
elephants. Which she did. They spotted us. Perhaps there had
been a curl in the listless stream of air, deflected by the mountainside. Anyway, the leading elephant threw back his ears, gave
that incongruous squeal "Whee!" and charged.

Here, as I have said, I learned I could run. Hoier, with quick
perception, already had a thirty yards' lead of us, racing for
the lake. As I passed Eve, I shouted: "Come on, sweetie!"
Also an incongruous cry! I made a snatch at her. Tembo was
rocking behind. Then he stopped. For some reason, he had
completely lost his "awareness" of us. He stood there, unde-
cidedly swinging his trunk. Then he gave it a disdainful flick,
and rejoined the other two, which were maliciously butting over
some thorn trees. But he left all three of us wondering what
really would have happened to us, if we *had* been forced to
plunge into that lake full of yawning hippos!

✦

From our car we removed the faithful spirit lamp, and made some tea for lunch. The ducks wheeled. The sun passed overhead. But still that wretched mechanic fussed with the engine. "Why don't we go out and hit it with a spanner?" I suggested to Hoier. "That usually makes boat engines start." We went out, hit it a frightful crack on the cylinder head—and it went off like a bird.

Then, as it was in gear, and this had jammed, we roared round and round our anchor chain. And this brought the hippos up. I don't know whether they were walking on the bottom or not, for the water was shallow in this bay. But they came towards us. "Aa-a-a-a-ah!" said one to me, flicking its little ears. One bumped into our chain, which brought both him and us up with a dreadful jerk. By this time our pseudo-mechanic's face had the pallor of a dead fish.

If you look at a map, you will see how these great African lakes lie between their walls of mountain chains. These mountains lie, one behind the other, in broken silhouettes. The near ones are vivid green. Those behind are blue. Then their highest ridges take a gossamer indistinctness, caused by the higher mists and setting sun.

A rain set in. The near rushes turned a vivid golf-course green. (An unpoetic way to put it, but that was precisely the image that flashed into my mind as I saw the long foreshore of rushes suddenly become this hue.) Three elephants stood out, coal-black in it. Thousands of hippos lay in the mirrored waters along the shore. For some reason, as the colors faded, everything became still. All Africa seemed at rest—or *waiting* for something! And then, in utter silence (for we had been unable to keep the engine going) we watched the three glaciers on Ruwenzori appear.

The clouds pulled away. And in that scene of smoke blues and dying green, a few flakes of white appeared high up in the sky. The sinking sun touched them for a moment, and they turned bright rose. Then the last snow peak glistened. And it was night.

Dark, African night, in which the hippos and the feeding elephants, and everything else, had been swallowed up. We might have been evil spirits, suspended in the air. There was no feel of the water around us. All was still. Until, with the master's touch, I clouted that damned engine on that head again.

*

*

29. Congo Administration

THE Congo marks a radical change of attitude from the East African idea of how to develop Africa. While Tanganyika might be characterized as a paternal Government watching brief (waiting until the natives can, if ever, rise to the point of governing their own independent territory) and Kenya might be called "white man's madness" (except for the practical efforts of the Kenya Farmers' Association), with the presupposition that the native is *never* expected to regain control of his former land, the Congo is a totalitarian state being developed and exploited along the latest big business lines.

Four big business concerns run the entire Congo. Individual white settlement is looked upon with such discouragement that it is practically prohibited. In the "holding company" which embraces all the above companies, the Belgian Government itself is an open half-share owner. Belgian officials in the Congo are working just as much to serve these business concerns as to fulfill the duties of administration, which are one and the same. Their control over the natives is primarily intended (and the Belgians are the first to point this out) to keep healthy and contented a dangerously limited labor supply.

As a consequence—since sentimentality is not mixed with a strictly business administration—the natives receive better medical attention in the Congo, and live in more comfortable and sanitary villages than anywhere else in Africa. (With the exception perhaps of Chester Beatty's model diamond-mining concession on the Gold Coast.) The natives are not educated to become Europeans or to produce a native *élite* (with no jobs for them), as they are in British possessions; they are limited almost entirely to manual trades, to fit them for holding jobs, such as those of locomotive drivers and first-class mechanics, in Africa. The Belgian Congo has no "Indian problem"; therefore, the lower posts which these Asiatics monopolize in Tanganyika, Kenya, and Uganda, are open for native occupancy.

Convicts, in striped blue and primrose jumpers, seem to be building a shocking amount of all the public works, the unbelievably good dirt roads which network the Congo, and the numerous new aerodromes being cleared in the depths of primeval jungle. Sometimes they are linked together with chains bound round their necks. A few are in this fix because of crimes such as theft and murder, but the overwhelming majority are delinquent taxpayers. The thought naturally presents itself: Was the tax placed high in order to produce plenty of unpaid labor? And then there is the *cultivation éducative,* as in the districts where each adult native is obliged to grow an acre of cotton. If he doesn't grow that, he will usually end in chains.

There is a point where the Belgian *Administrateur* will attempt to argue. "There is no forced cultivation," he will say; "if a native can pay his tax, he may do what he likes—grow nothing, if he wants to. But in that case, how is he going to earn money to pay his tax? So we say to him, grow cotton; you'll get real money for it, and you know what real money can buy!"

"So you are deliberately giving them the money urge?"

"Precisely. We find that once we have made a group grow cotton for a certain number of seasons, we no longer have to flog them (as we did do a short time ago), nor do we have to put them in prison for not paying taxes. They *want* to grow cotton. They *want* to make money. And we have no more trouble with them."

Thus do Government-Big Business-Church work hand in hand to place the Congo native on the inexorable endless-belt of modern progress.

This implacable determination on the part of Brussels, that

the Congo native must progress in spite of himself, is tinctured with a practicalness that leads to cynicism and not infrequent acts of petty brutality. But under it you find the astonishing growth of a native middle class, composed of clerks, railway employees, locomotive drivers, native chauffeurs driving the big motor lorries of the Vici-Congo transports into all parts of the Congo, and an amazing number of first-class mechanics. Incidentally, you find them at work in good, well paid jobs.

The way the African native has shown himself capable of doing such jobs is a practical index of his intelligence when it is given a chance. It is a lesson which should be taken to heart by Kenya, Tanganyika, and South Africa. And it more than makes up for any cynicism in the Belgian regime.

No white man goes to the Belgian Congo to live. He goes to serve so many years in a career, and then retire on a pension. Or he goes as a worker or executive in the mines or shops of the four big companies, in order to make enough money to leave Africa forever. The natives remain. The Belgians give them few false hopes. But they draw no color line; some of them will marry African girls and take them home. The sum total of this association of white and black under the Belgians is to raise village life and, while making plenty of money for Belgian shareholders, to create more and more jobs for intelligent Africans to fill.

The Congo will never again be a native country—not until its gold mines, diamonds, tin, iron and copper peter out, and palm trees cease to give kernels.

But, as I have said, the Belgians do not draw the color line, nor do the natives draw it against them. It is not at all unusual for a Belgian official to introduce you to a dark wife. Some natives are magnificent creatures, and you see that a career in the tropics has brought some commonplace little man from Courtrai or Ghent into cohabitation with an Atalanta. You wonder what she gets from Europe, the civilization which exported him.

At the opening of a new cottonseed-oil mill in the north

Congo, where all the officials and White Fathers in the region had gathered to bless the new machinery, to the accompaniment of champagne and an excellent buffet lunch, the most attractive woman of the occasion was the fawn-colored wife of the local *Administrateur*—gay, lissom, well dressed, quite able to carry on the usual sophisticated small talk which the intelligent priests demand. It was only her little girl, who seemed to have a questioning look in her large eyes, that made me wonder if there were *any* barriers she might find (and was keeping secret) between herself and her white playmates.

"Yes," said a Belgian woman of what the English would call the "county" class, "that one will feel it. There *is* a difference, despite what we say; we do feel we are different. I'm always sorry for these mixed-color children, for what is their future? This father here is madly in love with his wife, and can you blame him? She is a beautiful creature. And *very* good company. *As* his wife, she is fixed, already arrived. But their little girl has a problem ahead of her. She will go back to Belgium, to a convent. But when she gets out, then what? She won't want to come back to Africa; in fact, how could she? There is no large city population in which she could take her place. Her father will have been retired by then, will probably be living on a very small pension in Ostend. And, in Europe, a beautiful young girl 'with a touch of color' will find it difficult to get a good *husband*. And, my friend—you know what men are. Her father, you see, is a man of importance here; but in Belgium—*pouf!*"

"To which the answer is—?"

"That she will become a nun. A *religieuse*. Or, there's always Brussels and Paris— I do not approve of these marriages!" she added, with a sudden, fierce finality.

"There are some extraordinary cases of devotion," she said later, a little wearily. "I know of one case where an *Administrateur* here had two children by his colored mistress. His wife had left him and gone back to Belgium, when she found out the liaison he had been carrying on here. He died here in the Congo. And what did that white woman do? She sent for the children and adopted them. She is giving them precisely the same education as if they were her own. That's fineness of heart for you!"

I looked at that charming woman, whose pointed little chin looked as if it challenged the tropics to fade its owner. Faint moisture stood out defiantly, as if escaped from the mask of make-up. She was slender, chic, in a light frock that very possibly had come from Paris. She was the wife of the highest official in that province, a fat, jovial man, whose white tunic bore two rows of war ribbons. When, between his frequent trips to the buffet where the champagne stood in ice, he returned to us to make the two monsignors laugh with his good-natured badinage, she always smiled politely when the laughter around us showed that he had brought off a good jest.

She was keeping her part of the bargain.

And on such occasions she took advantage of the diversion to take out her compact and hurriedly repair the damage that the intolerable sun was doing to her face, even under the corrugated-iron roof of this shed. She was a nice woman, and I became aware that I was staring at her fat husband angrily. But, then, it was possible I was mistaken. They had only quarreled about his making her come to this boring ceremony?

On the whole I found the Belgian officials likable, patient, and very much overworked. They were not over-anxious to assist us to survey the particular "problems" of their individual districts, the *cultivation éducative*. But this was not because they had any motive of concealment; it was just that, if you want an official answer to your questions, ask Brussels—and we, here in the Congo, do not know how Brussels is phrasing this. They were polite, but it was the continental form of courtesy, and meant nothing. And letters which we brought from former Governors of the Congo, letters such as would have thrown all doors open in British East Africa, never feazed them. This we saw immediately, and, after one attempt, I seldom dug such introductions out from my dispatch case. It was just the opposite reaction I had expected from these Belgians, and their supreme paradox. We found we got much further in a district when we depended upon our own personal charm.

Belgian informality has its drawbacks. It is not long before you find yourself looking back yearningly to the unwritten standards which regulate life in British East Africa, the rigid routine of all the little things which give any life its peculiar flavor. The ritual "boy" with a cup of tea at six, the cool shower, shave, with fresh shorts and clean undershirt for going in to breakfast; the ritual of getting up a good sweat at tennis, golf, or polo, making your safety valves work; and then the cool "sundowner" at the club before your host takes you home to a fresh bath and change of clothes for dinner. The Englishman who puts on his dinner jacket in the jungle is fact, not fiction. And he knows what he's doing. He is sticking to a hard, painfully acquired, technique, a curriculum—the one *modus vivendi* by which a white man can resist being broken by a climate in which he was never meant to live, and by the dangerous boredom of seeing the same faces until one begins to hate them.

Sheer solitude is a luxury, even in Africa. That is why you will hear so many British officials declare they are much happier when they are out on safari in the bush. As they were in their early days.

The Belgian official has no such worries. By the law of his service he must be out on safari in his district, usually being carried along in a chair, *twenty-one days out of every month!* The result is that when he gets back to his station, or reaches some region in the mountains where there is a mine, he is eager for conversation. And in the twenty years or so that he will serve in the Congo only one week out of every four will have been spent being tied to a desk or facing the dull routine life of a station. This keeps him alive mentally, and I think most British officials would jump at such a chance to escape the desk work, the ever increasing writing of reports, which is growing like moss over the originally intrepid British colonial work.

The Belgians seem to have shown a great deal of uncommon good sense in handling their Congo problem. In the first place, they have realized the foremost importance of good roads. Then the vast transport combine, the Vici-Congo, which handles all the traffic and supplies to mines along these roads, knew long ago the civilizing effect of good hotels. The result is that in some of the most remote parts of the Congo you will find these good, red-brick hotels, built originally for the transport drivers, always used as the club by the Europeans in that district, and now grateful nights' rests for the travelers whom the Vici-Congo has begun to take on its services across Africa. Most of these hotels are as well run and comfortable as any roadside inns you will find in England or America. Comfortable, that is, as a white man can make himself in the steaming Congo.

These hotels, whenever we could get to one, meant oases in our drive across Africa. They made us sympathize with the main Belgian determination to discourage individual white settlers in the Congo. When chance landed us for the night in one of the few remaining private hotels, we never knew what we were in for. At the foot of Lake Kivu, for instance, is a hotel run by a Russian countess, with rows of roses rimming the rippling blue waters, arbored kiosks for the heat of the day, a cuisine such as you will find in few provincial hotels in France—a gorgeous mushroom omelette, for instance—and cool cement floors covered with circular rugs of leopard or zebra skins. You sleep under cool, thatched roofs in circular cubicles around the central hotel. And crisp biscuits are brought in with your morning tea.

This was the only hotel I have ever known which was built for spite. This beautiful Russian woman (she was of the borzoi type, long-legged, dressed in well cut buff corduroy slacks) had run a hotel with a French transport rider who was catering to some local mines. "I gave him the idea, raised most of the money, designed the whole place for him; then he tried to tell *me* how it should be run! *Pfui!*" They quarreled, separated; and then this unbeatable, clever woman came here and built this hotel not twenty miles from *L'Hôtel des Volcans*. She made it as nearly perfect as possible.

"To show *him* what a hotel could be?" I asked.

"Not a bit of it! He is not allowed to step foot inside the door! I have given strict orders that when I am away (I am going back to Paris, for a time) *he* shall not be allowed to stay here!"

"But isn't that illegal? Can a hotel do that?"

"Laws! *Pfui!* The Belgians, they tried to make me leave. They tried first to make me stop building it. Then they tried to buy it. Then they threatened me; all sorts of threats. I said: 'Bring on your advocates! I won't leave this place until you kill me!'"

She tossed her head. She wore a short, brown jumper and had a black bandanna tied around her graying hair. With waves of an imperious hand in six directions, she dispatched six gaping natives off to do six different jobs of work. "Belgians!" she said, dismissing the race. "They can't treat me like a dog!"

"I saw his hotel," I said. "It looked very nice. I was told the food was good there."

"Ha!" she choked.

That's how I got my *omelette aux champignons* for breakfast.

But then you may have fate land you for the night at an inescapable hotel such as I found in the mountains of Ruanda-Urundi. Here our cubicles were tin huts, partly made of gasoline tins, and standing on stilts to keep out the ground insects. They had overhanging tin roofs. They held the heat of the day all night, and you felt like bread being baked in a slow oven. A greasy proprietor who never buttoned his red polo shirt over his hairy stomach; a sore-eyed waiter who served soup with his thumb in the dish; floors slippery with yesterday's beer; the reeks of slops decaying in the sun; and a phonograph playing that tinpanny music which the Belgian lower classes love, all day long. The food was vile!

"It's hell!" said a young man at our table, breaking into the mournful conversation between Eve and me. "I am a German. As soon as I can sell my claim I'm going back to Tanganyika."

He was engaged in gold prospecting, another form of "individual enterprise" which the Belgians, particularly the big mining companies, ferociously discourage in the Congo. But here, in the mandate, they had to keep up the pretense of free entry for all nationalities.

"That's all bunk," he said. "They have spies on me. I've found two gold-bearing areas and filled in all the proper applications. Now they are trying to force me out, bringing every kind of pressure to bear on me."

"How old are you?" I asked.

"I am nineteen," he said. "Why?"

"I was just wondering how much success you would have, hanging on to your claims."

He laughed, and smoothed his immaculate, blond head. "That is understood. Well, I have not much hope; but I have taken my claim to one outside company and offered to turn it over to them. I now have them slightly worried, and these people here might make me a good offer. I hope to get enough money to give me two or three years over in Tanganyika. I'll prospect there."

He was an astonishing young man. The next morning I saw him setting off in his car with his one faithful "boy." The car held all his worldly wealth. "And this tent," he said, "which is much better than that hotel. I won't be back here for weeks."

He looked over my shoulder towards the veranda where the hotel proprietor stood watching us. The hotelkeeper wore the same claret polo shirt and black trousers with the red stripe down the side that he had graced us with the previous night. "He's another of the companies' spies," said the young German, loud enough for the other man to hear. "They've paid the natives around here to tell them where I'm prospecting, so that the companies may send a man in first. Look at him!"

The proprietor turned and went back inside.

"Well, so long!" called back the young German, as he took the wheel of his battered, box-body Ford. "I tell you one thing to remember about the Congo—what the white ants don't get the White Fathers will!"

His impudent self-assurance gave you the feeling that he was not altogether "on his own," that there was *something* behind him. I asked him point-blank if he was a Nazi, and he said no. But that didn't mean anything. It was not at all out of the question that he was a young mining engineer, furnishing the *Führer* in Tanganyika with some very comprehensive reports on minerals and politics in the Ruanda-Urundi Mandate. There were scores of such agents in Africa, some coming in as refugees.

This last thought was given us by a genuine (I suppose) German refugee who found us at the filling station. The rain was coming down in a steady sheet, and he asked Eve to take refuge in his house, which stood just by. It ended by us having luncheon with him. His books caught my eye; they were what is called "heavy," such works as those of Malinowski and Keyserling, and MacMillan's *Warning from the West Indies*. I asked him if he was an anthropologist.

"No," he said, "I am a hide buyer; a trader."

He made it plain he did not want to talk about himself. So I asked him if he had met the young German who was prospecting around there.

"Oh, that one? No, he wouldn't come near *me*. You see, I am a Jew."

His life was a scene from the story of his race which has been scattered over the face of the earth. In an odd way, his exile had led him to many of the things he wanted to do; he had, for instance, always wanted to shoot big game. He supposed this was due to the books he read, about the German explorers in Africa. So he had managed to bring a rifle with him. The chops we were eating came from a buck he had shot a few days before. He was interested in natives, and he had already begun to learn their languages. He bought from them direct, and sold his hides to one of the big Belgian companies. We left with him some damp Tauchnitz editions which I had brought out with me. And he gave us two loaves of bread, which his "boy" had just made; it is almost impossible to buy bread anywhere in Ruanda-Urundi.

I told him that over in Dar es Salaam I had met Dr. Ehrlich, brother of the famous discoverer of "606." He laughed. "Well, he's come to a good place to use it! We German Jews make our various contributions to world progress. Don't worry about me. The Belgians don't like me but they leave me alone—and that's a lot, isn't it?"

He gave me the impression of being much happier than he dared to admit. As if he would be tempting Providence if he did admit it and would be forced to move on again. He "walked softly."

"I wish you people could hang around here for a couple of days," he said. "That's the one thing that I miss—a good, long argument!"

*

*

30. Gorilla Hunting

WE found the Belgian *Administrateur* sitting in a dark, red-brick bungalow that was almost smothered in banks of giant rhododendrons. He was a silent, heavy man (he must have weighed close to 250 pounds), and on the dark veranda was a massive bamboo "chair," in which natives, running in teams of four, carried his great bulk about in the mountains of the gorilla country. He told us that the natives around here were not pacified; had not been considered "safe" until as late as 1925.

He was a bachelor. We found him with a dog and a cat sitting beside him, preparing to eat luncheon. He made his "boy" bring in the two pans of their food. "So that I may see for myself how much and what they get." And he made us share his own luncheon of chops and yams. He was not very much interested in food, he told us. And that was just as well. "You cannot get anything to 'taste,' not in the Congo." He would eat when he retired on his pension.

He was very dubious about the gorillas.

"It is not right to frighten them," he said; "if you do frighten them they will attack you. You may not take any firearms into the gorilla country. You may no longer have hundreds of natives to encircle them. The last gorilla we permitted shot was to obtain a big specimen for an American museum. We had 300 natives drive a giant gorilla to where our Belgian game warden shot it. It was a great beast; it had a nine-foot spread of arms.

"There was an Englishwoman here two years ago who gave us a lot of bother. She had letters. And because of her we had to shoot a baby gorilla and its mother. I had sent men out, with rifles, to protect the Englishwoman. I instructed them to fire only in case of real peril. But this Englishwoman persuaded the 'boys' to round up this poor gorilla they heard barking, and the mother, frightened for her baby, charged! Since then there have been no more 'encirclements.' And I am afraid I cannot let you disturb the gorillas, or risk your own lives, because, if I did let you go—you would have to track and chase after the gorillas *yourselves*. I could give you a dozen natives of that mountain, armed with spears. But with a gorilla I would want more than a spear, myself."

But we also "had letters"; and, after reading them, the *Administrateur* sighed. "Very well; I have a 'boy' here who talks French; you can have him. He is the son of a chief on that mountain; a mission boy. His name is Alphonse."

Alphonse was summoned. He was very mission, very advanced, in blue suit, raincoat, black patent-leather shoes with white tops, and what would be recognized in England as a black "foreign-office" hat. He was exhilaratingly intelligent, and his remarks, when he heard that he was to accompany us on a mad-gorilla chase into the jungle, glinted with sarcastic objections to the general damn-foolishness of the whole idea. He said (a) that it was an absolute impossibility to chase a gorilla on foot; you had to trap them—or encircle them; (b) if we *did* catch up, we would wish we hadn't.

"Not that I am afraid," he added, contemptuously. Nor was he.

But here the lethargic *Administrateur* also became sarcastic, saying that he was interested to hear Alphonse admit he knew so much about killing gorillas, as it was a well known fact that his tribe *had* killed several gorillas lately, and they were due for trouble because of it; and that Alphonse had better pack, as we were taking him up into the mountains beyond Lubero that very night.

"Two months ago," said Alphonse, as a last shot, "a gorilla

bit the calf off the leg of a man in my village, directly below the rest house where monsieur and madame will sleep tonight."

"I know all about it," said the *Administrateur*. "Monsieur and madame will be pleased if you show them this man. Now, go!"

"Fourteen years ago," smiled the *Administrateur*, "the father of Alphonse would have thrown a spear at you. But you will excuse my pride if I tell you that I think these ink-black men here are the finest natives in all Africa. I have spent fifteen years on the Congo River itself; I have had other districts. But I must instruct Alphonse; don't be put out if you find them surly and reluctant to do anything for you. They are shy, and I don't think they are used to us yet. And whatever you give them for your gorilla chase, or for eggs, they will make angry faces and shout that you have cheated them."

Below the *Administrateur's* park-like grounds lay the native village. In it was one of those amazing chain stores that the Belgians run throughout the Congo. We bought tins of Vienna sausages, cigarettes, lobster, and, as it was Eve's birthday, a pound tin of cream chocolates. When we expressed our astonishment at the range of goods, including a showcaseful of silver photograph frames, the Dutch manager of the store said: "They are for the wives of the engineers in the mines. They like these little gifts. They have little else to please them, poor dears. Contrary to what people imagine back home, a tropical climate does not help lovemaking."

Seated at two sewing machines outside a mud-and-wattle hut, and watched by a ring of loin-clouted Negroes carrying spears, were two swiftly pedaling native men, making into dresses yards and yards of purple cotton print gaudily patterned with yellow flowers.

"For the wives of the black men working in the mines," smiled the storekeeper. "A few years ago all they wore was a bunch of leaves fore and aft. They looked better that way."

A native dwarf, humped and bowlegged, cut painful capers as he worked the lever of the gasoline tank. He wore the scarlet jumper of a big mining company, with its name in white letters across his chicken breast. He laughed when he saw me staring at it, and made obscene gestures about his own body, to show that *he* could never work in any mine. A string of sullen prisoners, linked neck to neck by chains, shuffled past under a sloppy guard of police. And a shout from Eve brought me back into the white man's store. She was holding a bowl, which the storekeeper's wife had just given her—*filled with fresh strawberries!*

We slept that night at an altitude of well over 8,000 feet. Below us only the highest trees of the gorilla forest appeared above the mists of sunset. It was a lost-world scene in which all the verdure seemed out of proportion. For instance, along the wall of the jungle into which we were to crawl in the morning were ferns, some of them forty feet high. And although they were identical in shape with those you would find any day in England or America, you would pass like weasels beneath them. In those perpetual gray mountain mists there were giant lobelias which rose to twenty feet. And the dark hole in the green wall directly below us was, we were told, the mouth of the funnel from which the gorillas appeared, to raid the native yam and banana plantations.

There are believed to be some 800 gorillas in this mountain, rain-forest sanctuary, all living at altitudes of around 8,000 to 9,000 feet. There are supposed to be another hundred or so on the slopes of the volcanoes between the Uganda border and the Belgian administrative post of Rutshuru. But this is a sketchy census. Large areas of these jungled African alps have never known the presence of man, presumably not even a black man. And with a fine sense of values, the Belgian officials are united in the attempt to keep this gorilla sanctuary inviolate.

The village where we slept was another example of Belgian thoughtfulness in handling the Congo. It was built on a ridge, and had clean, well constructed mud huts lined up like soldiers.

There were whitewashed incinerators for burning the village refuse. And below, over the slope, was a row of latrines. The men, freed from the savagery of spear and loin-clout, were now dressed in whatever tatter or remnant of European costume they could come by. As they appeared to be shivering in these, you wondered how they ever managed to keep warm in the old days. I saw that the fires in the huts were kept burning all night. The women, round, stocky, and either frightened or unsociable, had all managed to obtain a strip or so of that violently patterned cotton cloth, which they wore, leaving one satin shoulder bare, as with togas. The children were naked, pot-bellied, nearly all with hideous umbilical hernias from the gases of the cereal diets which are the sole food of these always undernourished African people.

And with that love which the black mothers have for their children, the little girls wore minute "shame straps" of crimson beads.

Our hut was on a slightly higher knoll, across the road from the village. It was made of mud and wattle, with an overhanging thatched roof, and had around its interior wall an unbroken divan of bamboo. This had been limed fairly recently, as affording a sanitary precaution against some disease or plague which we did not care to think about, and we set up our beds with the feeling of going to sleep inside a chicken house.

I could picture the Belgian *Administrateur*, arriving here "on tour" in his chair, with his retinue of "boys" and cook, having his bed and his mosquito net and his table set up for him. Not having to do anything, or lift a finger; just an occasional barked command. And we tried to exact something of the same "service" from the dandified Alphonse.

But Alphonse was piqued. He had wanted to sleep in the hut with us. Having been weaned from his village, he did not wish to go back to it. He had now crossed over to the European side. And I, with great lack of understanding, was refusing to let him bide with us. It was painful, but when Alphonse appeared with his mosquito net in hand—this last greatly admired by the inhabitants of his childhood scene—I told him he must sling it somewhere else. Where, I never knew, because Alphonse did not appear that evening after sunset.

I can easily understand how the devil enters into a white man, when he is forced to depend upon surly, *deliberately* unhelpful natives. I went across to the headman with my usually urbane temper just fluttering along the edge of flash-point. With great restraint, and, I hoped, just the right intonation of menace in my voice, I demanded firewood, immediately!

For an appalled second it looked as if he were going to refuse. Then he gave an ill-humored command, and some men began to carry fagots across to us. I demanded water, and gave them a canvas bucket in which to fetch it. We always carried in our African water-bags a big supply of water, which we boiled ourselves. But we distrusted this water, which the natives grimly fetched us, so much that we hesitated even before washing the dishes in it.

The clouds came down over the volcanoes, and the antediluvian plants were swallowed by the mist.

And so, sitting on the edges of our camp beds, as we had done and would do for months to come, Eve cooked our usual dinner on the four-shilling alcohol lamp—soup, Vienna sausages and a tin of pears. The village, as if sending us to Coventry, was dead silent. We saw the silhouettes of men sitting around a big, central fire, but no sound came from them. And when we blew out our own hurricane lamps and went out on the edge of our ridge, hoping to hear some nocturnal prowlings in the gorilla forest, no sound came from there.

In the dawn we were awakened by drumbeats. It was time for Mass, the black priest calling the faithful to prayer. And for the first time we noticed that a big mud and bamboo structure in the center of the native village had a gilt cross on its ridge.

It blazed in the morning sun as we listened to the black people chanting in Latin, and as we watched the hot, rising ball burn away the mists from the glistening gorilla jungle.

Twelve unenthusiastic men appeared, with spears. With them, in patent-leather shoes, raincoat, and "foreign-office" hat, appeared Alphonse. And behind him hopped a man in shorts; one of his legs was twisted around a homemade crutch.

"C'est lui!" said Alphonse.

It was the man whom the gorilla had bitten. Proud of this distinction, he pointed to a plot of cultivation some sixty yards down the slope. He had gone down there at dawn, he said, to get some food, when the gorilla leapt up and bit him. When I was curious to find out whether the gorilla had made an unprovoked attack, and this question was finally conveyed to him, his face brightened; and he said, Oh, no, the gorilla was angry because he, too, had come into the clearing to get some food. He showed us where the gorilla's teeth had met through his calf.

The horse-like teeth had bitten through and carried away the flesh. I had, in the past months, seen many natives carrying frightful inflictions and mutilations; lepers, an Ovamba with an arm corroded by snakebite, those horrible monstrosities where a growth of yeast has started to grow in a football-shaped foot; and I have seen them lying in rows in hospitals, incurable, half eaten or half cut away. I never met anything in their blank and black faces but a silent question, "Master, is there any hope for me?" I heard no groans, saw no panic or even fear; just—this is fate.

And this half man—for he was now useless to his village—was no object of sympathy now. Perhaps they fed him (all blacks have this communism, unless the affliction is taboo), perhaps he made himself useful, tending a fire, hopping about on errands. But we, for these few minutes, gave him a fleeting glory.

He smiled as he tapped his crutch and gave a few bird-like hops, to impress us with the fact that this was the way he would now go on through life.

My own gorilla ardor began to cool.

We entered the jungle in single file, a man who was obviously the tribe's head hunter in the lead, then two more surly natives, with spears, then I, Eve, and Alphonse (how incorrigible he looked in that black "foreign-office" hat!), then nine more natives, with slender spears, looking equally displeased with this job. Tagging behind were three "boys" of about fifteen. They looked both frightened and pleased.

The jungle was impenetrable; I use that word in its purest sense. Most of the natives had reverted to their original nakedness to encounter this forest. It was amazing, the way they could slip through the undergrowth; no tangled liana or thorn seemed able to foul those silky black hides! When they pulled part of the green wall open and slipped through, they vanished

I didn't like crawling along wicker fish baskets (which was what these gorilla tunnels were), even when there were three sophisticated natives crawling along ahead of me. A gorilla coming head on would, I felt certain, just pluck the arms off us, like so many flies' wings. And at this juncture the eager Eve, with that maddening unawareness of the laws of cause and effect, or Newton's falling apple, or gorilla mentality, suggested that . take the lead. "Because," she said, "with these three black men in front of us, we won't see a gorilla when he *does* come!"

The idea did not appeal to me. "Besides," I said, "I'm no going to ruin my legs tearing apart all these creepers."

In the dark forests of South America I have seen a nativ blithely cut a path for himself through virgin jungle, with on of their deadly machetes. But that forest was a spongy, vege table-like, low-level growth. This in Africa was high rain forest a good 8,000 feet up, and the dangling lianas were tough a spring steel.

Nevertheless, in this choking mess, it was hot! The black backs of the natives glistened before me. My own safari shirt was soaked with sweat. For long stretches we had to crawl on our hands and knees.

In these rain forests, soaked in perpetual mist, all growth becomes abnormal. In an occasional open space we came out into ferns that broke in their curving spray a dozen feet above our heads. Then we would encounter impenetrable clusters of bamboo, thickly bunched at their feet, meeting in great feathery arches over us. And always there were the monstrous lobelias, twenty feet high.

This was the gorilla wonderland, and for all my misgivings that we might have an accident I felt the lust growing in me. We must come up to them.

For the greater part of that morning we never saw the sky. We were aware, because we came to their bases, of the giant, smooth trunks that were shooting upwards all around us. And every so often we came to where great trees had fallen, in their time, across the gorilla trail. It was between two of these that the head hunter held up his spear, and Eve and I stared down at a fern-lined depression, in which, said the huntsman, a gorilla had recently been sleeping. It might have been a bassinet! Then we came on three objects that gave me one of the few real shocks that I found in Africa—that country where, as I said, I spent eight months without ever seeing a snake! They were just three balls of dung. They looked like horse droppings.

But they were steaming!

That meant that a gorilla, badly frightened, had passed just ahead of us. It was there that I took a spear from one of the sullen, useless natives behind us. It was not much, I realized as I grasped it; a slender thing, seven feet long, with a thin, leaf-like point. I wouldn't have cared to try to push it into a gorilla, but it was *something*. I felt a little ashamed as I did this—it seemed so theatrical—and, to reconcile my own conscience, I moved up two pegs so as to be directly behind the head hunter.

Eve, like an insistent puppy, moved up immediately behind me.

At noon, with even the natives a bit disgusted and weary, the head hunter threw all bluff aside and, through Alphonse, made it clear that it was a mad-gorilla chase to try to catch up to them; they were much too quick-eared and fast for us; and the only thing to do (if we *would* insist upon going on!), was for us to pick a place on the ravine we had come to, and let them drive any chance gorilla towards us. This "encircle-ment," we knew, broke all commands of the Belgian gorilla mandate; and we were glad. On the lip of a ridge which looked down into a lobelia lined small valley, Eve and I and Alphonse sat down. So did the three "boys," wide-eyed, at a respectful distance. Then the twelve hunters slipped into the jungle, and were gone.

Then there was just silence. And greenness. We became as motionless as the trees themselves. I even did not smoke. Staring into the ravine, at the freak lobelias, ominous in their distortion, and watching the bushes below, I began to feel an *understanding* of this jungle. I imagined the giant gorillas, coming out from the forest and staring upward at the sun. I wondered if they put their hand up to shade their eyes, if there were any open patches where they lay and basked; or did they always live in this mesh of green mist and semi-darkness among the vol-canoes?

Then I saw the bushes move, directly across from us; a face, grotesquely Irish, appeared, and I saw the dark patch of a shoulder or back. The bushes closed. I pointed along the spear to show the place to Eve, but the gorilla did not return. Then I lit a cigarette. An hour passed. Directly behind us, within about sixty feet, there was a sharp bark. My hair just jumped upright. I had been brought up on various tales of the gorilla hunters; in them the gorilla always emitted a roar that made the jungle shiver. This was just a shrill yelp.

I turned, and found Alphonse watching me anxiously (he was really looking at the spear); and I saw that the three "boys" were absolutely popeyed with fright. But Eve, with her head turned toward the slope behind us, whispered, *"Lovely!"*

I don't think I ever hated her before, but to call that yelp lovely was too much to bear. I glowered at her when her eyes met mine. I was thinking, Does he know we are here? He did not sound like it; there was no sound of alarm in that voice. Do gorillas have a high sense of smell? What the hell shall I do if he does come down at us? Then the bark came again. Then two barks.

It was obvious that in the glade we had just left were two gorillas. They were approaching each other. Then a twig broke within twenty feet. I stood up, grasping that satiric spear, and the head hunter appeared from the brush just beside me.

He knew. They had heard the barks. And like a native when the chase is really on, these men were lusting to get to the gorillas as fast as we could. It was too tense to be frightening, and we had gone too far with our nerves already. I think that even if we had known they were coming towards *us*, we would have rushed towards *them!* So idiotic does excitement make you at times.

We came on them among the lobelias.

For what reason they had remained, or remained silent, I'll never know. But the moment we reached the rim of that open knoll they began to beat their chests. It's a horrible sound, meant to strike terror into everything in the forest, and it certainly worked with me, all right. That terrible shrill hammering—they don't yell; they just beat the caverns of their chests with their mouths open—hit me like a kick in the stomach. And for a moment I felt that uncontrollable sickness known as "wind-up." Eve did not have it a bit.

The natives all leaned back on their right legs, with spears held back, ready to throw them. Then run. Then I realized they never had had any intention of *facing* the animal; it was just, as a last resort, to hurl these things at him—and fly. The bushes within fifteen feet of us were being whipped about. The gorillas were right *there!* right in front of our eyes! and still we could not see them!

Then a bush immediately before me whipped down, and I saw a face staring at me, above a huge, humped shoulder. I set my feet—and the bush whipped back again.

I could say now that, yes, I have seen a gorilla, I have faced him within fifteen feet, but if I had to draw the picture of a gorilla from what *I* saw of one—well, it might be as much like a sea serpent as anything else. Except—for a second it swung its arms! And now I *know* why those pre-Elizabethan explorers brought back tales of serpents with beards, and "King Kong" monsters, and were not able to agree, even on the things they had seen in company. For, having no previous knowledge of, say, anything larger than a monkey—and *then* running on to a gorilla—why, he might have been twenty feet high!

The sight of him was worse than his shrieks! And the yells the two gorillas made as they tore on all fours into another one of their wicker funnels! We came close after them, tripping, falling, caught by the lianas. And here were more clusters of steaming dung.

Then the head hunter shook his head. We clustered around a large tree that flanked the gorilla walk. We could hear them yelping now, and hear one or two rasps as they tore across the lobelia-lined ravine. Then they were silent.

"The man say," explained Alphonse in his execrable Belgian French, "the gorillas they two kilometers away already. We no catch them again today. They won't come back."

I smiled. I did not want to "catch" them. And for an hour

or so we crawled back along the painful way we had come. We had seen a gorilla and had been as near, I dare say, as anyone will get to one in the Lubero forests these days. Seen as much as you will ever see without binoculars. I was satisfied; I would not want to have come any closer.

*

31. Leopard Men

THE main road across Africa is best where you would least
expect it to be. This is due to the tin, copper, and gold mines,
down in the mountains of Ruanda-Urundi and north of Irumu.
All their ore must be taken out by motor lorries. Amazing roads
have been built through virgin forests to get it out. The result
is that you can travel at about forty miles an hour through unbroken stretches of jungle for hundreds of miles, past an absolutely impenetrable wall of forest full of elephant, tribes of
pygmies, and rare okapi, on a red, sandstone road.

The only thing you have to be careful about is not to have a
breakdown that you cannot repair on the road, or to have so
many punctures or blowouts that you are left with less than
four tires. There is only one garage in the 600-odd miles between Lake Kivu and Stanleyville on the Congo.

And it was here that the lava of Lake Kivu took its toll
from us.

This amazing red road, running west of the Central African
Rift, goes along the feet of the main mountain range and its
volcanoes, then strikes sharp west at Irumu. You have to cross
the scores of streams, racing down from the volcanoes, in native
dugouts. It is a country of mahogany trees and ironwood, whose
gray trunks tower 150 feet before they spread out into a green
roof that houses another life above the choking undergrowth.
It is a scene that lends itself to either fine writing or verbal
"squash." The extraordinary thing about trying to describe a
jungle is that you must be precise about it. H. M. Tomlinson
demonstrated this superbly in *The Sea and the Jungle;* he took

each spraying palm, banana frond, and clinging liana, and gave its proper perspective in the complex jungle tapestry. He held himself well in hand. He was successful. But there are few writers who can resist taking a running jump into a flock of adjectives connected with "dense," "green," "impenetrable."

So I shall not describe this jungle. Except to say that it was still as death. I never saw a bird. Its only color, aside from varied greens, was an occasional scarlet flower, like a poinsettia. It was full of elephants, but I never saw one in it. Sometimes the bushes flicked-to ahead of us, as *something* retreated back into the forest. But whether it was an elephant, a rare okapi, or a pygmy, we did not know.

We were trying to reach Stanleyville, in order to go down the Congo on one of the palatial four-deckers. Needless to say, we missed it. This was luck, for we put the car on a barge and went down it several days on what was probably the smallest tugboat on the river. So small that we stopped everywhere, for cargo or to take on wood for fuel; we watched our captain fighting with the native stevedores, who never would load us fast enough from the cordwood fuel on the banks, and on these smelly banks, off which the big palace steamer would rush past a mile off shore, we picked up many an intimate detail, and bug, from native life.

We had originally intended to do this road to Stanleyville in six jumps from the gorilla country, stopping overnight at Beni and Irumu to sleep, eat, and fill our car with gasoline. Then stop with the American, Putnam, brother-in-law of the late Amelia Earhart, at his camp in the Ituri forest—Putnam who knows more about pygmies than any other white man. Then, in two more jumps (where there seemed no place to put up) to make a dash for Stanleyville. We did this, eventually.

But in one section, where the natives were clearing the jungle to begin a plantation, they had casually dropped a giant ironwood tree across the road. It took them all one afternoon to cut a section out so that we could get through. That broke one jump into two. Then, driving due west from Irumu, we had three blowouts in quick succession (the Lake Kivu lava getting back its own), and I spent an entire afternoon cutting up the oldest shoe to repair the least damaged one. Then we had to turn back to Irumu and beg the Vici-Congo company there to sell us one of its tires.

This was not bad luck, either. For we had intended to pass up Irumu, which lay off the main road. And now, going back to there, we suddenly discovered we had left the dark belt of jungle behind us and were in the deep, waving green of the savannah country. This was elephant grass, about fifteen feet high, waving over its rolling hills like a stretch of the Atlantic. Seen against a slate-gray sunset, this wide expanse was one of the most refreshing sights we had faced since Kenya.

The Vici-Congo foreman at Irumu was in bed with malaria. But he got up and tottered out. His eyes were the color of an egg yolk. He was shivering, and glistening beads of perspiration were all over his pallid face. "A-another attack," he chattered. "Bad, this one!"

It was not until I got the malaria myself that I realized what a prodigious favor he did for us.

You do not believe your first pygmy when you see him. Several times since we entered the dark Ituri forest we had seen little figures spring into the bush ahead of us. They clutched bows and arrows. And one or two seemed to have been wearing little crowns of feathers. But the bushes had ceased rustling when we came to the spot. Then we came on about twenty of the little people. They were carrying reddish nets over their shoulders. And one had slung over his shoulder a little, mouse-colored deer, about the size of a fox terrier. They had just trapped and killed it.

They had not had time to get away, because we came on them in a clearing of some deserted Bantu huts. So they submitted to our scrutiny. They did not smile. Their faces gave not the least change of expression. Ages of evolution lay between, and we could not cross. An old man among them was as wrinkled as a shriveled walnut. None of them came up to my breast. Most of the women had breasts that sagged like razor strops. And they were all stained with a pattern of dark-blue green. Except for a little string of leather around their thighs, this tattoo of dye was all they wore.

But there was something peculiarly *sympathetic* about them. They had the same impish charm that I had noticed about the Bushmen in South-West Africa. And, gradually, they began to smile. It is odd how universal that grimace is among the human race. It was the only way that I could sign to them that I was not an enemy. Not that they paid much attention to me! It was Eve who puzzled them. They seemed to be studying her. Their little arrows, which I suppose were poisonous, had leaves for feathers and did not have any notch; you just placed the flat end against a flat strip of bamboo that was used as a bowstring.

They were pot-bellied and had enormous behinds and fragile little arms that you felt would snap like pipestems. It was impossible to think that these frail little people, with their infantile faces, killed elephants by hamstringing them, or that they could build those ingenious liana bridges which they throw across the swift rivers. To kill elephants, whose eyesight is weak but whose sense of smell is to be feared, the pygmies sometimes smear themselves with elephant dung, then one walks up underneath the unsuspecting elephant, which merely thinks he smells another elephant, and shoves a spear upwards into its heart, while two comrades behind slash its rear-leg tendons.

They love putrefying flesh.

The Bantus of these forests sometimes pick up the old or crippled pygmies that the tribe has abandoned, and make slaves of them. Sometimes they catch young ones. We found an old couple in a Bantu village who were obviously doing duty in some form of servitude. When we came near them they looked at the Bantus, as if for orders or protection. And, when the lazy Bantus grinned, they stood still and let us approach them. When I gave the old man some cigarettes he dutifully walked across and handed them over to a fat Bantu. When I made him light one and smoke it himself, which he obviously enjoyed enormously, he looked at the Bantus very much as you will see a performing monkey on the stage look at his master when he is being scolded for not doing his trick. A "Please-don't-be-cross-with-me-for-I-don't-know-what-you-want-me-to-do" expression. And the silent Bantus grinned.

It suddenly struck me that these jungle Bantus considered themselves as far advanced above this grotesque little pygmy as I considered myself above them. We were both watching the antics of ancient man.

For about three days we passed through these pygmies. And in one place a Belgian *Administrateur* whom I found being carried along in his chair became sentimental about them. "Of course, we don't make *them* pay taxes," he said.

I had to laugh. "You can't," I said; "they'd be off in the bush in a minute. You'd never see them again!"

The Belgians, I knew, when they wanted to ascertain the whereabouts and the doings of any of these pygmies in the Ituri forest, had to come and ask Putnam. He had just brought back a young Mexican bride. His permanent home is in the Ituri forest. When we got to his camp late one night we received the bad news that the two had just gone off with a tribe of pygmies, to be gone two months in the bush.

We had just missed this man, whom I most wanted to talk to, by half a day. Stopping to try to help some Seventh Day Adventists had held us up. We came on an antique box-body Ford being watched by two pallid women, in enormous white sun helmets, and four spindly legged children. The children, when we drew up—you never pass anyone halted on the road in Africa without asking if you can help; at least, you're not supposed to—broke into a babel of raw American Middle-West.

"Say, where did *you* come from?" "Gee, look, mamma, he's got a leopard!" "Sez you!" "Say, mister—is that a 1938 model?"

A pale young man, in his early thirties, wearily held up a split inner tube. "Got anything," he said, "you think'll cover this?"

I asked him whether he had a spare tire. No, he said; they hadn't thought to take one from the mission. We had no patch that could cover the six-inch split, which he had obviously got from carrying on with a deflated tire, so we offered him our oldest tube. "Cut that up," we said. I got out and started helping him.

"Well, I don't think I ought to take this. Seems sort of presumptuous."

He gave us the impression that he was new to Africa. And by this time we felt *very* old. Less than two weeks before, our lights had gone out as we were rounding a precipice in the mountains of Ruanda-Urundi, with a drop of several hundred sheer feet on our right. With no lights, we spent the night exactly where I had managed to stop that car (with a lantern perched on its top to warn all traffic!); so we felt deep sympathy for him and those pale little children. "There's hardly an inch of my tube that hasn't got a patch on it already; you're welcome to it." Together, we got the tire off the wheel.

"Well, thanks," he said. "Guess I can fix things now so as we'll all limp home. Would you mind telling the mission when you pass?"

"Where is it?"

"Well—"

Then one of the women spoke. "On the far side of the second river that you pass from here. You'll see the sign all right— big one—'Seventh Day Adventist.' You tell 'em to send Willie out here on his motorbike. Willie's the only one around here that can fix *anything*. Tell Willie to hurry; we don't want these kids being chewed to death by the skeeters. You remember what I said—second river, on the right."

"Say, mister, where you going?" "Say, mister, what's *your* business?"

The pug noses and freckled faces crowded to the car. "Gee, *that* ain't a 1939—it's only a measly old 1937!"

"O.K.," I said cheerfully; "I'll tell Willie."

We found the mission. An old man and an old woman came out. He held out his hand, twenty yards before he got to me. "Welcome, welcome, stranger!" he said. "What brings you here?"

"Some people from your mission," I said, "have had a blow-out about fifteen miles back, across two rivers. They want you to send out a person called Willie. I think he had better take a spare tire for that Ford."

"Why, Willie's just gone *off!*" cried the woman.

"Hush, mother," said the man. "He'll be home to dinner. Madam, can't we ask you and your good man to stop the night with us? We can give you a right comfortable room to put up in! You're welcome. But don't think we're trying to press you."

It was hard to refuse. I wish, now, we had stopped. Those two good old people were so dying for a talk. And we would have learned lots of things. This man bore the weathered, wrinkled face of many years in Africa, with those strange, tell-tale creases around the eyes, from constant squinting to protect them from the sun.

"Mister," I said, "we've got seventy miles to do tonight before we pitch a bed. And we're in an awful hurry!"

He laughed. "Well, sir, I won't detain you for a moment. Good-by. Perhaps you'll drop in again some day?"

"Yes," I promised, "if I ever get by here. Good night, and *don't* forget to send Willie."

✦

By the time you have got this far, into the heart of Africa, you have forgotten your original conception of a land densely populated with black men sliding in and out the intricacies of low and steaming jungle. The unusual has become commonplace. From 7 foot Watusi to 3 foot 6 inch pygmies has been but a step; you may remain exalted, but you are not startled by the sight of snowcapped mountains glistening right on the equator; and it is perhaps only along this jungle road from Irumu to Stanleyville on the Congo that you realize you are sliding down off the great, red shelf, the western slope of the Central African tableland, into Africa as you have been led to believe it would be.

This is important. It explains swift rivers, where you had expected to find stagnant, muddy streams. You have been wondering why you have managed to keep comparatively cool in such zero latitudes, but along this road you cease to wonder; you are no longer cool, and the damp heat increases as if you were stepping down into a hot bath.

The natives along this road are called "Arabies." They are a legacy from the days of the slave trade, when the Arab traders passed through and either kidnapped these tribes to sell them on the East Coast for service in Yemen or Arabia, or, as the trade was suppressed, Mohammedanized them. They are not a pleasant lot. They have the slave mentality. And, from a near past in which they have lived in terror of becoming slaves themselves, they have become strident, like any man recently getting over a bad scare, and they at least try to bullyrag the pygmies—when they can't enslave them.

In this particular section—within a ring drawn with a 300-mile radius around Stanleyville—you will find today the most savage, hideous human beings left in Africa. The Moslem influence killed all the "witch-doctor" racket in the tribes—that religion has done a lot to civilize Africa! But—and I have nothing to prove this—it is believed that cannibalism still exists just north of Irumu. And it is a fact that the Society of the

Leopards still carries on, is even thought to be growing, in these parts; of men with steel claws who kill women and eat their breasts.

That I know because there were six "Leopard Men" in the prison at Stanleyville when I was there—the "Leopards" are never allowed out on road work—who were soon to be shot. And the Governor of Stanleyville, as you will see later on, told me that he believed a fair estimate would be to say that the Leopards had killed over 200 native women in his province during the past year.

This—*and I wish to point out that I have not been playing the "Darkest Africa" refrain in this book*—is the cold truth. This Society of the Leopards is so secret, so powerful, that even the native police are too terrified to inform on them. They are, as the Governor said, an almost insoluble African mystery.

You see queer sights along the road. This ribbon of civilization, thrust so arrogantly through surrounding barbarism; these two green walls, where the jungle is so thick that you feel your senses begin to choke with the confinement. One spectacle was a mission "boy," aged about sixty; he was dressed in European white trousers and a tweed coat, and wore an enormous sun helmet. He had silver-rimmed spectacles. He was carrying a bow and a handful of arrows.

The jungle falls away. You find yourself blinking in a wide, open space, blinding with white sunlight. It is a native settlement. For a mile back the jungle has been cleared. It may be full of blue smoke from the burning tree stumps and undergrowth. The natives may still be putting up their houses, in this part of Africa long, one-room oblongs with sharp roofs, made of bamboo ribs. The walls will be daubed with clay, to bake in the sun. The roof will be thatched with banana leaves. If the village has been there for a year or so, you will see the bright green splashes of the banana fronds shining in the sun between you and the distant blue wall which marks the resumption of the jungle.

The huts line the road. Fat little children run screaming to their mothers, and yellow dogs rush out to snap at your tires. There will be a big "palaver" shed, thatched with banana leaves. It will be in the center of the long lines of huts. Under it you will see the incongruous sight of naked men, lolling in deck chairs, and smoking and chatting. They make a remarkably good imitation of a deck chair, which they have copied from the Belgians, by using a fiber and ironwood. Quite likely one of the most patriarchal of these village elders is a Leopard Man.

If the clearing has been worked out—for nothing but police can make the native rotate his crops—you will see the long line of huts becoming bamboo skeletons again. The tattered roofs will blaze like white snow under the brutal sun. The blue wall of the distant jungle is not there; a light green growth shows where it is coming back over the land again.

Between villages you will see scrawny, naked women, their dugs hanging down like a dog's, staggering along the road under head packs. They will scream and fly into the bush if you attempt to get out of your car near them. It is embarrassing the way some withered old hen will shriek and flap about, as though you had a mind to rape her.

And here you will at last realize, if you haven't known it all along, that *the African lives all his life in a constant state of dread.* He's afraid of the witch doctor, he lives in terror of the evil spirits, he is afraid of the dark—the things that are in it— he lives in a continual horror (in this district) of offending the Leopard Men. And all the tribes who live back in the bush are afraid of the white man and his intentions.

We came on one vast clearing, for an aerodrome, where there were about 2,000 convict prisoners. Groups of them were tied together, in strings of six or seven, with neck chains. They were felling the trees and burning the brush in great piles. Others were hauling scoops of red earth to fill up depressions. Two posts, with an iron bar between them—a flogging stand—stood outside the convict settlement's office, which was also the Governor's thatched living hut. Soldiers in shabby green tunics carried rifles as they accompanied each group of convict workers. The convicts came from a wide range of country around Stanleyville.

The convict settlement's Governor, who said he hated his job, showed us a group of natives, boiling huge drums of beans over camp fires. He said they were all murderers. Some, with long cone-shaped heads, bound at birth to deform them, came from the Nyangara district, where, he said, sorcery was still in full vogue, and the favorite way of proving a person's innocence or guilt was to put him to the "poison test."

"*Remarkable!*" he said, in bored French. "They suspect, for example, that a man has killed his brother. So the villagers give him poison. If he is innocent, it will not affect him, they believe, these *sales bêtes!* Here is a case"—he showed us the dossier—"the man who gave that 'poison test' is now here." He pointed: "That big fellow there; he is serving twenty years."

He had these dossiers ticketed in bins, marked 1953, 1954, 1955, etc. "These," he said, as he ran a finger along the pigeonholes, "are the years when they shall be set free—but not by *me*, thank God! I shall be in Brussels!"

He carried a heavy whip in his hand. And on the sofa of his open veranda was an orange doll, long-legged, and wearing a Pierrot cap, such as you get as a favor at continental cabarets. The mud walls of his open veranda were hung with Oriental prints of naked, shadow-eyed *houris*.

"We are expecting sixty from Watsa, for having given the 'poison test,'" he said, with a salacious smile.

He had, it seemed, a bitter *flair* for the blunt truth. "Slavery?" he laughed, cracking his whip against his leg. "What do you think is the position of these native wives? These 'Arabies' around here, for example—they read the Koran and all that—but every one of them has four female slaves. The lazy—!"

He swished his whip. "Ten on the bare behind; why, that's nothing more than a morning tonic to these imbecile brutes!"

"*Voilà!*" he said, more gaily. "The aerodrome, it advances! And one day—*soon*, my friend!—I shall be flying home. I won't wait to take a boat. I'm impatient to enjoy what there is left of life!"

"All the pretty girls—?"

"*Oh, la-la!*" he said. He bunched his manicured fingernails against his lips, then shot them out towards us. He was shocking.

The rivers increased in number (all rushing down to the Congo) until it seemed we had to cross one about every hundred yards. There were no bridges. In some places they were so swift that a barge made of dugouts was slung from a steel cable that stretched across stream. This crossing was almost invariably just below a rapid. The far bank of the Epulu was fringed by a strange tree that had clusters of leaves the pink of a flamingo's wing at the end of every branch—like rose-colored candelabra. "Ya-yo-ya-yo-ya-yo," the natives chanted as they paddled us across them.

Midges increased. On one bank we were bitten by some strange black mites, raising pink blisters which festered days later and nearly drove us crazy.

At sunset the rivers shone bronze in the sun.

The Ituri itself was a half mile wide where we got across it this side of Bafwasendi. The dugout canoes were fifty feet long; a man could stand up in them, so deep down that only his head and shoulders appeared. "Ya-yo-ya-yo." A man with a drum beat taps for the paddlers.

We slept in an unfinished *Administrateur's* rest house at Bafwasendi, where there were six whites, and two convicts were given us for servants. So far from Irumu we had had five blowouts and six punctures. Our brakes were burning. We had used practically our last drop of both oil and gasoline. We had just managed to reach the one garage in 600 miles of Congo forest.

"It must be demounted," said the Italian mechanic, who

owned this miserable shed, to me the next morning. So de-mount it we did. The next day I sat and kept watch on the Italian to see that he didn't skimp his work, or fill us up with used oil, and the plump native girl he had in his sleeping quar-ters hung around, wrapping and unwrapping her bulging young breasts, rubbing them to attract my attention, making eyes at me.

The Italian, evidently, had been watching from the pit. He climbed out (he was a hairy little ape), and as he passed the girl called out to her to follow him into their communal hut. In there I heard the unmistakable noise of someone getting a hard punch in the face. If I had any doubts they were allayed at once; the little *café au lait* cutie came racing out of the hut, her mouth wide open, with a lip bleeding, and ran down the street towards the village, screaming her head off. She seemed to be running to catch up to the continual noise she made.

The Italian returned and selected a wafer gauge to test the points of my distributor. The "boys" never looked up from cleaning the brake shoes. Then a peculiar procession passed down the road before us.

It was two men, carrying a dead man, trussed like a pig, on a pole slung between them. The corpse was naked.

Africans turn a violet blue when they die. And this one had been badly mauled by a leopard, an elephant, or another man. There were great red slices down his neck and exposed ribs. I could see *inside* him!

"*Voilà*," said the Italian. "*Il est mort.*"

Then he stuck his cigarette stub behind his ear and dropped down into the pit.

*

32. Stanleyville and Big Business

WE reached Stanleyville—yes, we blew in there before a blinding, tropical thunderstorm, with all the oil palms blown flat in
the same direction and the half-mile-wide Congo lashed with
whips of flying spray. On our way we passed a motor lorry
that had just turned over. And I was glad, because three shouting Negro drivers had just tried to turn me over. They *would*
have a sight when they saw their four brothers of the convoy
staring at the underparts of their No. 3 lorry! Its wheels had
hardly stopped spinning when we came up to it; it looked like
a king crab turned on its side, about to die. And, driven deep
into the brush, nose down on the off side, was another native
motor lorry that had tried to pass it on this twisting road. So
do they handle the symbols of civilization. (Oh, native, I
thought; how would I feel if I had to live with you, in the
Congo, for over twenty years? Wouldn't I be a brute!)

"Your boat," smiled the proprietor, "has gone. It went down
the river this morning."   ‘

"Thank God!"

"There will not be another one for two weeks."

"*Allahu Akbar!*"

"And then it may be all full!"

"*Shuri ya Mungu!* It is the will of God!" I cried.

Then I rushed out to the car. "Out! Out!" I cried to Eve.
"We *can't* go on! we *can't* move! we can't do *anything* but lie
in bed and loaf for a whole gorgeous week!"

That's the way *this* African "explorer," fresh from his expedition into the giant and pygmy country, felt when he learned

that he was to be stymied for a week in the best hotel on the Congo. (For this Irumu-Stanleyville road and the falls above town had just been the scene of two "African expeditions.")

"But what about all our *things?*" said Eve.

"Out! Out with everything! Out with yourself, sweetie!"

"But the *t-h-i-n-g-s ! ! !*"

"BOY!" I clapped my hands. A half dozen assorted blackamoors slouched to obey. *"Tous!"* I cried. "Let the boy do it!" I said to Eve.

Then we went upstairs and bathed, and bathed, and bathed. It was the first time I had seen myself in a pier glass since Nairobi. I was interested to see that two rings around my knees, my arms from mid way above my elbows down, my neck, my face to about my eyes, looked as if I had been painted with iodine. That was sun. The rest of me was a pale, dead, fishbelly white, dappled with a strawberry rash. That was ticks. And—blessed trial by jungle! I had lost thirty pounds. I looked quite human again. (But I soon got over that!)

Eve thrust an arm out the bathroom door. *She* looked as though she were wearing long, brown gloves.

"Quick! A towel! Anything to stuff this with. This tub has a crack in it, and all our precious hot water is running out!"

There is no such thing as "The Book," in which a distinguished visitor should write his name, at the sentry-box before Government House at Stanleyville. In fact, I don't remember seeing a sentry. Perhaps he was somewhere among the bushes, in the grounds of that gray, gloomy Victorian mansion. But a brief note to His Excellency, sent by hand the night we got in, brought us an effusively courteous invitation the next morning to have luncheon with him that very day.

The letter began: *"Chère Madame, Cher Monsieur."*

Stanleyville is a lovely town, lying on the right bank of the river. It has its wide, pebbled streets, neat cement curbs, triangles of green parks, and every private home is banked with the scarlet flowers of the tropics. The streets are shaded with mangoes, oil palms with their clusters of coppery nuts, almond and monkey-bread trees, the monstrous baobab.

The river is about a half mile wide here, sweeping by in swirls from the Stanley Falls. It is dark, olive green, when you stare down straight into it, but clear, not muddy. It sweeps along at the steady pace of a good four or five miles an hour. Native dugouts, narrow as splinters, all the crew standing up and dipping their spear-shaped paddles with jerks, are carried swiftly down as you watch them cross. You hear their timed shouts. There is an incessant passage of tugs and dugouts to the far, low green shore, where you see several giant steel cranes waving their heads like giraffes above the oil palms, puffs of smoke from the wood-burning locomotives of the Ponthier-ville-Stanleyville railway, and the long line of big barges being loaded with "blister" copper and iron from the Congo mines.

Twice a month a big triple-deck passenger steamer fights its way up against this current from Leopoldville, 1,068 miles away, on the other side of Africa. The passage takes twelve days. It takes only eight to get down.

As this was the last place before we should reach Bangui, in French Equatorial Africa, where we could find even an imitation of a mechanic, I put the gallant Ford, with which I had fallen quite in love by now, into the garage for a complete overhaul. The roads we had traveled would be a picnic, we were told, compared with one or two spots we should find between Bangassou in French Africa and Duala in the Cameroons. And while the work was being done I had several days to hang about the waterfront, bargaining with tug captains.

We wanted to go down the Congo as far as Bumba, be put ashore, then drive up along the new road that has been cut through the jungle to Aketi, Bondo, Monga, and then cross the Ubangi River, in French territory.

Meanwhile, we ate lazy breakfasts out on our cool balcony, and watched the Congo sweep by. We caught up with our letters and air-mailed our precious films back to London. I declined more offers of iced gin slings than I care to remember. And at night, a bird—a mere bird, which had selected the mango tree some thirty feet from my pillow—made a continuous shriek as if someone were trying to file away a tin can.

Every dawn they cut the throat of a pig beneath our window. Our dinner.

The Governor of Stanleyville and his wife received us. There were no aides-de-camp. Thank God. We four sat at table with a light lunch and a bottle of 1921 hock. In the middle of the meal his two sons were brought in. Colt-like young things with ruddy cheeks and black bangs. "But they'll soon be going home!" he said, slapping their behinds lovingly. "To school, *mes enfants!*"

"*Non, non, non!*" they wailed, falling in with his game. He gave a nod, and the huge black "boy," wearing the white Moslem robe, grinned and bared his white teeth. He jabbered something at them in a language they clearly understood; then they each made us a little bow and were shoved out.

"These Leopard Men—" the Governor continued his conversation—"we find that mere hanging is not sufficient, not as an example to others. The natives do not believe they are dead. They must see blood. So, now, we are going to shoot them. We shall shoot the six we are now holding here." He shuddered: "*Ils sont sinistres!*"

"Are there many?"

He shrugged his shoulders. "Who can tell? Even our own police are afraid to inform on them; they are terribly dangerous men! A native will *never* inform on a Leopard Man."

He was keen on the subject, because he was just at the moment writing a report in his efforts to suppress the "Aniotos," as they are called there. He was conveying to Brussels some idea of the widespread activities of this secret society and its horrible initiation rites.

"It is there, you will perceive, that the very ferocious efficiency of the society begins, for none but a superman can get past the initiation rites. For example, one thing they must do is enter a village, go to a certain hut there, and steal a specified object from a selected person who is sleeping; then escape undetected. That is comparatively easy. If the innocent sleeper wakes he is usually murdered before he can cry out. But the next step is to enter at night a village which is guarded by other Leopard Men who are hidden in the huts and around the village!

"But they do it! The game is that, if any of the Leopard Men see him, they throw spears at him and try to kill him. He does the same if he sees one of them. The village, of course, has been cleared of everybody but the Leopard Men. No man becomes a Leopard Man until he has entered and escaped from a village under such conditions. You can imagine what it must be like for one of our policemen to try to arrest a man who has successfully done that!

"The Leopard Men tear out a child's eyes and put them in a bowl of oil with the little knives that they fasten to each of their fingers. This is so that 'the knives may have vision!' The knives are worn on the inside of the hand; they make marks like a leopard's claws."

The Governor put his hands on either side of his throat, and gave a jerk. "Like that!" he said. "You find the woman with these five cuts across her throat; it is the mark of the Leopard Men. Her jugular has been severed. Her breasts have always been cut off; the Leopard Men eat them."

"Oh, impossible!"

The Governor pointed towards the reports on his desk: "In 1938, 400 native women were killed around Wamba. One

Leopard Man, caught, took the white police to 38 dead bodies, all with their breasts cut off, and their hearts cut out. The Leopard Men had eaten them. *Who* knows *what* goes on; the district is full of dead bodies!"

There was a chief up a river which Eve and I had just crossed. The Administration wanted to build a ferry to cross it. The chief of the village refused to fell trees and make dugouts for the Belgians. The white carpenter said that he would go back and tell the Governor. The chief told him to do what he liked. Then, when the white carpenter was making his way across the "monkey bridge," made from creepers which overhung the swift stream, the chief cut his end of the bridge.

The white man managed to hang on to the lianas, and was swept against the far shore. He reached Stanleyville. An expedition was sent up, and the chief was brought back in irons to Stanleyville. The chief's wife (one of them) happened to be the daughter of an "Anioto," a Leopard Man. She stirred up her father to proclaim a campaign against the whites.

"It was the first time," laughed the Governor, "that we knew these Leopard Men were there! They had been foolish enough to break the law of their society to remain secret. When, to get at us, they murdered some of the people of that village, we caught them. The village was too terrified to betray them. But we got them 'on the job.' We hanged that lot. The ones we have here now we'll shoot as soon as I can find an occasion to make their death a good demonstration. *Pour encourager les autres!*"

"But how did you actually catch them?"

The Governor smiled, and ran a pale hand carefully over his sleek, gray hair. "Well, when the district officer went up, they tried to drown him, too; but we had another expedition hidden just behind the village. We rushed them."

At this juncture another child walked in by itself. It was small, with silk-like, blond hair. And it twisted its legs in embarrassment around the Governor's chair. It was dressed in a kilt.

"My youngest," said the Governor. "*It* wants to be a Scot!"

The curse of the Congo and of French Equatorial Africa are the vast concessions given to private trading companies. A formidable Government technique has been built up to conceal (in Europe) the fact that the natives of the Congo are nothing more than a black proletariat, being forced to sell to, or buy from, or work for a huge business trust, so complex in its ramifications (involving, as they do, the "interests" of high finance, the church, and the Belgian Government, with London capital) that it would require the "trust-busting" ardor of an American corporation lawyer of Theodore Roosevelt's day to expose them. Nothing less than an exposé could make this traditional African skulduggery clear to a European public.

The Government statement that only the lands "not occupied," or "not under cultivation" by the natives, have been preempted gives the idea to uninstructed Europeans that only waste land has been taken over by the State. *This is one of the most deliberate, unpardonable lies of all civilization.* Behind its shield, millions of African natives have been turned into a landless proletariat, and this is still going on, although to a decreasing extent.

What has happened is this: The natives, before the white man took his lands, believed that all land was held in common. There was no such thing as private ownership. An agricultural tribe cleared a patch of forest, put in its yams or tapioca or bananas, and waited for the crop. The ashes of the fires they used to burn the brush acted as manure or fertilizer for the land, for some time. When the land was worked out, that tribe moved on, cleared another patch of forest, planted again. A cattle tribe grazed a certain area of plain and burned the grass periodically, to make fresh green pasturage; and then, when the grass became too thin in that district, or there was not sufficient wild game, or the water failed, they moved on. There was always more land.

What the white man did—under the hypocritical lie pointed out—was to catch the native *static* at any one plantation or grazing area, and say: "*This* is the occupied land! *This* is the territory that *this* tribe is grazing over! All the rest of the land belongs to the State. Therefore, we have taken *nothing* away from the natives, when we sell or rent the rest of this territory to European concessionaires."

"We may even rent some of this 'waste land,' which they are *obviously* not using, back to the natives themselves," piously added the European Governments.

This was the explanation which the European and American general public got. This is what they have been swallowing, and are still gulping down. I ask you to believe me when I make clear this atrocity (I will give you concrete examples in a minute); and I ask you to see what it means.

To a native it means just this: He can't move. Africa no longer belongs to him. If he tries to collect palm nuts from his old trees, he is thrown in prison for trespassing. If he goes outside a reserve to graze his cattle, he is told he is on European lands. In Kenya, when the demarcations were made, it was found that the wells which these African pastoral tribes had been using were invariably on the European side of the line.

Proofs? Yes, plenty. Everywhere in Africa that you turn, except in Tanganyika, Uganda, Nigeria, the Gold Coast and Sierra Leone. From this I also exempt the Belgian Mandate of Ruanda-Urundi and the French Cameroons, which have always been kept free from such ruthless white man's exploitation by the restricting hand of the League of Nations Mandates Commission. French colonization in Senegal and Northern Africa is entirely outside this discussion, and is, one should note, usually a successful and happy colonization from both the native and the French point of view.

But in French Equatorial Africa—poorest paid, most understaffed of all French colonial possessions—two-thirds of the whole territory was originally leased out to forty concessionaires. Their abuses raised such a howl in France that, in 1912, they had to return 31,500,000 out of 87,000,000 hectares, alienated in 1889, back to the State. But, as compensation, many of these concessionaires received absolute freehold to diminished sections as *their* compensation, many of the concessions were extended to 1929, and, as Lord Hailey says in that impartial, magnificent tome, *An African Survey*, "The commitments of 1900 have thus been liquidated at a heavy cost to the natives."

The scandals of Leopold II in the Congo, the murder of thousands, more likely millions, of natives to gather "red" (*i.e.*, bloodstained) rubber need no retelling. It is not so well known, however, how he gave away huge parts of Africa to the Belgian railway companies, for example, to get money to build these railways, and for other schemes. The point to see clearly is that, to obtain these lands, Leopold II made the declaration that "all unoccupied or vacant lands are the property of the State." Then he gave "concessions" to get cash.

The present Belgian administration (before Leopold III ratted on the Allies) had as one of its aims (not expressed) to live down the reputation of Leopold II. It was also limiting the extent and the rights of concessionaires. But the *principle* that Leopold II established still held good; the natives *had* been disinherited, and the Belgian Government itself had the greatest difficulty in prizing loose the grip of the powerful concessionaires.

Here is a *present* situation: The *Comité Spécial du Katanga*. Two-thirds of the members of this committee represent the Belgian Government. One-third are company officials. The Belgian Government itself receives two-thirds of all the revenues made from exploiting this concession. The company gets one-third. This area holds some of the richest copper mines in Africa. And the section of the Congo placed under the administration of the *Comité Spécial du Katanga* amounts to 45,000,000 *hectares!*

The new *Comité National du Kivu*, established about 1936, in which the Belgian Government itself holds a controlling interest, is charged with "the development or colonization" of an area of 8,000,000 hectares.

Huileries du Congo Belge (which is "associated" with Lever Brothers, England, which is The United Africa Company, which holds a complete monopoly of the palm-oil industry and the major part of *all* West Coast African trade) has the right to lease 750,000 hectares, with the right (if in the five years preceding 1945 it exports 30,000 tons of palm oil) to the complete ownership of these 750,000 hectares.

The *place* for the selection of land was made in conjunction with the Belgian Government. But the absence of a defined boundary between native land and land claimed by the *Huileries du Congo Belge* has led to constant charges of trespass *by natives* when collecting fruit. Now an arrangement has been made that in each of the five blocs of land (comprising these 750,000 hectares) which are being developed by the company there is a certain area which is called *en division*. In this gradually narrowing area the natives (the original inhabitants) "may move freely and establish habitations where they choose, *until any land is appropriated by the company* for plantation, when it is marked off and fenced; after this natives are excluded from it; within the rest they may gather palm fruit as they please, *but they must sell it to the company.*"

They must sell it at a fixed price—fixed by the Belgian Government. A Government which is at least a half share-owner in all Belgian Congo enterprise.

So there you are. I know, when this is printed, there will be an uproar from various African-apologists who will try to prove that I am wrong, that I have misspelled some name! That I am Left-wing, or trying to mislead people, or have not been in Africa long enough to realize "how complex this situation really is." But you don't have to eat the whole egg to find out that it is bad, and even a layman can tell a broken leg when he sees one; and this Congo situation (with its duplicates in all parts of Equatorial Africa, with the exceptions I have quoted above) is too plain to be missed.

But you need not take my word for it. Leopold III betrayed the Allies. The king's cabinet has said that the king has no legal right to reign. Who and what is the legal Belgian Government must one day be established. When it is, it will be seen clearly to whom all the wealth of the Congo belongs; but you may be sure that *any* change of Government won't change the ownership claimed by the four big business companies which, with the Belgian Government, have been exploiting the Congo. But what the world will, one day, see—after these company claims have been established—is the role of the Belgian Government itself (and the place and vast claims of the Catholic Church) in the Congo.

Under the Congo Basin Agreement all European nations enjoy equal "open-door" rights to sell goods in the Belgian Congo. A Dutch company, for instance, runs an amazing string of chain stores in the older towns. But on the whole it can be said that Congo enterprise is coming more and more into the hands of the triumvirate named.

When Leopold III betrayed the Allies, the London press was full of articles exulting over the Congo raw materials which would fall into the hands of the Allies. Sentimental hope—the Allies already had these resources. The big Belgian companies were selling them. The Allies will continue to *buy* them. A new Belgian Government (if and when it can be formed, without the king) will naturally claim the share that went to the former Belgian Government. And the vast trade in palm oil was already in British hands—*Huileries du Congo Belge—i.e.,* Lever Brothers, which also runs its own chain stores throughout the Congo.

Gossip at Stanleyville was very much along these lines. The Belgian Government has been protesting that it is against any further "white colonization" of the Congo? Well, so it is; you're dead right, the four big companies (backed by the colonial officials and police) are doing everything they can to see that no more white or Indian settlers try to set up trade in competition with the big-business interests. They've got it all; they won't tolerate anyone else butting in! "Don't worry about that, old boy. They took those sixty-eight poor Indians out of Ruanda-Urundi, because they didn't dare try them under the laws of the mandate; they've got 'em in jail at Costermanville. That's the way they drive *them* out! The Costermanville justice is completely under the domination of the mining companies. In many cases, those Indians have been 'planted'— they are charged by the police with having gold dust found among the sweepings of their stores, but who do you think put that gold dust there? The police!"

"Yes, a big Indian lawyer flew up from Nairobi to defend the prisoners. But the Belgians told him they had held the trial the day before—ha! Then they reminded him that this was the Congo, not British territory, and he could do no good by trying to raise a squawk with the British Colonial Office.

"Yes, or threaten the Belgians with what 'India might think about it.'"

But the talk which infuriated most of the non-Belgian white men at Stanleyville (and I was shown the papers of the "trial") was the story of a Greek who had just been taken down the river, in a strait jacket—stark, staring mad.

The Greek was named Pataksvas. He was accused of illicit gold buying. Natives (whom the police were charged with torturing) suddenly made full confessions in court, declaring that their former statements against the Greek had been "torn from them," that they had been forced by the police to invent all the evidence which went to show that the Greek was an illicit gold buyer. And the Greek was acquitted.

But it had required five policemen to take this madman down the river from Stanleyville. Even his acquittal did not restore his mind—it had come too late.

None of this was idle gossip. I saw the report that went out on the Pataksvas "trial." I don't know the ultimate fate of the sixty-eight Indians in prison at Costermanville, but I believe the evidence against them was so poor that the British *might* be inclined to ask what it was. The mining companies claimed that they were losing 60,000,000 francs a year through this illicit gold buying.

An interesting figure in Congo finances is that some 44.3 per cent of the total budget goes for "the services of the national debt." This is the highest of any colony in the world—nearly double that of any other.

In fact, a table of these figures ought to give some idea of how colonies are run. I am taking the year 1935-36. The first table is the amount of revenue which comes from *direct taxation of the natives*. The second is the national-debt percentage in the budget, 1934-5.

Direct Native Tax as % of Total Revenue		Services of National Debt in Yearly Budget	
Tanganyika	35.8	Tanganyika	6.2
Uganda	33.5	Uganda	8.3
Belgian Congo	22.6	Gold Coast	4.3
Ruanda-Urundi	38.5	Nigeria	16.7
French Equatorial	32.0	Algeria	25.0
		Morocco	24.5
		Ruanda-Urundi	23.4
		Belgian Congo	44.3

But to show how the Belgians have invested immense sums to develop the Congo (as contrasted with British lack of enterprise in their possessions) it is interesting to see what is implied in the table below. This, up to the year 1934, shows the external capital invested in these colonies; it is divided so that Government and private investment are shown separately—all in pounds sterling:

	Government	Other	Total
Nigeria	28,712	13,117	41,829
Kenya and Uganda	27,443	7,128	34,571
Tanganyika and Zanzibar	28,992	15,529	44,251 *
Belgian Congo	32,986	101,727	134,713

* Of which £32 million was German capital.

From the point of view of present war needs, it is interesting to point out that the Congo supplies over half the world output of diamonds (used in the industries for boring and abrasives), over one-third of the world's production of cobalt (used for magnetic steels and alloys); some 6 per cent of the world's tin, and has a copper reserve estimated at over 10,000,000 tons. In addition, the Congo is one of the world's chief suppliers of radium. Gold has now become the Congo's major export.

As I have said about Belgian handling of the Congo, it is being developed by the latest big-business methods. The natives as a carefully conserved supply of black labor, get the best housing and the best medical attention in Africa. They are being encouraged to progress to hold skilled positions in all the trades. A black man in the Congo has double the chance for a good life than he would have in South Africa or Kenya, and a much more likely good job, in the immediate future, than he could hope to get in Tanganyika. (This last, be it said, is not a little due to the fact that the Belgians are determined to keep the locust-like Indians out of the Congo.)

Taken all in all, there is more to be said in praise of the practical Belgian method of handling the Congo than there is to be said against it. From the white man's point of view it is swift, well planned development and exploitation. From the native's, the growth of white man's enterprise provides practical jobs. The trend of the world towards a more humane and idealistic treatment of the natives brings these two forces in the Congo towards a point where the natives will—it seems almost certain—begin to hold positions in the higher ranks of Government.

That is an encouraging transition, to which the end of this war should give an immense impetus.

On our last day, Eve and I went up and "shot" Stanley Falls in a native dugout with forty shouting paddlers. It was an exhilarating passage. The natives of this sturdy fishing village actually fish in the falls themselves, working their way out to empty wooden fish traps held by weirs built right in the frothing rapids.

It is a stirring scene. You expect, always, to see a native prized loose by the flow of water. That often happens. When it does, the native rolls himself up in a ball, shoots down the falls, and straightens out to swim to shore a few miles below, at Stanleyville. The fish-eating natives of this village were the best built Negroes I saw in Africa. They showed what a black god the African can make of himself, an intelligent, laughing black god —when he gets enough of the right kind of food.

Down below, on the Congo, we saw hideous, misshapen people, so savage that they could only be classed as black beasts. They were alarming.

*

*

33. Congo River Tug

THE Congo is, like the Amazon, a river which lends itself to fine writing. But for most people it is just one everlasting, uneventful, unbearable wall of green. The river is twelve miles wide at Bumba, where we were going to get off, but you never know that, for you are always speeding down between islands. You cannot tell them from the main shore. And certainly the most beautiful sights on the Congo are the toes, or heads, of these islands, for you see the pattern of their palms and rushes, the tracery of the high mahogany or ironwood trees, with their lianas dripping like black lace against the sunsets.

And it was for these that I sat for four days, with my chin resting in my hands, watching the great river unfold ahead of me. It took on the nature of a spell. I became attuned to the variations of reflected greens. And then that emptiness, when, in a broad reach, the river ceased to have any identity and became colorless as the sky. The islands ahead seemed to float, then, like the faintest brush strokes of a sketch to be. They were mist blue. And they did not materialize, come down to water, until they had taken on that infuriating, sullen green.

The tug was the *Flandres*. She was run by the Otraco, that large and competent corporation which operates most of the heavy Congo traffic. Like all the other river steamers, she was a "wet-tailed Jane," which means that she had her paddle wheel at the stern. She was built like a large, steel slipper, and her shiny, steel deck was not more than two feet above water. She was filled with firewood. On the deck was the furnace, its red mouth constantly open for food, also the quarters of the native crew and all the Africans who could find sprawling space.

Above, standing on steel pillars, was the wheel house. This had two decks, with an open balcony around three sides. In the lower cabin slept Eve and I. In the upper was the wheel itself, standing in what was practically the parlor of an apartment inhabited by the captain, his delicate, blond wife from Bruges, and a child called Celestine.

Behind lay two steel barges of about 1,000 tons each. One was loaded with "blister" copper, taken on at Stanleyville and bound all the way down the Congo to Leopoldville, 1,068 miles away, where it would be shipped by rail to Matadi, then dropped into a steamer for Europe. The other barge was comparatively empty, waiting for the cargoes of cotton, oil nuts, rubber in flat blocks wrapped in sacking, bales of maize and rustling sacks of monkey nuts, which we picked up along the way.

Lashed across the curving iron hatches, over the copper cargo, was our car. To get it in that position I had to ferry it across the Congo, traverse a clatter of railway tracks and moving electric cranes, then negotiate the perilous passage of two dangerously bending planks, to get it aboard. There were two things to be guarded against; the first was that I did not tarry long enough on the planks to allow them to break under the weight of the car, or that I did not go so swiftly that I shot off at one side. The other—and this was ticklish—that I killed the momentum of my dash up the planks and came to rest on the top of those sinister, humped hatches, not carrying on to go off the barge.

This was, apparently, the very first time that anyone had tried this barge foolishness. There was no loading technique. And the most helpful person turned out to be a coal-black African—looking, in his tattered felt hat, like any Mississippi roustabout, with a face that had been so mutilated with cicatrices that it looked like a waffle. Little ridges of flesh, frilled like the icing on a chocolate cake, had been raised to beautify nostrils like a hippo's.

But he "knew his stuff." And it was a shocking, if encouraging, demonstration of the ratio of black to white man in the Belgian Congo to hear this black fellow yelling at the white foreman. Looking up, I noticed in the control boxes of the electric cranes—huge things—that it was a black, not a white, face that every time peered down at me. A man from Kenya, especially from South Africa, would have been infuriated by such a sight—"Blacks doing a *white* man's job!"

But they did it very well.

It was significant of the difficulties of Congo navigation that the captain refused to leave in that sunset. There was a maze of rocks below us and he said, "No; I will not try to go down through them *with the sun in my eyes!*"

No Congo steamer, even the palatial four-deckers, draws more than 6 foot 6 inches of water. Waffle-face and I hounded a gang of natives until we got a tarpaulin stretched over the car, to save it from being fried in that constant blare of sun, and then we lashed it with steel cable to every bitt in sight. When I gave him a tip he said *"Merci, M'sieu,"* and took off his hat, showing me a head that had been bound in babyhood until it was now shaped like a sugar cone. I was aching to ask him if these head shapings did not give him and his like perpetual headaches. But, from what white men tell me, the heads can be deformed until they resemble watermelons, without affecting the brain. Anyway, I reflected, Waffle-face had plenty of gray matter, no matter how it had been disarranged.

His magnificently white teeth had been filed to points.

That night, Eve and I ate a farewell dinner on shore with an Englishman, an American, and a German. This international trio, all long in the Congo, all hating it (and the Belgians) like hell, all agreed upon one point:

"The natives have got beyond these Belgians. In the first place, they know that the judges are so tired of sentencing them that they often won't convict. Reason being that the Belgians have begun to see the awful truth that jail isn't a punishment—

to these natives. They get better food and better housing in prison than they would at home. They get some nice, pleasant work out on the roads all day; go down to the prison any day, at 5 P.M., and you'll see the prisoners coming back, grinning. Eight lashes, they know, is the most they can get; anyway, here in Stanleyville. So how can the Belgians *hurt* them?"

"Ach!" the German protested. "That's nonsense! In the bush, I have seen—"

"Yes, we all have," said the others. "But we're speaking in generalities now, of the *official* point of view. And the *official* attitude towards the native is that he must be handled as if wrapped in cotton wool; he must not be 'bruised,' or have anything done to him that would *weaken him as a laborer*. Get that?"

"Hooey!"

"Damned hypocrisy!"

"Nevertheless," persisted the Englishman, "you've got to admit I'm right: *seen on the books*, the laws of the Congo are too lenient to be regarded as real punishment by the native— compared with what his own chief would have done to him in his own village. So the native—I'm thinking now of my 'house boy,' a thief if ever there was one!—makes fun of the *Administrateur* behind his back. They've got beyond the white man."

"Oh, if you put it that way, you've said a mouthful!"

"That is correct. The native needs a good beating."

Which was agreed.

"And French Equatorial Africa?" I asked the American. "What is *that* like?"

He grinned. He was a big, likable chap, from Texas, and he knew Africa from Timbuktu to Cape Town. He was now bound for the Rhodesias.

"Well," he said slowly, "last time I passed through there I had the malaria. I nearly died. Really. You know, when you get the deliriums? Well, my 'boy' came to me—he's from the

Gold Coast; good 'boy,' too!—and he sat down beside me, and he held my head, and he tried like the devil to get me well. Then he came in one morning, mad as hell about something.

" 'Massa,' he said, 'you get well! You get well quick! Massa, this damn country not fit to *die* in!' "

The husky young American leaned back and laughed. "Guess you don't want a fairer recommendation than that? That 'boy's' sitting out in my car now. Wouldn't part with him for the world. He and I have been all *over* Africa together."

"And he's your friend?" I asked.

"He? Bet your sweet life he is! Don't know what I wouldn't do for that 'boy.' Why—"

Then he stopped. "Yes, I see what *you're* driving at," he said to me. "You're right. When you see 'em over here, they're different, somehow. The Solicitor General of the Gold Coast is a Negro. And there's something *noble* about some of them! That's about the right word. They make you take another think, sometimes, and go over *yourself*."

This ingenuous admission made us all laugh. It was the truth, and there was something warm about it—something that made you feel there was an incredible amount of damned foolishness in the whole scheme of things, in the African world.

Celestine shrieked all day long. But sometimes it was the ship's siren. Eve declared that when she looked down, at sunset, on the lower deck, all coiled with twisting, naked bodies, and with this din going on, she felt like Dives staring down into hell. The furnace doors seemed always open, gaping for something to burn. And every now and then there would be an excruciating sound like the slitting of pigs' throats—a noise Eve had now acquired a horror of. But, upon investigation, it always proved to be Celestine.

The river was wide but the channel was narrow, marked with gasoline tin buoys painted black or red, and in some places there was hardly a ship's width between them. In such stretches there was always a tower on shore with a black ball raised or lowered to show when a ship was coming up. We did not run at nights, owing to the complexities of this channel, although the river was high at this time of the year from the rains in the mountains. But all day long there was the ceaseless "whish" of the stern paddles, the rattle and rub of the steering engines and chains. The *Flandres* went too slow to make a breeze for herself, but there was enough movement of air through our mosquito netting to make us sleep under blankets at night. And thus we slept, or sat and watched Africa slip by.

It was not at all what I had expected the Congo to be.

We should have been willing to have put up with a great deal more discomfort, for a little more change of scene. To begin with, this unbroken wall of green jungle, about 150 feet high, was always the same. The river might have been ten miles wide, as shown on the chart, but *we* never got a vestige of long vistas. And when you have seen a mile of this jungle wall, island or mainland, you have seen the lot. There were enormous distances between the villages. But, whenever the bank began to rise, and we saw the red of earth turning into high ground, there seemed to be always an enormous white man's trading shed of some sort, usually with a red, galvanized iron roof—although sometimes it was thatched—or else there would be just the long, low line of native mud huts.

But it was from these clearings that we took on this pale rubber in blocks, bales of cotton, and monkey nuts. Strings of Negroes, like a revolving belt or an endless centipede, ran up one line of planks and down another. Then the captain went out with a tape and measured the stacks of firewood, before all this was loaded in.

Always, when we swung about to come upstream and make a landing, swinging the barges behind us like a tail swinging its dog, a native stood in the bow, with the loop of our heavy steel hawser around his neck. Then he leaped into the Congo— *and swam to shore!*

The first time I saw him do this I waited for him to be drowned. I thought that steel cable must drag him down. But not him. With lusty, overarm strokes, such as were learned comparatively recently in Europe and the United States, this untutored African native did a finished double trudgeon to the bank. Little "totos," boys who could not have been more than six or seven years old, often swam midway out in the Congo to be within hailing distance as we passed. They also swam the overhead stroke. Their heads were like black coconuts on the water. And anything thrown over to them, such as a bottle, started a furious battle, like water polo, among them. When we left a landing the African marvel swimmer very often remained ashore to cast loose the hawser, then leaped in and swam off to the tug. The muscles of his glistening shoulders flashed with rippling power in the sun.

He was living every minute of his life!

I was often afraid that a "croc" would get him. But there were none, the captain said, although he thought that the lagoons in the centers of the islands must be full of them. This was another surprise—the complete absence of any life on the river.

We had expected hippos, crocodiles, monkeys swinging in the branches. There was nothing. Not even a raft of ducks, or a few cormorants to scutter off the water at our approach. Not even a heron or an ibis or a lovely white egret, such as had flashed about us on the great African lakes. Neither had the river, at this high water, any beaches or sandbanks. There was just this wall of jungle, going straight up, so dense and dark that, except in the clearings, you could not make out mahogany, palm, or bamboo. Implacable!

More firewood. A gang would be waiting. And then would begin that chorus of "ya-ha-ha-ha-ing" and "yo-ho-ho-ho-ing" without which no African seems able to make the slightest exertion. Little by little all the stacks would be carried up the bouncing planks and stowed in the hold, the bowels of the *Flandres,* and on we would go.

The children did a lot of this loading, especially of the sacks of unpressed cotton that we took on so often, and whether this accounted for the umbilical hernias that they nearly all had I cannot say, but truly awful they were, sometimes looking like elephants' trunks protruding from their unfortunate abdomens. But two doctors we found along the Congo both swore these hernias did not bother the natives, who took them for granted, and it was almost impossible to get them to submit to treatment.

Livid among the black children stood out an albino, with towlike yellow hair, weak eyes, and fish-like skin that was wrinkled like crepe over his scratched arms and poor knees. Shocked, Eve said to me: "Do *we* seem like that to the Africans, pallid, anemic, with the unnatural whiteness of worms and maggots? And of plants under stones? After all," she said suddenly, awed by the idea, "there is nothing revolting about those virile black bodies, but that wretched albino makes me think there *can* be about the white!"

But we came along shore to load firewood at one village which left us no inferiority complex about our pallid skins. These people were the most horrible human types I have seen anywhere in the world. It was not that they had been debased; it was just that they had not even begun to move along the road of evolution. So it seemed. The figures of even the women were not feminine, as we expect to see them. These tribesmen, who had come to the river from deep, interior jungle, were thin to the point of emaciation; the women had no hips—their breasts, leathery straps, were the only parts of their bodies which distinguished them from the scrawny men. They were a ghastly example of that chronic undernourishment which afflicts most natives all their lives in Equatorial Africa. And the chief objects of envy in their barter market on the bank were some smoked rats. Some of these rodents were the size of a cat. They were cut into sections.

Yet, in this assemblage which fell silent when Eve and I walked up—and it was a glowering, savage silence—there were some beautiful paddles to be bought or bartered, and a stand of those five-foot steel blades to fix in elephant traps. The paddles were long as spears, with sharp, spear-like blades; I handled half a dozen of them that did not vary, it seemed, an ounce in weight or a fraction of an inch in outline. It showed superb handicraft. These steel blades for killing the elephants had a scientific ribbing to give them strength; and this, too, might have been made with a pneumatic hammer, it was so exact. These blades are suspended over the elephant "walks," in the deep jungle, fixed into a heavy section of a suspended tree, a giant log. It must weigh tons. But so clever is the trap that when an elephant, plodding along his accustomed "walk," breaks a liana stretched between two trees, the huge log, with the spear, drops onto him. The steel blade, some five feet long and eight inches wide, must be driven right through him.

These people had been carved, with cicatrices, from head to foot. This raising of the skin—as if you had pinched putty up in ridges with your fingers—had been done in spray-leaf patterns across the women's backs. It had been done along the bridges of their noses, so that they went down from the forehead in a series of steps. And the outline of the full face, where a man's beard would ordinarily grow, had been raised in a fringe until you almost suspected they had raised the flesh in these permanent contortions to symbolize the beard.

Here was no answering smile, such as you might hope to get, after a time, from pygmy or Bushman or yellow Hottentot—here was just a blank. Here was the "darkness" of the savage mind that the missionaries speak about.

When you see it you get a conception of what that word "darkness" must mean to a missionary when he addresses, say, a meeting of the brethren in Scotland or Ohio—and you see the challenge that drags him back to Africa. After having seen it, I am on the side of mission work from now on. I don't care how many shady traders there may be among them as individuals—weaker brethren—the great work itself is just as imperative a *mission* as in the days when Stanley went back to England and tried to rouse the country. Tribes such as these, from the lagoons, black forests and deep swamps behind the Congo, live in a state of bestiality. They are beasts.

But the majority of the Congo River natives are happy, muscular—kept strong, I suppose, by having fish to eat instead of the everlasting cereals that blow the black man's stomach out like a balloon. There seems a lot of life lived in dugout canoes; the woman, it is hardly necessary to say, paddling, while standing; the man lying down under a thatch of banana leaves. The sun is barred by a cool sky of fleecy clouds; there is just the ticking of pistons; five hundred yards out from shore we see two natives poling a canoe up against the current. The river is so shallow.

The tug and the barges pass through a nimbus of white butterflies. Their noiseless flight is purposeless and beautiful. They have black edging on their wings, and, for a time, they light on the rail, flutter aimlessly in and out our superstructure. Then they are gone.

Basokos is off the main channel, and lies almost in a bay of islands. There is a long, low, white, crenellated wall. Has this been a fort? A Belgian flag flies over it. The doctor here tells us that his wife died three weeks ago. She went up to Stanleyville for her confinement. "She got fever, but the child survived." He tells us, with a worried look, as if anxious to know what *we* thought of his predicament, that he has written to his sister, in Belgium, asking her to take the child.

"But she is a young, unmarried girl; I don't think she will take it."

There is a mauve cathedral tower behind him, strangely like those you will see along the Lek, the lower Rhine, in peaceful Holland. This is a post; the red-brick bungalow of the *Administrateur* stands on a knoll, where another flag hangs listlessly from its white pole. There is a mill here; all night long the natives take the freshly picked cotton from the barge and pile it on the cement wharf. It will be pressed into bales here, for shipment to Europe.

Eve and I strolled along to another native market, stinking with the sour smell of the natives. We have remarked that, in Africa, sex is manifested in its most unpleasant and appalling shape. Here also they are bartering smoked rats and mice. These diseased people give you the impression of rotting as you watch them. Many have elephantiasis, and some are lepers.

But this is Whitsunday! Suddenly down the river bank comes the sound of singing. A little procession of children appears. They are waving palm leaves and marching. Among them walks a White Sister, a *Sœur Blanche*.

She is obviously a woman of breeding. She is beautiful. She handles the children with loving-kindness, and laughs as she tries to rally their straggling ranks. In the midst of that appalling dreariness she even manages to be gay.

I shall never forget her.

The river had a hypnotic effect on us, and so demoralizing was life on the *Flandres* that after the first couple of days we hardly had the energy to go ashore. I doubt if we should ever have got off at Bumba but for one excellent reason; the *Flandres* went no further.

Our captain, the only other white man on the tug, was a hard-boiled, competent person, with just that proper amount of arrogance that is essential for a skipper on the Congo. When he gave an order to a black man he stood within three feet of him and shouted as if the man had been a mile away. In this way the import, the *seriousness*, of his command sank in.

When it did not sufficiently quickly penetrate the thick African skull, then the captain struck at the well known sensitive spot, the curving shinbone. "*Thunk!*" would go his thick boot against that.

He and his wife talked Flemish between themselves, and to the shrieking Celestine. We experimented with French. He had made one literal translation into English which he used all, all day long. It was *pas du tout!* Whenever I thanked him for doing, or showing me, anything, he always waved his hands—as he imagined a gentleman should—and said:

"Nothing at all, *m'sieu!* Nothing at all!"

At Bumba I saw him kick a striped convict, who had impeded him, half way up the steep bank.

*

34. Native Mechanics at Aketi

IT is all to the credit of the Belgians that they have taken this very primitive mass of Congo natives and are yearly, and inevitably, giving them better living conditions and a practical education. The scheme is sound. It is to be doubted that if the big four companies were supplanted by a hubbub of private enterprise, a general settlers' free-for-all, the natives could progress at anywhere near the present pace. They would lack, for instance, the benefit of the present well synchronized teamwork. Moreover, the Belgian attitude towards colonizing the Congo shows a realism that is well in advance of other colonial powers, namely, that Africa will continue to develop *not* as an area for white planters, but as a territory of vast trust-run plantations, and that the white man's chief development in Africa will lie more and more in the operation of mines.

Congo! The word itself signifies a vast, humid area, teeming with black men. As a matter of fact, there are only 10,000,000 natives in Congo's 902,802 square miles, whereas Nigeria, the British colony, with only 372,599 square miles has a native population of over 20,000,000! Nigeria, bursting with oil nuts and cocoa, and admirably administered under the "indirect rule" first established by Lord Lugard, is the richest reservoir of black labor in all Africa. The Congo, when black man power is tabulated against its vast potential resources, is one of the poorest.

Therefore, an *Administrateur's* post in the Belgian Congo always calls your attention to the creative side of the work. That's the correct word, "creative." The Congo is in an intensely alive, creative epoch. It is going forward. It is alive. Tanganyika, it may be said without any disparagement of the fair British rule, is being held in abeyance, by contrast, and Kenya can be said to be still unco-ordinated, without any central plan, and left to the haphazard efforts of individuals. A move towards planned economy in Kenya, such as the Kenya Farmers' Association would like to bring about, would, at once, more than double the productivity and worth of that Government-neglected British colony. And this Government-sponsored enterprise (such as a London-subsidized settlement scheme) seems to be already on the cards as one of the inevitable awakenings in Africa as a consequence of this present war. I bring in here this apparently irrelevant subject of Tanganyika and Kenya because I think the war has already shown to the British public the sluggish mind of the conventional British colonial service in Africa, and the wasted potentiality of these possessions has at last been made clear.

I think the old attitude is gone.

When we got the car ashore at Bumba, and prepared it to take the new road up past Aketi to Bangassou in French Equatorial Africa, our thoughts did not linger on the adventures ahead of us. Perhaps the heat had cured us of being romantic? Perhaps, making this coast-to-coast drive across Africa without a "boy" to do the manual labor, we were getting enough small "personal adventures" in our stride without going out of our way to look for them. For a thousand miles or so we had taken the same road as two recent "African expeditions," sumptuous caravans with their own sleeping cars, movie vans, and retinue of black servants. We were tired.

At Bumba we lay two days in the Government rest house; sleepless nights with the constant filing of birds in the palm trees, the scuttering of rats in and out of our kit, the furious humming of mosquitoes which were bound to attack us, even though, smeared with citronella oil, we lay inside our nets. Several miles down the river lay 16,000 acres of a big *Huileries du Congo Belge* palm-oil plantation, and there, with our own jaded eyes, we saw the native technical workers living in small European bungalows, each with its own little flower garden, in a state of amenity idyllic in its perfection.

Perhaps it was at Bumba that I got the malaria? I don't know. I know that at the "sundowner," on the last night, when the *Administrateur* and his wife showed us their extraordinary photo albums of male and female circumcisions, many photographed in the process, with the girls' taut faces painted white, it all seemed part of the general nightmare. The next morning, when I dovetailed the last bit of kit into our car—there was hardly a square inch to spare by now—what with all the excess tins of gasoline and oil—I turned and glared at the cool Congo, moss green, slipping so complacently past. How marvelous it would be just to drift on and on down it, on the cool deck of some steamer! Then I slipped the car into gear and drove resentfully towards the green wall of jungle that awaited us.

One thing that should be noted about travel through Central Africa—a thing which differentiates it from, say, a traverse of the Shan States—is that you come to no remains, enchanting or otherwise, of older civilizations. The thing is just savage. You drive for miles, or hours, through this everlasting wall of jungle; then you come to a river. By this river, on the near or far side, is a collection of native huts. The Belgians have put them there, so that the menfolk of this village may work the dugout ferry. If the village is on the far side, and its men (as they usually are) are asleep, you will spend a considerable time squawking your horn, before a few lazy blacks totter down to the bank and begin to beat their monotonous refrain on the sides of their canoes.

But during these waits there is hardly a time when the spell of these rivers does not lay its hand upon you. They are so silent, so unconcerned about your presence. So dead. They flow, it seems, from out some great mystery—the life above the bends. I may rant, as I write, about delays and exasperations, but I never stood on the banks of one of these rivers without that almost painful urge to—well, just go around the bend below or above me. I wanted to see what was *there*.

And that, of course, is what kept us on.

Aketi was, to me, a green triangle, in the center of which, perched on a cement pedestal, was a wood-burning locomotive about the size of a Shetland pony. This was the first engine which the far-reaching Vici-Congo Company had put on its miniature rails to drag out the great mahogany and ironwood logs to the river. The river, brown, sullen, formed one side of this triangle.

The other side was a cement railway station and a vast, open railway yard in which puffed larger and later locomotives (about good scenic-railway size); and in which, in high iron sheds, hundreds of natives were working at machine tools, making locomotive repairs, and in the main power station, with only an occasional white foreman.

The base of the triangle was an oasis, the Vici-Congo's hotel. A cement veranda behind banks of green shade trees; a bar, which was never empty; and a green lawn covered with stucco bungalows for its guests. This hotel was full at the moment with a collection of cotton experts, both Government and private, some "experts in crop raising," and some visiting district officers who had come to Aketi for the ceremony of the opening of the first cottonseed-oil factory to be set up in the Congo. It was to be blessed by the priests, and the rose-pink church settlement outside the town was full of white-robed ecclesiastics.

Behind the oasis of the Vici-Congo hotel ran two parallel, palm-shaded streets. Along one were the Vici-Congo chain stores and filling stations, a well stocked establishment of the Dutch chain store trading company, its shelves holding a glistening treasury of tinned foods more extensive than you could get in

Holland; and then there came a small, "tolerated" bazaar of what looked like the scrapings of the British Empire, Hindu traders, Cypriots, etc., all suffering from that glum melancholia which comes from knowing that you are positively disliked.

The other street was a tree-shaded district of well built European bungalows. Stucco residences, with broad cement verandas and high, cool rooms. We dined there with all the amenities you would expect in British Dar es Salaam—cocktails, a well prepared dinner of several courses, soft-footed servants in spotless livery—with a young Belgian baron whose father was one of the directors of the Vici-Congo. He was stout, felt the heat, and seemed melting in his damp dinner jacket.

"The natives!" he replied in answer to my question. "They are not surprised by anything! A savage, he appears from the jungle, with his bow and arrow in his hands—sees one of our locomotives screaming past—you will notice that they scream like hell? That is because they are little; they scream to make up for their size. Inferiority complex, what?" (I might say this young man had gone to an English public school.) "Well, the native, he looks at the locomotive, then he turns to his companions, and says: *'C'est le blanc.'* 'It is the White.' That is all; there is no surprise.

"You would think they would be surprised by the aeroplane? *Pas du tout!* I have watched them. My first post—to break my spirit, I suppose—was way off in the damned jungle. We were to make an aerodrome there. *Voilà!* And one day, one came down. I was shocked myself to see three men step out of it; I had forgotten, in that damned heat, that there were aeroplanes. These blacks had never seen one, and as it circled over our heads I watched. You won't believe it; but *they did not even look up!* *'C'est le blanc'* again. I became so annoyed—it is this heat, you understand—that I resolved that if they didn't show surprise about *something*, then I would beat them. . . ."

He laughed feverishly. "But, of course, that was the *last*

thing that would surprise them; that would be merely *'C'est le blanc'* again.

"And, Mr. Farson, when you write this in your book, please do not put an exclamation mark after *'C'est le blanc.'* It should be merely a full stop, to show the impassivity, the infuriating impassivity of these black gentlemen."

In the course of my life as a journalist I have been walked through miles of steel works, automobile plants, irrigation schemes, Paris fashion shows, open-air brothels, the Ford works at Detroit, the G.P.U.'s home for illegitimate children—bored to desperation, yet forced to show a sufficiently polite interest until I could reach, without manslaughter, the one person I had come there to get a story from. Nothing is more intolerable than being "shown things."

Yet, in the locomotive works at Aketi, my interest reached almost a masochistic intensity. Amidst those flames and furnaces I saw a black man, his naked torso glistening like Vulcan's, take the red-hot end of a locomotive driving shaft and *pet* it with a trip hammer as gently as a kitten would play with a ball of knitting. He turned it over and over, gently tapping it until the color faded and it was just the correct width and shape. I saw another, spectacled, local virtuoso, working with slide rule and micrometer gauge, peel some thousandths of an inch off a brass journal.

"There is nothing in here," grinned the sweating white superintendent, tapping his skull, "to prevent the native from 'getting on'; you can see for yourself. This shop is almost entirely run by black men. *And they make first-class mechanics!*"

There were, working around and out of this hive of black industry at Aketi, the following native skilled workers: 42 locomotive drivers, 240 motor lorry drivers, 16 locomotive mechanicians, 75 auto mechanics, 82 carpenters, and 12 tire workers.

This, I think, gives you some idea of why my interest stirred, on finding this enterprise in the heart of the Belgian Congo. And

I might add that the Vici-Congo had two aeroplanes here, had eleven aerodromes already cut out in various parts of the surrounding jungle; that their motor lorries cover half a million kilometers every year, delivering mail and supplies to the mines; and that, in connection with the Sabena air lines, the Vici-Congo service maintains a six- or seven-day service to Europe from Bumba on the Congo.

The Vici-Congo supplies motor lorries which run to 300 "buying posts" in the surrounding jungle. All of this work, which includes a railway concession of 685 kilometers, began with the inauguration of thirty miles of this railway in 1926. There was absolutely nothing whatever at Aketi in 1924 when the Vici-Congo Company got the concession. It was just jungle, the home of savages.

There are only 126 white men there now.

At Aketi I found an exiled White Russian. He was the surgeon in the Vici-Congo's hospital. He took me into one of its clean little operating theaters, stripped the oozing dressings off my leg, and said, "How did you ever let it get like this? The bone is showing." And when I told him, he added: "Those other doctors have been trying to murder you." Like a locomotive—and feeling that I would occasionally like to let out a yelp like one—I was repaired.

"Now," he said, refusing to take any pay, "go on your way. You do *exactly* what I tell you; dress it twice a day; and you will probably get out of Africa."

"And you?" I was forced to ask.

"Okay," he laughed. "I don't mind the heat. And my wife, as you saw, is also a Russian refugee. We have no country."

*

35. French Equatorial Africa

OUR last night in the Congo was one of the best we spent in Africa. We had the Government rest house, facing the falls of the Uele River, at Monga. The falls came down in a series of cascades past rocky islands, some of them wooded. There was a continual movement of frothing white, in bars and noisy rapids, against the dark green of the forest. It was exciting movement, with a cool, scented breath from off the churning waters, but we felt a great peace as, by the light of a hurricane lamp, we cooked our dinner on the faithful little alcohol stove, on the broad veranda. An orange moon, like an illumination off stage, gilded the edges of some low-lying clouds.

It was seldom we had known such physical contentment. The usual striped convicts had been provided to unload the car and fetch cooking and drinking water. They were gone now. I had again experienced the peculiar disquiet of seeing in their anxious faces the desire to make some plea to me. For they did not know who I could be, and perhaps *here* was a chance for liberty. But the two armed Negro sentries shut them off like a wall; they even tried to take the cigarettes away from the convicts as I was giving them to them—until I cursed them roundly. And now we two were alone.

Someone had built a rose garden here. It was at the foot of the lawn that went down to the brown river. We saw two native women, with flaming torches, deeply preoccupied around some anthills. They were making little tapping noises with sticks on the hard ground; they were imitating rain. They were trapping white ants to eat. The ants, thinking the rains had come, spread their wings, crawled out of the anthill, and fell into the little pit that had been dug to receive them. They would be made into porridge in the morning. Some natives, with a light, were spearing fish by the falls.

In the morning, when the cascades seethed under the lifting mists, we watched the natives work their way out to their fish traps on the rocky islands. They swung themselves out, hand over hand, on lianas which they had rigged between the islands. Frequently we saw a fisherman bury himself in sluicing white water, like a fish, until he hauled himself to the rocks.

It was the last scene of the Congo play. The previous day we had driven unceasingly through the wall of high jungle. Then we came into bamboo forests. And here, along the edges of these vast sprouts and jungle, we were watched by impudent troops of long-tailed monkeys. It seemed that some, swinging themselves from tree to tree, missed their grip deliberately, to show us how simple a thing it was to catch and cling to the lower branches. Then they peered at us from leafy footholds.

Two things struck us, that day, as being notable. One was the appearance of some small, remarkably succulent pineapples, which we got from the natives by barter. Cut in half with my Norwegian knife, and then eaten with a spoon, as you would pineapple ice out of a bowl, they were delicious! The other thing was, we had forgotten to get any visas for French Equatorial Africa. . . .

It was a nice discovery to make in the heart of Africa; that we had got here, and did not have the inconsequential few words written on our passports that would allow us to cross the Ubangi River.

And Stanleyville was the nearest place where we could get them!

For that reason, when we stared across the river, about noon the next day, there seemed something more than sullenness in this slow, sluggish barrier. A half mile across, we saw the thatched sheds and the palm trees of the French frontier post, with the tricolor flying above. It looked very attractive.

"But do you think we'll get in?" said Eve, desperately.

"Certainly," I said, equally desperate. I was wondering how I could have been such a fool as not to have got my French visa in Cape Town, or Nairobi, where we could have pulled some wires. "It will be only a formality," I said.

Eve choked at my naïvete.

The paddlers here seemed more doleful than usual. But whether their morose "ya-ya-yaahing" and "yo-yo-yoohing" was because they were "French" natives, who would like to live in the Congo, or because they were "Belgian" black men who would prefer to live under the French, or whether it was just their idea of song, we could not tell. I became interested in the fact that the Ubangi River, at this point, was so remarkably shallow that we were poled nearly all the way across. And then an insolent looking Negro, in a sloppy French tropic uniform and a red fez, planted himself on the shore line to meet our car.

He looked ominous, and made an attempt to leap on our running board even as I was going up the steep bank. I accelerated a little to put him in his place, which was running alongside. Then, at the top, I stopped.

"*Le Commandant?*" I said firmly.

"*A la douane!*" he barked. "To the customs!"

My heart sank; for in Africa, I had learned, if native police or minor soldiery are insolent, they have either weak or rude masters. The giggles from a crowd of natives gathered round amplified this belief.

"*Le Commandant?*" I repeated, softly.

"*A la—*"

"LE COMMANDANT!" I thundered.

The effect was miraculous. "*Oui, monsieur,*" he said, humbly, and then, pointing sadly to where a dung-colored building lay—it seemed panting, under some mango trees—he said politely, "*Voilà.*"

The Commandant, on the other hand, was a tired, bowed little man, old; a *Chef du Province*, who told us, even as he shook hands, that he was going to retire. He was so delighted to have a chat with people who could talk about France that he merely said "Poof!" when we timorously admitted our passport deficiencies.

"*Mais pourquoi?*" he protested, raising his hands. "I shall now write that for you myself. *C'est une blague!*" "It's a joke!"

He sweated, and his blue-veined hand shook as he wrote the visas—he obviously had the "fever"—and, as he courteously handed them back, he said:

"*M'sieur et madame*, French Equatorial is the most underpaid, understaffed, and has the most abominable climate, of any territory in Africa. We welcome you."

On that encouraging note we left him, in his suit of worn khaki, so pressed and ironed by years of "boys" that its seams had become white—an old official just about to get his reward of a small pension, and a garden in cool, green France. The customs man, stocky, bumptious, who, obviously, must have been a trial to the other tired one, was equally contemptuous of official red tape.

"*Pfui!*" he said, when I admitted in advance that I had a rifle, a shotgun, and several hundred rounds of ammunition. "You're not going to shoot us, are you? Have you any English cigarettes?"

"Yes," I stuttered, "about 200."

"*Le Gold Flak?*"

"*Oui, tous.*"

"Could I have one?"

He wanted to talk about England. He had never been there. But he had been in a port—Dakar, I think—where his boisterous good nature had probably made him a welcome official to visit English ships. "Le vis-*key!*" he said, rolling his eyes. "And now, *m'sieur et madame*, I am here."

It was only the natives, sitting in cool rings under the mango

trees and listening, or not listening to the harangue from a native clerk, and the cluster which swamped our car at the general
store and filling station, that we found cheerful.

In the shop there was a white man—a Greek, I think—who
was unable to count. At any rate, for the gasoline and the supplies we bought for our long run to Ubangi-Shari, he managed
to mistake things so that he gave me 200 francs less change than
I should have received out of a 1,000-franc note. This was after
having already tried to gyp us on the exchange. When I made
him take a pencil and go through the exercise again, it was some
sixty francs less this time. Then it was back near the 200 again.
This may sound irrelevant and not worth relating. But I give it
because this man really could not do sums; his brain had gone
flat, and he was, in his small, desperate way—from drink, heat,
or dope—the first of several white men I found like him—one
a broken-down Englishman—in blazing French Equatorial
Africa. He was authentic "White Cargo" stuff.

French Equatorial comes nearer to the Africa of fiction than
anything you will find between the Indian Ocean and the Gold
Coast. It has heat, a heat that disintegrates you. And, unlike the
well run "business" administration of the Congo, this is one of
a small trader's country. A small thing, but Eve and I found
just one hotel between Bangassou and Yaounde, way over in the
French Cameroons, and we did not even sleep in that.

But its dining room—at least, the dirty space where people
ate—seemed a symposium of everything that can happen to the
white man under the equator's sun. The mean white proprietor
kicked the native waiters on their shinbones every time he could
get near them. It was the only place in the world where I have
seen almost the entire French community drunk at 10 o'clock
in the morning; they drank white wine with their breakfast—or,
more often, instead of it. A centerpiece, on a dais cluttered with
packing crates, was an object that had been placed on a pedestal
as if for worship; it was a large, enamel bidet.

There was a sense of values expressed in that symbol of

French candor which tokened, in that particular position, desperation itself.

Bangassou, of course, had no hotel. We were told that at a place called Kemba, about eighty miles on, there was a district officer, with, it was thought, a Government rest house. We might bed down in that. If not, there was always the car to sleep in, as we had done before.

The country opened out immediately, and, to us, became almost deliriously beautiful. Here was no choking jungle. It was green savannah, horizons of fresh, waving, green grass. Fresh as lettuce; we opened our lungs and breathed (it seemed almost with our eyes) more expansively than we had done for months. In the jungle we had, I realized now, always lived in undertones; the imminence of its green walls had crushed us. Now we lived again.

Such was the effect of long horizons, where the light greens turned into pastel blues, and a faint line of hills undulated silently along the lower sky.

And in one clearing, a glade—as if welcoming us back to the normal shape of things—a herd of soft-nosed antelopes stared at us reproachfully as we broke into the peace of their feeding ground.

This was cotton country, for the French, like the Belgians, had recently launched a forced drive to make the natives grow cotton. They declared that they had no compulsory cultivation—a native male was only forced, by law, to grow a certain area of food crop, the invariable tapioca—but the same old apologia was produced that, of course, "the native must pay his tax." This was only twenty francs a year in this district. But the native simply could not earn that unless he was growing cotton for himself or for some private planter. Result, all the way from Aketi, in the Congo, up to Lake Chad, the natives were growing cotton.

And it was three or four big combines, the same which worked the Belgian Congo, that were buying this crop. There was, I believe, little competition among them. The base price for cotton was fixed by representatives of these companies with the local Governors "to meet European conditions."

"But to get fifteen francs tax out of a native around here," one depressed French official told me, "is a heartbreaking task."

So along this fairly new road across French Equatorial Africa you will come on villages which have just been created. The natives have been "put down" there to begin cultivation. For a quarter mile or so there will be a long line of these mud-and-wattle, windowless, thatched huts flanking the dirt road. They were so clean and respectable that they made you wonder whether it was the French who had done it, or, if given half a chance, this was not the way the African natives would ordinarily live if they could get away from the arbitrary despotism of their witch doctors and greedy chiefs.

For this, it must be admitted, is one thing that the white man, whether he be British, French or Belgian, has done for the great mass of the African natives; he has destroyed the most cruel, unfair system of petty despots in the world—except where it suits his own purpose to use them.

The next question presents itself: What type of rule, or fairness, has the white man put in its place?

There is a widespread misconception that the French idea of colonization is "assimilation"—to make every native a *citoyen* of France. That is dead wrong. As far back as 1923, this idea was dropped by Albert Sarraut, Minister for the Colonies, for a program called "parallelization." The natives would not be encouraged to become Frenchmen; they would not have the right to elect deputies to the Chamber of Deputies; they should remain Africans. A native *élite* is to be encouraged which is expected to voice the views and wishes of the African population to the French officials on the spot, and which, in turn, is supposed to interpret French civilization to the natives. The great bulk of the French African natives will from now on be regarded as *sujets*, not *citoyens*, of France.

(If you have ever seen the precise teeth of Sarraut meeting through a slab of salami—as I have often witnessed, when he was ambassador to Turkey—you will realize the practical, ruthless sharpness of this distinction.) The other aim of Sarraut's practical colonial policy was that the French colonies must be *made* to produce, besides soldiers, practically all the raw materials which France buys from over seas; the colonies should be complementary to French industry. And—this is where the pinch came—the French people must provide the money to put the colonies on this producing basis.

I give this here because it is in marked contrast to the *laissez-aller* British conception of how to handle colonies, whereby instead of a broadly conceived plan to develop the colonies as one great, integrated whole, there was no plan, not even for a single colony. I give it because, now that the dead hand of the British civil service has been uncovered back home, the British, after this war, will be in a mood to put live men in charge of colonial administration, of all administration. In which case something like Sarraut's businesslike comprehension of the subject will be called for.

That is, of course, if there is not some great spiritual revolution in the attitude towards *all* colonization. This will not come from the black men; they are helpless. But in the shaping of a new world a great deal of the hypocrisy must be done away with in African administration.

With the French, for instance. Dakar and Casablanca have native quarters where the Senegalese and Moroccans teem like ants, and are treated with about that much deference by the French population. On the other hand, it is not an uncommon sight to see a French officer walking out with his colored wife, leading their little *café au lait* child by the hand. There is no aloofness there. I have sat in the sidewalk cafés of both these great ports and watched the white and black *élite* mixing fraternally. Yet, out in the jungle, dealing with the great black mass of natives, the French *Administrateur* can be, and usually is, as ruthless and contemptuous of the people under him as, say, the manager of a steel works as he drives through his Polish laborers in South Chicago. They are just raw material. From what I saw in Africa I believe that it is only the Englishman who can entertain feelings of a sentimental nature towards the natives under him, and this will be only from an official.

The average British "trader" or business man in the tropics is of a coarse and vulgar nature, swollen with the conceit of living far above his natural level—with the ability to lord it over so many servants, for example—and if he is tolerably kind to his own personal house "boy" he feels that he has fulfilled the Englishman's reputation for fairness in Africa. As a business man he is every whit as rapacious in his dealings with the natives as is a Belgian or a Frenchman.

But the official French attitude towards the equatorial native (this does not apply to French North Africa) is a bewildering combination of the intellectual conception of equality, and ruthless brutality.

For example, one French *Administrateur* declared to me, "We were told for this season, 'Double the amount of cotton, and there will be no questions asked.' "

He said that the first responsibility he placed upon the local chiefs. "We pay the chiefs; they usually get about 5 per cent of the poll tax. And there can be a certain bonus paid for cotton." But the final responsibility, or blame for failure, he said, meaningly, rests upon the *Administrateur*.

"And will you get double this year?" I asked.

He smiled. "My friend, what will you? *Of course!*"

On the other hand, the natives have been so badly "done" by the local French traders that, in Ubangi-Shari, the sale of native products to Europeans is allowed to be held only on certain days of the month. This is so that an *Administrateur* can be there to protect the natives, to see that they get a fair deal.

It was a big English trader who complained of this to me at

Bangui. He said that it greatly interfered with his business of buying palm nuts, coffee, and cotton.

"*I'd* like to buy," he said, "when, where, and how I want to. *My* company wouldn't 'do' the natives."

But as he said it I had to smile. I knew one specific case, a case that should have been a colonial scandal, where his company had entered into a secret combination with other companies to fix the price they would pay the natives for their one and only product—a slick business trick that would have brought their directors into court in England or the United States.

I would never accuse white trading interests in Africa of altruism.

French Equatorial Africa is over four times the size of France. It is, as I have said, the most understaffed, underpaid, unpopular of all the French colonies. It is hard to enlist French officials to go out there.

I'd like to show this grueling trip from Bangassou across to Yaounde, in the French Cameroons, in a series of pictures, for that's how I saw it.

Take, for the background, the wide horizons of the elephant-grass country. The light green savannahs. In the far, far distance there is usually the misty blue silhouette of mountains, as nebulous as smoke. Each river, as you come to it, will be marked by a dark green belt of tangled jungle. The thatch of the round native huts, with their queer tufted tops, blazes like burnished metal in the sun—it is so hot!

The road is vivid, sandstone red, some of it only a year old, and a horror. A torrential tropic rain turns it into gullies and rivulets. It leaves it a wreck of potholes. It was so bad at the time we went across it that it broke my front springs three times before I got to the border of the French Middle Congo, wrecked my speedometer—a grave accident, when you *must* know how many miles to the next place where you may hope to get help or gasoline; and when we finally limped into Yaounde, the capital of the Cameroons, this last stretch from Bangassou had done more to wreck our Ford V-8 than had all of Tanganyika, Kenya, Uganda, and the Belgian Congo.

On the other hand, it was what I had expected from tropical Africa.

Perhaps the first thing I'd like to say about the natives we met along this road—and I like to say it in fairness to the Frenchmen—is that these natives were happy. There was not a village we passed through, new or old, where the little potbellied "totos" did not rush out to wave at our car. Not a village where we stopped that the headmen did not approach us with a smile on their likable faces. And this was in primitive country where, for long stretches, the women wore nothing at all but a bunch of mango leaves fore and aft (it made me believe in Eve and the fig-leaf), and the men, although most of the headmen seemed to have acquired a European felt hat, went about in G-strings. In one village, where the women seemed to have maimed or malformed themselves in every way possible, with cicatrices and with disks stuck through their ears, the one who I suppose was considered the best dressed woman in the district wore, dangling in some extraordinary way from her nostrils, the three-inch blade of a European penknife.

But they were happy. And they showed it in the way they treated us. In this particular village, the chief was a woman. I wish you could see this village—the two rows of long, thatched huts leading into the sunset, and before each hut a little group, squatting, of the family. There were muzzle-loading, gaspipe guns in evidence, and spears, and their beloved peanut-colored hunting dogs, which look like yellow bull terriers and can't bark, or were just the ordinary village mongrel dog with curly tail and every fault, except lack of courage or faithfulness —there were all these things, but there was no meat in the pot. The woman of each hut—these natives seemed monogamous—

was cooking the inevitable tapioca in a black, earthen pot, taking out little handfuls now and then to push into the mouth of her baby, with the man sitting on the ground in dignified inactivity, waiting for dinner to be ready. There must have been some fifty or sixty of these huts on each side of the road. And down at the far end was an unused, thatched hut which was oblong in shape, and which, we were given to understand, was where a white man would put up, if he came there.

It hadn't been used for years. The sons of the woman chief ran ahead to sweep its floor. This was clay. So were the walls. And, as the walls only rose for less than four feet under the thatched covering, we were on exhibit in everything we did. We could not see out because the entire village, all that could get there, was trying to lean over our wall.

But it was a good thing they were there. For just as Eve was sitting down on her camp cot, which I had hastily erected before darkness, a "boy" gave a shout, shoved her aside, and brushed something onto the floor. Then he killed it. It was a scorpion.

This scorpion had dropped from a bamboo matting which was stretched across under the thatch to make a ceiling. And that bamboo matting gave us one of the worst nights we spent in Africa. The reason was that there was a heavy snake on it. It had probably been sleeping there, or hibernating, and the heat from our hurricane lamp must have wakened it. The first we knew was that, in the dead silence of the African night—unbroken except for the humming of insects—we heard the matting rustle. And, looking up, we saw it bending under a heavy weight.

Our first impulse was to run. But where to?

I finished my daily notes in a hurry. Then we crawled under our mosquito nets, and tucked them in around us under our sheets, so that we lay under two cones of gauze. Then I blew out the light and prayed for morning.

The snake seemed rather unsettled and sleepless himself.

We lay there listening to his rustles for a long time. And I don't know which one of the three of us went to sleep first. I don't know if you can imagine how terribly inadequate a mosquito net seems when it is all there is between you and a black mamba or a cobra?

Leopards are thick in these parts, all the way to Duala on the Bight of Benin in the French Cameroons. And in the morning we saw the work of the village artist on the wall. It was a primitive but extraordinarily vivid painting of a leopard hunt; six African soldiers, in uniforms and bayonets, with a noncommissioned officer, facing a conventionalized leopard, opposite a snarling dog. The fact that the colors were only black and raspberry pink did not detract from the validity of the work. There obviously *had* been such a leopard hunt, and this was its testimony.

In this amazing village, so full of savagery and decency, the first sight that met our eyes, after we had dressed in public that morning, was six girls being oiled and having their kinky hair plaited, for a ceremonial dance. They were, we were given to understand, the coming village ballet. That night they would dance their initiation. Two veteran dancers were primping them, highly conscious of our interest, and the six little beauties sat like a row of blackbirds on a log, but just as much aware of their importance, and just as nervous, as any six little ballet dancers of the imperial ballet in Czarist Petrograd.

Fantastically enough, their completely new tufts of mango leaves were so fresh and bunchy that, as they sat there, they gave the appearance of billowy green ballet skirts.

These natives were not the misshapen creatures which live in the dark jungles of the Congo. They were savannah people, who lived in open air and wide spaces. And they were extraordinarily beautiful. The slim waists and hips of these women in this part of French Equatorial Africa easily explained the remarks of one French official to me that life "in the bush" was not without its consolations.

✦

Then there was the bed of the wife of the French District Officer at X.

X—that is, the D.O.'s bungalow and a chance rest house for strangers—rests on the top of a red bluff overlooking a broad, swift, dangerous river. An adventurous tribe of native fishermen work their wicker fish baskets in the frothing rapids. There is not another white man within a hundred miles of this lonely Frenchman and his wife.

But did they want company? No! When, after a rickety crossing on the usual raft made of dugouts, I put the car to climb the steep bank, I found at the top a Frenchman, sullen, sweating with fever, unshaved, who glared at me almost vindictively from under a sun helmet much too big for him. In its battered, soggy condition it looked like an overturned coal scuttle. A place to sleep? He eyed me with his yellow orbs. Then he nodded.

Looking in the direction indicated, I saw a long, low, white bungalow with a red, corrugated-iron roof—a box that I knew instinctively would be hotter than hell. Could he give me some water? He eyed me again and said, "*Oui.*" Could I buy some gasoline from him, or anywhere around here? "*Non!*"

"What are you here for?" he asked.

I told him, saying that I had started this drive over in Tanganyika; my front springs were broken, so was my speedometer; I was almost out of fuel.

"*Bien!*" he said. Then he turned and went into his bungalow.

A few minutes later a "boy" appeared, climbed on our running board, and directed us to the other bungalow. I began the long evening ordeal of unpacking beds and cooking kit, and setting them up. Two "boys" appeared and left a four-gallon gasoline tin of water on the veranda. We had put the beds up on this stone veranda, and I was stringing the mosquito nets while Eve made some tea, when an elephant walked hurriedly past—a *red* elephant. Behind him, poking him occasionally with a stick, was a light-colored native who, I knew, could not come from these parts.

"Of course," said Eve, "we should have been sophisticated enough to know that when people have lived alone for a long time they don't *want* to see strangers. We got that way ourselves, out in British Columbia. It's only in places like the Riviera that you welcome passers-by. Not in outposts, or desolate spots. One always flatters oneself that one will be such a treat for them, when they never see anybody—but one isn't!"

"We haven't done him any harm," I said.

"We've disturbed their peace."

"Peace be damned!" I said.

We sat down on our camp cots, opened up a tin of Swiss strawberry jam, went berserk with peevishness, opened our last tin of biscuits, and prepared to endure a rainy night. I looked up, and saw that, although the house was new, the whitewashed rafters under the corrugated-iron roof were rotting with red dust; there were little piles of it, like European anthills, all over the cement veranda. I asked Eve if she remembered the scene in *White Cargo* where the drunken planter hit the rafter, and just such a red, rotting dust fell to the floor. "Well, here we are," I said. "And our French friend across the way seems to have gone the way of this wood."

At that moment a "boy" in immaculate khaki tunic and shorts appeared, saluted stiffly to his red fez, and handed Eve a note. Written in a well bred, female hand, it asked us would we come to "five o'clock."

When I brought the car to a stop a dapper Frenchman in white duck and a blue polo shirt leaped down the steps and opened the door for Eve to alight. I hardly recognized him. "My wife," he said, leading us into a cool room where a very pale young girl lay back in a chair. "You must excuse us; she has the fever." She was blond, with blue eyes made almost spectral by the blue flesh around them. She was very beautiful.

The floor was cement, but polished like glass. The chairs were of carved, dark African woods. There were circular mats, made of leopard skins, on the floor. And a tiny deer, about the size of a cat, made a rattle like castanets as it scampered to her side. A long-tailed black monkey, with a white mask, regarded us like an Egyptian statuette from its perch on the back of her chaise longue.

"So you," I smiled to the Frenchman, "own that red elephant?"

"*Oui, m'sieu.* He is red because he likes rolling in the dust. He is a baby—we had him up in Lake Chad—and he walked all the way here, 1,200 kilometers! *C'est bon, n'est-ce-pas?*"

The woman was trembling. "Lake Chad? Yes."

She seemed to forget what it was she intended to say about it. She let her white arm dangle beside her chair. Her husband frowned, and gave us each a quick smile. "We shall be going home soon," he said.

"How long do you get?"

"Usually, after two years here, we get six months back in France. When I get there I usually find some excuse to make it a year. This time—" He stopped, and gave his wife a long, firm smile. "This time—?"

She shook her head. "*Non, non;* I shall be all right." Then she stood up, and, almost as tottery as the little deer, she led us into her incredible bedroom.

I suppose he found her on the stage, or else she was a mannequin. Yet she was not at all that type. But this bed was a Hollywood director's dream of something suitable for the Empress Josephine. One almost expected to see an "N," in laurel leaves, at the head of its blue silk canopy. And it stood on a dais of polished cement, up which you had to ascend two steps.

"*C'est beau!*" she laughed.

And then we saw, through her laughter, that she saw the joke of the whole thing.

She led us back, with her debonnaire totter, into the room

with the leopard-skin rugs, where some beautifully iced cock-tails were served by a "boy" in a jibbah and red fez, and where, on looking round again, I began to see there was some lyric note of mirth in its entire *décor*—the grinning black ebony masks, with their ivory eyes; the prodigality of leopard skins, the little deer, the white-masked monkey—these were all part of a pattern, with the red elephant. It was her spirited response to the ordeal of Africa; she was burlesquing it.

Despite the amazing French reserve of refusing to discuss their personal affairs with strangers, she was ill enough, and he was worried enough, for it to come through, how much they were depending on this trip home to make her well again, so that she would return, and he could get his pension, earned at an age when they would both still be young. Writing this now (after Pétain has capitulated), knowing just how many French men and women there are all over Africa, just like that, living for their pensions and their villa in France, I can understand their confusion, poor souls, as to just which side they should fight on!

I must also state that this pair were the only two of the French official class that we met all through French Equatorial Africa who were courteous and pleasant. We surprised them by refusing firmly to stay to dinner, in common humanity, for she was too ill. But we had hardly settled down to our own miserable meal from tins when a safari of "boys" appeared out of the night, bringing a basket of pineapples, oranges, avocado pears, eggs, milk, bread (a great treat in Africa); and even an extremely well made chocolate soufflé.

But the pair were unique.

The bats repeatedly drove us out of the wooden latrine that night.

The next night, the *Administrateur* remarked that if we did not shut the door of the guest house and sleep inside, we should probably be eaten by leopards.

"But that, madame, is to me *naturellement parfaitement égal.*"

And the night after that, another 200 miles further on, the *Administrateur* even refused to supply us with a packing crate for a table, because, he said, the Under Minister for the Colonies had stolen the last table he had lent!

During all this time we were working along the banks of the Ubangi River, anticipating the delights of a hotel in Bangui itself. Names prominently marked on the map, such as Fort Sibut, looked encouraging. Yet, when we got to the fort, we did not know we were in it; there was just nothing there at all. And at Bambarri, where we had been told there was a French garrison, these were all black, with a few of the surliest type of French noncoms, and the district officer here was certainly one of the most unpleasant Frenchmen I have ever met. He refused absolutely to accept our explanations of our trip, and even challenged the authenticity of our passports. It was his mean eye which discovered that we had had no visas at all for French Equatorial Africa until after we had entered it at Bangassou.

"That man there," he said, "was a fool to give them to you. It is irregular; *irregular,* do you understand?"

Notable happenings along this bit of heartbreaking road. A French boy—from Martinique—*made* two leaves to reinforce our springs. He was the mechanic of a large coffee plantation. A wooded village which had hundreds of gray parrots, with red tails, sitting on top of its huts, or walking unconcernedly in and out of them. Two American evangelical mission workers regarding a lion which someone had just shot from the bridge that morning as it came down to drink, and which seemed still able to scare. And, Eve declares, the longest snake in Africa, which whipped across the floor behind me as I was putting up the beds. I never saw it!

Fifteen miles out of Bangui we dropped again into the dark

equatorial jungle. Then we came out on the banks of the Ubangi once more, here broad and sullen, with yellow bubbles floating toward the Congo, and, on the far side, some sheer red cliffs. On the river front we found the one hotel between here and Yaounde in the French Cameroons—and it was named *Hôtel Pain!*

This was the hotel with the famous bidet in the dining room. Most of its guests were drunk at 9.30 in the morning. But they really had some excuse. At Bangui when I tried to get some films developed the photographer said: "It is impossible. The water here is too hot. It would melt your films." Bangui, aside from being the seat of a Governor, was a trading center for pygmy deer hides and beeswax.

The Governor, M. St. Felix, was suffering from a *crise de la Paradise* (malaria), we were told. In reality he was in the last stages of dengue fever, lying on his face, having his spine punctured to extract the spinal fluid. Governor St. Mars, who had been flown out from France to relieve him, told us that he had also had it, and it was *très grave, madame!*

It was at Bangui (although I did not know it) that I was hit with the malaria I had picked up somewhere along this road in Equatorial Africa. It was also at Bangui that we hired the first and only "boy" we had in all Africa. His name was *Jean!*

I think we got Jean because I was tired of doing things; I had learned what it means to travel and live months in Africa without a "boy." I would at least taste the experience of having one. Malaria plays queer pranks, and mine began with a ferocious gloom. Also, I had been eating antibacillus tablets ever since Aketi, and these—I discovered afterward I had taken enough to kill a man—are also conducive to melancholia. I ate them to prevent an infection setting up in my leg, where the shinbone itself was now bared, with an ulcer the size of a cent.

The *Hôtel Pain* was better named in the English sense of its spelling than in the French; we had found a room in an empty bungalow, where I was lugubriously beginning to set our beds up, for use until an entire new set of springs, etc., could be found or made for the Ford V-8, when this equally lugubrious African appeared at our door. He had a letter from a former employer, saying: "This 'boy' worked for me six months. His work was good. I cannot say as much for his honesty."

He looked to us rather a nice "boy." We hired him for four days, at the end of which time he was arrested by the police for the theft of a tin of extremely nasty, oily biscuits, which I had given him and which he was carrying home. As we drove from the police station after setting him free, I wondered whether the former accusations were also false or whether it was upon his record that the police had acted.

He had seemed strangely at home in that police station.

We made up a song, "Every day is mango day, in Bangui!" For every morning, at six o'clock, as the natives trooped into town to work, they knocked the mangoes off the trees with long sticks. Lying there, in the eye-sizzling heat, I would hear a "plop," then the shouts of "boys" rushing to get that mango. Down by the hotel those not employed by somebody sat and watched the mango trees for a fruit to drop. When one did, someone blew a bugle, and the whole waterfont raced for the mango.

The river ran malevolently past. I had nothing to do except feel worse and worse. A London newspaper had cabled me, asking whether I would fly to the Gold Coast and write a series of articles on its colonial administration. A more enterprising paper, it seemed, had sent a correspondent there, by ship, to write a yarn about its misadministration. I wired that I would, asking what terms could I get. Then the London editor, apparently unused to handling foreign correspondents, forgot to answer my radiogram. Unable to believe this, for four days I fought with the French post office and radio officials, making myself one of the most hated men in Bangui. Furious, I then sent a cable which I hoped would escape both the French and British post office Mrs. Grundys. It read, "For Krissakes Answer."

I got the answer, weeks later, over at Duala in the French Cameroons. It offered a handsome sum.

I would see the new Governor. I found one of his aides drinking riesling with the French in the *Hôtel Pain* as I was eating my breakfast. My irritability was so intense that it impressed him with my importance. I did see the Governor. He was of a smiling Parisian type, a *bon vivant,* with the memories of good living still recent enough to give him fortitude. He began by telling me that of the twenty men he first came out with to French Equatorial Africa, seventeen were now dead. But *he* wasn't! He asked me to mark that. He was still on the job.

"But after thirty years' service," he said, sadly, "a French Governor only gets 50,000 francs a year to retire on—£300!" He said that any French official, while serving, got less than one-third of what his English counterpart would be paid.

Government House stood on a red hill, and through the darkened blinds we could see the implacable Ubangi flowing below us to the Congo. He said that he found that sight very beautiful, and encouraging. The river was low now, and no boats could come up. But one day he would take a boat and go down it to the Congo, down the Congo to Brazzaville, then he would board, at Pointe-Noire, an oceangoing African liner for the last time, and sail back across the cool sea to *La Belle France!* (Always that dream; the villa in France, and, unquestionably with this man, the boulevards.) And as we were staring a sloppy soldier came in and saluted him.

"How many black troops do you send the French army?" I asked.

"As many as France asks for. We keep a dossier of all the

ablebodied men in Equatorial Africa. When Paris asks us to
send so many, we send so many. We shift them about to
acclimatize them. They enlist for five years, with usually three
years abroad. But it is bad—I don't like it—to send these black
men to France; we lose prestige."

"Why?"

"Well, they see France. You know what the prostitutes are
like in Marseilles. And, then, French politicians are fools!
Ubangi-Shari, *m'sieu*, is just recovering from the Popular Front.
Those idiots even wanted to introduce the 40-hour week in
French Equatorial Africa!"

"How long does it take you to make a native a soldier?"
I asked.

"Oh, in twenty-eight days, even if we catch them wild, we
can make them obey commands and carry a rifle. They are not
supposed to know much. It is the noncoms."

It was a nice, casual, little definition of "cannon-fodder."

At luncheon the drinking party in the hotel is still going on.
They are now buying each other cocktails. A Czech Bata man,
selling shoes, sits staring at his meal. It is the same luncheon
he had yesterday: Sorrel soup, European tinned vegetables,
tinned Dutch butter, condensed milk, local coffee, a slab of a
steer that has just been butchered over in the native bazaar.
Some Arabs walk past us disdainfully out into the blazing sun.
Black "boys," or slaves, are holding huge umbrellas over some
of them. The Arabs wear vast, wound turbans. And their boots
of crimson-red morocco leather are embossed with gold. They
look at the table of the heavy drinkers, laugh in their beards,
and nudge each other. A transport lorry covered with red dust
draws up. Three Frenchmen fling themselves in chairs on the
cement terrace and order Pernods. Their lorry is high with
bales of the tiny gray deer skins.

A few Africans hold high places in the Ubangi-Shari administration, particularly in the treasury. As such they are

entitled to be members of the *Cercle Bangui*, where drinking parties begin Sunday night and do not terminate until Monday morning. But these fortunate black men, I am told, do not drink; they are jealous of their high position. One is entertaining a party of white officials and their wives in the *Hôtel Pain* now. The proprietor kicks aside some chickens that have wandered in among the chair legs to see what they can pick up. He kicks, with a savage "clunk!" on the shinbone, the black waiters, in order to make them serve faster. The black man host, who has a very intelligent, sensitive face, appears not to see these things. I notice him, once or twice, glancing towards the table of the drunken French traders as if he were apprehensive they would shout some rude remark about him. You can see that, much as he enjoys this meal, he is anxious for it to be over.

One of the drunks, greasy with sweat, has been wearing for the last two days nothing but the same pair of shorts, shoes, and dirty white shirt. He now unbuttons it down to the navel. He has "got off" with the woman next to him. They make playful slaps at each other.

"It's not the administration, it's the administrators," growls a sallow Englishman who is having luncheon with Eve and me. He is waiting for a 'plane to take him to Leopoldville (we met him up at Stanleyville), and the 'plane which stopped today had no place. He faces another week of Bangui. "The French have their arms around the native's neck one day, and, the next, they're kicking him in the behind. The natives never know where they are with them!"

He complains of the monotony of no seasons. He has, worse luck, he says, to remain in the Congo. Back home he can make nothing like the money paid here. He tries to get all his work done before breakfast, 6 or 7 to 8.30. Then he lives for the best hour of the day. "That's your first drink, at 6 o'clock, as the sun goes down! By Jove, sometimes that makes up for everything!"

I found another Englishman that day—or, he found me. He was following the three French traders that I have just mentioned. He was trying to wheedle them into giving him a job. To duck the crowd of drunks in the *Hôtel Pain*, I had gone along to a tiny saloon on the waterfront. I was sitting there, staring at those implacable bubbles floating down on the Ubangi, when they came in, with him following. He stopped.

"English?" he asked.

I shook my head. I didn't want conversation—not with such a human wreck. That showed the malaria must have been rotting me, because, usually, I like listening to the alibis of waterfront bums.

"German?"

"Hell, no!" I said.

"Oh, Yank! Well—"

"Have a drink," I offered.

He licked his lips. "Honest, I wish I could," he said, "but I can't take time *now*. I've got to talk to these Frenchmen. Get some work."

He started to go through the door. Then he came back. "I used to own a plantation out here, right up that river. Pretty place."

"Did you?" I exclaimed politely.

"Yes. Pretty place."

"I'm sure it was," I said.

"Have a drink," I repeated.

He hesitated, took off his topee, and mopped a fish-white forehead. "Nope," he said, "can't be done. I've *got* to get a job!"

That night, when the French colonial officials were sitting on the *Hôtel Pain* terrace in their white drill uniforms with the gold-striped epaulets that make them look like naval officers, the drinking party broke up—literally. What happened was that the fat little man, with the unbuttoned shirt, leaned across to embrace his fair lady, rested his weight on the table, and the whole combination toppled over. Unperturbed, he arose like a phoenix from a ruin of broken bottles and glasses, assisted his lady to her feet, and, amply patterned with Dubonnet—for they had started on that now—they wandered off below the mango trees, like two sticks of a tripod.

At 8.30 the next morning he tacked into the dining room, flopped into a chair, and began on another bottle of riesling. He had lost his lady, but found a dachshund.

Once every fortnight a motor caravan leaves Bangui, goes west across French Equatorial Africa, crosses a slice of the French Middle Congo, then travels to Yaounde, the capital of the French Cameroons. We gave it a two-day start, hoping to be able to use the *cases de passage* (cabins) which have been put up for its drivers and passengers. The day after it departed we were told that the rains had washed the roads away a hundred or so miles further on, and that nobody would get through.

We accordingly packed the last free cubic space in our car with tins of gasoline and oil, bought some spare spring leaves, paid off the faithful Jean, and set off at dawn the next morning, to challenge our fate. Eve had to catch a German steamer, sailing on a certain date from Duala, in the Cameroons, and there was not a day to be lost now. We found the motor caravan, broken down, at the first *case de passage,* and we never saw it again. The drivers were already taking it easy in their striped pajamas, and the ladies of the drinking party, we discovered, were among the convoy's passengers. So was the little fat man. They were at it again, the little man stalking around with a bottle in his hand; and, as our speedometer was working again, I was able to inform Eve that it was just 165 miles between their "binges." They were bound for France!

We slept in a village hut that first night, but, after that, we held every *case de passage*—where we hurriedly set up our beds —before they could get to it. We often wondered what would happen if they did turn up. We had taken a vow that nothing less than force (and there would have to be a lot of that) would turn us out.

The Cameroons and the Middle Congo are said to possess some of the greatest forest wealth in all Africa. I believe it. Coming out of Ubangi-Shari we skirted the foothills of the red mountains, where the brush was fairly open; with the Middle Congo we plunged into the dark equatorial jungle again. You have heard enough about it. And now, with the fever grilling my bones, I no longer had the heart to make notes about it.

It was just drive—drive—drive; unload—load; unload— load; then, *crash!* went the springs again.

Then, in the heat of the day, we let the car slide gently down a gully that had once been the road, and natives paddled us across a swift river; and there, wide, with a deep ditch on each side, was a broad highway. It may have been only made of dirt, but, with our crippled Ford, to us it was welcome as a boulevard. It was only four years old. We were in the mandate of the French Cameroons! A few hours later we reached the French frontier post of Batouri, slid down a hill of clustered native huts, passed the ruins of the old German fort; and there, shining on a red hill, was the long, white structure of the French administrative post.

These French mandate officials were as different from their weary brothers in French Equatorial Africa as a well paid, healthy man from an underpaid, overworked, desperate brother. One of these young men was haughtily haranguing a huge circle of white-robed Mohammedan Hausa headmen from the north Cameroons. The other, while his clerk was filling out our papers, invited us into his office, where he was just then interviewing an interesting "case."

This was a murderer, in hand and leg shackles, fixed with padlocks. He had just shot a poisoned arrow completely through his wife. "In one side, madame," said the Frenchman, politely, indicating on himself where the arrow had entered, "and out *here!*" He touched his other ribs. The mute murderer, in spite of his terror, nodded. The young Frenchman then proudly held up the bloody arrow. Then he showed us the bow. "You pull it with your foot, madame. He will get fifteen to twenty years, madame. We have the death penalty in the Cameroons, but we seldom enforce it. These natives are so impetuous!"

Saying that there were only sixty-four white men in the whole vast Department of Batouri, the Frenchman produced a file and handed Eve a few cards. One was of an Englishman, rated as "bachelor," but with four children. "*Et de toutes les couleurs, madame! Oh, la-la!*"

Such abandon, after the depressing heaviness of Bangui, went to my head. Looking out from the high, red hill, I saw the long, green sweeps of light savannah grass dancing before my eyes, and, leaving Eve to exchange witticisms with the gallant Frenchman, I seized the car and drove down to the shops again. Here I watched an expert French mechanic demount my front spring—splayed like a hand of cards again—and insert the reserve leaves. We reamed shallow holes to prevent the shackles slipping, and I bound them with twine. I suddenly noticed that I was covered with glistening little globules of sweat; yet I was shivering; my head was spinning.

Then for the first time in a year and four months I asked where there was a liquor store. I bought a half bottle of Martel, drew the cork, threw back my head, and drained half of it.

"*C'est bon!*" said the mechanic.

I smiled, and shared the other half of the brandy with him. "How far is it to Yaounde?" I asked.

"About 350 kilometers, *m'sieu*. Good road all the way; this is the Cameroons." He saw me eyeing some natives who were sewing on a row of outdoor Singer sewing machines. They were making cotton prints into skirts. "In 1926, *m'sieu,* this village was naked. That's what we French have done!"

He jerked a thumb towards the tricolor fluttering so proudly from the headquarters on the hill. It was an inspiring sight.

There were two things that I had to do before I put Eve and the car aboard the *Wadai* at Duala, and flew to Accra. I wanted to see a German, a tobacco grower, who was running the biggest plantation in the Cameroons. The other matter—and it was a desire which increased with every mile I drove—was to see the Governor. For what the French have done in road building in the Cameroons is a model for all the rest of Africa.

There were only 500 kilometers of road in the Cameroons in 1918; there are now 7,000 kilometers of probably the best roads in Africa.

Our troubles were over.

Seventy-two kilometers this side of Yaounde we turned up a pleasant drive of eucalyptus trees and came into the usual hive of German industry. This plantation of 25,000 acres sends (or sent!) 70,000,000 leaves of Sumatra tobacco to Germany every year. There were the usual Apollo-like German youths stalking about in chamois shorts, and with embroidered braces. A former big game hunter for the Hamburg zoo—of the "bring-'em-back-alive" species—was superintending the erection of a new power plant. The manager, an ex-German army officer, and brother captain to Buxell, the coffee grower whom I had gone to see way over on the slopes of Ngorongoro Crater in Tanganyika, was sweating in his office, making out the plantation's accounts so that they might be sent to Berlin.

"You see," he said, "we *sell* our tobacco in Hamburg. But we don't get all the money for it. That is decided in Berlin—against *this.*" He tapped the accounts. Berlin it was which decided how much money the plantation *really* needed, and that they were allowed in foreign exchange. The remainder stayed in the fatherland.

"It is hard," he said, patriotically, "but it is necessary. The Reich must come first these days."

It was like an actor's line, this declaration. And I had heard its like so often from desperate Germans that I did not even challenge it. This jovial chap, in a French mandate, was just as much a slave of Berlin as were the Germans I had talked with over in Tanganyika. And, to be honest about it, this was the way that they wanted things to be.

It doesn't do our own minds any good to tell ourselves fairy tales about the Germans in Africa. They all felt (except the pure anti-Nazis) that they were playing their parts in a great new life that the *Führer* was opening for the fatherland.

The Germans, in what is now the British Cameroons, had something like twenty-five major plantations. When these were put up for auction in London after the last war, the Germans bought back twenty-four of them. The French, in their 166,000 miles of the Cameroons they acquired by mandate, got at auction or pre-empted 362 German properties, but there were only eighty-six Germans in the Cameroons, of 2,000 European population.

This was now the largest plantation, however, in the Cameroons. Therefore it was only natural that Herr Leuch should give a start when I asked him what was the latest news about the war.

"What war?" he asked.

"The one that seems to be coming."

"*Ach!*" He waved his fat hand. "Don't talk like that, my friend; there is no chance of war. Our *Führer* doesn't want it."

"Do you really believe that?"

"I do," he said.

"So do I," I said, utterly surprising him. "But Hitler wants things that will *make* a war. And *then* what will happen to this splendid plantation?"

He shook his head again and again, as if trying to throw my words out of his ears.

Yaounde rests on the last ridge of the red uplands in the Cameroons before you plunge down into a tropical jungle more suffocating, I think, than you will find anywhere along the Gulf of Guinea. This might account for the peculiar gaiety among the 250 white people in this capital. They seem always conscious of their good fortune in being stationed where a man can breathe.

But it was a bit startling to get in there, just after the six o'clock darkness had dropped, and find every soul in the hotel playing bridge. It was, we discovered, the social hour. Both manners and dress were formal; all the French colonial officials were in their white drill. The stone lower floor was divided into three divisions by a circular bar. By the door were pool tables and bare drinking tables for transport riders who did not care to dress, and for the less distinguished among Yaounde's white population. On the far side of the bar were the bridge tables. Haughty stares would greet you if you ventured there. To the left were the long lines of dining tables where all, dressed or in the battered shorts and polo shirts of the road, would eventually eat their meals. Sitting on the plebeians' side of this circular bar, and cursing the Governor loudly, was one of the most unpleasant Germans I have met.

"The Governor," he said, "is a ——! During all the years we have been here he has never once invited either my wife or me to one of his receptions!"

He was a pure caricature of a German—bald, no back to his head, rolls of pink flesh down the back of his thick neck. I gathered, from the way he bellowed, that he was a person of some local importance, and that he was also going home. (Eve "drew" him on the *Wadai!*) And listening to him rant about the Governor made me all the more anxious to meet the Governor—who seemed a man of good taste.

When I did meet M. Brunot, the Governor, I realized that I was in the presence of a man of the world.

"Do you know why the natives respect the French?" he asked. "Because we have beaten them. We have beaten them up at Lake Chad. We have deposed their emirs and chiefs. We are warriors. Therefore they respect us."

"But what about the Germans?" I countered. "They, too, are warriors."

"The German Major Dominick," said the Governor, icily, "dug trenches and burned the natives alive, in gasoline. And before he had to clear out before us he hanged the King of Duala. That is history. These natives have memories.

"Furthermore, we have made a native *élite* here. All the younger generation is being educated in French schools; most around here speak French; we have a large body of native clerks, postal officials, radio men and interpreters. They take a deep interest in European newspapers. These educated natives are shocked by the things they read there, the declarations of Hitler's Germany. Hitler's treatment of the Jews has terrified thousands of Africans. This native *élite* knows that if the Cameroons are given back to Germany it will be reduced to a black slave class again. Am I right?"

He was right, I knew, because everywhere in Africa today the educated African is frightened of Germany. Hitler's constant ranting about racial superiority has chilled the Africans with the fear, considering what he has done to the white man, of what he would do with them. They are pathetically articulate on that subject. And it is an interesting thing to call attention to, that *if* by any mischance the African races were put under German rule again, it would be only the primitive, untutored savage whom the Germans would not find bitterly opposed to them. Not that that would make any difference to the Nazis.

"And how do you feel, *M'sieur le Gouverneur*, about this question of color? I believe you are a Socialist?"

"Yes," he said, quickly; "but that doesn't mean that I consider all men, white and black, equal, or that I think all natives should have French citizenship. The British have a very good attitude in that way. They are great 'gentlemen,' and they always slightly despise all native peoples, and yet they have an enormous respect for the liberty of the individual.

"I always remember that when I was an unimportant *Administrateur* in one of my first posts in Africa, I made friends with a British official across the frontier. When I went to Bathurst on my way home, the Governor, Sir John Denham, was kind enough to ask me to dinner. And at dinner His Excellency turned to me and asked me about an extradition case concerning a British native from Gambia. Now, the Governor was a very great and important man, and I was nothing at all. And yet he had all the particulars of that case in his head, knew the man's name and all the details of the case. Whereas *I* had just taken it in the day's work, and thought nothing of it."

M. Brunot, now the Governor of an important French mandate himself, gave me a wise smile.

"Just like an Englishman, wasn't it, that deft little compliment of inviting me to dinner and then"—the Governor sighed—"getting everything he wanted, so casually!"

"Quite painless," I said.

M. Brunot, whom the tropics had bleached, nodded solemnly. "They have a 'way,' these English officials. Now the natives here, they say to me: 'You are always bothering us! Bothering us about road work, about taxes, about vaccination, about military service; there's no end to it!'

"And I say to them, 'Well, why don't you move over the frontier and live in British territory?'

"'No,' they say; 'we don't want to do that. We would live better there, and make more money. But you *think* of us differently.'"

I smiled, and answered as politely as I could that he need not use such bald-faced propaganda with me. I repeated the usual German accusation against French administration: "One day they take the native's arm, and he is a brother. The next day they kick him."

"Yes!" The Governor laughed, delightedly. "That is very much the French temperament. There's a good deal of truth in that! Still, you must admit, there *are* those days when we treat him like a brother. Do the Germans show such days?"

Brunot was one of the French colonial governors who took the allied side when France collapsed. But pressure was put on him, and I am afraid he wavered—good man as he was.

Only one who has seen these French Equatorial officials in action can realize the bitterness with which they must have scorned the offer of capitulation by the Pétain Government. As I have shown, for ten, twenty, thirty years they all lived with one day in mind—the day when they should receive their pensions and go back to live in cool, green France. They all had the same dream—the villa, a garden, wine under the arbor, the delight of a *fine*, dominoes, and some sparkling conversation in the café after dinner. The ecstasy of just physical ease. Some spoke to me of a river they would fish, some of a lazy, poplar-shaded canal, to be bobbed for yellow perch. Some winked, and spoke of the boulevards. They all talked of food; oh, the salads they would get! "*M'sieur*," laughed one, "I shall eat when I retire—but not here. It is impossible!" They all had this dream. Well, Pétain offered it to them. And they turned it down.

That refusal was, in my opinion, one of the most heroic acts of this war, for service in French Equatorial Africa was so unpopular that the officials had to be paid a bonus to go there. At one time this was 120 per cent; it was 100 per cent up to the eve of this war. And in a territory which, as I have said, is over four times the size of all France there were, aside from the military who administer most of the territory around Lake Chad, not many more than 600 white French officials.

Service in French Equatorial Africa is not the smart, gay, sometimes romantic life that it is in French North Africa. Nor do you have the cafés of those two glittering ports, Dakar and Casablanca. There are no "clubs" when you get into the equatorial bush. The work is, for most of these men, a one-man job. So, having seen them, I think these men who have willingly accepted exile from France, temporary or final, are possibly the most gallant Frenchmen I have ever seen.

For their bravery is not the act of a moment, or of things done in company; it is just the bitter resolution to stay out of France until they and the British can take it back from the Germans. And that's long-distance courage.

As a result of this spirit, there now stretches, from the French Cameroons on the Gulf of Guinea to the Anglo-Egyptian Sudan, a huge *bloc* of Allied territory, across Africa from almost ocean to ocean. This completely dispels the Axis dream of the Germans capturing Duala and marching up to meet, at Lake Chad, the Italians marching down from Libya. That rendezvous will never take place.

Also, the British and the free French now command a vast territory producing a valuable cotton supply, and, with forced cultivation, will be able to increase its output quickly.

Although the Governors of both Ubangi-Shari and the French Cameroons stressed to me the need of their keeping a sizable force of trained troops in their territories against any attempted Axis *coup*, it must be admitted that up to the time I write this (September 15, 1940) the Pétain Government, ruling from Dakar, still holds sway over the finest French African troops, the ebony-black Senegalese. These huge natives have had to face the peculiar choice between Frenchmen and Frenchmen—if they have ever been aware there was such a choice. The happy-go-lucky warriors will probably continue to be happy, as long as their pay and rations continue. It has probably never occurred to them that they were unconsciously making a choice between French and German domination.

It is a strange situation—first, because there has never been a choice, since they are still under their old officers; and, second, the Senegalese, except for a few who may have fought in the last war, do not know what a German *is*. And the same goes for the natives of French Morocco.

When you realize this truth, the decision of French Equatorial Africa to throw in its lot with the British and free French takes on an added importance. And here, it seems, is the chance for a great propaganda blow against the Pétain Government now holding Dakar and Casablanca—don't attack them from the sea; attack them from inland, with the African mind. In this the free French might now make a splendid use of the *élite* they have been cultivating so assiduously in French Equatorial Africa.

And Governor Éboué, who brought Lake Chad in on the side of the British and the free French, is a Negro.

The Cameroons are to the French very much what Tanganyika is to the British. Both are administered with the same purity of purpose. Men who know both territories intimately have called my attention to the remarkable road building of the French in comparison with the official British lethargy in developing Tanganyika. I must say that, on the surface, the difference is marked. These men have also pointed out that the most progressive plantations in both territories are run by Germans. That, too, is obvious. On the other hand, my own impressions were that the rather scholarly, pedantic attitude of the British administration towards the Tanganyika native is the rigorous adherence to an experiment in a genuine attempt to lift the great mass of Tanganyika natives towards self-government. It is the opposite, anyway, of an official desire to exploit the native, or let him be exploited. Whereas, with the French, despite their fraternization with the natives, I never got that impression at all.

That is important. I find it impossible to give concrete proof of it. But I always felt, when I was there, that the French attitude towards the equatorial native was cynical. I know critics will demand that I be precise. But I won't try to be such a fool. It is just like asking a Frenchman to come over, and be precise about the United States, or state definitely whether the Republican or the Democratic party has the best plan for government. Millions split on that. But I feel that few men who know Equatorial Africa intimately will disagree with me when I draw this distinction between the ability of the British official view to be altruistic towards the native, compared with what must be called the chronic cynicism of the French.

The French have a nonchalance that is part of this very practical point of view. They do not invest their equatorial governors with anything like the official British pomp. There is no "signing of the book" at the gates of Government House, no stamping and crashing salutes from sentries with bayonets, no pestiferous aides, acting as if they were ushering you to the throne of God when they lead you into the Governor's presence. To see the Governor of the French Cameroons, a most important mandate, I merely walked with his *Chef d'Affaires Politiques* as far as the side steps of Government House, where the *Chef* pointed to the Governor's office, and said, "He is in there." I went up and knocked.

The French are jealous of the high salaries paid to British officials. A British resident in Nigeria retires on £1,000 a year; a *Chef du Département* in the Cameroons or French Equatorial Africa retires on £300. And they are paid proportionately while in service.

At first, this all makes you feel that the British officials could dispense with some of their pomp and think a little more about the physical and economic development of the territories entrusted to them. They could think about business—for a change.

With some Governors I should say that this unquestionably holds good. With others—and I have just called attention to their aloof, altruistic attitude—there must be some impartiality and justice in that God-like dignity with which the British like to invest their colonial Governors.

With one outstanding exception, I never entered a British Government House in Africa without thinking of Noel Coward's skit, in that charming revue where he took off the colonial Governor with the song, "Mad dogs and Englishmen go out in the midday sun!" I began to sing it to myself as I shook hands with the aide.

You can see, from what I have said, that there were not many class distinctions in Yaounde. My most profound political conversations were carried on with two of the highest officials under the Governor while we were playing billiards in the back room of the other hotel's bar. And, as an example of what one can pick up by insistent questioning, I give you the opinions of these two men on the Cameroon native.

Said one: "I find them intelligent and very hard working. If you were a planter you would have no trouble getting good men, if you paid them three francs a day."

Said the other: "They are stupid and lazy. It is almost impossible to get them to work. It's hard to get them to work up here, as they prefer the cocoa plantations of the coast. You would be a fool if you paid them more than two francs a day and their 'chop.' "

So much for first-hand information.

The beautiful girl behind the bar had been a planter herself. She was an adventurous creature, for she had actually come out from France, obtained a small plantation, then sent for her young man to come out and marry her. Then they went broke during the slump, as did nearly all the small planters in the Cameroons and in French Equatorial Africa. He was now working the farm while she worked in the hotel. Her beauty made it popular.

She seemed an ideal person to interview on the color question.

"*Moi? Impossible!*" she cried, when I asked her if she felt herself a sister to the fashionable colored ladies I had watched playing bridge over in the other hotel. Then she made the gesture of spitting, and asked me in pungent French the equivalent of "How do you get that way?"

"Why, you're *mad!*" she said.

We reached Duala through the steaming jungle, just in time to comply with the formalities which must be gone through before Eve could board the *Wadai*. One of these was having our fingers punctured with rusty pins, so that our blood could be tested to see that we did not have the sleeping sickness. We expected to get blood poisoning from the pins so officially jabbed into us by a native medical assistant in a white coat. But that was nothing to our fear that they would find the sickness—we had been months in tsetse-fly country—for if they did find a trace we would be put into concentration camps! We spent a bad night.

The trip together was over. We had driven across Africa. Gray, black, and white ocean liners and tramps lay along the piers of Duala. The Gulf of Guinea lay just down the river. I strained my eyes towards it longingly. I envied Eve. And she, perverse, unkillable creature, envied me! She had not yet had enough of Africa. We split our kit, I taking just two suitcases and a typewriter, for my flight to the Gold Coast. We left the rest of the stuff in the car and slung it aboard the *Wadai*. Dusting my hands, I said, "Well, *that* one is over."

She shook her head. "We might have gone up to Timbuktu," she said, sadly.

"Haven't you *ever* got enough?" I asked, angrily.

"*No!*" she said.

That night the *Wadai* slipped down the river. The German

colony of Duala, which had gathered to see her off, gave themselves a party in the hotel garden around midnight. I was invited to it. About two in the morning I found myself having a furious argument with a fat German, who, I discovered—in the middle of it—was the *Führer* for the French Cameroons. The French ended the argument by scaling saucers from the bar at all the electric lights in the hotel's garden. It was too late to go to bed. Three of us who were taking the morning 'plane sat there and waited for the sky to lighten. And at dawn an immaculate pilot of Air France, wings up on tropic white, stood before us.

"Dahomey and the Gold Coast?" he asked us.

We got up, wearily. But the names thrilled me. The wheels of the 'plane gave their last "tap-tap-tap" before we took the air. In a little while I looked down into the green delta of the Niger.

*

THE GOLD COAST

36. Gold Coast Capital

THE long, lemon seas race across the African shelf and thunder against the Gold Coast. The palm trees rock and wave their heads in breeze and spray. You hear the roar, as if your ears were singing, even in your sleep. After a time you would feel incomplete without it. All ships must lie about a half mile off shore; you go out to them in surf boats, mounting the incoming waves, and you are swung on board in "mammy chairs," or just large canvas buckets, like a cargo of nuts. The Negroes sit on the thwarts of these surf skiffs; their stumpy paddles have broad fingers, like the black man's hands; they wear red toboggan hats, with dangling tassels, and their red sweaters have the name of the lighterage company embroidered on their chests.

This coast has been called, with dreadful truth, "the white man's grave."

And, looking back from the rail of some steamer that in an hour or so will pull up her anchor and take you away—your heart already beating more tranquilly, freed from the effort of trying, in the Gold Coast humidity, to force the necessary amount of oxygen into your lungs—you see a white, battlemented castle rising straight from the foaming surf. This is Christiansborg, from which, it is said, no Danish or Dutch Governor ever returned alive throughout 140 years.

Today the Gold Coast is just tolerable—I wouldn't give it more than that. Those Dutch and Danish Governors died as much from drink and dissipation as they did from malaria and the coastal fevers, in the old slave-trading days. Days when it was sometimes a year before they could get a letter from home, if then. And whole complements of the garrison, with the possible exception of a rigorously self-disciplined factor, died between the calling of one ship and the arrival of another. The old barracoons, with their shelves for slaves and their iron-barred doors, still line the inner walls of this massive, white-washed fortress. And below, as you look down from your bedroom, as the surf booms and surges away from the cliff, you see the rusted, muzzle-loading old cannon that for a century thundered almost continuously against natives and the ships of England and France.

The man who was the resident of that castle when I was there, Sir Arnold Hodson, is of such a nature that he would resent it if I paid him any compliments. I can merely say that *he* would not have died in the Dutch or Danish days, and that it is a pity he did not live in them; for here, in my last Governor in Africa, I met a true Elizabethan.

Sir Arnold would rather sleep in a tent in the deep bush than in Buckingham Palace. And he would rather be alone. He goes off alone, with no "boys," to shoot bush cow, the most dangerous animal in Africa. The bush cow does not wait to be wounded, like the buffalo, before he starts to hunt you. The minute he is aware of your presence in his territory he begins to stalk you. He is all set on killing you. Sir Arnold shoots them with a .500 "because you haven't, usually, much time to stop them." His books on lion shooting in Abyssinia are considered by big-game hunters in Africa to be classics on the subject. And, as I have said, he doesn't like compliments thrown at him. I leave it at that.

I can say three things: The natives of the Gold Coast call Sir Arnold the "Sunshine Governor," because they know he has a heart and looks after their interests. Many European residents in the Gold Coast and Nigeria think that he is a little scant in his official receptions; he doesn't hold many, and he thinks a bottle or two of beer is enough for anyone. Finally, this British Governor is such a man *qua* man himself that he detests second-raters and "gentlemen"—the type you think of in quotation marks. He is much greater as a *man*, even than as an official; and when I heard some underling Nigerian officials saying they didn't like him "because he is much too pro-native," I knew, even before he invited me to come out and stay at Christiansborg Castle, that our conversation would not be hampered by any aide-de-camp.

I knew, when I saw him in gray alpaca and black mosquito boots, sitting on his sofa, and lean, leathery, hard as nails, that here was a man I could learn a lot from. He had the same quality as Major "Cocky" Hahn, the Native Commissioner I had lived with seven months before down in closed Ovamboland—the practical, realistic, sympathetic understanding of Africa and its people, as if they had become attuned to them, that ignores, or brushes aside all the pomp of office and official red tape like interfering underbrush. For it is not easy for men in these positions to be themselves.

We had finished dinner. And we had just embarked on the fascinating topic of the impact of Africa upon a character—the fact that a thinking man *must* realize, when he goes there, that he must make the laws for his own life for himself—when the solid walls of Christiansborg Castle began slowly to turn before my eyes. This castle, which had seen so many degenerations! I took a grip on myself. Yes, I replied to the Governor, I had seen one or two men of whom I could say that they had *expanded* beyond the bounds of ordinary human limitations; you were aware that they were thinking in terms beyond the rim of your own mental process. Almost another dimension. Was this gained by loneliness and years of constant introspection, or was it possible that Africa, itself, held things which fertilized such a growth? That would account for the "characters" and the lives of some of these disturbing men you met "behind God's back."

I shall always regret that that talk was never terminated. But just as we were "going good" and I was getting some of the same mental exhilaration that I found in India—chiefly with Mahatma Gandhi—lucidity pouring from my mind like gasoline from a punctured tank, the room whirled. I ran for my room, and was violently sick. I took off the white coat of my dinner jacket and leaned out across the thick fortress windows —there are no panes of glass, of course, except in shop or office windows, along the Gold Coast—and when I tried to focus my eyes on the rusty cannon below me, they, too, seemed moving and moiling about in the soapy surf. Then I thought it was about time I went to bed. Instead, I sat, for an instant, on the long, bare African sofa by the cool window—and woke up there the next morning.

At breakfast, when the Governor came in, spick and span from his seven-mile walk, I apologized for the state of my tropic drill; I was wet with sweat.

"I can't understand it," I said.

"I can," said the Governor, giving me a sharp glance; "you've got malaria. And you're going to hospital."

I went. A charming Scots doctor, who had served as a sergeant major throughout the last war, and was gentle as a woman, took my blood. A little later he returned, smiling, with his microscope. "There they are," he said. I looked at the smear, my red corpuscles intensely magnified; and in one or two I saw a little curled-up object that looked grotesquely like a shrimp.

"I like shrimps," I said.

"Well, you've got it," he said. "You had better get into bed."

I had seven months to look back on. All the way back to that day when I came ashore from the German steamer at blazing Walvis Bay. I thought of my rival, a very capable journalist, racing down from London to write an exposé of colonial misadministration on the Gold Coast. Well, I had seen plenty of things to make a sensation, if I were hunting them: The attempt to destock the cattle of the Wakamba natives in Kenya, and their near-revolt; the arbitrary imprisonment of the Indians by the Belgians in the Ruanda-Urundi Mandate (and how they lugged them over into the Belgian Congo for their alleged trial); the still burning resentment of the Kavirondo against the white man's gold rush into their promised reserve; the way most of the road work in the Belgian Congo seems done by convicts; and the forced cultivation of cotton in both the Congo and French Equatorial Africa.

Running over these first-class stories for scandalmongering, I wondered why I had not written some of them. One or two would have made quite a stir. Then I thought of others, dozens of minor exposés. It was too easy. I then saw that running through nearly all of them—present as that shrimp was in my red corpuscles—was a salient fact. In nearly all these cases it was business, sometimes big business, running amuck, often despite the attempts of local officials to prevent it.

And here, I thought, is a major story. If it could be shown how often, and how universally, the colonial officials themselves had been, at heart, on the natives' side in these instances, some useful purpose would be served. The spotlight would be thrown where it belonged—not upon some more or less helpless officials, but upon our attitude towards the ethics of governing black people "for their own good."

Here is a case in point:

The little Gold Coast is—although very few except the chocolate interests know it—the largest cocoa-producing country in the world. For the past ten years it has exported yearly over 42 per cent of the world's supply of cocoa. This is grown entirely by natives on their own small plantations. This fact is something in the nature of a miracle, for these natives, certainly not *aided* by Europeans, have created this amazing industry, surpassing Ecuador and Brazil, from a single cocoa pod which a Gold Coast native smuggled into the territory forty years ago.

To repeat—consider, as a demonstration of what the African natives themselves can do, that these African peasants, on their one- to five-acre farms, are growing (because some of the finished product is now diluted with palm nuts) over half the chocolate that the entire world eats!

So much for the natives.

There is the correlative enterprise of the fourteen huge European business combines, most of them British—one of them controls the entire West Coast and Belgian Congo crop of palm oil—which are buying the cocoa crop as well as operating the merchandise stores selling European goods to the natives.

In November, 1937, in order to abolish their own ruinous intercompany competition, these European companies entered into a secret "buying agreement"—and, it is believed, a secret "selling agreement"—which produced a disastrous eight-months' strike of the native cocoa growers as well as a boycott of the European, mostly British, goods imported by these companies.

As cocoa dominates the entire life of the Gold Coast—it supplies, directly or indirectly, some £2,500,000 out of the entire Government revenue of £3,700,000 and provides the sole or almost the sole means of livelihood of the 3,000,000 natives and 3,000 white men making their careers in this country—every Briton who is in any way interested in Britain's colonial administration of overseas development should read the report of the government commission sent out to the Gold Coast to clear up the mess and suggest the settlement of the future relations of the native growers with the London business interests.

The report is an African drama more thrilling than a magazine exposé article. It costs 3s. 6d. at His Majesty's Stationery Office.

In it you will read how the Secretary of State for the Colonies in London—*without even reading the agreement which the buyers reached in secret and without consulting the Gold Coast Government or the native cocoa growers*—accepted the oral explanations of two of the most important members of the London combine and wired the Gold Coast Governor that he should advise the natives to accept the buying agreement as it was "in their own best interests!"

You will see that the Governor hastened to reply that the one thing the Africans dreaded was a European "pool" combining to fix a buying price, and that the agreement would certainly arouse determined native opposition throughout the colony. The Governor of the Gold Coast was not allowed to see the secret agreement. He had not yet seen it, when I met him in June and July, 1939. And, as far as I know (I don't know whether the disconcerted Secretary of State was ever, afterwards, allowed to have a peep at part of it), the Governor of the Gold Coast has not yet seen a full copy of this agreement, a European buyers' monopoly-understanding which affects vitally the sole commodity on which the entire life of the colony, social, economic, as well as political, rests.

I know that when one of these two major representatives went out to the Gold Coast—he is a man whose family has a great name for philanthropy—and tried to "kid" the African chieftains into accepting the agreement unread, he got the following humiliating response, at a huge mass meeting:

"We don't think for an instant that you mean wrong by us," said, in effect, the chiefs. "We are quite sure you mean what you say when you say it is for our own good. But if it is so *good* for us, why can't we *see* it?"

"I have never," a European who was present at that meeting, said to me, "felt sorrier for anyone in my life! He *did* look like such a damned fool."

Of course, the secret buying agreement was of such a nature that he *couldn't* show it to the chiefs. So the chiefs led their "untutored" subjects in an eight-months' strike, which, aside from paralyzing the Gold Coast and costing the European merchants heavy losses for the perishable goods they had in store, gave the natives a complete *moral* victory (as shown by the report of the government commission) and a partial economic one.

Barbaric rites and taboos were invoked by the resolute Gold Coast chiefs to keep the native front firm. The chiefs swore "fetish oaths," binding upon their subjects, not to sell cocoa, and this news was published by "gong gong," the beating of a tubular bell in each chief's district. Whereat the chief's oath was read out, with the news that anyone who broke the order would be arrested and punished. This had no legal binding force, as the State wouldn't have backed the chiefs up, but the natives obeyed it to a man.

Wrestling with this complete strike and boycott of their goods, the European companies complained that (a) the chiefs encouraged the strike and led their people; (b) the Government was weak in handling them; (c) it was the work of agitators.

After its findings, the commission reported: (a) Who else could lead the natives but their chiefs, and events had shown that this was a popular, almost 100 per cent native protest and represented the true native feeling; (b) "we consider that the local Government acted throughout with tact and that credit is due to Sir Arnold Hodson and his officers for the handling of a very delicate situation"; (c) and as to the European companies' complaints of "agitators" being at work, this official British Government Commission rose to fine, ironic scorn. It said:

"The term 'agitator' is somewhat tendentious, being freely used by those who hold a particular belief to indicate an improper motive in others who presume to oppose them."

It is a definition that could be used, with great benefit to our judgments, elsewhere than on the gallant little Gold Coast.

If there is one thing that this cocoa strike and the Commission's Report show incontestably, it is that if alleged slackness in colonial administration is to be investigated, the investigations should begin in Whitehall and at the top.

How is it possible for the British Secretary of State to order the Gold Coast Governor to sponsor an agreement when he hasn't read it? How is it possible that a man in that responsible position can be so ignorant of the psychology as well as the economic position of the natives over whom he is supposed to be the ultimate administrator that he disregards the local Governor's protests that the attempt to enforce the agreement can only lead to a wholehearted native strike and boycott?

One answer is obvious: The office of Secretary of State is a political plum. Behind that is the lethargic British attitude towards the colonies. And a direct outcome of these is the lack of any broad economic thinking by the Whitehall colonial staff. In such a situation a private business interest, if it is big enough, can exploit any colony it wants.

This story is not, perhaps, so sensational as the Trinidad, Jamaica, and British Guiana commotions, but it is along the same line of the official Whitehall economic complacency of which Africa reeked—until six months after this war was on.

As regards the big London buyers, the story is not all black. The commission unearthed an almost incredible amount of skulduggery among the natives. Native brokers, intermediate buyers for the big European companies, were cheating their own brethren right and left. The favorite device was a short-weight scale which made 80 pounds read only 60. And African brokers were lending money, in the middle of the season, against a price which they knew would be below the season's price, and getting the native's crop at that figure. There was an unbelievable number of native "share croppers" and absentee landlords —products of the vices of plutocracy—even on the five-acre farms.

And, on the company's side, it should be remarked they were nearly all operating chains of trading stores on the Gold Coast and therefore wanted the natives to have as much purchasing capacity as possible. The year 1937 was expected to be a boom cocoa season, and these stores were stocked with European merchandise—which the natives did not buy.

It was a beautiful mess. When I left the coast the present situation was that the Governor and his staff had been complimented, by the commission, on remaining neutral; the group of European buyers were maintaining stoutly (and incredibly) that there *was* no secret buying agreement. Nobody believed anybody, and the commission had left with strong recommendations that the Government, or someone, should help the natives to combine in one *selling* organization in order to protect their private welfare from another possible buying combination.

This would have been a storm in a tea—or cocoa—cup, were it not for the fact that over half the outside world's supply of chocolate was involved.

The one thing which the cocoa fracas did show was the appalling absence of any economic conception from Whitehall, not only to protect but to develop this miraculous trade.

When Englishmen talk of their colonies being of no use to them they might take a look at the ships loading cocoa off the Gold Coast, and think again. What seems vitally needed is a rousing publicity campaign on the colonies to wake up the Britisher (and Whitehall) to what they've got.

And—I stress this here—they should keep it. For I think it is under the Englishman that the black man has the best chance to progress and will receive the fairest minded treatment while he is doing it.

The real story of the Gold Coast lies in the fact, sometimes giving rise to the complaint in London of mismanagement, that the colony has reached an advanced stage of native evolution in which it is undergoing the inevitable growing pains. Too many Africans are being educated for too few jobs. And there is too much higher education.

Unlike the case in South Africa, where the native is debarred, almost legally, from entering any skilled occupation in which he could compete with the white man, the Gold Coast's present Supreme Court judge is an African; so are the Solicitor General and the Secretary of Native Affairs. Governor Sir Arnold Hodson's policy was to place 50 per cent of Government jobs in Africans' hands. By this I mean the important jobs, for when I was there in 1939 there were already 850 Europeans on the staff list, against 4,000 Africans.

Africans were in all ranks and branches of the Government service, down to barely qualified typists on a rising salary of £4 a week, which is considerably more than the equivalent worker receives in London.

The latest trouble in the Gold Coast, which erupted just before I got there, was a three-days' strike of 106 *native* railway locomotive engineers for more pensionable jobs, more uniforms, and a quicker advancement in pay. In fact, so "Africanized" is this colony that there is not one white locomotive engineer on the Gold Coast.

It cannot be said that the British administration is holding the native back.

Yet, with the Africans progressing so rapidly, there is inevitably an *élite* of educated natives demanding the pay of Europeans as well as more "European" jobs. The very advance that the British have given to the natives is being held against the British. On the Gold Coast there is a surplus of doctors, potential school teachers, and out-of-work lawyers; the condition is somewhat similar to that in India. It may not be a large surplus. But there is this troublesome (and trouble-hunting) element of the intellectual "discontenteds."

These Africans are not wrong in desiring what they want, but government jobs cannot be created fast enough to absorb them. Now you see, when you view this scene, why the Belgians ruthlessly insist that an African native's education must be along the lines of practical trades, to fit him for life in Africa—*life as it is.* And why the French dropped "assimilation" for "association," or "parallelization." They have seen the unwisdom of creating a class which can find no means of subsistence. The British seem to have been too far advanced, perhaps theoretically, in the extent to which they have given their Africans "education."

These intelligent, frustrated Africans, hunting jobs which they know they could fill, have a legitimate grievance. They have been, so to speak, "brought into this world," and find there is no place for them.

Therefore the five native newspapers of the Gold Coast (I don't think there is a European one) are filled with leading articles and letters criticizing the present (some say too pro-African) Government, chiefly on the ground that the official programs do not dispense with Europeans fast enough and give the Africans the posts.

Read in London, or listened to, their grievances would seem to indicate a deplorable state of affairs. But you must visualize them against this background: As a cold matter of fact, the Gold Coast is probably the most "African" colony on that sun-smitten continent. When the British economic development catches up with their idealistic educational program, the Gold Coast should be one of the happiest countries in Africa.

In the meantime, and despite the thirty-five to forty thousand natives who work in the gold mines and diamond fields, the Gold Coast is still the world's foremost cocoa country. Still awaiting a planned economic development—from Whitehall.

37. Earthquake

LABADI 30th June, 1939.

To
His Excellency's Private Secretary
   Christensborg Castle,
     Xborg:

Your Excellency—

Sir: We the Lepers of the C.D. Hospital, Labadi Road, Accra, do beg to tender our sympathies to you and the people of the Gold Coast especially Accra for immediate death, accident, destruction of properties and sorrow. Which they have sustained on the 22nd inst. by the Earthquake.

Having heard through the Radio of His Excellency's efforts in regards for the safety and guide of the homeless inhabitants of the City of Accra we greatly admire His Excellency's active activities, no wonder he is styled Sunshine Governor.

Be it remembered that when a person's life has been in immediate danger and that has been restored, no doubt for some purpose and what is that purpose! Be still and know that I am God. "Psalm 46 verse 10."

We as patient of the C.D. Hospital have sustained no accident of any kind.

We pray that may kind Nature watch and guide all of us.

   Sec. S. G. Natt.   We have the honour to be
Ast. Sec. G. Q. Morton.   His Excellency's Poor & Loyal
                             Patient.

"It was a sight to break a man's heart!" an up-country district officer admitted to me.

"And then what did the natives do?" I asked.

"They sat down and waited. They had done all they could. They had placated every god they could think of. Then they sat down to rest. There was nothing more to be done. They were cool as cucumbers!"

As everyone ought to know by this time—it has been told often enough by us writers—night, in the tropics, drops at 6 o'clock. The veil comes down. I was sitting in my bed in the European hospital at Accra, in the middle of my bout with malaria. When the quake hit us I was eating my dinner. Then came the roar. As I said, it was astonishingly like the roar and trembling of the earth as an express train rushes past you. For a split second I thought of that. Then my bed began to buck like a goat. The lights went out. I felt a mutton chop on my chest. And a soft trickle of plaster descended upon my head.

I then made the important announcement to myself, and made it aloud: "*You* are in an earthquake."

There was no exclamation mark. I just sat there. What to do? And as I sat I heard cries, as if from a rising flock of startled seafowl, then silence.

"*That*," I said, again aloud, "was from the native quarter; there must be a lot of people killed there."

Then I got up.

It is extraordinary, how in the biggest moments you will think of the smallest things. I knew where my drill suit lay. In the darkness, I found it. But I could not find my necktie. I was grubbing about for this when a light approached along the veranda. It was a candle, on a saucer, carried by my male native nurse, a Mr. Johnson.

Mr. Johnson was an educated African, getting some £280 a year. He was kindly, humorous, respectful—and forgetful. The previous day, at luncheon, he had forgotten my pill. I had said to him, "Johnson, you must not do that; you know this malaria treatment must be adhered to; a pill with each meal; that is essential."

"Yessuh," said Mr. Johnson.

Now he stood before me. The candlelight illuminated the mess the overturned plates had made of my bed. It showed the alarming cracks in the plaster-covered masonry. It showed my bed where it ought not to have been, in the center of the floor. Then I asked Johnson to help me find my necktie. But Johnson was holding another saucer; he shoved it towards me.

"Sir," he said, "your pill."

Then the idiocy, the madness, of the whole scene struck me, and I shot out of that room, along the veranda and down the stone steps out onto the driveway. There I found the four other European inmates of the hospital who could walk. There was a dim moon. We stared at the hospital.

"Well," said one, "I don't think I want any more dinner tonight."

At that moment the matron of the hospital came past. She is an "old Coaster," a remarkable woman; for over thirty years she has watched Englishmen come and go—or die. She had just bumped into the Negro cook of the hospital, hiding in the bushes.

"Missie," he stammered, *"be this God?"*

"Yes, Francis," she answered, sadly; "I'm afraid it is."

Miss Rigby walked straight under the dangerous stone arch, up the steps, into the hospital. We grinned, and followed her.

There was a consultation. One man had had most of his insides taken out and couldn't be moved. There were a couple of malaria cases who couldn't stand up. It was decided that, as the hospital had a wooden roof, they had better remain where they were. Then the towhaired Scots doctor arrived in his motor car, bearing the first European casualty. He was a very minor official who had leaped from the window of his bungalow, breaking the bones of his foot. He was still popeyed with fright; his eyes were round as watch crystals.

Dr. Gillespie, muttering something about metatarsals, dislocation or fractures, might have been back in Edinburgh. And I, having a newspaper to write for, said to the matron:

"Miss Rigby, may I use your car?"

"I'll go with you."

It was a brand-new one, a German Opel, I think; and a few weeks before she had overturned herself in it while learning to drive it, and had broken two ribs. But this, apparently, meant nothing to her. We got in and drove towards the lightless, silent town.

I have said that this was an upheaval where I saw the black man behaving better than the white. But that in no way implies that the white men did not behave admirably. In fact, one of the most poignant things about this calamity was the deep consideration which both peoples felt for each other. It was as if one touch of disaster makes the whole world kin. And in the following days, for we had more calamities, I saw sight after sight that aroused my interest in human behavior. Deep, genuine kindliness that washed away all the pomp and red tape of officialdom, all the bosh and trivialities, and brought black and white man face to face and shoulder to shoulder in a common sorrow that made you wish with all your heart this decency that was felt between them could be "fixed," made established so that it could be continued with in normal life.

But that was not to be. This raised things to heroic heights. Afterwards we would return to our beastly inhibitions and self-righteousness. It would be long before another disaster would make us kind again. And it would require a disaster. There seems to be something to meditate upon in that; we know how to behave decently on heroic occasions, but the ordinary run of our daily life is too sordid.

Anyway, that is one of the questions which kept returning to my mind that night as I watched the black population of Accra, stricken dumb as sheep, moving silently about among the rubble of their mud-and-wattle houses, trying to succor each other in the dark. The idea of panicking never occurred to them, though there might be another quake at any moment, bringing down the rest of the buildings. Later, twenty-one dead natives were found under the ruins. At one place in the road, where our lights showed that a crowd was blocking us, the matron and I found a group of low-voiced natives curiously regarding a man who had leaped from the third floor of a near-by European office building. An old native said, with that drawl I had known in the United States, "I think he must have broken his back."

"Well then, don't *move* him," said the matron.

"We're not trying to, madam. We're waiting for an ambulance. Do *you* know where we can find an ambulance?"

The matron and I suggested that they get a door, slide him gently on that, then lift him into the first procurable motor lorry.

"But don't lift him!" said the matron.

"No, madam, we all heard what you said. Do *you* know where we can find a motor lorry?"

"No," she gasped, a bit testily; "you must find that for yourselves."

That—this quiet little scene in the dark—marked the essential difference that night between the behavior of the white man and that of the black. The superstitions of the natives, which had given them their philosophic resignation and freedom from fear, had also robbed them of their initiative. They were still waiting—even for recovery to *happen*. The white men, on the other hand, had gone at once into an automatic reaction of reconstruction.

At the power station, where Miss Rigby knew the superintendent, we found him under a massive block of machinery which was being held up by four steel columns. These had taken a slight list. And he was under them with a hurricane lamp.

"John," she said, "isn't that a dangerous position? There might be another shock at any moment."

"Well, Mary, we've got to get the lights going."

We had twenty tremors in three days.

At the telegraph and cable office we found the three Englishmen in charge gazing at the wreck of their batteries. The acid was still running out of them, and we were warned not to step in it. "Our life blood," grinned one. "The cable's not broken, but we've got no juice. Yes," he said to me, "your cable will go as soon as we can get through again. Don't worry about precedence."

"I always worry about precedence," I said; "I'm a newspaper man, working for the *Daily Squirt*."

"Well, we're not," he said, facing me stoutly.

It was an endearing rebuke.

The next morning he invited me into his bedroom over the wrecked cable office, to have a drink. Dangling from the ceiling was a hunk of masonry that must have weighed forty pounds. It was being held for the moment by a piece of steel reinforcing wire.

"Are you going to sleep under *that?*" I asked.

"Certainly. If my name's in the book, it's in the book."

"That's not bravery," I said; "it's bravado. Besides, it's damned silly."

"No; it's not." He smiled; he was a big, sandy-haired man, with the white eyelashes that go with his type. "It's just damned laziness. See this."

He picked up a Chinese statuette of a woman, which was standing with its face to the wall. There was a crack in the porcelain and a chip taken iff its base.

"*That* happened last year in Manila. Another earthquake.

Last night all the earthquake did was turn her around. That's the way I found her this morning, face to the wall."

Nevertheless, he changed his mind; he did not sleep in that room that night, which was just as well.

The officers of the Gold Coast Regiment had rushed to their barracks, thinking they would find their men in confusion. Not a bit of it. They were lined up under their native sergeants. They thought the Germans had come.

There was another lesson in cool, philosophical deportment.

But there was one place where there was terror. The quarters of the European superintendent in Fort Usher, which is now the prison, were completely wrecked by the quake. Behind the grim walls the African prisoners were cut off, isolated, from all their African background. And they were screaming.

It was an unnerving sound, as I drove past. But they were released the next day and paraded in the prison square, where the warders quieted them by playing the harmonium.

From a near-by village church bells began to ring after the quake, and rang incessantly. Habitants paraded the streets beating gasoline tins and chanting hymns. And, I learned the next morning, each village had its own choir, which, the previous night, improvised concerts until dawn.

Dust clouds made the moon appear green. The shocks were felt in Lagos, 250 miles away. And the local correspondent of a famous press agency lost his reason and filed a cable (later printed in London) saying that the earthquake *had lasted nine hours.*

There was plenty of irony in that topsy-turvy night. Accra, like most British colonial seats, is a horrible site of pomposity and poverty. Vast, vulgarly ostentatious Government buildings, of totally unnecessary grandeur, lording it over a warren of native wattle huts. And what happened in the earthquake was that the mud-and-wattle native dwellings stood the strain much better than the European buildings. The huts heaved and swayed, ending up at impossible angles, but most of them stood up. Whereas, with the European buildings, the façades and all the stone gingerbread icing fell off. The streets were cluttered with Grecian ruins.

There is a bank, which I shall call Netley's. It shed its stone garnishments *in toto;* it was just a square, respectable building when I stared at it in the green moonlight. Vastly improved. A light was moving about somewhere on the second floor; I could see it being reflected on the ceiling, and, thinking that it might be a woman or someone injured and not able to get out, I tried a side door to see if I could go up and help things.

"What the hell are you doing there?" came a ragged European voice behind me.

"I am," I said, "trying to get into Netley's Bank; someone seems caught up on the second floor."

"Damn it, man, *I* am Netley's Bank!"

"All right, then," I said; "there *still* seems someone trying to get down from the second floor."

The secretariat, a pillared near-Grecian affair, had shed its façades, gables, and stone balustrades. It was empty when I stared at it along about midnight; it was condemned the next morning as being unsafe. I found a group of English officials contemplating the ruins. And while we were doing so a body of native clerks stepped nimbly past and entered the ruined building.

These African "educateds" had received with joy the news that the secretariat was condemned, because, for a few hours, until new quarters could be found, they would not have to do any work. But this morning they trooped into the rickety building, nevertheless, sat down at their desks, and typed letters off to their relatives up country, telling them all about the quake.

"Well, I'll be damned!" said a young Englishman, wearing an Old Wykehamist tie. "Do you know what happened to me last night? I don't mind telling you. I was having my bath, when the quake came along, and I popped straight out the window. Completely starko. There I was, standing on the lawn, naked as the day I was born, utterly terrified to go into my bungalow, when out came my 'boy.' He gave me one look, then he gasped, 'Massa no fit!'

"He was horribly shocked. So he popped back into the bungalow and brought me some clothes. All he could find, in the dark, was my wife's nightdress and the top part of my dinner jacket!"

"Did you put them on?"

"You're damned right! I was cold."

I suppose the original British idea, in erecting these unnecessarily large and pompous buildings wherever they plant the Union Jack overseas, was to impress the natives. But I think it no longer works. From what the Indians told me, the incredible pomp of Sir Edwin Landseer Lutyens' government buildings at New Delhi only infuriated them. "When you consider," they said, "the state of the Punjab peasants." And at Accra there were one or two buildings which brought one up short, they were so unwarranted.

One of these was the supreme court building. It cost, it is officially admitted, at least £70,000. It is larger, higher, longer, more imposing than the capitol of many an American State. There is in Accra only one European barrister and twenty-four African, and elsewhere in the colony there are only four European barristers and thirty-two African. Yet—and God knows how little use it has been in preventing the natives from being exploited by the European trading companies—supreme court it is called.

I drove there eagerly on that disjointed night. But, unfortunately, not a tile had dropped from it.

Perhaps the most uncanny experience I had that night was with the Accra lighthouse. I was standing below, staring up at it for some time, *feeling* that there was something wrong. Then I realized that although the light was still burning, the beam had stopped rotating. One of the most important lights on the African coast had become a false beacon.

The keeper of the light had had a terrifying experience. He was up in the tower, inspecting the lamp, when the quake hit Accra. The tower swayed and all the mercury ran out of its mechanism. He saw it stop.

He could not catch the mercury to put it back. What should he do? Put the light out entirely, or let it burn as a false light? What would the captains in the ships off the coast do? A stationary light, hundreds of miles from where they should find such a thing!

It was a mad night.

When we drove out to Christiansborg Castle to find out what had happened to the Governor, Sir Arnold Hodson, we found that ancient fortress, where I had spent my first night on the Gold Coast, guarded by a ring of sentries. Its massive, white masonry was seamed with cracks. The Governor was sleeping where he much preferred to sleep, in a tent on the lawn.

Outside the castle walls I found a strange example of human values. There are some comparatively palatial homes out there. They belong to rich Syrian traders. These had all left their homes, but, at the risk of their lives, they had all salvaged their precious motor cars. They were sitting in groups beside them in the green moonlight.

Only four Europeans that I know of, and not one native, slept under a roof in Accra that night, or the next three nights.

As we drove back to the hospital we found the natives setting up households along the curbs. Some had lamps, and were holding parties of sorts. Many were sleeping under the fishing skiffs which are found everywhere in the streets of the town's native quarter. Near the hospital, after we passed the bungalows of the European officials, we saw their "boys" putting up tents on the lawns.

Outside the hospital gates we found a group of Negroes. One had a guitar. The rest were dancing jigs in the splattered moonlight under the mango trees.

Then the rains came. Two nights later Accra was struck by the worst tropical cloudburst within memory. With 70,000 natives camped out in the streets, this second blow of "kind nature" threatened to cause more deaths among them than the earthquake. The sandy town squares, where the black soldiers of the Gold Coast Regiment had been magically (from a white man's point of view) erecting bamboo and palm-frond huts, became lakes. The gutters sluiced until their roaring rivers flowed over the sidewalks. Seventy thousand natives, stricken almost flat by the force of the downpour, sought shelter like slugs.

They crouched under tables they had rescued from their wrecked houses. They put beds on boxes and lay like tinned fish, under sodden mattresses. They lay under overturned skiffs. Seventy thousand of them! I heard white officials groan when they argued over the impossible task of providing cover for them.

The whites were having no paradise themselves. The European population of Accra varies between 900, at the height of the cocoa season, and 600. Practically all of these people, men, women and children, were living in tents. The waters, rising, and red from the soil, swept through their kit boxes, washed away clothes, and rose towards the level of their green canvas camp beds.

The European bungalows of the Gold Coast officials are erected on pillars of concrete, and about twelve feet off the ground, in order to protect their foundations from the ravages of the white ant and other insects. Safely, I thought, perched in one of these buildings that night, like an ancient lake dweller, a colonial official, his American wife, and I, rode through the last major shock. There were two roars; one of thunder, the other that undulating, ripping sound of the quake. The house shuddered. Then, in the comparative silence, we heard the rain redouble its battering attack on our roof. The house was a sound box, and filled with a small roar itself, as if someone were rubbing steel brushes on our roof.

Through this we drank whisky and read poetry. My host was a poet himself, with a rich, cadent voice. And as we swayed in our nest he read, with great feeling, such poems as he could find which dealt with God's inhumanity to man—"The Angelus," for instance.

By now I knew that I wanted to get away from Africa. The malaria had left me in an unreasonable mood of melancholia. Perhaps the pill that Mr. Johnson forgot did it. But anyway I wanted to get free from the tropics. I vowed that when next I traveled it would be to a land of perpetual ice. I found a kindred spirit, a distinguished official, who agreed with me. He began his morning round of drinks at 10 o'clock in the club. You could always find him there, glass in hand, hand shaking, slightly apologetic, his handsome face puffed and flushed, his intelligent eyes already getting that deadly milk-white circle around the iris. He was close to the danger line.

"The only exercise I get," he muttered to me, "is walking as pall bearer behind the funerals of my friends. People die out here for no reason at all."

The English at Accra are a very pleasant lot. And I enjoyed my evenings in the favored circle that sat under the tree out-

side the club. But I drank far too many whiskies than were good
for me. I went out beyond Christiansborg Castle and spent three
nights with the chief of the native fishing village. Here, where
the breeze from the surf ceaselessly swayed the palm trees, we
sat in a ring under the moon, and talked—well, of everything.
Wading with them at dawn, I climbed into a fishing skiff, and,
with everything lashed to the thwarts, rode the surf, to sail
miles off the hot coast where they fished all day. They scraped
the bamboo mast, blew a cigarette into the fluff, and made fire.
On an earthen pot filled with sand they made a fire of charcoal.
And on this, in a tin that had been full of slimy fish and bilge
water, we cooked the spines of the mackerel they had cut up for
bait. The salt water gave it tang, and the heat sterilized the fish
spines which had been floating about among three pairs of black
feet all day. It was an excellent dish.

By now I had set a "boy" to watch the coast. As I feared, the
Italian tramp steamer did not show up. For three nights I had
everything packed, and gave farewell parties with my friends.
The *Piave* was only going to lie off Accra for an hour or two,
I was told. I could not afford to miss it; there would not be
another one for weeks.

On one of these white-hot days, when I lay, almost knocked
out, along the thwarts of the fishing skiff off the coast, I announced that I was going to strip and dive overboard. The chief
held up a horrified hand:

"No, *no*, master! Plenty big sharps!" (Sharks.)

I almost told him I didn't care. After another farewell party
with the Europeans that night, I drove out and found the fishing village sitting again in a ring under the moon. By now they
had become used to me, and some of the little "totos" danced.
To me the thing brought up vague memories, for I was reared
by Negro servants, and their ancestors had come from here. The
face of an old Negress who sat on the sand beside my chair
was the same as Rhodie's, our cook. I told her so.

"You stay here, master," she said.

But driving home that night I said to the "boy":

"Boy, don't you go to sleep tonight. You sit on the beach. You watch for ship. The moment you see the ship come, you run and tell me. Savvy?"

"Yes, master; I watch very precisely for boat."

So he did, bless his heart! Dawn was just breaking when I saw his big, black face appear over my window sill. He opened his pink mouth:

"Massa, massa!" he said, hurriedly. "Boat come!"

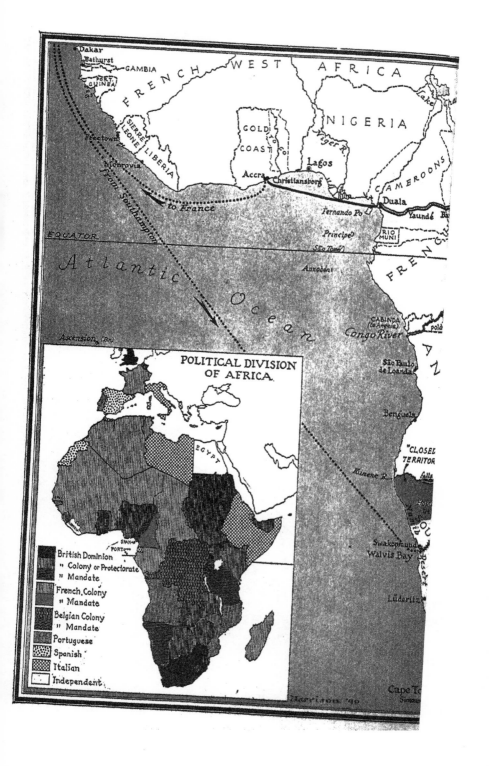

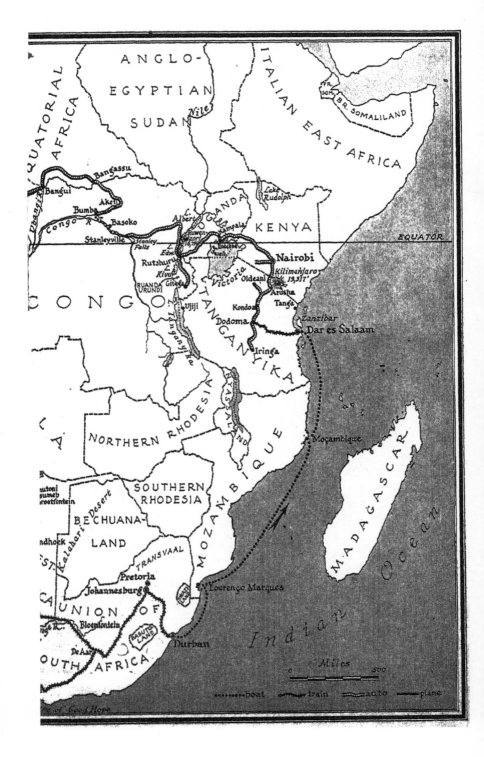